The World of the Indian Ocean, 1500–1800

M.N. Pearson

The World of the Indian Ocean, 1500–1800

Studies in Economic, Social and Cultural History

ASHGATE
VARIORUM

Published in the Variorum Collected Studies Series by

Ashgate Publishing Limited
Gower House, Croft Road,
Aldershot, Hampshire
GU11 3HR
Great Britain

Ashgate Publishing Company
Suite 420
101 Cherry Street
Burlington, VT 05401–4405
USA

Ashgate website: http://www.ashgate.com

ISBN 0–86078–962–4

British Library Cataloguing in Publication Data
Pearson, M. N. (Michael Naylor), 1941–
    The world of the Indian Ocean, 1500–1800 : studies in economic, social and cultural history. – (Variorum collected studies series)
    1. Acculturation – Indian Ocean Region – History 2. Europeans – Indian Ocean Region – History 3. Medicine – Indian Ocean Region – History 4. Indian Ocean Region – History 5. Indian Ocean Region – Commerce – History
    I. Title
    909'.09824

Library of Congress Cataloging-in-Publication Data
Pearson, M. N. (Michael Naylor), 1941–
    The world of the Indian Ocean, 1500–1800 : studies in economic, social, and cultrual history / M.N. Pearson.
        p. cm. – (Variorum collected studies series ; 813)
    ISBN: 0–86078–962–4 (alk. paper)
    1. Indian Ocean Region – History. 2. Indian Ocean Region – Economic conditions. 3. Indian Ocean Region – Social conditions. I. Title. II. Collected studies ; CS813.

    DS340.P45 2005
    909'.09824'0903–dc22   2004062694

Printed and bound in Great Britain by TJ International Ltd, Padstow, Cornwall

VARIORUM COLLECTED STUDIES SERIES CS813

CONTENTS

This volume contains x + 324 pages

INTRODUCTION

This collection consists of articles published between 1968 and 2001. The first, one of my few ventures into the history of Southeast Asia, was also my first publication. I still remember the gratitude I felt towards Denis Sinor, then and now editor of the *Journal of Asian History*, for his acceptance of this piece of juvenilia. Sinor relied on Charles Boxer to referee my submission. This publication thus marked only the first of many kindnesses that I received from Boxer over many years.

There is a certain thematic unity in these fourteen pieces. All are located in the early modern period, and all, except perhaps the first, describe people living on the coasts of the Indian Ocean. Another linking factor is that most of them are based, at least in part, on Portuguese materials. However, throughout my career I have presented myself as one who uses European documentation to write about Asian history. I hope that this collection continues to bear out this claim. Nevertheless, it is essential that scholars, both those from the region and those from far away, now make a more concerted effort to find and use indigenous sources. To do this will obviously involve laborious linguistic training, and also some acquaintance with palaeography. More fundamentally, their view of history is likely to be very different from that of a modern western researcher. One example is the Swahili chronicles. Regardless, the effort to use them will make possible a much more nuanced view of this early modern period in the lands around the Indian Ocean.

A final broad theme in all of them is the claim that in most areas of society and economy early modern Europeans and Asians had much in common, with the newly arrived Europeans having no particular advantage over their Asian interlocutors. The four pieces on medical history seem to demonstrate this especially well. This is not a matter of being "Asian-centric", or of denigrating the achievements of the first Europeans to enter the Indian Ocean. Rather, it is a matter of seeing a certain commonality when we look at most of human kind. This ended, at least in a material sense, when Europe began to industrialise late in the eighteenth century.

These articles and chapters are reprinted without alteration except for the correction of a few typographical errors and some minor updating. Rereading them was a sobering task, for often I wanted to amend sweeping statements made in earlier, more dogmatic, stages of my career as an historian. Especially cringe-worthy is my antiquarian explanation for the decline of Spanish trade in the Philippines, which I attributed to "a decline in the spirit of the Spanish"! [I, 128] As I reread these pieces I also became very aware of the parsimonious way in which I used some material on more than one occasion. I hope readers will not be too put off by this auto-plagiarism. I am grateful to all the original copyright holders for giving me permission to reprint these pieces and to Dr. John Smedley for suggesting this collection, and for putting up with many delays as the project limped towards completion.

M.N. PEARSON

New South Wales, Australia
5th October 2004

ACKNOWLEDGEMENTS

Grateful acknowledgement is made to the following persons, institutions and publishers for their kind permission to reproduce the papers included in this volume: Denis Sinor, Editor, *Journal of Asian History* (I); Cambridge University Press, Cambridge (II, XIV); Jayant S. Budkuley, Registrar, Goa University, Goa (III); Oxford University Press, New Delhi (IV, V, XI); Steve Mullins, General Editor, *The Great Circle* (VI); Hendrik E. Niemeijer, Editor-in-Chief, *Itinerario* (VII); Modern Humanities Research Association, London (VIII, XII); University Press of Southern Denmark, Odense (IX); Ohio University Press, Athens, Ohio (X); Institute for Research in Social Sciences and Humanities of MESHAR, Kerala (XIII); Editions Rodopi, Amsterdam (XV).

PUBLISHER'S NOTE

The articles in this volume, as in all others in the Variorum Collected Studies Series, have not been given a new, continuous pagination. In order to avoid confusion, and to facilitate their use where these same studies have been referred to elsewhere, the original pagination has been maintained wherever possible.

Each article has been given a Roman number in order of appearance, as listed in the Contents. This number is repeated on each page and is quoted in the index entries.

I

SPAIN AND SPANISH TRADE
IN SOUTHEAST ASIA*

In the history of early European commercial contact with East
and South Asia, the Spanish case stands out as unique. The Portuguese prospered from their small colonial territories in Asia in the
sixteenth century, as did the Dutch and English in the seventeenth.
This prosperity was based on the inter-Asian "country" trade, for
in this period most European goods did not find a ready market in
Asia. The profits of the country trade were invested in the spices,
cloths, and other Asian products which were sent to Europe, although
the English and the Dutch were also forced to export some bullion
from Europe to pay for these goods. But the Spanish lost their share
of the country trade after a short period of active and profitable
engagement in it, and for most of their time as a colonial power in
Southeast Asia their exports were paid for by bullion sent from
Acapulco on the celebrated Manila Galleon. Indeed, even the Spanish
Government itself in the Philippines was kept from insolvency only
by these annual infusions of American gold. This paper is not concerned directly with this imperial trade between Spain's Southeast
Asian and Central American colonies, but with the country trade,
centered on the Philippines, during the first century of Spanish
control. A short overview of Philippine trade during this period will
be given first, showing its period of prosperity and its decline. Then
Philippine trade with the several countries of East and South Asia
will be described. From this area by area study should emerge several
general factors which together were responsible for the decline of

* I have to thank Professor C. R. Boxer, and Professor David Joel Stein-
berg of the University of Michigan, for their valuable comments on earlier
drafts of this article. Neither of these gentlemen has seen this final draft.

Philippine trade. This in turn will throw light on the nature of the Spanish colonial effort in Southeast Asia, demonstrating, for example, the consequences of the religious factor in Spain's colonial policy, and the results of the attempt to govern the Philippines in the interests of a homeland on the other side of the world.

The prosperity of the Philippines in the early years of its time as a Spanish colony is well documented. This prosperity was necessarily based on trade in the products of the surrounding countries, for the Spanish found almost no Philippine product suitable for them to export. As early as 1587 ships from other Asian countries were calling at Manila, lured by stories of the wealth of the galleon.[1] In 1609 Morga painted a picture of a flourishing trade based on Manila. Goods were coming "from China, Japon, Maluco, Malaca, Sian, Camboja, Borneo and other districts" including Mexico. From this "great and profitable, and easy to control" trade "large and splendid profits" were being made by the Spanish.[2] Certainly Coen and other Dutchmen were well aware of Manila's prosperity and possibilities, and for this reason made numerous attempts to take the islands for Holland. In 1626 another contemporary source spoke of Manila's wealth and of the many foreign ships coming there.[3] Grau Y Monfalcon pointed out that "in Asia and the regions of the Orient, God created some things so precious in the estimation of man, and so peculiar to these provinces, that, as they are only found or manufactured therein, they are desired and sought by the rest of the world."[4] At first it seemed that the Spanish were going to get a share of the profits to be made on these goods even if none of them were produced in her territories.

To this end the position of Manila relative to the rest of Asia was of great importance. Thanks to this, and her magnificent harbor, it seemed she was ideally suited to become the emporium of the East. Indeed, Philippine trade before the Spanish arrival must have

---

[1] H. de la Costa, *The Jesuits in the Philippines*, (Cambridge, Mass., 1961), p. 111.

[2] E. H. Blair and J. A. Robertson, *The Philippine Islands, 1493—1898*, I—LV, (Cleveland, 1903—05), XVI, pp. 176, 187. This indispensable collection of source materials, upon which most of this paper is based, will be referred to as "BR" in the future.

[3] BR, XXII, pp. 93—94.

[4] *Ibid.*, XXVII, p. 88.

been of a far-flung nature. A party sent out by Legazpi soon after his arrival captured a Moro junk which carried iron and tin from "Borney", porcelain, bells, benzoin and tapestry from China, and pots and pans from India. The Moro pilot of the junk had traded in the Moluccas, Borneo, Java, Malacca, India and China.[5] Legazpi himself saw that Manila was well suited for trade with "Japan, China, Java, Borneo, and the Moluccas and New Guinea, as one can go to any of those parts in a short time."[6] The early missionaries realized that, as a result of their position, "de la possession des Philippines, dépend la conservation de presque tous les posts ou débuts de chrétienté en ces régions."[7] It seemed that Manila could continue to be "the first mart of the East", an earlier and greater Hong Kong or Singapore.

The early Spanish had two other advantages—capital and determination. The trading capital of Spain and Portugal together, after their union, has been calculated to have been 5,000,000 florins (about £ 417,000), while the Dutch United Company started with only 290,000 florins (about £ 24,000).[8] The spirit of the early Spanish is plain to be seen in the deeds of such men as Legazpi, Juan de Salcedo, Gomez Perez Dasmarinas, Martin de Rada, OSA, Acunha, who retook Tidore and Ternate for Spain in 1606, and Juan de Silva, who in 1609 melted down church bells to make cannon with which to repel the Dutch.[9] The reckless conquistador arrogance was evident in the deeds of Blas Ruys and Belhoso in Cambodia, and in Sande's claim that 4,000 to 6,000 men would be sufficient to take China.[10] The spirit of the religious could be seen in China, Japan, Formosa, and the Philippines themselves. Even in commercial matters the early Spanish showed plenty of initiative. The remnants of Magellan's

[5] *Ibid.*, II, p. 116. A "Moro" (Moor) was a Muslim native of Mindanao or other islands in the Southern Philippines.

[6] Quoted in C. R. Boxer (Ed.), *South China in the Sixteenth Century*, (London, Hakluyt Society, 1953), p. xli.

[7] Henri Bernard, *Les Iles Philippines du Grand Archipel de la Chine*, (Tientsin, 1936), pp. 70—71; see also *ibid.*, pp. 135—36.

[8] M. A. P. Meilink-Roelofsz, *Asian Trade and European Influence*, (The Hague, 1962), p. 182. Throughout this paper conversion to English pounds is based on C. R. Boxer, *The Great Ship from Amacon*, (Lisbon, 1959), pp. 335—38. 338.

[9] Bérnard, *op. cit.*, p. 163.

[10] BR, IV, pp. 58—59.

expedition competed successfully with the Portuguese in the Moluccas by offering prices eight times higher than their rivals.[11] An early opportunity to missionize and trade in China in opposition to the Portuguese was seized eagerly by the Spanish, though this chance was soon spoiled.[12] In 1598 a determined effort was made by a Spaniard to open up trade with Siam.[13] Between 1613 and 1619 three unsuccessful attempts were made to start a trade between Spain and the Philippines via the Cape.[14]

This early dynamic phase soon passed. In the political and military sphere Spain retreated in the face of the Dutch and other enemies. Formosa was abandoned in 1642, Mindanao and the Moluccas in 1662. Commercially, Manila began to stagnate, until she was "little more than a way-station between China and Mexico."[15] The general decline is considered by many historians to have started after the death of Juan de Silva at Malacca in 1616, though Bernard prefers to make 1641—42 the turning point.[16] Chaunu says trade was bouyant until the late 1610s, but then declined steadily to a trough in the late 1660s, followed by a moderate expansion from 1680.[17] Certainly the feverish prosperity of the first thirty years was never recovered. In the period 1586—1780 customs revenue as a percentage of the total receipts of the Manila *caja* were highest in 1611—15, when they were 70 *percent*. After 1635 they were never even half of this proportion.[18]

Yet although Philippine trade declined, this does not seem to have been a general tendency in the area. The Dutch had started their Southeast Asian trade in much the same spirit as had the Spanish. When the first ships got back in 1596 "toute le République sembler se lever pour aller ravir les trésors fabuleux de ces régions marveilleuses, et vingt-deux bateaux se réengagèrent aussitôt sur la périlleuse

---

[11] Meilink-Roelofsz, *op. cit.*, p. 155.

[12] Boxer (Ed.), *South China in the Sixteenth Century*, pp. xlv—l.

[13] BR, XV, pp. 184—86.

[14] C. R. Boxer, "Portuguese and Spanish Rivalry in the Far East during the Seventeenth Century", *Journal of the Royal Asiatic Society*, pp. 150—64, (December, 1946), pp. 91—105, (April, 1947), pp. 156—57.

[15] W. L. Schurz, *The Manila Galleon*, (New York, 1959), p. 26; see also BR, XLVIII, pp. 311—12.

[16] Bernard, *op. cit.*, pp. 193, 223.

[17] Pierre Chaunu, *Les Philippines et le Pacifique des Ibériques*, (Paris, 1960), pp. 244—56.

[18] *Ibid.*, pp. 78—83.

route." The later profits were commensurate with this spirit—shareholders in the Dutch East India Company got dividends of between 20 and 40 *percent* from the 1630s onwards. According to Bernard, during their first century in Amboyna the Dutch regularly made profits of 300 *percent* on their trade with this island.[19] In the 1640s the Portuguese galliots were bringing back about 3,000,000 cruzados (£ 600,000) a year in bullion from Japan. This represented the capital of Chinese, Japanese and Portuguese merchants.[20] At Tonkin both Portuguese and Japanese traders had an extensive trade in the late 1630s. There are records of a flourishing trade from China to Batavia, Cambodia, Cochin China, Siam and Patani in the 1620s and 1630s.[21]

The problem is thus set: why did Philippine country trade decline so quickly when there were apparently still profits to be made in the area? To answer this question, we must first consider Spanish trade in East and Southeast Asia in more detail, and from this try to draw out the general causes of the decline.

Within this area, the trade with China was always the basic one. Chaunu talks of the "caractère incomparable du trafic avec la Chine. La colonie espagnole ne peut vivre sans une liaison régulière et abondante avec le continent chinois", and adds later that fluctuations in the general prosperity of the Philippines depended largely on fluctuations in the China trade: "c'est bien, malgré les apparences, les heurs et malheurs du trafic avec le Continent chinois qui commandent les heurs et malheurs du trafic du galion lui-même."[22]

Officially, Chinese were not allowed to engage in foreign trade, though there was no prohibition on foreign ships bringing tribute from countries "that were impressed by the virtue of the celestial court."[23] But this prohibition was apparently not enforced at Fukien, for this province had a regular trade with the Philippines long before the arrival of the Spanish.[24] Legazpi did his best to befriend the

---

[19] Bernard, *op. cit.*, pp. 144—45, 154, 191; D. G. E. Hall, *A History of South-East Asia*, (London, 1964), p. 308.

[20] Boxer, *The Great Ship from Amacon*, p. 169.

[21] J. C. van Leur, *Indonesian Trade and Society*, (The Hague-Bandung, 1955), pp. 215, 242, 198, 374.

[22] Chaunu, *op. cit.*, pp. 54, 266—67.

[23] Meilink-Roelofsz, *op. cit.*, p. 77.

[24] Edgar Wickberg, *The Chinese in Philippine Life, 1850—98*, (New Haven, 1965), p. 3; Boxer (Ed.), *South China in the Sixteenth Century*, pp. xxxix—xl.

Chinese traders he met with, and by 1572 the basis of the junk trade with Luzon was laid.[25] There were early complaints of the poor quality of Chinese goods,[26] but the Chinese soon learnt what was required by the Spanish. In 1609 Morga spoke of thirty or forty large junks coming to Manila each season with a great variety of goods.[27] These included re-exports, goods bought at Malacca, Patani, the Moluccas or Japan and transhipped from Fukien to the Philippines.[28]

In the early years this trade was large and flourishing. Until the 1630s between twenty and thirty junks came each year, with the total number in the forties in 1588, 1596, 1609, 1610, 1612, 1635, and 1637. The junks were as large as 350 tons. But from 1642 to 1700 the number of junks only twice rose over twenty a year. This trade was also valuable—the cargoes of ten junks taken by the Dutch in 1617 were worth 750,000 florins (£ 62,500). According to Coen the Spanish collected 500,000 reals (£ 12,500) from the tolls on silk exports from Manila, and the Chinese Governor of Fukien claimed he got 80,000—100,00 reals (£ 2,000—2,500) a year from tolls on the trade with Manila.[29] The trade was carried on by the Chinese, not the Spanish. Apart from a few early attempts, the Spanish made no effort to break into it at its source by establishing posts in China. They were content to stay in Manila and let the goods be brought to them. There seemed to be no need for undue exertion while the galleon brought bullion with which they could pay the Chinese and take a profit for themselves.

The Macao-Manila connection also flourished early in the seventeenth century, although trade between the Spanish and Portuguese

[25] Edward J. McCarthy, *Spanish Beginnings in the Philippines, 1564—72*, (Washington, D. C., 1943), pp. 79, 124, 129.

[26] BR, IV, p. 58, VI, p. 269.

[27] *Ibid.*, XVI, pp. 177—80.

[28] T'ien-Tse Chang, *Sino-Portuguese Trade, From 1514 to 1644*, (Leyden, 1934), pp. 94—95; de la Costa, *op. cit.*, p. 50. Dr. Chang's book should be read in conjunction with a detailed review of it by Paul Pelliot in *T'oung Pao*, XXXI, pp. 58—94, (1934).

[29] Meilink-Roelofsz, *op. cit.*, pp. 263—65; Chaunu, *op. cit.*, pp. 148—77. Chaunu's figures frequently do not agree with stray references in other sources, as for example, in Schurz, *The Manila Galleon*, pp. 71, 114. Actually, all the statistics in this paper should be regarded as at best only informed guesses.

colonies was forbidden by Philip II after he became King of Portugal in 1580. This prohibition was occasionally re-issued.[30] Pedro de Baeza said that "The Spaniards who live in the Philippines do not communicate with them [the Portuguese in Macao], although both Spaniards and Portuguese communicate with all the other nations and provinces of those parts. This greatly scandalizes the natives of those regions, seeing that only Spanish and Portuguese do not deal or communicate with each other as would be expected of fellow-Christians and vassals of the same king."[31] No doubt the Spanish King liked to believe this, but it was not the truth. For most of the period between 1580 and 1640 the Portuguese carried on an illegal but lucrative trade with Manila.

This trade was apparently well established by 1591, for in this year seven Spaniards asked to be allowed to trade in Macao. They said the Portuguese traded in Manila, and made good profits.[32] In 1609 Morga said Portuguese ships came from the Moluccas, Malacca and India as well, with spices, slaves, cloth, jewels, carpets and atpestries.[33] The Portuguese trade with Manila increased as Dutch attacks in the seventeenth century made voyages to Malacca and Goa more risky—three galliots came to Manila from Macao in 1621 with rich cargoes.[34] In 1626 four galliots arrived, one with a cargo worth 500,000 pesos (£ 100,000).[35] But there were complaints from the Manila merchants about the Macao trade—they said the Portuguese were paying good prices for Chinese goods, and so the Chinese did not bother to come to Manila to trade. The Portuguese then took advantage of their semi-monopoly position in Manila.[36] In the early 1630s Manila's imports from Macao were estimated at 1,500,000 pesos (£ 300,000) a year, and as late at 1640 two or three ships were apparently still coming each year.[37] In this year Portugal seized her independence, and until 1668 she was officially at war with Spain. But

---

[30] Schurz, op. cit., pp. 132—34.
[31] Quoted in C. R. Boxer, The Christian Century in Japan, 1549—1650, (Berkeley - Los Angeles, 1951), p. 425.
[32] BR, VIII, pp. 174—75, 180—82.
[33] Ibid., XVI, 184—85; see also Meilink-Roelofsz, op. cit., p. 160.
[34] de la Costa, The Jesuits in the Philippines, p. 341.
[35] Boxer, The Great Ship from Amacon, p. 114.
[36] BR, XXV, pp. 111—17, 124—28, 136—38.
[37] Ibid., XXIX, 306; Boxer, The Great Ship from Amacon, pp. 134—35.

apparently trade continued nonetheless, though at a greatly reduced rate.[38]

This extensive trade was almost completely in the hands of the Portuguese, although legally it was forbidden to them just as firmly as it was to the Spanish. It seems that the Portuguese were more ready to take firm action against Spanish attempts to trade in Macao than were the Spanish to stop Portuguese trade in Manila. As was the case with the Chinese, the Spanish soon gave up their attempts to trade direct, and let the Portuguese monopolise the Macao-Manila trade.

The Portuguese had maintained their precarious position at Macao since 1557, and profited greatly from the rupture of relations between Japan and Ming China consequent on the depradations of Japanese pirates. For several decades Portuguese citizens had a monopoly of the silk-bullion trade between China and Japan. Thus they opposed the Spanish not only because they were potential competitors, via Manila, in this trade, but also because they feared Spanish missionary work in China might antagonize the Chinese towards all foreigners and lead to their expulsion from Macao. Further, China was part of the Portuguese *Padroado*, and any mission work that was to be done there should be in Portuguese hands. So they warned the officials at Canton that the Spanish were "ladrones y levantados, y que eran gente que se alcauan con los reynos donde entravan."[39] In 1590 they foiled a Spanish attempt to trade in China.[40] Eight years later the Spanish, despite the "hate and enmity" of the Portuguese, got permission to establish a trading post at El Pinal. According to Morga, the Spaniards got on well with the Chinese, but the Portuguese drove them out even so.[41] This was the end of Spanish efforts to trade direct in China—apparently a few Spaniards later went to Macao on sufferance,[42] but the Macao-Manila trade remained completely in Portuguese bottoms.

---

[38] Boxer, "Portuguese and Spanish Rivalry in the Far East", p. 163; C. R. Boxer, *Fidalgos in the Far East, 1550—1770*, (The Hague, 1948), p. 163.

[39] Quoted in Boxer, *The Great Ship from Amacon*, p. 61.

[40] BR, VIII, pp. 177—78.

[41] *Ibid.*, XV, pp. 162—63; Boxer, *Fidalgos in the Far East*, pp. 46—47. The site of El Pinal is uncertain, but according to Chang it was 12 leagues from Canton (Chang, *Sino-Portuguese Trade*, pp. 109—10). Professor Boxer prefers to leave the matter open (Boxer, "Portuguese and Spanish Rivalry in the Far East", p. 152 and footnote).   [42] BR, XXIX, p. 306.

Spanish trade with Japan was for a while fairly extensive. There had been some Japanese trade with the Philippines before the Spanish arrived, and this apparently continued, for the Japanese section of Manila was established at least by 1585.[43] Two official "Red Seal" Japanese ships were coming to the Philippines each year at the end of the sixteenth century,[44] and in 1609 this trade was still in progress, with the Japanese ships bringing foodstuffs and taking back raw silk and other goods.[45] Between 1604 and 1606 Ieyasu authorized at least thirty voyages from Japan to Luzon.[46] Some idea of the size of the trade can be got from the increase in the number of Japanese residents of Manila—in 1593 there were between 300 and 400, but by 1606 there were over 3,000. This trade began to decline in the late 1610s after Christianity was forbidden in Japan in 1614. By the 1620s it had nearly completely petered out.[47]

The Japanese connection was not maintained by the Spanish. In 1602 Ieyasu sent an embassy to the Philippines asking Spain to trade in Japan. Some Spanish ships were sent to Japan in the next few years, not so much because the Spanish hoped to profit from such trade but rather because they wanted to stay on good terms with Ieyasu so that their friars could continue to work in Japan. At one time the Spanish even had a small settlement in Japan, but again this was maintained for religious rather than trade reasons.[48] The strength of the Spanish desire to trade in Japan can be gauged from the aftermath of the *Nossa Senhora da Graca* affair in 1610. The dispute over this ship led to a break in Portuguese-Japanese relations, but Ieyasu was soon forced to re-open them because neither the Dutch nor the Spanish were capable of replacing the Portuguese as suppliers of Chinese silk.[49] Yet the Spanish must have had plenty of silk—obviously they were not interested in trading with Japan. Apparently the Spanish felt that they did not need Japanese silver, for they could get it from Mexico. More importantly, it seems that

---

[43] M. T. Paske-Smith, "Japanese Trade and Residence in the Philippines", *Transactions of the Asiatic Society of Japan*, XLII, (1914), p. 692.

[44] BR, XV, p. 305.   [45] *Ibid.*, XVI, pp. 183—84.

[46] Boxer, *The Christian Century in Japan*, p. 264.

[47] *Ibid.*, pp. 302, 367.

[48] *Ibid.*, pp. 301—302; Paske-Smith, *op. cit.*, pp. 700—702.

[49] Boxer, *The Christian Century in Japan*, pp. 270—83; Boxer, *Fidalgos in the Far East*, pp. 62—63.

Madrid accepted the Portuguese contention that Japan was in their trading sphere. The Spanish Government thus discouraged any attempts by Manila merchants to break into the Portuguese trade.[50]

In any case, opportunities such as that of 1610 were rare, for usually Japanese-Spanish relations were rather strained. For most of the time, the Spanish could not have traded in Japan even if they had wanted to. These uneasy relations were partly a result of Spanish economic policies—not only did the Spanish Government disapprove of Spaniards trading anywhere apart from with other Spanish colonies, but also it opposed Japanese attempts to trade with Acapulco. Thus Date Masamune's embassy in 1613—14, which seems to have been backed by Ieyasu himself, met with a cold reception in Mexico and Spain. He asked the Seville authorities "to send him several pilots to instruct him to navigate between the Indies and Spain, as he intended to yearly send his vessels to Europe, and thus show his good will and resolution by frequent and direct intercourse between Japan and the old continent." In 1616 Date sent another ship to New Spain, and while it was there the complete prohibition of all such trade was announced.[51] There were also political strains. The ruling Tokugawa family was always afraid that the Europeans had designs on Japanese soil, perhaps in alliance with dissident Daimyo elements within Japan, while the Spaniards were alarmed by the possibility of Japanese attacks on the Philippines in 1592, 1597, 1621 and 1630.[52] And the question of missionaries in Japan was closely related to these Japanese fears, for the Tokugawas saw the missionaries as a "fifth column" undermining Japanese allegiance to the state. The root cause of the uneasy Spanish-Japanese relations was the determination of the friars to get to Japan, a determination which increased after Christianity was forbidden. The Spanish failure to control these zealots led to the Japanese severance of relations with Spain and her colonies in 1624, and the formal expulsion of all foreigners twelve years later.

The Spanish seem to have had a fairly extensive trade with the Moluccas before the arrival of the Dutch, but this trade was con-

---

[50] Boxer, *The Great Ship from Amacon*, p. 3.

[51] Schurz, *op. cit.*, pp. 125—28; C. Meriwether, "A Sketch of the Life of Date Masamune and An Account of his Embassy to Rome", *Transactions of the Asiatic Society of Japan*, XXI, (1893), *passim*.

[52] Paske-Smith, *op. cit.*, pp. 696—99, 704, 706.

spicuous by its absence after about 1600—indeed between 1606 and 1662, when Spain held Western Ternate and Tidore, Chaunu claims only two ships came from there to the Philippines.[53] Yet the Spanish knew very well that the spice trade was an extremely lucrative one. The cargo of the *Victoria* had been worth at least 25,000 ducats (£ 5,000) in 1522, and in 1529 Charles V, by the Treaty of Saragossa, received 350,000 ducats (£ 70,000) from Portugal in return for his giving up Spain's claims to the Moluccas.[54] While Spain held two of these islands, several Spaniards wrote of the great profits that they could continue to make from the clove trade. Grau Y Monfalcon spoke of this as "the most noble product, and that which is most earnestly desired, as it is of the greatest profit and gain,"[55] and around 1620 one writer said Spain could make 3,290,000 pesos, (£ 658,000) a year from the clove trade.[56] In 1621 another writer claimed that the Dutch were making (less expenses) a profit of 2,796,000 ducats (£ 559,000) a year from this trade, while Spain was spending 218,000 pesos (£ 43,600) a year on keeping a foothold in the Moluccas.[57]

The Spanish failure to profit from the spice trade was partly a result of lack of initiative. In the 1610s the English found the natives eager to sell spices to them,[58] but following de Silva's death in 1616 the Spanish seem to have looked on while the Dutch made the trade their monopoly. In 1640 a Jesuit said Spain "rather holds those islands [Tidore and Ternate] for the conservation there of the faith ... than for the profit that is derived from them,"[59] yet actually

---

[53] Chaunu, *Les Philippines et le Pacifique des Ibériques*, pp. 152—65. This claim is apparently false, as the Spanish sent ships from Manila to provision and reinforce the garrisons on Tidore and Ternate; often a small fleet was sent each year (e. g. BR, XXIV, pp. 330—32; XXVII, pp. 40—41). Some of these ships must have returned to the Philippines, but, judging by the contemporary comments quoted in this and the next paragraph, they seem to have returned empty.

[54] E. G. Bourne, "The History and Determination of the Lines of Demarcation Established by Pope Alexander VI, between the Spanish and Portuguese Fields of Discovery and Colonization", American Historical Association, *Annual Report*, 1891, (Washington, D. C., 1892), pp. 116—19.

[55] BR, XXVII, p. 97.   [56] *Ibid.*, XIX, p. 304.

[57] *Ibid.*, XIX, pp. 291, 296; see also *ibid.*, XVIII, p. 109.

[58] Meilink-Roelofsz, *Asian Trade and European Influence*, p. 199.

[59] BR, XXIX, p. 309.

Spain seems not to have done much missionary work there either. The Moluccas were regarded as being in the Portuguese sphere of interest. This had been stipulated by the Treaty of Saragossa. Urdaneta was warned that "you are not in any way or manner to enter the islands of the said Muluccas, because the treaty which his majesty has made with the most serene king of Portugal is not to be broken."[60] Thus although the Spanish made several attempts between 1582 and 1606 to retake the islands from the native rulers and later from the Dutch, this was always done on behalf of the Portuguese.[61] A year after the success of 1607 the clove trade was reserved to the Portuguese, and it was decreed that it was to be carried on via India.[62] Portuguese-Spanish co-operation soon ended, except in cases of emergency such as those of 1615—16 and 1622, and the Dutch effectively stopped the Portuguese from sailing the Moluccas-India route. But the Spanish still made little effort to fill the gap, even after 1640 when they were not bound to keep out of Portuguese areas. Instead, the Dutch were allowed to control the trade, and most ignominiously, America was supplied with spices by them.[63] The abandonment of Tidore and Ternate in 1662 was typical of the whole inglorious Spanish performance in the Moluccas after about 1600.

Philippine trade with the rest of Southeast Asia must be surveyed here, not because it was of much economic importance but for the sake of completeness. Until 1640 some Portuguese ships came to Manila via Goa and Malacca, and later in the century trade with India began, only to languish after a few years.[64] There was no trade with Java until peace was made with the Dutch in 1648, and even after this trade with Indonesia reached no great heights, thanks to the exclusionist policies of both the Spanish and Dutch. In the early seventeenth century some native craft came to Manila from Borneo each year, but according to Morga the Portuguese got all the fine diamonds found on this island.[65] Annam and Tongking were in a state of almost perpetual war between 1620 and 1674 as a result of rivalry between the Trinh and Nguyen groups, but despite this the

[60] Quoted in McCarthy, *Spanish Beginnings in the Philippines*, p. 23.
[61] Hall, *A History of South-East Asia*, pp. 227—28.
[62] BR, XXVII, p. 100.
[63] Schurz, *The Manila Galleon*, p. 142.
[64] *Ibid.*, pp. 134—35.
[65] BR, XVI, p. 185; see also *ibid.*, XXIX, p. 306.

Portuguese and Dutch and English all traded there at various times. The Spanish apparently did not.[66] Similarly, the Portuguese cloth trade in Cambodia continued well into the seventeenth century,[67] but despite Cambodian requests for trade with the Philippines in the 1590s, and the exploits of Blas Ruys and Belhoso, Philippine trade was never important in this country.[68] The same can be said of Siam. Early in the century the Dutch and Japanese opened relations with Siam at Patani and Ayutia, and trade soon flourished. Later in the century Narai tried to free himself from his economic dependence on the Dutch, but the English and French, not the Spanish, took advantage of this.[69]

We must now consider the reasons for this progressively poorer and poorer showing on the part of the Spanish. Chaunu, who has produced what is by far the most detailed statistical account of Spanish trade in the Pacific, seeks to link the fortunes of this trade with the economic health of Europe. He claims to have established "une corrélation positive élémentaire entre les grandes lignes de la conjoncture des prix (en Hollande et en Espagne notamment) et la conjoncture de l'activité générale des trafics dans l'océan Pacifique. Cela, aussi, nous pensons l'avoir démontré et, peut-être, avons-nous démontré d'un même coup qu'il existe bien dès la deuxième moitié du XVI siècle, au moins, présomption solide d'une économie-monde, une économie-monde qui fait, derrière Magellan, le tour de la terre."[70] Chaunu admits that his study is an incomplete one, and it does seem very unlikely that this thesis provides a full explanation for the fluctuations of Philippine trade. Certainly he has established a correlation between Philippine trade and European prosperity, but this could be largely coincidental. Yet it is not my intention to deny the influence of European factors on the Spanish country trade centered on the Philippines, but simply to suggest that non-economic European factors should also be examined. More specifically, it is possible to show that, as a result of these influences coming from Europe, the early prosperity of the Philippines was not firmly based, but rather had within it from the very beginning the elements which

---

[66] Hall, *op. cit.*, pp. 393—96.
[67] Meilink-Roelofsz, *op. cit.*, pp. 165, 189.
[68] Schurz, *op. cit.*, pp. 144—50; BR, XVI, pp. 185—86, XXIX, p. 306.
[69] Hall, *op. cit.*, pp. 335, 338—41; BR, XVI, pp. 185—86, XXIV, p. 207.
[70] Chaunu, *op. cit.*, p. 265.

later caused this prosperity to vanish. These elements will emerge as we consider the general reasons for the decline of Philippine trade.

The first of these general reasons is the restrictions which were placed on Philippine trade from 1565, which gradually became more and more all-embracing. But the regulations from Madrid were never firmly obeyed; indeed if they had been the Philippines could hardly have traded anywhere. Some idea of the nature of the restrictions can be gained from the following decree: "It was ordered that the ships that go from Nueva Espana to Filipinas must sail from the port of Acapulco by the end of March, without extending even a day into April. And inasmuch as we are informed that that is inconvenient, we order that the ships be prepared with all that is necessary by December, so that at the end of that month, they may leave the said port of Acapulco, so that they may be able to arrive at the said islands, at the latest, some time in March. It is our will that this be executed inviolably, and it will be made a charge of omission in the residencia of the viceroys of Nueva Espana; and, if they do not so do, we shall consider ourselves disserved."[71] But the number of times such laws had to be repeated, with increasingly draconic penalties and increasingly petulant expression, showed clearly that the more unrealistic restrictions at least were not obeyed.[72]

Spanish foreign trade focused on the port of Seville, through whose *Casa* all New World trade had to pass. Her merchants, combined with Spanish manufacturers, especially those making silk, formed an extremely powerful lobby at Madrid. In response to their pressure, Spanish economic policy was formulated and preserved. This policy cannot be described as purely mercantalist, for no attempt was made to meet the demand for the large merchant marine which was essential for mercantalism, and at times colonial industries were allowed to develop.[73] The system is better described as monopolist, with a saving addition of inefficiency.[74]

As monopolists, Spanish merchants and manufacturers could only view early Philippine trade with horror. Manila was profiting from

---

[71] BR, XXV, pp. 33—34.

[72] For example, *ibid.*, XVII, pp. 27—50, XXV, pp. 23—37.

[73] J. H. Elliott, *Imperial Spain, 1469—1716*, (London, 1963), p. 190; C. H. Haring, *Trade and Navigation between Spain and the Indies*, (Cambridge, Mass., 1918), pp. 7—8, 125—26.

[74] Elliott, *op. cit.*, p. 173.

trade which was not with the mother country, nor even with another Spanish colony. Foreign silk was underselling native Spanish silk all over South America. Spaniards were trading in foreign ships. And worst of all, bullion was flowing from Peru to Manila, and from there into the hands of infidels. Such economic tendencies were regarded as so dangerous that at one time there was a move in Spain for the exchange of the Philippines with Brazil, so that the anomaly could be ended.[75] Such a drastic step was never taken, but in 1586 Madrid nearly abolished the all-important silk trade with China, and in 1720 it actually did, though fortunately this was reversed four years later.[76]

More petty restrictions abounded. Their number increased over the years, but some were imposed at the very beginning of Spain's colonial career in Asia. Thus Legazpi's final instructions forbade private trade except through the royal officials, the Cortes of Tomar (1581) forbade trade between Portuguese and Spanish colonies, Philippine citizens were forbidden to trade in China in 1593, and Japanese were excluded from the Philippine trade in 1609. But the degree to which these were observed can be gauged from an incident in 1629—in this year the Portuguese who bought the captaincy of the Japan Voyage bound himself to send at least three ships to Manila in the next three years. Similarly, Philip II ordered that trade between Macao and Manila must go via Malacca, but this was generally ignored.[77]

Other restrictions covered the galleon trade between Manila and Acapulco. The ownership, size, tonnage and number per year of the galleons was strictly laid down, as was the place where they were to be built and their route. Officials, soldiers, individual religious, and officers of the galleons were forbidden to take part in the trade. The value of the cargoes was restricted, and trade between the Philippines and Peru was prohibited in 1581. Nor were Chinese goods to be re-exported from Acapulco to Peru. All these regulations were meant to limit the competition to Spanish goods in South America.

---

[75] Haring, *op. cit.*, p. 147; Bernard, *Les Iles Philippines du Grand Archipel de la Chine*, p. 65.

[76] BR, VI, pp. 279—83, XLIV, pp. 253—57, 265—68, 306.

[77] McCarthy, *Spanish Beginnings in the Philippines*, p. 26; Boxer, *Fidalgos in the Far East*, p. 109; Bernard, *op. cit.*, p. 63; BR, XLVIII, pp. 310—11, XVII, p. 50.

Many of them were flouted, yet such a basic one as that limiting the number of ships could not be.[78] The general tenor of these restrictions, and indeed of all government policy in the seventeenth century, was well summed up in 1629. Governor Tavora proposed to Philip IV an imaginative scheme to increase Spanish trade with the Moluccas. In Madrid a decision was written at the end of his letter: "The fiscal declares that the form is laid down by the decrees and ordinances which treat of it, and he thinks it undesirable to make any innovation."[79]

These restrictions were imposed in order to make Philippine trade conform to the Spanish ideal of colonial trade. Their total effect is difficult to assess. Some Spaniards blamed them alone for the decline in their trade. Grau Y Monfalcon wrote "And if commerce is regarded as the greatest splendour of kingdoms (as it certainly is), this greatness is not lacking to the Philipinas; for they have so rich a commerce that, if they could enjoy it free, there is no city known to the world that would surpass, or even equal, Manila."[80] Certainly the restrictions stopped Japanese trade in the Philippines and Mexico. They were influential in preventing the development of a Spanish trade with China and Macao, though here Portuguese opposition was probably most important. Generally, they must have had an enfeebling effect on Philippine trade, and helped to discourage any spirit of innovation. But many of these restrictions were imposed as soon as the Spanish took the Philippines. Thus much Philippine trade during its early period of prosperity was carried on in violation of royal decrees. No matter how openly these decrees were flouted, such trade cannot be regarded as healthy and liable to continue. Sooner or later the prohibitions would have some effect, and this indeed happened as a more law-abiding spirit of routine replaced the early conquistador bravado. Spanish trade in Asia had to decline once it began to fit more closely the model laid down in Madrid for colonial trade.

Closely related to this reason for the decline of Philippine trade were Spanish relations with the Portuguese. In the seventeenth century

---

[78] Schurz, *op. cit.*, pp. 165—77, 193—99, 366—70; BR, XII, pp. 60—61, XIII, pp. 257—59, XIV, pp. 214—27; Haring, *op. cit.*, pp. 145—47.

[79] BR, XXIII, pp. 30—35.

[80] *Ibid.*, XXX, p. 33. Father de la Costa agrees that the Philippines' stagnation was a result of "the repression of its expanding commerce" (de la Costa, *op. cit.*, p. 416).

the Spanish paid great deference to the prohibition on interference with Portuguese spheres, and thus they effectively eliminated most of South and Southeast Asia as places where they could trade. In the Moluccas the ridiculous situation developed of the Spanish holding Tidore and Ternate, yet not trading with them, even when the Portuguese were prevented from doing so by the Dutch. Japan also was left alone by the Spanish, while in Macao and China they let the Portuguese stop them from trading, while at the same time the Portuguese were enjoying an illegal but profitable connection with Manila. For a country like the Philippines, with limited natural resources but an excellent position, a prosperous trade could only be developed if she managed to become an emporium dealing in the goods of other countries. These goods need not necessarily have been carried by the Spanish—most of them were not in the period of prosperity—but when other countries were not trading with the Philippines the Spanish should have gone out themselves and traded. This was not done. Monopolist trade theories in Spain, together with the Spanish desire (in Europe) to conciliate the Portuguese, led to restrictions. These were present almost from the start, but it was some time before their effect was felt.

The galleon journey across the Pacific was always a hazardous one, as Schurz has so graphically depicted. The Spanish Friar Navarrete once described how "at Cavite, a wave took thirty-six Men out of another ship . . . There's a Wave! Some were sav'd, the rest perish'd."[81] Such dangers were constant, but in the first half of the seventeenth century the Spanish were afflicted by a particularly bad run of luck. Six galleons were wrecked between 1600 and 1609, while in 1616—17 four were forced back to Manila after unsuccessful attempts to reach Acapulco.[82]

A greater hazard at this time was the Dutch attacks on the Philippines, on Spanish shipping all over the Pacific, and on Portuguese, Chinese and Japanese ships bound for the Philippines. These attacks were, of course, part of the worldwide Spanish-Dutch hostility of this time, and thus were an element in the Dutch struggle for economic and religious freedom from Spanish dominance. In Philippine waters

---

[81] J. S. Cummins (Ed.), *The Travels and Controversies of Friar Domingo Navarrete, 1618—86*, I—II, (Cambridge, Hakluyt Society, 1962), I, p. 91.
[82] Schurz, *op. cit.*, pp. 258, 261.

the Dutch raids seem to have reached a peak in the 1610s. But the second decade of the seventeenth century was also the time when Spanish prosperity in the Philippines was probably at its greatest. Between 1625 and 1640 the Dutch generally left the Spanish alone, though their Moro allies did not always, yet this was when the Spanish decline began. It seems that the Dutch attacks at first stimulated the Spanish to greater efforts, as evidenced militarily by the battles of Playa Honda. But these exertions had the effect, over a period of time, of exhausting the Spanish, so that once the Dutch threat ended for a time in the 1630s they sank into lethargy. When the attacks were renewed the Spanish were less capable of combatting them, even in the Philippines. They were quite incapable of stopping the Dutch from consolidating their tight monopoly on trade with Indonesia. Yet the Dutch were not irresistible—the English, French, Portuguese and Chinese all competed with them with at least some degree of success. So again there were factors present in Philippine trade during the period of its prosperity, namely Dutch hostility and the hazards of the sea, which in this case at first had an invigorating effect. But over a period of time these factors also contributed to the decline of Philippine trade.

Another element was the religious one. This also was present throughout, and its influence on Philippine trade with Japan is an outstanding example of Spanish chickens coming home to roost. In the Spanish conquest of the Philippines, and indeed, in the basic aims lying behind their expansion in the sixteenth century, God and Mammon and Caesar were inextricably mixed. In the case of the Philippines, however, the glory of God seemed to have taken first place over the glory of Spain or of the King. It was the influence of the Orders which prevented the abandonment of the Philippines, despite the fact that about 15 *percent* of Spain's total profits from the Indies were, in the seventeenth century, spent on maintaining the islands. In the first half of this century abour half the receipts of the Manila treasury were in the form of aid from New Spain.[83] As Chaunu says, the Spanish king spent "pour permettre l'oeuvre de quelque trois cents missionaires, impensables sans la présence politique de l'Espagne, une fraction non négligeable des revenus de son Nouveau Royaume espagnol, . . . et non seulement Philippe II,

---

[83] Chaunu, *op. cit.*, pp. 268, 78—83.

mais bien plus que lui, ses successeurs, Philippe III et surtout Philippe IV." [84]

This religious dominance was the main cause of the growing Japanese hostility to the Philippine connection. At first relations were reasonably good, thanks to the Japanese desire for trade, but in 1622 the Japanese reply to a Spanish embassy was "that such Embassages came not of themselves, but procured by religious men, dwelling in those [Philippine] Islands; and that the Xogun Lord of Iaponia would receive no Embassages from places broaching a law most false, diabolical and seditious, turning the state upside down and deceiving the subjects. That already he had been deceived in that kind, and that under cover of traffick and merchandize this pernicious law and the Authors thereof had been brought in, whom he now had banished under vigorous paines and would receive no more." [85] Four years later a Spanish ship seeking trade was told it must leave Japan at once, and "no vessels should go from these [Philippine] islands under pain of death, on account of the religious which they conveyed from here." [86] Thus such later attempts as were made by the Spanish to trade in Japan were blocked by their association with the hated and feared missionaries.

The Spanish connection with militant Roman Catholicism also had an effect on their trade with other areas. Flagrant Spanish attempts at conversion did not endear them to the mandarins of Canton, and these attempts were stressed by the more secular Portuguese in order to discredit their rivals. Dutch hostility to the Spanish was partly religious antagonism, fostered by the work of the Inquisition in the Low Countries and by Spanish treatment of Dutch prisoners of war. In the seventeenth century the English tried to get permission to trade between India, Bantam and Manila, but this was not allowed, presumably as a result of economic policy and religious antagonism. [87] Bernard criticizes the Dutch and British for their "mercantilisme tristement prosaique et banalement areligieux" and for their "notion de patrie s'était dissociée de celle de la fidélité au souverain et à la religion traditionelle," [88] yet these stric-

---

[84] *Ibid.*, p. 20.
[85] Boxer, *The Christian Century in Japan*, p. 368.
[86] BR, XXII, p. 96.
[87] *Ibid.*, XXXV, pp. 209—11; Schurz, *op. cit.*, p. 135.
[88] Bernard, *op. cit.*, pp. 187, 150.

tures cannot be considered valid. If the Spanish were going to merge God and Mammon, they had to be prepared to accept the possibility that one of these allegiances might work to the detriment of the other. Once again an element was present in early Philippine trade which finally had the effect of limiting it.

Underlying all these factors was a decline in the spirit of the Spanish. The stock which had produced men like Cortes, Pizarro and their Philippine counterparts seemed to be exhausted. This was of crucial importance for Spanish trade; as a cautious, conservative spirit of routine replaced the earlier daring, the elements which tended to limit trade came to be more effective. The Spanish had been opposed by the Moros and the native rulers of the Moluccas right from the start, Dutch attacks had started in the late sixteenth century, they had been forbidden to trade with Portuguese colonies from 1581, other trade restrictions had been in force before then, the Philippines never provided important articles of trade for the Spanish until the eighteenth century, and religion had always been interwined with the secular strain. But the early spirit of the Spanish was sufficient to overcome all these obstacles. Manila prospered despite them all.

To some extent the decline in initiative resulted from these early large profits. The Spanish did not perceive the precarious basis of their prosperity, hedged around as it was by so many hostile factors. They thought they need not work too hard to do well, and so they began to ease up in their efforts. Yet soon this led to a situation where they were not capable of the active role needed if Manila was to continue to flourish. Thus these same early profits had a stultifying influence, which opened the door for the other inhibiting factors to take effect.

There were other factors contributing to this decline in initiative. The Spanish have never been noted for being a great trading nation and this was doubly true after the Jews and the Moors, the main trading elements in the home society, were expelled in 1492. To some extent the decline of the early thrustful commercial spirit was simply a reversion to the usual Spanish lack of interest in trade. The whole galleon system and the restrictions on it were not conducive to initiative. In particular, the dependence on the Chinese silk trade hindered attempts to develop other markets, but the Mexican silk manufacturers, who often invested heavily in the Manila trade,[89]

---

[89] Schurz, *op. cit.*, pp. 363—65.

did not want any other product except silk. The regularity of the arrival of the junks made it seem unnecessary to try and establish a Spanish post in China. And the Spanish in the Philippines seem to have shared in the general decline of the Spanish nation. According to Bourne, in the seventeenth century the power of the Dutch, French and British was rising, but in Spain there was only "the absence of the spirit of progress, hostility to new ideas, failure to develop resources, and the prevalence of bribery and corruption."[90] A good example of this conservatism was seen in the Northerly route taken by the galleons from Manila. The galleons always sailed South from Manila, East through an extremely dangerous passage, and then North up the East coast of Luzon. Had the galleons gone North from Manila up the West coast much time could have been saved and danger avoided. Yet even such an obvious reform as this was never undertaken in the seventeenth century.[91]

It was the growth of such a spirit as this that let all the other inhibiting and restricting factors take effect. The long economic decline of the Philippines in the seventeenth century resulted. A continuance of the early prosperity would have required either root-and-branch reform in the Spanish state, amounting to a change in the very economic, religious and political foundations of the Spanish nation, or an endurance of the conquistador spirit, devoted now to more mundane pursuits. The decline of Philippine trade was not inevitable—this was proved by the Governors of the late eighteenth century. But given all the inhibiting factors present, it would not have been easy to avoid this decline.

---

[90] BR, I, p. 47; see also *ibid.*, XLIV, p. 228 f. n.
[91] Schurz, *op. cit.*, pp. 224—26.

II

Brokers in Western Indian Port Cities
Their Role in Servicing Foreign Merchants

The merchant who arrives in a locality unknown to him must also carefully arrange in advance to secure a reliable representative, a safe lodging house, and whatever besides is necessary, so that he is not taken in by a slow payer or by a cheat.[1]

It has been the ancient customes of the Indians to make all bargains by the mediation of Brokers, all Forreigners as well as the natives are compelled to submit to it: the Armenians, Turks, Persians, Jews, Europeans and Banyans.[2]

* * *

Over many centuries of trade and exchange there evolved in western Indian port cities a refined and complex set of structures designed to facilitate this trade. A very high degree of functional specialization was found in these ports. This article attempts to flesh out the role of one link in a very complex chain of economic relationships, that is, the brokers who dealt with foreign merchants. After a general discussion, brief case studies of Calicut, Diu and Cambay will go some way towards showing the actual mechanisms of the system in operation in the sixteenth century.

The role of merchants in India in the sixteenth and seventeenth centuries has recently been much discussed. The first volume of the *Cambridge Economic History of India* provides useful summaries of this recent research.[3] In his first monograph Ashin Das Gupta surveyed

---

[1] 'The Book of Knowledge of the Beauties of Commerce and of the Cognizance of Good and Bad Merchandise and of Falsifications', in Arabic, 1318, quoted in Ann Bos Radwan, *The Dutch in Western India 1601–1632* (Calcutta, 1978), p. 16.

[2] Annesley of Surat, quoted in K. N. Chaudhuri, *The Trading World of Asia and the English East India Company, 1660–1760* (Cambridge, 1978), p. 71; quoted again in K. N. Chaudhuri, *Trade and Civilisation in the Indian Ocean: An Economic History from the Rise of Islam to 1750* (Cambridge, 1985), p. 226, with one change.

[3] *The Cambridge Economic History of India* [*CEHI*], vol. 1 (Cambridge, 1982), pp. 340–5 by T. Raychaudhuri; and pp. 418–25 by Ashin Das Gupta for sea-going merchants.

456

mercantile roles in Malabar,[4] while A. L. Chicherov analysed economic relationships in the whole of India.[5] Surat's merchants have been much studied.[6]

Eric Wolf has reminded us that 'When the European sea traders intruded into other continents . . . they often found long-standing networks of commercial relationships that involved principles and operations with which they were wholly familiar.'[7] Braudel's magisterial *Civilization and Capitalism* provides an attractive entrée to these European comparisons.[8]

Two very recent books provide stimulating overviews of trade and commerce in the Indian Ocean area and further afield. K. N. Chaudhuri's *Trade and Civilisation in the Indian Ocean* is a brilliant synthesis, packed with insights on, among much else, the economic and social roles of sea traders and land merchants.[9] Philip D. Curtin's *Cross-Cultural Trade in World History* is equally stimulating but perhaps a little more problematical.[10] His book concentrates on the notion of the 'trade diaspora', that is 'socially interdependent but spatially dispersed communities'.[11] The argument is innovative, the overview courageous in its scope, yet I feel he tries too hard to fit too many traders into the 'trade diaspora' rubric. The result is that he stresses similarities at the expense of differences. Nor, I feel, does the fact of their wide geographical dispersion really make them very different from any other traders. In any case, except for Africa he has scant concrete data on what 'cross-cultural brokers' actually *did*. Nor does he have much to say about local brokers who played the same role as these people, who by his definition are foreigners. Thus my article at the least fleshes out, with reference to India, and adds to his more general analysis.

[4] Ashin Das Gupta, *Malabar in Asian Trade, 1740–1800* (Cambridge, 1967), pp. 103–23.

[5] A. L. Chicherov, *India: Economic Development in the 16th–18th Centuries* (Moscow, 1971), *passim*.

[6] Ashin Das Gupta, *Indian Merchants and the Decline of Surat, c. 1700–1750* (Wiesbaden, 1979), pp. 74–88; B. G. Gokhale, *Surat in the Seventeenth Century* (London, 1979), pp. 117–36; Ann Radwan, *Dutch in Western India*, pp. 16–20; Surendra Gopal, *Commerce and Crafts in Gujarat* (New Delhi, 1975), *passim*, but especially pp. 218–37; M. J. Mehta, 'Some Aspects of Surat as a Trading Centre in the Seventeenth Century,' *Indian Historical Review*, I, ii, Sept. 1974, pp. 247–61 .

[7] Eric R. Wolf, *Europe and the People without History* (Berkeley, 1982), p. 84.

[8] F. Braudel, *Civilization and Capitalism, 15th–18th Century*, 3 vols (New York, 1981–84), esp. II, 114–230, 374–457, III, 125.

[9] K. N. Chaudhuri, *Trade and Civilisation in the Indian Ocean*, op. cit.

[10] Philip D. Curtin, *Cross-Cultural Trade in World History* (Cambridge, 1984); and see Chaudhuri, *Trade and Civilisation*, pp. 224–6 for a critique of the basic concept.

[11] Curtin, *Cross-Cultural Trade*, pp. 2–3.

The term 'merchant' is of course a very general one. Das Gupta usefully divides merchants into four types: shippers, merchants, brokers, and *sarafs* (money changers; the correct spelling is *sarraf*). We are concerned with the third, the brokers, in Arabic *dallal*. Mediterranean parallels can be followed in Lieber's useful article,[12] while J. K. Fairbank has analysed in detail the role of the *hong* merchants in Canton in the two centuries before the Opium Wars.[13] In the context of Surat Das Gupta suggests a subdivision into general brokers, who did all the sales and purchases for a large merchant, and brokers who dealt in specific commodities, such as cloths, or spices, or saltpetre. He stresses the ubiquity of brokers: 'In short wherever there was an economic transaction in the city, you would very likely find a broker to smooth your way and take his cut.'[14]

A. Jan Qaisar, in an article which is absolutely fundamental to our understanding of brokers in Mughal India, makes clear the difference between brokers on the one hand, and *sarrafs* and *dubashis* (interpreters) on the other. He delineates four types of brokers: those who were regular employees or agents of merchants, companies, etc., and who were paid either by a salary or a commission (these could perhaps best be called agents rather than brokers); those who worked for more than one employee; those who worked ad hoc; and those who were appointed by the state. He notes that most brokers also traded on their own account. This is a most useful reminder of the dangers of being overly schematic, and of the complexity of the actual situation. In fact everyone traded, even if they were primarily not merchants but, for example, rather *sarrafs*, *dubashis*, or sailors.[15]

The subdivisions of brokers suggested by Qaisar and Das Gupta enable us to see more clearly commercial roles in Indian port cities. Our concern in this paper is with one sort of broker, that is those who connected with sea traders, especially foreigners. Such people can be seen as a specific category within the broad rubric of 'brokers', even though there is no doubt that they also played other economic roles at other times. In particular, they would service other traders, apart from foreigners, and they would also trade on their own account. Before fleshing out the function of these people who serviced foreigners, it is

[12] Alfred E. Lieber, 'Eastern Business Practices and Medieval European Commerce,' *Economic History Review*, 2nd series, XXI, 1968, pp. 230–43.

[13] J. K. Fairbank, *East Asia: The Modern Transformation* (Boston, 1965), pp. 73–8. See also a short but more up-to-date account in Curtin, *Cross-Cultural Trade*, pp. 242–5.

[14] Das Gupta, *Surat*, pp. 84–5.

[15] A. Jan Qaisar, 'The Role of Brokers in Medieval India,' *Indian Historical Review*, I, ii, Sept. 1974, pp. 220–46; T. Raychaudhuri in *CEHI*, I, 342.

458

useful to fit them into a more general framework, drawing on neo-Marxist theory developed by Eric Wolf and Immanuel Wallerstein.

Wolf has put forward a concept of a tributary mode of production, which he finds in all the major world agricultural areas around 1400 and later. State power varied greatly from region to region, but in general terms these states all 'represent a mode of production in which the primary producer, whether cultivator or herdsman, is allowed access to the means of production, while tribute is exacted from him by political and military means.'[16] Tribute collection involves the accumulation of surpluses, and these surpluses were circulated either socially or geographically. They could be siphoned upwards, or redistributed downwards. It was in this process that 'commercial intermediaries' or merchants played a role, for they handled the actual transfer or exchange. The acquisition of luxuries by the elite was especially, though not exclusively, important.[17] In fact luxuries, and even some basic commodities, were circulated over very wide geographical areas. Here is where Wallerstein's concept of the world-economy is important.

He finds a 'modern world system' beginning to evolve in western Europe in the sixteenth century. However, there was also in existence at this time 'a flourishing world-economy,' or at least proto-world-economy, in the Indian Ocean area.[18] This world-economy included very diverse people, and was integrated to a degree by equally diverse traders, people originating not only from the littoral areas of the ocean but also from as far afield as China, the Mediterranean and western Europe. The diversity of these traders, who played the crucial role of making this vast area into a system sufficiently integrated as to be described as a world-economy, created its own problems. In particular, the heterogeneity of these traders necessitated a mechanism by which they themselves could be integrated and serviced in foreign ports; such mechanisms were essential for the viability of the whole system. The rest of this article will sketch these mechanisms.

Ashin Das Gupta has gone some way towards explaining the role of brokers who dealt with sea traders. Shippers, and merchants engaged solely in imports and exports, relied on specific commodity brokers for specific goods. Sea traders, however, he depicts as 'tied to an alter ego

[16] Wolf, *Europe*, pp. 79–80.

[17] *Ibid.*, pp. 82–4. See also a succinct analysis in K. N. Chaudhuri, *Trade and Civilisation*, p. 16.

[18] Immanuel Wallerstein, *The Modern World-System: Capitalist Agriculture and the Origins of the European World-Economy in the Sixteenth Century* (New York, 1974), p. 331.

in the shape of a general broker who would operate a vast network of middlemen to supply his principal with the range of commodities desired for export, or help sell the varieties of goods imported.'[19] This is useful, but we can attempt to modify and elaborate on this broad sketch.

The crucial distinction to be made concerns the degree of knowledge and support available to a foreign merchant when he (for I know of no female travelling merchants) disembarked at a port in western India in the sixteenth century. It is unlikely that any foreigner was completely ignorant of what he would find. At the very least he would have picked up scattered information from his fellow-traders in his home area. If he was European, he would possibly have read Marco Polo, and later in the sixteenth century Linschoten, Cesare Federici, or one of the Portuguese authors. Conversation on the ship as it approached the port would provide extra detail. Thus even a trader with no local connections at all was still far from being a *tabula rasa*.

More likely the foreigner was not on his first visit anyway. Van Leur's famous pedlars travelled incessantly. Gujarati trade with the great centres of Aden and Malacca operated on a regular and routine basis. The Portuguese shepherded large annual convoys of local ships between Cambay and Goa, and on other routes also. The number of 'new chums' on board any ship was limited, and they would be socialized by their experienced fellows into local mores and customs.

Further to break down the problem of particularism was the fact that most visitors would be 'known' at a foreign port. Most were not *sui generis*, but rather were members of loosely or tightly integrated mercantile communities: Arabs of Mascat, *chettyars* of Coromandel, Portuguese of Goa, *moplahs* of Calicut. Individuals from these groups often travelled in company, and one or more members would have local knowledge or expertise all over the vast Indian Ocean area. Even if a Portuguese private trader, let us say, arrived alone and ignorant in an Indian port city, he would almost certainly find there an agent or broker who was used to dealing with Portuguese, and who probably spoke some Portuguese. Much more often a visitor would already have a recommendation to a particular local broker. In other words, he would be 'known' in any major port, and would easily find a local person to integrate him, and mediate on his behalf.

The furthest end of this continuum, the people for whom integration in a foreign port was most easy, were those who had their compatriots

[19] Das Gupta in *CEHI*, I, 420.

already settled there. These latter are the people Curtin calls 'cross-cultural brokers'. Sea traders met by such people may well have been the majority of all sea traders. Many merchant groups found it worthwhile to have representatives, often kin members, settled in all the major ports of the Indian Ocean, rather than rely on a local. This would apply even to the so-called pedlars, who frequently were either travelling on behalf of a shore-based principal, or had connections of some sort with people settled in foreign ports. Hindu agents were found at many foreign ports and trade centres, and were connected with large Indian broking families.[20]

As a more specific example, the great Muslim traders of Rander had their fellows settled, and usually married to local women, in all the major ports of the Indian Ocean.[21] A visitor from Rander to, say, Aden simply disembarked and went straight to his compatriot, who then provided him with all the local advice and assistance he needed. In major ports such 'foreigners' lived in specific areas, governed them-selves, and lived generally under conditions later described as 'extra-territorial'. Certain local brokers serviced these groups both generally and in regard to particular commodities. Here, then, there was a layer of locally-settled 'foreigners' to mediate between the visitor and the local environment.

The best example we have of this is the Armenian merchant Hovhannes.[22] Wherever he went, both on the coast and inland, in Shiraz, Surat, Agra, Patna, even Nepal and Tibet, in his late-seventeenth-century travels he was looked after by locally-settled Armenians, some of them kinsmen, others known to him from other ties. He seems to have never had to deal alone with local officials and merchants; he always had a fellow Armenian by his side. Thus he always entered a ready-made network of credit, supply, information and local expertise.

It is unlikely that the brokers who dealt with the locally settled Armenians, or other foreigners, had this as their only occupation. These brokers no doubt traded on their own account also, and acted as brokers for other merchants. It is in fact often difficult to discern the various roles a broker played. Those specializing in a particular

---

[20] Qaisar, 'Brokers', p. 225, and see my 'Indian Seafarers in the Sixteenth Century,' in *Coastal Western India* (New Delhi, 1981), pp. 116–44.

[21] Radwan, *Dutch in Western India*, p. 17.

[22] Lvon Khachikian, 'Un marchand armenien en Perse, en Inde et au Tibet,' *Annales ESC*, 22nd year, March–April 1967, pp. 231–78; see also Lvon Khachikian, 'The Ledger of the Merchant Hovannes Joughayetsi,' *Journal of the Asiatic Society* (Calcutta), VIII, 1966, pp. 153–86.

commodity dealt with all merchants, whether local or foreign, who wanted their particular category of goods. When we talk of the brokers who dealt with foreigners we are then concerned more with general brokers who, as we will see, provided many services, not all strictly economic, for visitors. These general brokers in turn dealt with brokers specializing in particular commodities on behalf of their foreign principal.

This is not to say that these general brokers did not deal in the same way with locals also, but foreigners would have more need than would locals for the all-encompassing services these men provided. The people most dependent on such general brokers were the comparatively unusual group of total strangers. In the middle were the vast majority of foreigners who had some local contacts, or even a fellow-countryman resident in the port. At the furthest extreme were locals. One should not, however, see these general brokers as functionally totally distinct from other brokers. In the most general way, all made their living primarily by acting as an intermediary, either within the production process or between buyer and seller.

Some of the evidence points to particular brokers specializing in servicing specific foreign traders, but in general, as we will see, at least in Cambay these specialists in servicing visitors made no communal distinctions at all; they looked after any foreigner. Three senior scholars in the area of Mughal economic history, K. N. Chaudhuri, Ashin Das Gupta and Tapan Raychaudhuri, all stress the lack of business dealings between Hindus and Muslims in India, and within Hindu India even caste and community exclusiveness.[23] However, my evidence shows rather a *lack* of communal divisions. Barbosa noted the *vanias*, who 'dwell among the Moors with whom they carry on all their trade.'[24] Qaisar, in his authoritative article, says the vast majority of brokers were Hindu, and even Muslims preferred to use Hindu brokers.[25] It seems that here as elsewhere Mammon triumphed over religious particularism.

One underpinning of the hold of brokers over foreigners was the matter of language. This is an area about which very little is known. At 1500 the majority of sea traders, that is those who actually visited foreign ports, were Muslims, and presumably used a form of Arabic or Persian to communicate. In the sixteenth century isolated European travellers and traders, such as Varthema, Federici, and Le Blanc,

[23] K. N. Chaudhuri, *The Trading World of Asia*, p. 150; *CEHI*, I, 424, 343.
[24] Duarte Barbosa, *The Book of Duarte Barbosa*, 2 vols (London, 1918–21), I, 110–11.
[25] Qaisar, 'Brokers', p. 224.

usually approached India from overland, via the Middle East. Presumably they picked up a smattering of language on the way.

Such was usually not the case with Europeans who arrived in a more organized fashion, that is the Portuguese in the sixteenth century and the English and Dutch in the seventeenth. The English East India Company encouraged its servants to learn Indian languages, but had little success. By this time, however, a form of Portuguese which the English called 'Negro Portuguese,' presumably a mixture of Portuguese and Indian languages, was widely spoken in Indian ports. Nevertheless many visitors, and especially northern Europeans, increased their reliance on brokers by their linguistic incompetence. In 1641 in Qandahar, Manrique was told he needed a broker because 'the people of your nation do not speak the language of these countries, so you are sure to encounter difficulties unless you find someone to guide you.'[26] Such linguistically-incompetent people were easy to cheat. Brokers, on the other hand, often learnt one or more European languages.[27]

It may be that it was language difficulties which led to the development of an intriguing form of silent bargaining in Calicut. This method was well described by Varthema, and his account also shows clearly the mediating economic role of the broker:

The merchants have this custom when they wish to sell or to purchase their merchandise, that is, wholesale: They always sell by the hands of the *Cortor* or of the *Lella*, that is, of the broker. And when the purchaser and the seller wish to make an agreement, they all stand in a circle, and the Cortor takes a cloth and holds it there openly with one hand, and with the other hand he takes the right hand of the seller, that is, the two fingers next to the thumb, and then he covers with the said cloth his hand and that of the seller, and touching each other with these two fingers, they count from one ducat up to one hundred thousand secretly, without saying 'I will have so much', or 'so much'. But in merely touching the joints of the fingers they understand the price and say: 'Yes' or 'No'. And the Cortor answers 'No' or 'Yes'. And when the Cortor has understood the will of the seller, he goes to the buyer with the said cloth, and takes his hand in the manner above mentioned, and by the said touching he tells him he wants so much. The buyer takes the finger of the Cortor, and by the said touches says to him: 'I will give him so much.' And in this manner they fix the price.[28]

The brokers in the great ports were of course happy to service any foreigner, for thus their business increased. A newcomer could,

---

[26] Quoted in Braudel, *Civilization and Capitalism*, III, 489.
[27] Qaisar, 'Brokers', pp. 223 f.n., 230–1, 235.
[28] *The Travels of Ludovico di Varthema* (London, Hakluyt, 1863), pp. 168–9.

however, meet opposition from other merchants, whether foreign or not, who were already established in a particular trade and who were concerned to limit competition. Brokers could thus be caught in the middle, between a desired new customer and a jealous established one. The many accounts of the English in Surat in the seventeenth century have copious detail on such problems. The English, nevertheless, were forced to trade as best they could within the existing network of commercial relations.

The Portuguese response in the early sixteenth century was rather different. When they reached Calicut they were faced, not surprisingly, with competition from the foreign Muslims who dominated the spice trade of this great port city. But it is clear that local suppliers, and local brokers, were happy to service the Portuguese, seeing them as simply one more group of customers. The threatened foreign traders were, however, able to hinder (using strictly commercial methods) Portuguese trade, and this resulted in a Portuguese attempt to break out of the traditional network and trade on a basis of monopoly enforced by naval power. The varying success of this attempt has been much discussed. Two points in the present context can be made. First, in areas where Portuguese power was weak (really everywhere except western Indian coastal waters) Portuguese, both those working for the official system and the vast majority who were trading on their own account, *did* trade within the bounds and structure of the existing framework. It was only in certain areas, and with respect to certain products, especially spices, that the Portuguese tried to establish a new system. Second, to the extent that this official Portuguese system was successful, it was something of a historical freak. In India it was only replicated (using slightly different means) in the later eighteenth century as the British established political control.

Although the Portuguese failed to achieve all their aims, their presence in the sixteenth century did distort traditional networks and relationships in several Indian Ocean port cities. This was obviously the case in the cities they conquered, such as Goa, Malacca and Diu. Other cities also were affected. Calicut suffered greatly from Portuguese hostility. The brief case studies which follow look at three port cities in the period before the changes caused by the Portuguese occurred. The commercial structure of Calicut will be sketched in the very early sixteenth century, Diu in the period before the Portuguese conquest of 1535, and Cambay, largely unaffected by the Portuguese, over the whole sixteenth century. These three examples will serve to flesh out our general account of the role in the traditional, pre-

464

European, period of brokers servicing foreign traders in sixteenth-century western Indian port cities.

Around 1500 Calicut was a city very largely dominated by foreign traders. Mme Bouchon has stressed the unique configuration of Malabar states at this time, with power shared between Hindu rulers and Muslim sea traders.[29] It is clear, however, that at least in Calicut Gujarati *vanias* were also very important traders who contributed to Calicut's prosperity.[30]

The Muslim population of Calicut was divided into foreign traders and local converts, the *moplahs*. While some *moplahs* engaged in coastal trade (and continued to do so throughout the sixteenth century despite Portuguese opposition), the high prestige and high-profit long-distance trade in spices was very largely controlled by foreign Muslims. Varthema claimed there were 15,000 Muslims in Calicut, 'who are for the greater part natives of the country.'[31] In 1502 there were claimed to be 4,000 households of Muslims just from Cairo and the Red Sea in Calicut.[32] The Muslim 'foreigners' came from very diverse areas, including Persia, Gujarat, Khorasan, the Deccan, Cairo and the Red Sea area. Ibn Batuta had earlier found the head merchant in Calicut to be Ibrahim, the *shahbandar* from Bahrein.[33]

Although these foreign Muslims were not totally dominant in Calicut's commerce, they did occupy a very important political and economic position in the town. A Portuguese account of 1500 said 'These Muslims are so rich and powerful that they almost govern all Calicut.'[34] Some of them owned fifty ships, and every year at least 600 ships came to Calicut.[35] Barbosa, more soberly, talks of ten to fifteen ships of foreign merchants trading to the Red Sea each year.[36]

As we noted, groups of foreigners in Indian port cities and elsewhere usually managed their own affairs for themselves. Thus Barbosa tells us that in Calicut the foreign Muslims had a head or governor, who ruled and punished them without reference to the Hindu ruler, the Zamorin.[37] It seems, however, that such was the economic power of the foreign Muslims in Calicut that they sometimes went beyond this; not

[29] G. Bouchon, *Mamale de Cananor* (Paris, 1975), p. 182.
[30] Barbosa, II, 73.
[31] Varthema, *Travels*, p. 151.
[32] João de Barros, *Da Asia*, 4 vols (Lisbon, 1945–46), I, vi, 5.
[33] Mahdi Husain, *The Rehla of Ibn Batuta* (Baroda, 1976), p. 189.
[34] A. B. de Bragança Pereira (ed.), *Arquivo Português Oriental*, I, ii, p. 140.
[35] Fernão Lopes de Castanheda, *História do descobrimento e conquista da India pelos Portugueses*, 9 vols (Coímbra, 1924–33), I, xiii.
[36] Barbosa, II, 77.   [37] *Ibid.*, 76.

content with the customary autonomy for themselves they also at times pressured the Zamorin when their interests were threatened.

The person who represented them on such occasions was the head of the foreign Muslim merchants in Calicut. His role at the time of the arrival of the Portuguese was crucial in blocking (by non-military tactics) Portuguese attempts to get adequate cargoes of spices. The result was continuing hostility between Portugal and Calicut.[38]

Relations between visitors and local brokers were mediated through the many foreign Muslims who were settled permanently in the city. Some of these residents were agents of groups of Muslim merchants based in other great trade centres, especially the Red Sea area and Egypt. As Pires tells us, 'Many nations used to have great factories here.'[39] Most of these foreign residents were married (presumably to local women) and had children.[40] (But even if they had been settled for generations, they still distinguished themselves from the *moplahs*, who were local converts.) In terms of our general analysis, a Muslim visitor to Calicut would thus find his fellows well established, indeed politically quite important, and quite capable of mediating between the visitor and local brokers and suppliers.

Some impression of the mechanisms for doing business in Calicut can be gained from a fifteenth-century account:

Security and justice are so firmly established in this city, that the most wealthy merchants bring thither from maritime countries considerable cargoes, which they unload, and unhesitatingly send into the markets and the bazaars, without thinking in the meantime of any necessity of checking the account or of keeping watch over the goods. The officers of the custom-house take upon themselves the charge of looking after the merchandise, over which they keep watch day and night. When a sale is effected, they levy a duty on the goods of one-fortieth part; if they are not sold they make no charge on them whatsoever.[41]

Things were not always so easy, however. A French traveller, Vincent Le Blanc, found some problems in the 1570s: 'The Strangers and Merchants are upon their arrivall put [to a great inconvenience] to buy

---

[38] For these events see Barros, *Da Asia*, I, v, 6–7; Castanheda, *História*, I, xix, xxxvi, xxxviii–xxxix. The Portuguese accounts also contain much detail on the government structure, and role of merchants, in Malacca before 1511. Details of this, and of these merchants' attempts to counter the Portuguese, can be found in Barros, II, vi, 3, 6, 7; Tomé Pires, *The Suma Oriental of Tomé Pires*, 2 vols (London, 1944), II, 254–5, 264–5, 273; Gaspar Correia, *Lendas da India*, 4 vols (Lisbon, 1858–64), II, 253; *The Commentaries of Afonso Albuquerque*, 4 vols (London, 1875–84), III, 87–8, 128–9, 166–7.

[39] Pires, *Suma Oriental*, I, 78.   [40] Barbosa, II, 76.

[41] Abd er Razzack in R. H. Major (ed.), *India in the Fifteenth Century* (London, 1857), p. 14.

466

houses to dwell in, which troubled us very much, being forced at our departure to leave it for half it cost us; you buy women for your service, and put them off again, but not without some losse.'[42] Obviously his situation was different from that of the earlier foreign Muslims. Unlike the isolated French traveller, they were met by a network of compatriots who owned houses and were married.

We get glimpses of the role of local brokers in early sixteenth-century Calicut. This role seems to have been more important than one would expect, given the permanent presence of so many foreign Muslims in Calicut. Varthema confirmed that merchants, when selling wholesale, always used a broker as an intermediary between buyer and seller.[43] There was in fact an established network to incorporate foreigners into the local commercial milieu. The second Portuguese expedition of 1500, commanded by Cabral, was at first well received. The factor, Aires Correa, was allowed to set up a factory. He was given a house for this purpose, and its owner, a Gujarati Muslim, was given the task of teaching him 'the customs and trade of the country.'[44]

This mechanism applied not only to new and isolated foreigners like Le Blanc and the Portuguese, but also to new foreign Muslims. Given what we have said above about the large number of locally settled foreign Muslims, this is surprising. Nevertheless, Barbosa is quite clear that these visitors also had provided for them by the state various helpers designed to integrate them into the local scene. He described how ten or fifteen ships belonging to foreign Muslims settled in Calicut sailed to the Red Sea each monsoon.

In this trade they became extremely wealthy. And on their return voyages they would bring with them other foreign merchants who settled in the city, beginning to build ships and to trade, on which the king received heavy duties. As soon as any of these Merchants reached the city, the King assigned him a *Nayre*, to protect and serve him, and a *Chatim* clerk to keep his accounts and look after his affairs, and a broker to arrange for him to obtain such goods as he had need of, for which three persons they paid good salaries every month.[45]

If Calicut was largely dominated by foreign Muslims, the situation in pre-Portuguese Diu was rather different. We can say nothing definite about how foreign merchants were treated, for we have no evidence at all of the role of brokers. It is clear, however, that there were many foreign Muslims in Diu as well as in Calicut. Varthema in 1504 expatiated on the wealth and trade of the port, and said there were 400

---

[42] Vincent Le Blanc, *The World Surveyed* (London, 1660), p. 58.
[43] Varthema, *Travels*, p. 168.
[44] Bragança Pereira, *Arquivo*, I, ii, p. 134.   [45] Barbosa, II, 77.

Turkish merchants in residence; indeed, he called it 'Diuobandierrumi, that is, "Diu, the port of the Turks."'[46] Accounts from later in the century point to a more diverse foreign population: Linschoten found *vanias*, Muslim Gujaratis, Turks, Persians, Arabs and Armenians there.[47] Nor is there any doubt about the wealth of these merchants. In 1537 governor Nuno da Cunha spoke of merchants with funds of 100,000 *cruzados* (about Rs 180,000) or more.[48]

It is likely that local brokers, in this case Gujarati vanias, had less of a role in Diu than in Calicut or Cambay. Diu, unlike the other two, was very much a transhipment centre. Its hinterland, the Saurashtran peninsula, was poor and unproductive. Its role was to act as a way station between the great ports and production areas of the Gulf of Cambay and the destinations for the Gujarati goods, in other words, all the major port cities of the Indian Ocean. Calicut and Cambay both operated in part as transhipment centres too, but they, unlike Diu, had productive hinterlands as well. It is likely that transhipment of goods would involve less of a role for brokers; rather large merchants could handle this matter face to face. Such is at least likely, though the matter is still to be fully investigated.

What we can say with some assurance is that the state played a much larger role in commercial activities in Diu than was the case in either Calicut or Cambay. Thus we can assume that agents of the government, people who were virtually employees rather than the more autonomous brokers of the other two ports, played an intermediary role in commercial transactions in Diu.

When we talk of the government in pre-Portuguese Diu we are really talking of Malik Ayaz, who controlled the port with a considerable degree of independence until his death in 1522.[49] He participated vigorously and successfully in trade. In 1519 he was buying all the pepper which could run the Portuguese blockade and get to Diu.[50] More generally, Castanheda said that most of the goods which came to Diu were sold to Malik Ayaz, who afterwards sold them to merchants from the interior, or re-exported them, and so made huge profits.[51] After his death, the sultan of Gujarat, Bahadur, also participated massively in Diu's trade on at least one occasion.[52]

---

[46] Varthema, *Travels*, pp. 91–2.
[47] J. H. van Linschoten, *Travels*, 2 vols (London, 1885), I, 58.
[48] *Studia*, nos. 13–14, p. 86; no. 10, p. 191.
[49] For his career see my *Merchants and Rulers in Gujarat* (Berkeley, 1976), pp. 67–73.
[50] *As Gavetas da Torre do Tombo*, IV, 216.
[51] Castanheda, *História*, II, lxxv; cf. Barros, *Da Asia*, II, ii, 9.
[52] *The Mirat-i Sikandari*, Persian text edited by S. C. Misra and M. L. Rahman

468

Such state involvement in trade was most unusual in sixteenth-century India. It raises questions about the role of coercion, if any. I have discussed this matter elsewhere;[53] suffice it here to point out that 400 Turks and many other foreigners were not going to stay in Diu if Malik Ayaz was hindering their trade. In the present context, the point to be made is that we can assume that this government involvement in trade, plus Diu's role as almost exclusively a transhipment centre, meant that local brokers played a less autonomous and less important role in this great port city than in our other two.

The evidence from Cambay is much fuller. We can see here, in this great trade centre, sophisticated integrative mechanisms at work. Unlike Calicut, whose trade was dominated by foreigners, mostly Muslims, and Diu under governor Malik Ayaz's firm control, in Cambay local merchants, both Hindu and Muslim, controlled the cream of the trade. This had not always been the case. In the early fourteenth century Arab merchants had been important, even dominant.[54] Around the middle of this century Ibn Batuta described Cambay as 'one of the most beautiful cities . . . The reason is that the majority of its inhabitants are foreign merchants, who continually build there beautiful houses and wonderful mosques . . .'.[55]

By 1500 this had changed. Local residents were now dominant. Pires noted various foreign Muslims settled and driving a great trade in Cambay, but immediately pointed out that the trade of the locals was much greater.[56] The indigenous vanias were especially important, but local Muslims, some no doubt of foreign extraction, were also flourishing. True, there were important foreign Muslims in Gujarat at this time, but most of them were not merchants but rather served the sultans in military and political capacities.

Pires and others have left us good descriptions of Cambay's trade. The pattern is of Cambay's merchants having their agents in all the major trading centres of the Indian Ocean littoral, and indeed far inland too. Thus everywhere they had a level of fellow Gujaratis mediating between them and the locals. Such, however, was not the case with foreigners visiting Cambay. They, on the contrary, were usually only sojourners, waiting to complete their business, or for the

(Baroda, 1961), p. 274. Braudel notes that foreign merchants in Venice in the fifteenth century were subjected to a considerable degree of state control: *Civilization and Capitalism*, III, 125.

[53] *Merchants and Rulers*, pp. 15–16.

[54] S. C. Misra, *The Rise of Muslim Power in Gujarat* (London, 1963), pp. 63–4, 67, 96.

[55] Husain, *Ibn Batuta*, p. 172.

[56] Pires, *Suma Oriental*, I, 41–2.

monsoon to change before proceeding with their voyage. Frequently a trader from, say, the Red Sea would arrive in Cambay, engage in trade, and then ship himself and his goods on a Gujarati ship and so continue on to Calicut or Malacca.[57]

In Cambay these foreign traders were usually received and serviced not by their fellows who were resident in the town, but rather by local Gujaratis who specialized in this brokering or intermediary role. We are most fortunate to have two accounts from about 1564 and 1575 of the mechanisms of this procedure. We will first quote both accounts in full. The Venetian Cesare Federici (often incorrectly called Caesar Frederick) described commercial practice in 1564:

There is in the city of Cambaietta an order, but no man is bound to keepe it, but they that will; but all the Portugall marchants keepe it, the which is this. There are in this city certain Brokers which are Gentiles and of great authority, and have every one of them fifteene or twenty servants, and the Marchants that use that countrey have their Brokers, with which they be served: and they that have not bene there are informed by their friends of the order, and of what broker they shall be served. Now every fifteene days (as above sayd) that the fleet of small shippes entreth into the port, the Brokers come to the water side, and these Marchants assoone as they are come on land, do give the cargason of all their goods to that Broker that they will have to do their businesse for them, with the marks of all the fardles and packs they have: and the marchant having taken on land all his furniture for his house, because it is needfull that the Marchants that trade to the Indies cary provision of householde with them, because that in every place where they come they must have a new house, the Broker that hath received his cargason, commandeth his servants to carry the Marchants furniture for his house home, and load it on some cart, and carry it into the city, where the Brokers have divers empty houses meet for the lodging of Marchants, furnished onely with bedsteds, tables, chaires, and empty jarres for water: then the Broker sayth to the Marchant, Goe and repose your selfe, and take your rest in the city. The Broker tarrieth at the water side with the cargason, and causeth all his goods to be discharged out of the ship, and payeth the custome, and causeth it to be brought into the house where the marchant lieth, the Marchant not knowing any thing thereof, neither custome, nor charges. These goods being brought to this passe into the house of the Marchant, the Broker demandeth of the Marchant if he have any desire to sell his goods or marchandise, at the prises that such wares are worth at that present time? And if he hath a desire to sell his goods presently, then at that instant the Broker selleth them away. After this the Broker sayth to the Marchant, you have so much of every sort of marchandise neat and cleare of every charge, and so much ready money. And if the Marchant will imploy his

---

[57] See on this Pires, ibid., I, 41–7; II, 269–74; Castanheda, História, III, cxxx; Barbosa, I, 154–6; Varthema, Travels, pp. 105–11; Conti in Major (ed.), India in the Fifteenth Century, p. 20; Santo Stephano in ibid., p. 9; for Gujaratis overseas see Bragança Pereira (ed.), Arquivo, I, ii, 139; Barbosa, passim; Linschoten, Travels, I, 252–6.

470

money in other commodities, then the Broker telleth him that such and such commodities will cost so much, put aboord without any maner of charges. The Marchant understanding the effect, maketh his account; and if he thinke to buy or sell at the prices currant, he giveth order to make his marchandise away: and if he hath commodity for 20000 dukets, all shalbe bartred or solde away in fifteene dayes without any care or trouble: and when as the Marchant thinketh that he cannot sell his goods at the prise currant, he may tary as long as he will, but they cannot be solde by any man but by that Broker that hath taken them on land and payed the custome: and perchance tarying sometimes for sale of their commodity, they made good profit, and sometimes losse: but those marchandise that come not ordinarily every fifteene dayes, in tarying for the sale of them, there is great profit.[58]

About ten years later a French traveller, Vincent Le Blanc, left us a remarkably similar account of trade practice in Cambay:

Trade is very faithfully carried on there for the Factors and Retalers are persons of quality, and good reputation; and are as careful in venting and preserving other persons wares, as if they were their own proper goods; they are also obliged to furnish the Merchants with dwelling houses, and ware-houses, diet, and oftentimes with divers sorts of commodities: the houses are large and pleasant, where you are provided with women of all ages for your use, you buy them at certain rates, and sell them again when you have made use of them, if you like them not you may choose the wholsomest and the most agreeable to your humour: all things necessary to livelihood maybe made your own at cheap rates, and you live there with much liberty, without great inconveniences; if you discharge the customs rates upon merchandizes, nothing more is exacted, and all strangers live with the same freedom and liberty as the Natives do, making open profession of their own Religions.[59]

He goes on to expatiate on the probity of business practice in Cambay. A companion was involved in a case of fraud. He and Le Blanc were helped by 'our host, a rich broker or merchant'. The case was satisfactorily settled. 'This I have related to the faithfulnesse and integrity of our Landlord, and really their sincerity and integrity is such, that the Justices esteem their words and writings to equal sacred things; and when a Merchant happens to die, leaving his goods in one of these persons hands, they are very faithfully restored to his heir, or next of kindred.'[60]

Before analysing briefly these two accounts, we must digress to evaluate their reliability. Both have been curiously ignored by historians. Federici, it is true, is quoted in passing in several recent

---

[58] Published in Richard Hakluyt, *The Principal Navigations*, 12 vols (Glasgow, 1903–05), V, 375–6.

[59] Le Blanc, *World Surveyed*, p. 47.

[60] *Ibid.*, p. 48.

works, but his extended description of business practice, in many ways the best and fullest we have, has not received anything like the attention it deserves. To my mind it is of very great value and interest indeed. Nor, despite complaints of muddled chronology, has anyone questioned seriously the authenticity of his work.

Le Blanc presents some problems. His work has been almost totally disregarded, partly no doubt because there is no modern edition. Indeed, I myself discovered his account only recently thanks to a reference in an unpublished paper by my friend Dr Aniruddha Ray of Calcutta. It is regrettable that the original French edition was unavailable to me. There is also the problem that Le Blanc died about 1640, some years before the French edition of his travels appeared in 1649. The English translation dates from 1660. Penrose questions his reliability, though not concerning his account of India.[61]

We will have to wait until Donald Lach reaches the seventeenth century in his magisterial *Asia in the Making of Europe* before we can pronounce definitively on Le Blanc's reliability. In the meantime, I think we must take the passages quoted above seriously. The first confirms, and adds to, Federici's account but, despite the prevalence of plagiarism at this time, there is no evidence that Le Blanc stole or added to Federici. He claimed to know the west coast of India well;[62] despite errors and muddles elsewhere in his book, I can find nothing improbable in the passages quoted above. At least for now they should be taken at face value, that is, as a reliable and interesting account by an eye witness.

Both accounts, by Federici and Le Blanc, really speak for themselves. They point to a sophisticated mechanism designed to facilitate foreign trade and integrate foreign traders. The question is to explain why, at least on the basis of existing evidence, this system was unique to Cambay, for its details differ markedly from what we know of practice in Calicut. The answer seems to be that Cambay merchants, backed by centuries of expertise, relative political stability, and a productive hinterland, could be expected to be more dominant, more capable of providing themselves all the facilities a visitor would need, than were, say, the locals in Calicut. Given their efficiency and probity, there was simply no need for most foreign merchants or trading families or groups to go to the trouble of establishing a kinsman or compatriot in Cambay. Such a person could add nothing to the facilities already available locally.

[61] Boies Penrose, *Travel and Discovery in the Renaissance* (Harvard UP, 1952), p. 219.
[62] Le Blanc, *World Surveyed*, p. 43.

The sketch provided here will, it is hoped, point to the crucial role of brokers servicing foreign merchants in these three port cities. Indeed, to the extent that the Indian Ocean world was an integrated world-economy, this was achieved by the work of these brokers. Nevertheless, as it will be obvious from this rather sketchy account, there are still huge gaps in our knowledge. I have found no sixteenth-century data on the rate of commissions charged, a vital lacuna. Perhaps even more important, who provided the capital? Did brokers outlay funds themselves, or were they totally dependent on the capital of their principals? And was the position of the broker similar in other littoral areas of the Indian Ocean? Recent studies of southeast Asia seem to point to a situation more akin to that of Diu than of Cambay, in other words, substantial state interference. All these matters, and others, await the attention of researchers.

III

GOA-BASED SEABORNE TRADE
17th-18th CENTURIES

IT is the received opinion that the Portuguese *Estudo da India,* and its capital of Goa, entered a period of decline early in the seventeenth century. Various reasons for this decline have been presented; these need not detain us here, but the fact of decline is generally accepted, even if its precise meaning has not yet been adequately specified. Both contemporaries and modern authors agree. J.H. Plumb wrote "Rigid, orthodox, decaying, mouldering like an antique ruin in the tropical heat, the Portuguese empire slept on."[1] In the late seventeenth century Manucci wrote that the Portuguese had previously been religious and just, but now "they are unbelievers and pretenders. The cause I know not -- whether it be because they are a mixture of Jews, Mahomedans, and Hindus, either having an admixture of their blood, or having drunk it in their nurse's milk -- but in place of just they have become unjust; robbers and oppressors instead of disinterested men." [2]

A Jesuit observer in the 1660s was a little more specific (though also more picturesque and extravagant than accurate) about what this decline meant. Padre Manuel Godinho introduced his book by pointing out that

"the Lusitanian Indian Empire or State, which formerly

dominated the whole of the East, and comprised eight thousand leagues of sovereignty, including twenty-nine provincial capital cities as well as many others of lesser note, and which gave the law to thirty-three tributary kingdoms, amazing the whole world with its vast extent, stupendous victories, thriving trade and immense riches, is now either through its own sins else through the inevitable decay of great empires, reduced to so few lands and cities that one may well doubt whether that State was smaller at its very beginning than it is now at its end."

He went on to conclude, in a morbid passage, that

"if it has not expired altogether, it is because it has not found a tomb worthy of its former greatness. If it was a tree, it is now a trunk; if it was a building, it is now a ruin; if it was a man, it is now a stump; if it was a giant, it is now a pygmy; if it was great, it is now nothing; if it was the viceroyalty of India, it is now reduced to Goa, Macao, Chaul, Baçaim, Damão, Diu, Moçambique and Mombaça, with some other fortresses and places of less importance -- in short, relics and those but few, of the great body of that State, which our enemies have left us, either as a memorial of how much we formerly possessed in Asia, or else as a bitter reminder of the little which we now have there." [3]

The final verdict was pronounced by the famous traveller and savant Richard Burton, writing in the *Madras Mail* in 1890 and reflecting very clearly late Victorian certitude about the superiority of the British and the failings of all others:

"The fact is that Goa is politically and commercially extinct. Once the most important trading centre on the Western Coast of India, it has been left far behind by rival cities with more backbone and enterprise, qualities which the Goanese have lacked ever since the days when they gave themselves up to luxury and ostentation, and so lost all the energy which distinguished them when they still had fortunes to make, and enemies to fight." [4]

These accounts and descriptions all see an unrelieved decline: everything went down and decayed. Our concern is with trade, and we will find when we discriminate a little that the story here is not just of complete and absolute collapse. The glory days of the sixteenth century had gone, no doubt, but many Goans still could make money and be innovative as they traded all over the Indian Ocean and beyond. In other words, we need to try not to be too influenced by political decline, and look beneath the surface at the everyday activities of Goans in these two centuries. Anthony Disney has very usefully distinguished between several elements in Goan life in the seventeenth century:

"First there was the Goa of the Portuguese crown and administration which was conceived of as a distant royal possession maintained for its strategic, economic and religious importance to the metropolis, and for imperial prestige. Then there was the Goa of the local elites -- European merchants, settlers, and officials in their private entrepreneurial capacities, together with the Indians, mostly Brahmins and Banyas, who collaborated with them in business and administration. To these groups Goa was principally a funnel for commercial enterprise. There was the Goa of the religious establishment, especially of the great and powerful Roman Catholic regular orders, for whom Goa was an administrative and educational centre, and significant source of both recruits and income. Finally there was the more mundane Goa of the rural majority, which included both the traditional landowning class in the villages, and the great mass of landless labourers, fishermen and other underprivileged groups." [5]

This essay is concerned with the second of these four strands. The problem we face immediately is that so little research has been done on this topic. There is massive data available in the archives in Goa and Lisbon, but so far no researcher has used this to construct a detailed picture of Goa's sea trade after 1600. Nor are secondary works of much use. There are many studies of trade and commerce on the coasts of India in the seventeenth and eighteenth centuries, but in all of them the Portuguese, or Goans, are seldom mentioned. Thus Holden Furber's large and very comprehensive survey of this period has copious details on the Dutch and English, even the Danes and French, but almost nothing on the Portuguese.[6] Nor has the equally large and authoritative *Cambridge Economic History of India*[7], K.N. Chaudhuri's two recent surveys [8], Arasaratnam's recent excellent study of Coromandel trade[9], or Ashin Das Gupta's two fine monographs on areas, Malabar and Surat, where the Portuguese once had been very prominent.[10] Watson's study of British private traders says little about their Portuguese peers, and nor does Nightingale's account of the rise of the British in western India in the late eighteenth century.[11] The only exception to this general neglect of Goa in surveys of trade and commerce in our period is in works on East Africa. Recent excellent books by Gervase Clarence-Smith and Malyn Newitt[12] do give considerable space to the activities of traders based in Goa and other Portuguese possessions.

It must be stressed that the data is available; all that is needed is keen young researchers who are prepared to use it. A recent study of Macao's trade at this same time[13] shows what can be done, and provides a model for a future researcher working on Goa. Souza has constructed a very detailed account of Macao's trade from the mid-seventeenth to the mid-eighteenth century. He had to use data from Dutch and English as well as Portuguese archives, but he shows us what the possibilities are, and this for a port much less documented than is Goa. In his book he has a total of 36 tables and three graphs relating to trade movements and other matters to do with trade based on Macao between the early seventeenth and the mid-eighteenth century. This is precisely the sort of study we need for Goa. In its absence, much of what I have to say in this essay will be very preliminary and tentative, stressing gaps and lacunae in our knowledge as much as presenting reliable information.

The first general point we can establish with some certainty is simply that Goa's total trade indeed did decline precipitously in our period. We will modify this broad statement later, but the general fact is that there was a major decline. One qualitative illustration of this, which points to the demoralisation of Goa's traders, was contained in a letter from the viceroy to the king in 1630. He described how Goan merchants now went in sailing ships which were lightly armed, and sometimes carried no arms at all. This was because when an enemy appeared they could then beach their ship quickly, take with them their bullion and portable valuables, and escape inland. The viceroy noted that this was prejudicial to other merchants who carried more bulky goods on these ships, as they lost everything. He had tried to remedy this by passing an order that in such cases the goods saved, which were mostly gold and small valuables, were to be divided up *pro rata* among all who had cargo of any sort on the beached ship. The viceroy hoped that this order would mean that those with portable valuables would now be forced to fight instead of just beaching their ship and running away.[14]

Quantitative evidence confirms the fact of a general decline. Disney gives us data for Goa's customs returns which show a substantial decline from early in the seventeenth century. In *xerafins*, these went as follows:

c.1600	226,666
1610	200,000
1627	150,000
1628	125,000
1629	132,000
1634	130,000

As this was a time of high inflation, the decline is actually even more serious than these figures show.[15]

Other figures, this time for the value of Goa's sea trade in the seventeenth century, confirm this rapid fall. In rupees, the value went as follows:

c.1600	72,00,000
1605	53,14,000
1616-17	36,00,000
1635	27,60,000
1685	10,20,000

Finally, customs revenues, which once made up the bulk of Goa's revenue and showed the importance of sea trade in the area's economy, fell sharply as a percentage of the area's total revenue:

1545	customs duties made 63% of total revenue
1586-87	57%
1600	56%
1616-17	44%[16]

An excellent little book by Magalhães Teixeira Pinto gives a good, but melancholy picture of the situation at the end of our period, that is in the 1820s. The only people in Goa, Daman and Diu

III

with any wealth were *Vanias*, not that this was a new situation. Diu had a total of three merchant ships, where once it had been a major port. Goa's sea trade by this time was totally moribund, indeed almost non-existent.[17]

This general decline of trade does not, however, mean that everyone in Goa was poor. Far from it; rather we have good evidence of the existence of rich people in a poor state. The government's finances certainly were in a state of permanent crisis, but some individuals still did very well indeed. Among them were the Jesuit Order, which from skilled investment in land and trade remained a powerful economic force until their expulsion by Pombal later in the eighteenth century. They were dominant in their *taluka* of Salcete, of course, but the Order also owned much land in Ilhas. Many seventeenth century viceroys made large fortunes during their tenures from trading in diamonds and with East Africa. So did some Goa-based Europeans, both Portuguese and others, who often were agents for large business houses in Europe. Thus the Portuguese Manuel de Moraes Supico, who died in 1630, and the Flemish de Couttre brothers, made large fortunes from the diamond trade. A recent book by Boyajian[18] shows the wide financial networks of Portuguese Jews or New Christians in Europe; these financiers usually had agents in Goa also. Yet here also a decline did occur during the seventeenth century. Increasingly Goa was not an essential base for such European merchants. They moved to settlements established by the Dutch and English, or to major Indian ports, and used Dutch or English ships to send goods to Europe.[19]

Other groups in Portuguese India also continued to prosper. This applies especially to those who held land. Several travellers in the late seventeenth century commented on this. Careri in the 1690s noted generally that "The Portuguese Live very great in India, both as to their Tables, Cloathing, and number of Cafres, or Slaves to serve them..." More particularly, he visited Bassein and then travelled inland to where the gentry had their country estates. He went fifteen miles through countryside where there was nothing "but delightful Gardens, Planted with several sorts of the Country Fruit Trees, as Palm, Fig, Mangoes, and others, and abundance of Sugar Canes. The Soil is cultivated by Christian, Mahometan, and Pagan peasants, inhabiting Villages thereabouts. They keep the gardens always Green and Fruitful, by watering them with certain Engines..."[20]

Much the same phenomenon, that is private wealth based on land, was noted by the Scot captain Hamilton around 1700. He found that Bassein "is a Place of small Trade, because most of its Riches lay dead and buried in their Churches, or in the Hands of indolent lazy Country Gentlemen, who loiter away their Days in Ease, Luxury and Pride, without having the least Sense of the Poverty and Calamity of their Country." [21]

The point is that while there was still wealth in seventeenth-century Portuguese India, it was now based much more on land than on trade. It is true that we know almost nothing of the extent of land trade at this time, that is trade with inland areas contiguous with the Portuguese possessions, but we can assume it was rather small. Two sets of figures can serve to show the importance of land for government revenue, and so by implication for private fortunes. Disney [22] uses the important account of Bocarro, from the 1630s, to show how important land revenue was in the total. The following table shows the percentage of government revenue derived from land as compared with total revenue:

Daman	90% +
Ceylon	80% +
Bassein	75%
Salcete	74%
Bardez	50%
Goa and Ilhas	2%
Diu	0%

Overall, 31% of crown revenue came from land, and 47% from seaborne commerce.

Another set of figures shows the movement of sources of government revenue away from trade and into land. The table [23] on the next page shows percentages of government revenues derived from various sources:

Yet although revenue from land for both government and private individuals became more important in the seventeenth century than was sea trade, the general point is that Goans still tried hard to trade and profit. A common theme is the importance of economics in the lives of Goans from this period, and earlier and later. Wars and politics could be left to the viceroys and their armies, religion was a matter for the priests and Orders except perhaps on holy days. What

was important was trade, even in the bad times of the seventeenth
century. Three complaints quoted by C.R. Boxer make this point
very clearly for the earlier period, but can be applied to ours as well.
A priest complained that the Portuguese "will go to the ends of the
earth in search of riches, but will not take a step from the love of
Christ." St. Francis Xavier himself noted in 1546 that "we have such a
brisk trade with the heathen, and so little religious zeal, that we
more readily treat with them about temporal profits than about the
mysteries of Christ Our Lord and Saviour," while in the same year
another Jesuit said that "The men who come out to India, come to
get money to take back to Portugal, and not to save souls." [24]

Year	Customs	Quit Rents	Tributes	Horse Duties
1581	58	24.8	12.3	4
1588	59.8	24.5	13.6	2.1
1607	58.9	25.1	13.8	2.2
1609	62.4	16.3	15.3	6
1620	63.1	19	17.8	0.2
1635	23	18.1	58.8	0.1

But while trade remained of central importance for Goans in our
period, it was not so much the Portuguese and *mestiços* who did best
from it, it was local people, in other words Hindu and some
Christian Indians, especially the former. Recent studies have shown
how crucial Vanias and Saraswat Brahmins were in Goa's general
economy[25]; this applies to her seaborne trade also. This is a theme
which will run through the rest of this essay. Again Bocarro sets the
general scene. In the 1630s the investment in Goa's interport trade
(not in the carreira to Portugal) was put at 2,850,000 *xerafins*, and of
this 2,000,000 belonged to non-Christian Indians, often invested in
partnership with Portuguese, both local and from Portugal.[26]
Rudolph Bauss, in his important but as yet unpublished study of the
Portuguese economy between 1750 and 1850, finds that 90% of the
economies of Goa, Diu and Daman were controlled by Indians.
After 1785 the trade of the Portuguese Indian Ocean empire was
approximately half of the value of commerce between Portugal and
Brazil. However, while the metropolitan Portuguese economy and

her Atlantic trade were largely controlled and financed by British money, in the Indian Ocean Portuguese trade was dependent not on the British but on local, Indian, finance and participation.

Another, more concrete, example shows again this Indian dominance. In 1739 Goa was under attack from the Marathas. A disorderly crowd of soldiers and Augustin priests looted the house of a Goan Hindu called Phondu Kamat, "the wealthiest merchant in Goa," on suspicion that he was harbouring Maratha enemies. His own inventory showed that 130,000 *xerafins* was taken in cash, diamonds, gold ornaments, and fine cloths. Soon after this he donated, or perhaps had extorted from him, another sum of 130,000 *xerafins* to help in Goa's defence. As a comparison, at this same time the notoriously wealthy Jesuit Order, which had already contributed 80,000 *xerafins*, now offered a further sum of only 20,000 *xerafins*.[27] Phondu Kamat must have been either more patriotic, or more wealthy, than the Jesuits; the latter is probably true.

Two final matters will serve to end this general discussion of themes to do with Goa's sea trade in the seventeenth and eighteenth centuries. Both of them constitute examples of the general malaise of the time. The first is the matter of migration from Goa, the point being that people do not leave an area where they have strong home and cultural ties unless they are forced to by lack of economic opportunity. Goans have of course been famous for their willingness to migrate in the nineteenth and twentieth centuries, moving first to British India and to east Africa, and during the last two decades to the Gulf area. This was a trend much earlier too. In the prosperous sixteenth century Goans travelled far and wide to trade, but this was not usually a matter of migration. By 1700 however many inhabitants of Portuguese areas in India had voted with their feet and left, either permanently or for a time, their home area.

The eminent modern Portuguese historian Vitorino Magalhães Godinho surveyed Portuguese India around 1700, and found decay far advanced. Diu and Chaul had been supplanted by Surat and Bombay. Daman and Bassein were harassed by the Marathas. In the whole colonial area, there were less than 3,000 male Portuguese and *mestiços*, and the urban elite was mostly Indians. Many Portuguese migrated. In Coromandel they moved from San Thome to Danish Tranquebar, French Pondicherry, and especially to English Madras, where there were 3,000 Portuguese in the 1670s, and by the early 1700s, 9,000. In Bengal, outside of the Portuguese empire, there was a Portuguese-speaking population of between 20,000 and 34,000, with 8,000 in Hugli and over 2,000 in Chittagong. Now that the long war with the Dutch had ended, Portuguese also settled in the prosperous Dutch cities of Malacca, Colombo, Negapatam and Cochin. These migrants had varying statuses. Some were skilled artillerymen serving in Indian armies and doing well. There were some wealthy merchants in Batavia and Madras, but in Hugli, Ceylon and Malabar the Portuguese population was very poor. Most of these people were of course *mestiços* rather than ethnically "pure" Portuguese, yet they did retain the Portuguese language and the Catholic religion.[28] This trend continued and increased in the nineteenth and twentieth centuries. The census of 1900 showed that 11% of the population of Salcete were migrants, and 16% of Bardes. In 1921 the total population of Goa was 469,494, but it was estimated that there were almost 200,000 Goans living elsewhere, in British India, in Burma, in east Africa and in what was then Mesopotamia, now Iraq. No less than 50,000 were in British India, especially in Bombay. More precise figures from just before the end of Portuguese rule, in the 1950s, show that Goa's total population was 547,448, but there were also the following outside of Goa:

Bombay	80,000
Rest of India	20,000
Karachi	10,000
Rest of Pakistan	20,000
Kenya and Uganda	30,000
Persian Gulf	20,000
Total	180,000[29]

The point is that this was not a new phenomenon in the twentieth century; from the seventeenth century Goans had been driven away from their homeland by its declining economy.

A second subject also shows the problems of the economy, and is directly relevant to our theme of overseas trade, for what we find is that Goa's authorities for at least some three centuries ignored a chance to develop a major export market based on a local product. The product was iron ore, and the existence of large deposits was known from at least the early seventeenth century. A report from about 1623 said that artillery and cannon balls could be made very cheaply in Goa because very close to Portuguese territory there were *minas de ferro*. An English expert noted in 1802, during the British occupation of Goa, that "There were mines, in the Province of Ponda, which could afford considerable quantities of very good Iron, if proper Engines were built: there is Water enough in their Neighbourhood to work Mills."[30] More decades passed, and still nothing was done. In 1931 it was noted that

"No geological survey has been made of Goa....The principal minerals are manganese, iron and aluminium. No serious attempt to prospect or exploit these minerals has been made, though recently some foreign interests have acquired certain concessions for working the manganese mines from which the ore is exported to the Continent (of Europe). Mica also exists but is not quarried on any important scale. Goa is known to possess rich mineral resources and if these were scientifically explored their exploitation would be a source of wealth to the country and its people. The apathy of the latter and the poverty of the Government, however, combine to render this a possibility almost as remote as it is highly to be desired."[31]

As late as 1947 the great Goan savant D.D. Kosambi yet again noted the existence of iron ore deposits in Goa, but they were still not being developed. It was only after this that Dr. Salazar's regime, desperate for revenue and anxious to justify its claim to retain Goa, began to develop these mines. Once it started, production shot ahead. The following table shows tonnes exported in selected years[32]:

1947	14
1950	72,054
1955	1,528,797
1960	5,652,087
1961	6,527,695

Since liberation production has of course increased even further. For our purposes, the point is that there was available a local resource which could have bolstered, indeed transformed, Goa's trade and exports, but for at least three and one half centuries an inefficient government did nothing to promote this.

Before analysing in detail the *carreira* (Portuguese-Goan trade) and *cabotagem* (coastal trade) we need to set the scene by investigating first of all general trends in the Portuguese empire in our period, and then the political context in which the Estado da India operated in the Indian Ocean in the seventeenth and eighteenth centuries.

The two in fact and closely related, for Goa's vicissitudes in the seventeenth century were in large part a result of a change in the focus of the empire. India was ignored, Brazil received all the attention and resources. Godinho characterises the Portuguese empire in the fifteenth century as dominated by west African gold, the sixteenth by Asian pepper, and the seventeenth by Brazilian sugar. In the seventeenth century "O açucar substititui a pimenta, a rota do Brasil relega para a penumbra a rota do Cabo, o imperio, de oriental, torna-se atlantico."[33] Brazil boomed while India stagnated, as the following tables for Brazilian sugar production and population show:

Year	Number of mills	Annual production in arrobas
c.1570	60	180,000
1600	200	600,000
1645	300	1,400,000

Population:	White	Slave	Total
1546-8	2,000	4,500	6,500
1583	24,750	32,600	57,350
1600	30,000	120,000	150,000[34]

By the middle of the seventeenth century these population numbers had all doubled as compared with 1600.[35] By the end of the century this trend to the Atlantic had become writ even larger. At this time the population of Portugal itself was some 2,000,000, with at least 165,000 living in Lisbon. In Brazil there were some 500,000, one-fifth of them European, while in Goa only 50,000 remained, and in the whole of the Estado there were perhaps 10,000 Portuguese.[36] By this time at least it was Brazil which maintained Portugal's prosperity, governed metropolitan affairs, and meant a lack of interest in the rest of the empire. This found practical expression even in the late 1630s. Faced with Dutch attacks in both Brazil and the east, in 1638 41 ships and 5,000 men were assembled to relieve Brazil, but to help India at the same time only a few ships and 500 men were sent.[37] Metropolitan Portugal in the first half of the seventeenth century was providing cannon fodder for Spanish armies, and from 1640 to 1668 was fighting a long war against Spain; it was trying vainly to hold on to its areas in west Africa, and was defending the long Brazilian coastline. There was little left to defend the Estado da India, and this enforced neglect was an important reason for Portuguese losses of territory in the seventeenth century, these in turn limiting greatly her overseas trade.

As we have seen, in the sixteenth century Portuguese trade was closely tied up with the military and political effectiveness of the government in Goa. As the latter declined, so too did the former. In the most general terms, the Estado da India had always been not a territorial state but rather a network of maritime connections between bases. Along these networks food, supplies and military equipment were moved. Partial dominance in the sixteenth century was replaced by major attacks in the seventeenth. The Estado was obviously peculiarly vulnerable to such maritime threats; as its opponents became more and more successful the essential lines of sea communication were severed and the small land bases left isolated and bereft.

Three general points need to be made about Portuguese military setbacks in the seventeenth century. First, while the Dutch were the main enemies, several local powers also contributed. Second, the overwhelmingly effective Dutch attacks in the Indian Ocean area, and especially in India, came only from 1636, not from the 1590s when the Dutch first arrived in Asia. Third, long before these open Dutch attacks, their effectiveness in competing on various trade routes had already seriously undermined the Portuguese state, which turned out to be unable to compete. The figures for Goa's customs quoted earlier make this point clearly; they decline precipitously long before Goa was blockaded or Portuguese forts in India had been lost.[38]

III

The list of losses is a long one, and only the most significant will be mentioned here. The Dutch quickly drove them out of Moluccas, the source of spices. Persian forces, backed at sea by the British, captured the important base of Hurmuz in 1622. In 1639 Japan was closed to them. Two years later the Dutch took Malacca. By this time the focus in the hostilities between the Dutch and the Portuguese was on Brazil. The Dutch had captured Pernambuco in 1630. The Portuguese inhabitants revolted in 1645, but it was not until January 1654 that Recife, the last Dutch stronghold, was recaptured. It was only after this that the focus moved back to Asia. Between 1655 and 1663 the Dutch inflicted major blows, driving the Portuguese from Sri Lanka, Macassar and Malabar. Meanwhile Goa itself was subjected to yearly blockades, from 1638 to 1644, and again from 1656 to 1663.

Two other opponents, one on the sea and one on the land, then replaced the Dutch and were equally successful in whittling away at the remains of the Estado. At sea the naval forces of the Ya'arubi Imams of Oman had important successes. After the loss of Hurmuz the Portuguese had been able to continue the same sort of trade using Mascat as a base; in 1650 the Omanis took this port. Bandar Kung was a less successful third alternative in the Persian Gulf area. In 1661 the Omanis sacked Mombasa town, and in 1668 the town of Diu; in both cases the forts were not taken. But two years later the great fort of São Sebastião at Mozambique was nearly taken, and in 1698 the Portuguese were driven from the Swahili east African coast after the Omanis took Mombasa.

On land the main opponents were of course the rising power of the Marathas. Shivaji himself launched a minor attack on Goa in 1667. After his death, a major attack from Sambhaji was on the verge of success when his forces were diverted by a Mughal attack on him. In the eighteenth century the Marathas were more successful. Most of Goa was occupied by them between 1739 and 1741, and while they were forced to withdraw, the Province of the North, or at least the very valuable and comparatively large area of Bassein, was lost to the Marathas between 1737 and 1740. The acquisition of the New Conquests in Goa soon after was some compensation, but the fact is that the Portuguese empire in India now consisted merely of Diu, Daman and Goa, and all three of them were largely moribund anyway. Indeed, it could be argued that the loss of these possessions was not the real cause of Portuguese

Year	Portuguese	Dutch	English	Danish	French	Total
1581	3					3
1582	4					4
1583	4					4
1584	6					6
1585	4					4
1586	3					3
1587	2					2
1588	5					5
1589	6					6
1590	4					4
1591						0
1592	1					1
1593	1					1
1594	2					2
1595	3					3
1596	1					1
1597	4	3				7
1598	3					3
1599		4				4
1600	6	8				14
1601	2	7				9
1602	2	10				12
1603	4	13	4		1	22
1604	6	8				14
1605		8	1			9
1606	1	7	2			10
1607	1	3				4
1608	2	6				8
1609		4	2			6
1610	3	1	1			5
1611	2	4	1			7
1612	3	1				4
1613	3	7	2			12
1614	1	2	5			8
1615	1	5	2			8
1616	3	5	3			11
1617	2	4	5			11
1618	4	8	2		2	16
1619	3	5	3			11
1620	2	6	2			10
1621	1	6	1			8
1622	1	8	5	2	1	17
1623	3	8	5			16
1624	2	6	3	1		12
1625	3	4	4			11
1626		10	6	1		17
1627	3	7	3			13
1628		7	4			11
1629	2	7	5			14
1630	1	9	4			14[39]

decline; rather it was a symptom of that decline. The Dutch had out-competed the Portuguese commercially before they began to take Portuguese possessions. In other words, the Portuguese could have kept all their forts and still their trade would have declined in the face of the greater finances and efficiency and better commercial techniques of the Dutch and English.

It is important then not to assume that sea trade, let alone individual commercial success, is exactly correlated with these sieges and battles and losses of territory. As we noted, many individual Portuguese continued to prosper in the seventeenth century and later. Similarly, Souza's book shows Macao's traders competing and even prospering in particular places and various times. What can we say of Goa's trade in these two centuries?

As is well known, the *carreira*, the voyage of Portugal, declined rapidly from early in the seventeenth century. The main problem was simply the competition of the Dutch East India Company. Niels Steensgaard has provided figures which show how quickly the Portuguese lost out in more or less peaceful competition. The table opposite shows the number of ships returning to Europe from Asia.

These figures make clear the decline of the *carreira* In aggregate, between 1600 and 1609 the Dutch sent 74 ships to Asia, the Portuguese 24 and the English 9. Or, between 1600 and 1630 344 European ships were sent to Asia, of which 194 were Dutch. And not just ship numbers, but obviously the cargoes too declined. Disney has worked out that during the sixteenth century an average of 18,000 or 19,000 quintals of pepper were loaded on Portuguese ships in India. Between 1610 and 1630 the average fell to 10,355, and later of course pepper shipments to Portugal virtually vanished. Other data also points to this decline. As early as 1606 it was profitable for a French ship to go from Marseilles to Lisbon with a cargo of pepper. By the 1620s Dutch imports to Europe were greater than Portuguese imports at their height, in the last quarter of the sixteenth century; this despite the fact that the Portuguese had had a monopoly, while the Dutch were competing with the English and the Portuguese. In this last quarter of the sixteenth century, the Portuguese returned to Europe 2,000 or 3,000 tons of shipping a year, but by the middle of the seventeenth century the Dutch alone were sending back 10,000 tons.[40] Decennial data over three centuries provides a graphic measure of the decline of the *carreira*. These figures are for ships leaving Portugal; not all of them got to India.[41]

1500-09	138	1600-09	68	1701-10	22
1510-19	96	1610-19	56	1711-20	20
1520-29	76	1620-29	67	1721-30	30
1530-39	80	1630-40	30	1731-40	24
1540-49	61	1641-50	44	1741-50	27
1550-59	51	1651-60	32	1751-60	17
1560-69	49	1661-70	21	1761-70	16
1570-79	54	1671-80	25	1771-80	13
1580-89	56	1686-90*	5	1781-90	15
1590-99	44	1691-1700	23	1791-1800	9

* Note that five years are missing here.

By the late nineteenth century the trend of the decline of the *carreira* had been writ very large indeed. By this time, even after the loss of Brazil, trade with India was almost invisible. In 1886 61% of Portugal's colonial trade was with Angola, 22% with São Thomé in west Africa, and 12% with Cabo Verde. Trade with Goa and with Mozambique was each only 1%.[42]

As we noted, the main reason for the decline of the *carreira* was Dutch competition, rather than Dutch attacks, though some of the great ships were taken in European waters by English and Dutch enemies, and the blockades of Goa also of course hindered the *carreira*. Yet it must be said that the Portuguese contributed themselves to this decline, especially by their failure to man their ships professionally. Boxer has written of a deeply ingrained contempt in Portuguese society for the profession of sailor, and this in a country largely dependent on sea trade. As a concrete, and comical, example of this failure, he noted how in 1650 a ship bound for India put in to Luanda, in Angola on the west African coast, "*cuidando estar ja na India, que tal piloto levava.*"[43]

Once the Portuguese realised how effective was the competition of the companies, and especially that of the Dutch East India Company, there were moves to try and imitate them by founding a Portuguese East India Company.[44] After prolonged discussion the old system of a crown monopoly on the *carreira* was terminated, and a company formed in 1628. But the problem soon became clear, namely a lack of capital. Only about half as much as was needed was subscribed, and of this the vast majority came from the crown. Even the directors of the company refused to subscribe, so that out of a total capital of 1,380,926 *cruzados*, only 1500 came from private investors. The company collapsed and was wound up in 1633.

Another attempt in the 1690s also failed, and for much the same reasons of lack of capital and overwhelming competition from other Europeans.

The *carreira* then declined very rapidly in the seventeenth century. However, Bocarro in the 1630s estimated that Goa's regional trade, in other words cabotagem based on Goa, was worth fifteen times the trade to Portugal. We must now turn to Goa's trade in the Indian Ocean area and assess its fortunes in our period.

We need first to distinguish between the various participants in this trade. The following groups can be differentiated, even though there were sometimes some overlap, and often members of two or more groups would act in conjunction with members of other groups. The part-time participants, that is people who were not full-time traders, consisted of officials, from the viceroy on down to the lowliest clerk, and clerics, including members of the Orders, and even Inquisitors. Among European full-time commercial people, some were agents for large firms in Portugal and other parts of Europe; these men typically would not be permanently resident in Goa, but would return to Europe after their tour of duty in India. Other traders of European origin, mostly Portuguese but some others also, were *casados* in the sense that they were permanent residents of Goa or some other Portuguese area. Included in these two European commercial groups were many New Christians, that is converted Jews. Next among the casados were the *mestiços*, a large group and an important one.

Among traders who were ethnically Indian, the Indian Christians were probably the least successful most of the time. Non-converted Indians played a much larger role. They included two very prominent caste groups, the famous Saraswat Brahmins of Goa and the central west coast of India generally, and the equally prominent Vanias, who derived from Gujarat but were prominent in Goa as well as in Diu, Daman and Bassein. One difference between these two Indian groups is that the Saraswats were local people in Goa, and indeed their activities were largely restricted to Goa. But the Vanias of course were members of the dominant trading community in the great economic area of Gujarat; ties, and finance, for these Vanias in say Diu could well come from their fellows resident elsewhere in Gujarat.

When we look generally at Goa's sea trade, the most notable phenomenon is the dominance of these Indians living in Portuguese areas, rather than either Portuguese or *mestiços*. The second general theme is a decline in this trade also as a result of Dutch and English competition and of the losses of possessions which we sketched earlier. Finally, we will discuss the way in which Goa's traders were able to operate within the entrails of stronger trading networks, making minor profits by filling the gaps, operating in the interstices, in the wider imperial systems of first the Dutch and later the English.

C.R. Boxer has given us a good sketch of Goa's trade routes in the middle of the seventeenth century.[45] On the route from Goa to Mozambique, Zambesia and Sofala Indian textiles were exchanged for ivory, gold dust, ebony and slaves. Traders and ships from Daman, Bassein and Diu shared this trade with those from Goa. Further north in east Africa, the trade to the Swahili coast, and especially to Mombasa, was dominated by ships from north of Goa, from Diu, Daman, Chaul and Bassein. Ivory was the main trade item, along with some gold and slaves. In the Persian Gulf area horses, seed-pearls and dates were acquired. Closer to home, the local coastal trade on the west Indian coast brought rice and pepper from Kanara, and clothes from Gujarat. From Sri Lanka came cinnamon, but Portuguese trade in the Bay of Bengal was all in the hands of private traders based in the area. Coir for rigging came from the Maldives and Laccadives.

We can see how territorial losses had already changed the nature of Goa's trade by this time, and how they would do so further later in the century. By 1650 Hurmuz and Malacca had already been lost, as had the Moluccas, while the Portuguese had also been denied entry to Japan. In this very year, 1650, Mascat was lost to the Omanis, who at the end of the century also took Mombasa and so terminated the Portuguese trade in ivory on the Swahili coast. And even when the Omanis did not take territory, their craft still harassed Portuguese ships. Mombasa, Diu and Mozambique were sacked in 1661, 1668, and 1670 respectively, while small craft sailing off the west Indian coast had always to beware of Omani and Malabari raiders. And in the late 1650s and early 1660s the Dutch drove the Portuguese from Sri Lanka and Malabar.

Bocarro's important survey of 1635 gives us an excellent impression of the values of various routes sailed from Goa at this time, and also of the extent of the decline even this early.

Goa-Portugal: 1600, 2,000,000 *cruzados*, now 3,000 *cruzados*
Goa-Mozambique: 1,000,000 *cruzados*
Goa-Mombasa: 10,000-12,000 *xerafins*
Goa-Sind: 80,000-100,000 *xerafins*
Goa-Gujarat: 1600–2,000,000 *cruzados*, now 150,000 *xerafins*
Goa-Kanara: 300,000 *xerafins* for rice
Goa-Cochin: 110,000-130,000 *xerafins*, including pepper
Goa-Sri Lanka: 150,000 *xerafins* for cinnamon
Goa-Malacca: 50,000 *xerafins*
Goa-Maldives and Laccadives: 30,000 *xerafins*

The total investment in the mid 1630s was 2,850,000 *xerafins,* and as we noted 2,000,000 of this belonged to non-Christian Indian traders.

As Goa's trade declined her great merchants often moved out. The European agents of great business firms in Lisbon and elsewhere increasingly found it possible and profitable to settle in other Indian ports, some European like Madras and later Bombay, others local, such as Surat. Those working for themselves also often left Goa as it declined and as the Dutch blockades hindered its trade. These people traded far and wide in a multitude of products and in many places. Boxer has reconstructed the career of Francisco Vieira de Figueiredo [46], an important trader in south and southeast Asia in the seventeenth century. He traded in sandalwood from the Lesser Sunda Islands, cloves from the Moluccas, gold from China, the Philippines and Sumatra, tortoiseshell from Macassar and Indian textiles from Gujarat and Coromandel. He even played a role as a diplomat at times, acting as an agent for the rulers of Macassar, and for Mir Jumla of Golconda. In another work Boxer presented sketchy details on the careers of four other seventeenth-century private traders [47] and in yet another publication an account of the trading activities of Lopo Sarmento de Carvalho.[48] Virginia Rau published *O "Livro de Rezão" de Antonio Coelho Guerreiro*[49], a very rare opportunity to look at the actual account book of a merchant. Finally, Souza also was so fortunate as to find an account book of a local merchant, in this case Francisco da Gama, for 1619-1621.[50] This man, based in Macao, was a ship owner, a merchant and an agent. He owned one ship, and part owned another. As a merchant he invested in at least seven Portuguese country traders' ships, including one of his own. As an agent he got freight, letters of exchange and bullion destined for ports from Cochin to Malacca and back to Goa. He imported from India, on his own account and for others, cotton and silk piecegoods, and silver bullion consigned by the Jesuits. From the south China sea area he imported cloves, gold, sugar, zinc and porcelain.

Goa under the Portuguese was always a rice deficit area, and had always imported food from neighbouring Bijapur, from Gujarat, and especially from Kanara. This trade in a necessity continued in the seventeenth century despite Dutch blockades and attacks from Omanis and Malabaris. In the 1630s, according to Bocarro, it was still worth some 300,000 *xerafins* a year. This trade apparently continued throughout our period, but presumably decreased as Goa's population fell.

One problem for local traders who owned allegiance to Portugal was that the officials tried to enforce the old monopoly and control system which had been put in place in the sixteenth century long after Portuguese decline had meant it was really a farce, and indeed counter-productive. Even in the eighteenth century they continued to seize Gujarati ships if they did not have *cartazes*. This of course now happened very infrequently, as everyone had learnt to ignore the Portuguese as powerless. Indeed, the important English merchant Robert Cowan joked about this saying "it was the means of livelihood of the necessitous *doms*." [51] More detrimental was the attempt to continue to insist that all Portuguese craft trading on the west Indian coast must call at Goa and pay duties, regardless of whether or not they did any trade in Goa, and indeed regardless of whether or not they even wanted to call at Goa. In the late seventeenth century Macao's traders were affected by this. Blocked from trading in the south China sea, they began to develop a trade on the west Indian coast, buying pepper in the Dutch Malabar ports and trading with it to Surat. These traders had no desire or need to call at Goa, but the viceroys tried to insist that they call and pay duties anyway. Finally Macao's traders were able to get a concession from Lisbon freeing them from this irritating and anachronistic requirement.[52]

The greatest local trade from Goa in the sixteenth century had been the route north to Gujarat, especially Cambay, with stops along the way at Chaul, Bassein, Daman, and Surat. This *cafila* sailed several times each season, and consisted of 200 or 300 small ships laden with Gujarati products on the southward voyage, and bullion on the northern. The decline of this trade was noted by the Dutch merchant Van den Broecke as early as the 1620s. The value of the cargoes had fallen sharply, and the number of ships had gone down to only some 50 or 60.[53] Diu, once the jewel of the empire and the producer of a massive surplus from its customs house, also declined, thanks in part to attack from the Omanis. In the sixteenth century the port had boasted 200,000 wealthy vanias, but by the 1660s it had only 7,000 or 8,000. The customs house had once raised Rs.1,50,000 a year, but by the 1660s this had fallen to Rs. 54,000.

By the eighteenth century Portuguese trade with Gujarat had almost vanished. In 1743 English ships took 16,000 bales of cotton from Surat to China, French ships 1300 bales, and Portuguese ships only 700.[54] Portuguese interests in Surat, such as they were, were looked after early in the century by the great Parsi broker Rustumji Manakji [55], and then, ironically in view of Portugal's long record of anti-Semitism, by the Jewish merchant Moses Tobias. In the eighteenth century the main Portuguese interest in Gujarat was centred on Diu and Daman, where a few Portuguese cooperated with the dominant Vania merchants in the east African trade, to which we must now turn.

As traditional trade routes declined, it seems that trade with east Africa, that is with Mozambique, Zanzibar and the Zambesi interior, and with the Swahili coast centred on Mombasa, became of much greater importance for the Portuguese. Mozambique had of course always been important as a way station for the *carreira*, but increasingly in the sixteenth century it also became a trade centre in which cloths and beads from Cambay were exchanged for gold from the Zambesi area, and slaves. The other important product was ivory, and until 1584 this was a crown monopoly. In that year this trade was handed over to the captain of Mozambique in return for a large annual payment. These captains seem to have been particularly extortionate; their illegal attempts to get bribes and favours acted to limit the trade of Mozambique island. At this time and later the Portuguese expanded far into the Zambesi interior, setting up quasi-feudal *prazos* or landed estates, over which the nearest representative of Portuguese authority, the captain of Mozambique, had very little control indeed. In this expansion Indian finance was crucial. Vania money, controlled by Indians who lived in Portuguese areas in India, both Goa and Diu, was invested in the cloth and ivory trade of Mozambique island.

A sign of the importance of Vania finance came in 1686, when the monopoly of the captain of Mozambique was ended. Now the Portuguese contracted the right to import Gujarati cloth into Mozambique to a merchant group from Diu. Goans, usually Catholics and Indo-Portuguese, moved from Goa to the Zambesi area, intermarried, and took up *prazos*, thus becoming land-owning as well as trading elites. By the early nineteenth century the majority of the leading "Portuguese" in Zambesia were probably of Goan origin. The profits from trade, and the tributes exacted from the *prazos*, were usually remitted to Goa, and the Goans who made these profits in east Africa usually retired to Goa. As Clarence-Smith noted, "The gold, ivory and slaves of East Africa had been part of the commercial network of the Indian Ocean, exchanged for Indian cotton cloth and other goods. Indian subjects of the Portuguese crown controlled this trade and were largely responsible for keeping Mozambique in the empire over the centuries."[56]

Further north, on the Swahili coast centred on Mombasa, ivory was the main product. In the sixteenth century Portuguese control here had been minimal, until Turkish raids in 1585-6 showed them how tenuous was their sway. To remedy this, the great Fort Jesus was built at Mombasa in 1593. Until this fort was lost to the Omanis in 1698, the trade in ivory from this coast was a flourishing one, making large profits both for officials, private Portuguese, and Vania participants. The Swahili coast played a central role in the Portuguese attempt to revive the idea of establishing a Portuguese East India Company to compete with the Dutch and English. In 1693 such a company was set up in Lisbon, with a capital of 500,000 *cruzados*, unlike in the 1630s all of this being from private sources. Eight Portuguese and four Genoese were directors, the latter being heavy subscribers. The hope was that this company would profit from tobacco sales in the east. This company was meant to revive the *carreira*, but another one, established in Goa in 1695, was to concentrate on the Indian Ocean trade. Goan capital was heavily involved in this second company. In 1700 the Portuguese crown arranged a merger of the two, with a total capital of 700,000 *cruzados*, two-thirds of which belonged to Goans. These companies, like their predecessor in 1628-33, were virtually still born. Hopes of a profitable trade in east Africa were doomed by the loss of Mombasa in 1698, and the lack of government control over the trade and inhabitants of Mozambique and Zambesia.[57]

The importance of Indian money, both Goan and Vania, in Portugal's east Africa trade was revealed again early in the nineteenth century, in this case in the unsavoury matter of the slave trade. Early in the century the British moved to abolish this trade. The treaty of 1815 between Portugal and England made the Portuguese limit their continuing involvement in this trade to south of the equator. Through to mid-century Portuguese merchants, with some (illegal) British participation, did well from a large trade in slaves between Angola and Brazil, where the importation of slaves was only prohibited in 1850. There was also a flourishing, though smaller, trade in slaves in the Indian Ocean area, based on Mozambique, in the first half of the nineteenth century. Some 200,000 slaves were traded over this period. The actual capture and their transportation to the coast was done by the prazo holders and officials of Zambesia (often they were the same people), but the finance and shipment out was handled by Indian trading houses, especially Vania ones, on the coast in Zanzibar and Mozambique island. These Vanias, as Portuguese subjects, could operate with impunity as they were not subject to the prohibition of the trade which their fellow - Vanias who were subjects of British India were liable to.[58]

The participation in the slave trade of the early nineteenth century is an example of the way in which increasingly Goa's traders operated within the gaps, or interstices, of more powerful and successful imperial and trading systems. There were other examples of this adaptation: a discussion of them will close this essay. It must, however, first be stressed that this sort of trade was not completely new for Goa's traders. They had always been ready to find a gap and make a profit. In the sixteenth century they had defied, when they could, the official system of controls and monopolies. Thus Portuguese, both *casados* and officials, and even clerics, were from time to time accused of trading in spices, which were meant to be a crown monopoly. Similarly, they traded to prohibited areas, such as the Red Sea, when they could. Now the official Portuguese system lay in ruins, but others, the Dutch and the English, tried to impose monopolies and restrictions of their own. Goan traders were able to operate in the entrails of these systems and still make profits. They could do this because they were not Dutch or English subjects, and so could use their Portuguese status to ignore various prohibitions. Vania and Portuguese participation in the slave trade in the first-half of the nineteenth century provides one example of this.

Other smaller examples of a considerable flexibility are legion. In the seventeenth century the important diamond trade in Goa was meant to be a strict crown monopoly. As we noted, several Goans even so made large profits from trading in this product. In the 1670s this was done by selling diamonds to English private merchants on English ships which called at Goa in November and December of each year, ostensibly to take on provisions.[59] A similar willingness to circumvent their own government, and a considerable lack of what we would now call patriotism, was to be seen north of Goa in the 1720s. The Angrias, originally the Maratha navy but by now independent, operated effectively off the Maharashtra coast at this time, and in the 1720s some Portuguese traders from the Province of the North, in an ironic reversal of the sixteenth-century situation, took *cartazes* from the Angrias so that they could continue to trade.[60] Similarly, to beat the Dutch blockade in the 1640s and continue to trade with Mozambique, some Portuguese sailed under the English flag. As one example, in 1640 the governor of Daman leased the pinnace "Francis" from the English East India Company. It took on a cargo of cloth and beads in Gujarat; in the manifest these were described as belonging to the Indian governor of Surat. The ship sailed to Mozambique, and then Madagascar, and traded with impunity. Meanwhile the Dutch were seizing Portuguese-flag ships.[61]

Souza's recent study of Macao's trade shows this city's traders operating within the confines of the stronger Dutch and Chinese systems as best they could. As one market was closed they moved to another. The Dutch quickly established control over the Moluccas, the source of mace, nutmeg and cloves, but for a time were unable to end a clandestine trade in these products to Macassar, which under its Muslim rulers became an important centre for the spice trade. In this port city Portuguese merchants from all over the remains of the empire traded and even settled. In the 1620s between ten and 22 Portuguese galliots called each year, and there could be up to 500 Portuguese in the town. In the next century the Dutch ban on country trade to their areas by other Europeans was frequently ignored by Portuguese traders. Portuguese ships on the Macao-Manila-Goa run also called in at Galle, in Dutch Sri Lanka. Similarly, in 1717 the Ch'ing dynasty imposed a ban on overseas trade in China. The Portuguese in Macao were exempt from this, and did well filling in this gap while the ban lasted. In the second-half of the seventeenth century English trade from

Coromandel to Spanish Manila became important. Textiles were exchanged there for tobacco, copper, sugar and especially silver. The problem for the English was that the Spanish allowed only Portuguese and Asians, but not other Europeans, to trade in Manila. Thus this English trade was done in partnership with Portuguese subjects, and also Armenians and various Indians. The ships in this trade sailed under Portuguese, or Indian, flags. The Portuguese involved were Indo-Portuguese settlers from San Thome and Madras.[62]

Late in the eighteenth century Portuguese traders, and the state, received another windfall. The metropolitan trade with India revived in the 1780s as Portugal was neutral in the European wars of this time. Until the French invaded Portugal in 1807, and indeed until the end of the wars in 1815, Lisbon was revived as a major entrepot for the importation of Asian goods into Europe, especially Chinese tea and textiles from Bengal and Gujarat.[63] In the late 1790s a Portuguese company sent ships and money to Surat to buy piece goods, and they also left a resident agent there. The English were annoyed at this competition, but as Portugal was neutral they could do little to stop them. And as Portugal and France were at peace in Europe, the Portuguese made large profits importing these goods into the European continent, while other traders were stopped by the British blockade.[64] But once peace came to Europe this Portuguese trade was undercut by competition from the English; more generally, the Indian textile industry was now in fast decline thanks to competition from Manchester machine-made cottons.

The career of one, perhaps typical, Portuguese merchant shows clearly the role of the Portuguese as British power expanded in India. He, and his fellows, worked within the system set up by the dominant British. Miguel de Lima e Souza, a resident of Bombay and a Portuguese subject, had various partnerships with English traders resident in Bombay. He had resided in Bombay since 1775, and had connections in Goa. When Jonathan Duncan was Governor he used Lima e Souza in all his official dealings with the Portuguese authorities in Goa. He also had good contacts with various local Indian rulers, and used these on behalf of the British. His contacts in Gujarat enabled him to play an important role as British rule expanded in Gujarat in the 1800s; thus he gave Duncan important advice when he took over for the English East India Company the government of Surat in 1800.[65]

Our final example of private Portuguese trade in the period of imperial decline concerns the opium trade to China in the early nineteenth century. Opium had been traded in small quantities from Gujarat and Goa even in the sixteenth century, but it became more important late in the seventeenth century. In the eighteenth century the English East India Company restricted exports of opium to China, even then the major market, to Bengal opium, which they monopolised. However, in the 1810s this trade was liberalised, and private traders now turned to cheaper, though inferior, Malwa opium, which had the added advantage of coming from an area not ruled directly by the English. Faced with this competition, in 1813 the English prohibited the export of Malwa opium from Bombay and its other west coast ports. This left open an opportunity for Portuguese subjects and Portuguese-flag ships, which were not affected by this ban, to enter the trade. They did so with gusto, and this trade from Daman, and also Diu and the Portuguese factory in Surat, expanded greatly. The East India Company tried hard to stop it, and even got the British government to apply pressure on Lisbon, but to no avail. Finally, the company accepted this private trade, and tried to force it to go through Bombay. The result was a tariff war between Daman and Bombay in the 1830s, which the English finally won. By 1840 90% of Malwa opium was exported through Bombay.

Much of this trade was handled by subjects of British India, especially Parsis resident in Bombay, but using Portuguese itermediaries to circumvent the ban. In the Portuguese areas two groups profited from this trade. It was done through Portuguese Indian commercial houses, and these were run not by Portuguese but, as we would expect, by non-Christians who were Portuguese subjects. The Goa government also did well from this, making large revenues from customs duties and the sale of Portuguese papers for opium ships. No data is available, but Clarence-Smith suspects that the expensive new capital of Portuguese India, Panaji, was built between 1827 and 1835 largely from the profits the government made from this trade.[66]

Even though our data is so sketchy, and so much research remains to be done, the broad trends in Goa's sea trade in the seventeenth and eighteenth centuries seem to be clear enough. The *carreira* declined, thanks to Dutch commercial competition, from very early in the seventeenth century. Apart from a brief revival during the Anglo-French wars of the late eighteenth and early

III

nineteenth centuries, it was of very little importance over the whole of our period. As for cabotagem, the traditional routes declined also as the Dutch out-competed Portuguese traders and then rubbed salt in the wound by conquering most of the main Portuguese trading centres. In the later seventeenth century it seems that trade with east Africa was the most lucrative, done not only from Goa but also from Diu. The loss of Mombasa crippled this trade, which however revived in the early nineteenth century as the Indian Ocean slave trade expanded. The general pattern from the mid-seventeenth century is one where Portuguese and Portuguese-Indian traders, often in partnership with each other, roamed the Indian Ocean seeking gaps in the monopoly system set up by the Dutch, and later the British. At particular times, in particular places and particular products, gaps were found and profits were made. But the whole context was very different from the palmy days of the sixteenth century, when it was Portugal which established the monopoly system and used it for its own benefit and for that of her private traders.

REFERENCES

1. Introduction to C.R. Boxer, *The Portuguese Seaborne Empire*, London, 1969, p. xxv.
2. Niccolao Manucci, *Storia do Mogor, or Mogul India, 1653-1709*, trans. W. Irvine, Calcutta, 1965-67, 4 vols., III, 127.
3. Quoted in C.R. Boxer, *Portuguese Seaborne Empire*, pp. 128-9.
4. Richard Burton, *The First Four Chapters of Goa and the Blue Mountains ... with Articles which recently appeared in the Madras Mail and Madras Times*, Madras, 1890, p. 79.
5. A.R. Disney, "Goa in the Seventeenth Century," in M.D.D. Newitt, ed., *The First Portuguese Colonial Empire*, Exeter, 1986, pp. 85-6.
6. Holden Furber, *Rival Empires of Trade in the Orient, 1600-1800*, Minneapolis, 1976.
7. *The Cambridge Economic History of India*, Vol. I, ed. Tapan Raychaudhuri and Irfan Habib, Cambridge, 1982.
8. K.N. Chaudhuri, *Trade and Civilisation in the Indian Ocean*, Cambridge, 1985; K.N.Chaudhuri, *The Trading World of Asia and the English East India Company*, Cambridge, 1978.
9. S. Arasaratnam, *Merchants, Companies and Commerce on the Coromandel Coast*, Delhi, 1986.
10. Ashin Das Gupta, *Indian Merchants and the Decline of Surat*, Wiesbaden, 1979; Ashin Das Gupta, *Malabar in Asian Trade*, Cambridge, 1967.
11. I. Bruce Watson, *Foundation for Empire*, New Delhi, 1980; Pamela

Nightingale, *Trade and Empire in Western India*, Cambridge, 1970.
12. G. Clarence-Smith, *The Third Portuguese Empire*, Manchester, 1985; M.D.D. Newitt, *Portugal in Africa*, London, 1981.
13. G.B. Souza, *The Survival of Empire*, Cambridge, 1986.
14. Historical Archives of Goa, *Livros das Monções*, Vol. XIV, ff. 166-6v.
15. A.R. Disney, *Twilight of the Pepper Empire*, Cambridge, Mass., 1978, pp. 50-51.
16. M.N. Pearson, *Coastal Western India*, New Delhi, 1981, pp. 75, 87.
17. Gonçalo de Magalhães Teixeira Pinto, *Memorias sobre as possessões portuguezas na Asia*, Nova Goa, 1859, pp. 30, 31, 41-3, 53, 59-63.
18. James Boyajian, *Portuguese Bankers at the Court of Spain, 1626-1650*, New Brunswick, 1983.
19. A.R. Disney, "Goa in the Seventeenth Century", pp. 89-92, and see also C.R. Boxer, *Portuguese India in the mid-seventeenth century*, Delhi, 1980, pp. 39-42.
20. S.N. Sen, ed., *Indian Travels of Thevenot and Careri*, New Delhi, 1949, pp. 159, 168-9.
21. Alexander Hamilton, *A New Account of the East Indies*, ed. W. Foster, London, 1930, 2 vols., I, 105.
22. A.R. Disney, "The Portuguese Empire in India, *c*. 1550-1650", in John Corr'eia-Afonso, ed., *Indo-Portuguese History*, Bombay, 1981, p. 151.
23. Artur Teodoro de Matos, "The Financial Situation of the State of India during the Philippine Period, 1581-1635", in Teotonio R. de Souza, ed., *Indo-Portuguese History*, New Delhi, 1985, p. 97.
24. Quoted in C.R. Boxer, *Francisco Vieira de Figueiredo*, The Hague, 1967, p. 50 and f.n.
25. See G.V. Scammell, "Indigenous Assistance in the Establishment of Portuguese Power in the Indian Ocean", • in J. Correia-Afonso, ed., *Indo-Portuguese History*, pp. 163-73; T.R. de Souza, "Mhamai House Records", in International Seminar on Indo-Portuguese History, II, *Proceedings*, Lisbon, 1985, pp. 931-41; M.N. Pearson, "Banyans and Brahmins: Their Role in the Portuguese Indian Economy", in *Coastal Western India*, pp. 93-115.
26. C.R. Boxer, *Portuguese India in the Mid-seventeenth Century*, p. 47.
27. P.S.S. Pissurlencar, *The Portuguese and the Marathas*, trans. P.R. Kakodkar, Bombay, 1975, pp. 276-81, 302.
28. V.M. Godinho, "Portugal and her Empire, 1680-1720", *New Cambridge Modern History*, vol. VI, Cambridge, 1970, pp. 518-9.
29. B.G. D'Souza, *Goan Society in Transition*, Bombay, 1975, p. 203; *Times of India Illustrated Guide to Goa*, Bombay, 1931, p. 38; *Peace Handbooks*, vol. 13, London, 1920, pp. 32, 38, 46.
30. British Library, Add. MSS. 13703, f. 92v.
31. *Times of India Illustrated Guide*, p. 28.
32. D'Souza, p. 193.
33. V.M. Godinho, *Os descobrimentos e a economia mundial*, 2n. ed., Lisbon, 1981-3, 4 vols., I, 49; see also V.M. Godinho, *Ensaios*, vol. II, Lisbon, 1968, p. 177.
34. Godinho, *Ensaios*, II, 198-9.
35. A.H. de Oliveira Marques, *History of Portugal*, vol. I, New York, 1972, pp.358-9.
36. V.M. Godinho, "Portugal and her Empire", *New Cambridge Modern History*, vol. V, Cambridge, 1964, pp. 384-5.
37. J.B. Harrison, "Europe and Asia", *New Cambridge Modern History*, vol. IV,

III

Cambridge, 1970, p. 664.

38. Generally see C.R. Boxer, "Portuguese and Dutch Colonial Rivalry, 1641-1661", *Studia*, no. 2, 1958, pp.7-42; C.R. Boxer, *Portuguese India in the Mid-Seventeenth Century*, pp.1-22; L. Blussé and G. Winius, "The Origin and Rhythm of Dutch Aggression against the Estado da India, 1601-1661"; in T.R. de Souza, ed., *Indo-Portuguese History*, pp.73-83.

39. Niels Steensgaard, *The Asian Trade Revolution of the Seventeenth Century*, Chicago, 1974, p. 170.

40. A.R. Disney, *Twilight of the Pepper Empire*, p. 109; D. Rothermund, *Asian Trade and European Expansion*, New Delhi, 1981, p. 22; N. Steensgaard, "Asian Trade and World Market," *L'Histoire a Nice*, tome III, Nice, 1981, pp. 133, 140.

41. C.R. Boxer, *Portuguese Seaborne Empire*, p. 379.

42. G. Clarence-Smith, *The Third Portuguese Empire*, p. 65.

43. C.R. Boxer, *Portuguese India in the Mid-Seventeenth Century*, pp. 25, 30-33.

44. See Disney, *Twilight*, passim; Godinho in *New Cambridge Modern History*, vol. V, 386, 388; vol. VI, 516-7; G. Winius, "Two Lusitanian Variations on a Dutch Theme", in L. Blusse and F.Gaastra, eds., *Companies and Trade*, Leiden, 1981, pp.119-34.

45. C.R. Boxer, *Portuguese India in the Mid-Seventeenth Century*, pp. 43-6.

46. C.R. Boxer, *Francisco Vieira de Figueiredo, passim*.

47. C.R. Boxer, "Casados and Cabotagem in the Estado da India, 16-17th centuries", International Seminar on Indo-Portuguese History, II, *Proceedings*, Lisbon, 1985, pp.121-35.

48. C.R. Boxer, *The Great Ship from Amacon*, Lisbon, 1959, pp. 90-139.

49. Lisbon, 1956.

50. G.B. Souza, *Survival of Empire*, pp. 35-6.

51. Das Gupta, *Indian Merchants*, pp. 91-2.

52. Souza, pp. 177-9.

53. Om Prakash, ed., *The Dutch Factories in India*, New Delhi, 1984, pp. 151, 155, 235.

54. Furber, *Rival Empires of Trade*, pp. 274-5.

55. See J.J. Modi, "Rustom Manock", *Asiatic Papers*, IV, Bombay, 1929, pp.101-320; P.S.S. Pissurlencar, *Portuguese Records on Rustomji Manockji*, Nova Goa, 1933-36.

56. M.D.D. Newitt, "East Africa and Indian Ocean Trade: 1500- 1800", Ashin Das Gupta and M.N. Pearson, eds., *India and the Indian Ocean, 1500-1800*, Calcutta, 1987, pp.213-4; Newitt, *Portugal in Africa*, p. 10; G. Clarence-Smith, *The Third Portuguese Empire*, p. 3.

57. See Godinho in *New Cambridge Modern History*, VI, 516-8; Eric Axelson, *Portuguese in South-East Africa*, Johannesburg, 1960, pp. 175, 181-2, 186-7.

58. See Newitt, *Portugal in Africa*, pp. 15, 17-18; Clarence-Smith, *Third Portuguese Empire*, pp. 31, 34-6.

59. I. Bruce Watson, *Foundation for Empire*, pp. 17-18.

60. C.R. Boxer, *Portuguese Seaborne Empire*, p. 137.

61. Axelson, p. 121.

62. Arasaratnam, *Merchants, Companies and Commerce*, p. 154.

63. Clarence-Smith, pp. 1-2.

64. P. Nightingale, *Trade and Empire in Western India*, pp. 154-5, 161, 170, 173.

65. *Ibid.*, pp. 171, 184-5, 192-3, 196-202, 225-9.

66. Clarence-Smith, pp. 25-8.

IV

Asia and World Precious Metal Flows in the Early Modern Period[1]

This survey is based on recent secondary sources, and does not, most of the time, represent more than an overview of the literature. Its aim is to look out from Asia at world bullion[2] flows in the period from 1500 to about 1750. It is a commonplace observation that the establishment of routine connections between Europe and the Americas and Asia resulted, for the first time, in a genuine world circulation of bullion, this in turn creating for the first time a relatively integrated world system at least for this commodity. Both contemporaries and modern scholars have written at length about this global circulation. It was known that both before and after American production began much silver flowed through Europe and on to the East, so that Iberia was 'The Indies of the Genoese' or 'the Indies of other foreign kingdoms.'[3] Godinho writes of this flow as a 'blood letting' ('*sangria*') or as 'this irreversible haemorrhage' ('*essa hemorragia implacável*').[4] He also, however, in a more recent book has put the matter in a wider and more useful perspective. He writes that:

The Cape route can only be comprehended and understood within the world network of routes; trade in spices and drugs, as also in silk, only functioned tangled up in the complex circuits of precious metals and coins which created, beyond the economies of the world, a world-economy.[5]

Godinho estimates that, around 1500, 1,750 kgs of gold, equivalent to 20,500 kgs of silver, flowed from Europe to the East, this being about one-quarter of total European production, and he says this is a low estimate.[6] Braudel also noted that this flow was not new. In a typically florid passage, he wrote:

Away to the east flowed these currencies, out of the Mediterranean circuit into which it had often required much patience to introduce them. The Mediterranean as a whole operated as a machine for accumulating precious metals, of which, be it said, it could never have enough. It hoarded them only to lose them all to India, China, and the East Indies. The great discoveries may have revolutionised routes and prices, but they did not alter this fundamental situation, no doubt because it was still a major advantage to westerners to have access to the precious merchandise of the East . . .[7]

Later he wrote:

This Italy-China axis, beginning in America and running right around the world either through the Mediterranean or round the Cape of Good Hope, can be considered a structure, a permanent and outstanding feature of the world economy which remained undisturbed until the twentieth century.[8]

Careri, travelling in Mughal India in the late seventeenth century, overestimated the inflow to India, yet his general description of flows is so evocative as to merit quoting:

That the Reader may form some Idea of the Wealth of this (Mughal) Empire, he is to observe that all the Gold and Silver, which circulates throughout the World at last Centers here. It is well known that as much of it comes out of America, after running through several Kingdoms of Europe, goes partly into Turky, for several sorts of Commodities; and part into Persia, by the way of Smirna for Silk. Now the Turks not being able to abstain from Coffee, which comes from Hyeman, and Arabia Felix; nor Persia, Arabia, and the Turks themselves to go without the commodities of India, send vast quantities of Mony to Moka on the Red Sea, near Babel Mandel; to Bassora at the bottom of the Persian Gulgh; and to Bander Abassi and Gomeron, which is afterwards sent over in Ships to Indostan. Besides the Indian, Dutch, English, and Portuguese Ships, that every Year carry the Commodities of Indostan, to Pegu, Tanasserri, Siam, Ceylon, Achem, Macassar, the Maldive Islands, Mozambique and other Places, must of necessity convey much Gold and Silver thither, from those Countries. All that the Dutch fetch from the Mines in Japan, sooner or later, goes to Indostan; and the goods carry'd hence into Europe, whether to France, England, or Portugal, are all purchas'd for ready Mony, which remains there.[9]

There is a major problem with European-oriented accounts which concentrate on the flow of American silver to Europe. We can put Asia back into the picture in three ways. As we have just noted, historians are becoming increasingly aware of the extent of the drain of American silver to Asia, but we need to stress, contrary to earlier accounts, that the majority of the flow of precious metals from Europe to the East for most of our period did not take place in European ships via the Cape, but rather in Asian, and some European, ships via the Levant. Second, few historians have made the effort to evaluate exports of gold from southeast Africa. Third, we have only recently begun to take account of the vast production and exports of silver from Japan over the period 1560 to 1668, and even later, to China. Thus, contrary to a European focused stress on the effects of American silver on Europe, three of the major aspects of world monetary flows in this early modern period have to do with Asia: the drain of much American bullion across the Pacific, or through Europe and so to Asia, often carried in Asian ships, and two major production areas apart from the Americas, that is gold from East Africa and silver from Japan. Indeed, the role of Europeans has recently, and somewhat extravagantly, been described merely as that of 'intermediaries in the trade between the New World and China'.[10]

Why did precious metals flow?[11] Briefly, one reason had to do with variable exchange ratios between gold and silver. This is emphasized by Flynn and Giráldez in their recent article, for they find the reason for bullion flows to be not a European inability to sell goods in Asia, but rather the very favourable price of silver in China.[12] In the eighteenth century the English East India Company (EIC) benefited because the ratio between gold and silver varied greatly between Europe and Asia. In Europe it was around 15:1, in Asia between 9:1 and 12:1. So silver flowed to Asia, and some gold went back to Europe.[13] Ratios in fact could vary enormously. In Japan the ratio earlier in the sixteenth century was 1:5 or 1:6. Thanks to the increase in silver production it fell to 1:10 later in the century. At the same time in China the ratio was 1:7 or 1:8, but in some areas it was as high as 1:13.[14] Even silver alone was worth quite varying amounts in different places. In Goa from the 1560s big profits were made from the sale of silver reals of eight: between 25 per cent and 40 per cent profit when silver bullion from Portugal was sold in Goa to money dealers from Goa and other parts of India. In 1629 the profit was 70 per cent.[15]

Another, and probably more important, explanation for the flow is simply that Europeans wanted Asian commodities, while the reverse, by and large, was not the case. Hence Europe had no choice, in our period, but to export precious metals. As Furber noted, 'if silver had not been available to the Europeans in sufficient quantities, the East India trade could not have been carried on'.[16] More recently Om

Prakash has made this same rather obvious point, that the trade of the Europeans in Asia was entirely dependent on American gold and silver, for without it they would have had no resource with which to buy Asian goods.[17]

American production of precious metals, first gold and then silver, and later Brazilian gold, has been much discussed. The American discoveries of course increased supplies in Europe. Braudel claims that before them there were some 5,000 tonnes of gold and 60,000 tonnes of silver in circulation in Europe and the Mediterranean, while between 1500 and 1650 America added to this stock 180 tonnes of gold and 16,000 of silver.[18]

Barrett's recent survey[19] of American production and flows seems to be based on the most recent estimates, and provides an up to date overview. However, it may be that his estimates of exports from Europe are too low. In the seventeenth century he finds that in each 25-year period Europe retained more silver and equivalent than it exported. These are average figures, in tonnes, over 25-year periods:

European Export and Retention of Precious Metals (tonnes)

	Exported from Europe	Retained in Europe
1601-25	100	145
1626-50	125	165
1651-75	130	200
1676-1700	155	215

Source: Ward Barrett, 'World bullion flows, 1450–1800', in James D. Tracy ed., *The Rise of Merchant Empires: Long-Distance Trade in the Early Modern World, 1350–1750*, Cambridge, Cambridge University Press, 1990, pp.242–3.

Vilar's figures[20] are based entirely on Hamilton, and so can no longer be taken seriously, though they do at least show how gold was outdistanced by silver from the 1550s. Cross's more recent estimates[21] seem to be at variance with Barrett's, even though Cross is discussing only silver production, while Barrett's figures, as noted, are for silver and equivalent. Cross also attempts an estimate of the share of New World bullion in total world production from 1500 to 1800. I feel that his method distorts the significance of Japanese silver production, which was vast but split between the last decades of the sixteenth and early decades of the seventeenth centuries, thus making a nonsense of his century-wide comparisons. Nevertheless, his figures[22] do broadly show how dominant American supplies were in the world total. He finds in these three centuries the new world producing respectively 68.5 per cent, 84.4 per cent, and 89.9 per cent of total world production of silver, and 39.1 per cent, 66.1 per cent and 84.9 per cent of gold.

The rise in the gold percentage in the eighteenth century is of course mostly a result of an influx from Brazil, which between 1712 and 1755 sent on average 10,867 kgs of gold a year to Lisbon,[23] this being roughly equal to South American silver production at the same time. In any case, my concern is not really with American production but rather with flows from America.

We have several recent excellent, though not necessarily compatible, descriptions of flows of precious metals from the New World to Europe and so on to Asia in our period. For the sixteenth century we have only spotty data on the flow of this bullion via the Cape of Good Hope in Portuguese ships to India and the Indian Ocean area, and even worse information on flows via the Levant, that is from the Mediterranean through the Red Sea or Persian/Arabian Gulf to the Indian Ocean. This situation as regards the Levant continues for the rest of our period, but we have good data on bullion transfers by the Dutch and English East India Companies to the East from 1600 to 1750. Reasonable estimates of the flow from Acapulco to Manila and on to China have been available for some time. I will now elaborate on each of these flows in turn.

Barrett has provided an overview of the flow from America to Europe;[24] as we would expect, in our period, from 1500 to 1750, of a total production of 3,580 tonnes of silver and equivalent, 2,705 tonnes arrived in Europe.[25] Much of the rest went across the Pacific to the Philippines. My concern is with the flow on from Europe. Chaunu tells us that about 4,000 or 5,000 tonnes of silver got to the Orient via the Pacific between 1570 and 1780, and 17,000 via the Levant or the Cape of Good Hope between 1503 and 1650. Roughly one third of American's silver production then ended up in the Orient.[26] This is useful as a broad estimate of flows, and in specifying the three main routes: the Pacific, the Cape and the Levant. Unfortunately, Chaunu also gives us an example of the lack of precision which is often a feature of himself and his fellow Annalistas, for it appears that by 'the Orient' he means only China. Braudel quotes this figure approvingly, though he also likes Gernet's estimate that one half of all silver mined in America between 1527 and 1821 ended up in China.[27] Later Braudel notes that the main route for the flow to the East was via the Levant 'as late as the seventeenth and eighteenth centuries.'[28] This is true, but I think we can be a little more precise than this.

What was the main route followed by precious metals as they went from Europe to the East? Attman has produced two interesting overviews. In 1986[29] he found the following flows (he calculated in millions of rix dollars, which I have converted to tonnes, assuming a rix dollar to be equal to 26 grammes):

Destinations of American Precious Metals (tonnes)

	1550	1600	1650	1700	1750
Am Prod	130	286-364	260-338	338	702-780
To Iberia	78	260	208-234	273-325	468-650
To East	(52-78)	114.4	156	221	317.2

Source: Artur Attman, *American Bullion in the European World Trade, 1600–1800*, Goteborg, 1986 p.78.

It is to be remembered that the flow to the East came both via Iberia, and via Acapulco and Manila. Subsequently he tried to estimate European exports of precious metals over various routes,[30] and again I have converted rix dollars to tonnes:

European Exports of Precious Metals(tonnes)

	1600	1650	1700	1750
To Levant	(26)	(52)	(52)	(52)
To Baltic	44.2-52	60-78	60-78	60-78
Via Cape	26	44.2	85.8	148.2

Source: Artur Attman, 'Precious metals and the balance of payments in international trade, 1500–1800', in Wolfram Fischer, R. Marvin McInnis and Jurgen Schneider, eds, *The Emergence of a World Economy, 1500–1914*, Wiesbaden, 1986, p.115.

Several comments are in order here. First, the figure of 44.2 tonnes for 1650 includes some silver from Japan. Second, as he says, these are minimum figures. Third, it will be noted that his figures for the Levant are only estimates. On the one hand, unlike in an earlier version he does at least see some variation in the Levant flow, but on the other hand he seems to be still too low for this route. Finally, we need always to keep in mind that flows to the Levant are not necessarily flows to the Indian Ocean area, or to India and China. Much precious metal stayed in Safavid Iran and Ottoman Turkey. But despite all this, Attman's efforts are better than Barrett's.[31] In his recent survey he finds Europe exporting each year 50 tonnes of silver and silver equivalents via the Levant for the whole period from 1601 to 1780. His figures come from an early effort of Attman's, and his complete failure to attempt to estimate variations on this route is really a total abdication of responsibility. For the six successive 25-year periods from 1601 to 1750 he finds 50 tonnes per year of precious metals going each year via the Levant to Asia, and via the Cape 8 tonnes, then 19, 20, 53, 85 and in 1726–50 101 tonnes. These figures are also, as we will see, dubious, for most authors find the flow via the Levant greater than that carried in East India ships via the Cape well into the eighteenth century.

The data for the sixteenth-century flow from Europe to the East is spotty indeed. We do not yet have any detailed study of Portuguese bullion imports to Asia in the sixteenth century. There is nothing comparable to the studies for the two northern European companies in the seventeenth and eighteenth centuries. Godinho says that over the second half of the sixteenth century the Cape and the Levant combined took 72,000 kg of silver or its equivalent per year; at this time European mines were producing 21,000 kgs, and American 130,000.[32] Over the whole sixteenth century, Moosvi finds the Portuguese alone bringing in to the Indian Ocean area over 60,000 kgs of silver a year via the Cape.[33]

We have much better data for the seventeenth and eighteenth centuries for the Cape route, thanks to better records, and better modern research by Gaastra and Chaudhuri. For the English East India Company, Chaudhuri has presented a table showing its total exports of treasure, and another showing five-year averages, both covering the period 1660 to 1760.[34] The figures fluctuate wildly, and gold, thanks to a change in the exchange ratio in the early eighteenth century, vanishes completely after 1715. Overall, his figures show that a very high percentage of total English exports to the East were bullion, despite this being in theory an age of bullion hoarding, and that English exports of precious metals were very substantial indeed: on two occasions they were worth more than £1,000,000. Prakash shows, using Chaudhuri's data, that over the period 1660–1720 only 20.6 per cent of English imports to all of Asia were made up of goods: the rest was bullion.[35] Attman produced a useful table which showed that until 1758–60 the EIC on average sent 75 per cent of its total imports to the East in bullion and only 25 per cent in goods. After Plassey and the beginnings of political dominance the percentage fell immediately, to 40 per cent and later much lower.[36]

Gaastra's figures[37] for the Dutch East India Company [VOC] show that the trend is towards a steady increase, unlike the wild EIC fluctuations. His figures for the total for each decade after 1602, up to 1730, in tonnes of silver (I have converted his guilders to metric weights at 100 guilders being roughly equal to one kg of silver, and rounded them off a little) show a rise from 52 tonnes in 1602–10 to 124 in 1620–30, then a decline to 119 tonnes in 1660–70, and thereafter a quite steady rise to 392 tonnes in 1700–10 and no less than 667 in 1720–30.

More useful, as it introduces the aspect of comparison and relativity, are his figures for total VOC exports of precious metals from three areas from 1640 to 1660: Europe, Persia and Japan.[38] Again I have converted his guilders to tonnes, and it may be noted that exports from Japan and Europe at this time were all silver, while some gold is included in the Persian figures. Disregarding minor fluctuations, he shows that in this twenty-year period the total from Europe was 192 tonnes, 90 from Persia, and from Japan a massive figure of just under 300 tonnes.

In a similar but more general overview, Gaastra[39] compares VOC exports of precious metals from Europe, and from Japan, over a longer period; again I have converted millions of guilders to tonnes:

VOC Exports of Precious Metals (tonnes)

	From Europe	From Japan
1640s	88	152
1650s	84	131
1660s	119	145
1670s	110	115

Source: Femme S. Gaastra, 'The Dutch East India Company and its intra-Asiatic trade in precious metals', in Wolfram Fischer, R. Marvin McInnis and Jurgen Schneider, eds, *The Emergence of a World Economy, 1500–1914*, Wiesbaden, 1986, p.104.

Thus over these forty years, 400 tonnes came from Europe, 540 from Japan. The general point to be made here is that the availability of Japanese silver to the VOC enabled them to rely much less than their competitors, especially the EIC, on exports of bullion from Europe. Such exports were often politically touchy in the seventeenth century. The Dutch were also able to generate revenue in Asia from their successful involvement in the 'country trade', that is inter-Asian trade. This also reduced their requirements of bullion from Europe.

We will discuss other implications of the vast exports of silver, and later gold, from Japan presently. In the meantime, and despite our comments in the previous paragraph, we still need to stress the huge VOC exports of bullion from Europe, just as was also the case with the EIC. On average two-thirds of VOC exports from Europe were in bullion; in the seventeenth century Peruvian silver, in the eighteenth-century Brazilian gold.[40] Similarly, Prakash has found that between 1660 and 1720 Dutch imports into Bengal, one of their major trading areas, were only 12.5 per cent goods, the rest being bullion.[41]

So much for the quite good data which we have concerning the companies and the Cape route from 1600. Much more difficult, but also more interesting, is the matter of flows via the Levant, that is from the Mediterranean and so through Ottoman Turkey to the Indian Ocean, or to Persia. We must first stress that not all the bullion which entered the Middle East went right on to the Indian Ocean or to China. Much stayed in Ottoman Turkey and Safavid Iran. But what sorts of flows did end up in the Indian Ocean, as compared with the figures just quoted for the Cape route? We may first remember again the unsatisfactory figures produced by Attman and Barrett, which we noted above. They are too general, and too small. We cannot in fact do much better than them in terms of precise figures, but we can revise their low estimates. What we find is that the flow through the Levant was greater than that via the Cape until well into the eighteenth century. We must, again, not be blinded by the later success of the Europeans so as to overestimate their role in Asian trade in the period to 1750. This is a general theme in modern writing on the Europeans in Asia from 1500 to 1750, and it applies to bullion flows as well as to more general commerce.

Sanjay Subrahmanyam has provided a useful overview. He notes that Steensgaard and Barrett claim that the Cape route was dominant, but he finds the data of Moosvi, Brennig and van Santen to be more convincing. He concludes that at least through the seventeenth century much more bullion entered the Indian Ocean area via the Levant than via the Cape: the former 'easily dwarfs' the latter.[42] Moosvi's careful survey is based on the outputs of Mughal mints, a useful technique in that all bullion entering Mughal India was recoined in an official mint. She stresses fluctuations. There was a spurt in silver entry via the Levant and so in mint output between 1625 and 1645. Over the next thirty years mint output fell as silver imports declined, but they revived again after 1675. In sum she finds that imports from the Levant were vastly greater than those via the Cape. In the period 1660–1705 she finds 44.5 tons of silver entering Gujarat alone from the Levant each year.[43]

Joseph Brennig has produced some specific data for the most important Mughal port and mint, Surat. He has detailed figures for the years 1643–44. He finds that 19 per cent of the silver imported was from Japan. Only 28 per cent came via the Cape, but 61 per cent of the total was handled by Europeans; that is, the companies brought bullion from the Red Sea and Persian/Arabian Gulf along with locals.[44] It is interesting to note that the European percentage fell sharply after this, reflecting the fact that their dominance comes only in the later eighteenth century. In the period 1690–1720 Brennig finds Asian merchants bringing in 76,500 kgs of silver a year to Surat. This was vastly more than that imported by Europeans. The European percentage of total bullion imports fell from around 50 per cent in the 1640s to 17 per cent in the early 1700s.[45] So much then for too great an emphasis on the activities of the Europeans at this time: they were still being out-traded by their Asian rivals both in the area of bullion and in general commerce.

To complete this survey of flows and production we must turn to East Asia, and investigate flows from Spanish America to Asia via Manila. Estimates of the flow via the famous Manila galleon, from Acapulco to Manila and so on to China, vary enormously. Chaunu estimated that Spain sent 4,000 tonnes to Manila between 1570 and 1780, while in these two centuries the VOC sent 5,900 tonnes via the Cape.[46] Moosvi claims that in a big year in the 1590s Spain sent 500 tonnes of silver across the Pacific, nearly as much as it sent to Europe. The average however was much less, perhaps one-third of this or 175 tonnes.[47]

Barrett, who is much stronger on America than on Asia, produced some very low figures for American silver flows across the Pacific. He finds[48] annual averages, in tonnes of silver, for the six twenty-five year periods starting in 1601 and ending in 1750 as 17, 16, 6, 15, 15, and 15. Flynn has been very critical of these figures, noting that there may have been 128 tonnes per annum in the early seventeenth century, and one report claimed 307 tonnes had been smuggled in 1597.[49] Atwell says cautiously that in the early seventeenth century between 58,000 and 86,000 kgs a year went through the Philippines to China, though he notes that other estimates are much higher, up to even 345,000 kgs a year.[50]

TePaske has put the matter in a rather different perspective. He notes[51] that overall the Philippines took very little American silver. Over the period 1581 to 1800, 83 per cent went to Castile, and only 17 per cent across the Pacific. However, this percentage did vary widely, as this table shows:

Flows of American Silver

	To Castile	To the Philippines
1580s	88%	12%
1590s	95%	5%
1600s	90%	10%
1610s	71%	29%
1620s	65%	35%
1630s	70%	30%
1640s	57%	43%
1650s	74%	26%
1660s	74%	26%
1670s	86%	14%
1680s	71%	29%
1690s	61%	39%
1700s	81%	19%
1710s	88%	12%
1720s	76%	24%
1730s	85%	15%
1740s	79%	21%

Source: John J. TePaske, 'New world silver, Castile and the Philippines, 1590–1800', in J.F. Richards, ed., *Precious Metals in the later Medieval and Early Modern Worlds*, Durham, NC., 1983, pp.434, 444.

Thus in certain periods the Philippines took very substantial proportions of Spain's total production: over one-quarter in the period 1600–50, and over 40 per cent in the 1640s. At present the state of research for this period is such that any attempt at explanation of these variations would be not only hazardous but in fact nugatory.

We can now leave the matter of flows of American bullion to Asia, and turn to our two other main concerns, that is production of bullion apart from America, specifically from East Africa and Japan. In general, we must remember that there was some local production also, and quite complicated flows within Asia. As an example of the latter, the EIC ships took quite large amounts of bullion from India to China[52] and at times, as we have noted, gold was exported from India to Europe. As to the Asian production, there were minor workings in various parts of Southeast Asia[53] but the main thing here was the production of gold from East Africa, and of silver, and later gold, in Japan, which played a major role in East Asia in the sixteenth and seventeenth centuries. Even today not all scholars have come to terms with the implications of these vast flows. Thus K.N. Chaudhuri excludes Japan from his otherwise useful map of bullion flows.[54]

We will first assemble what is known about gold production and export from East Africa, from the fabled mines of Munhumutapa, in modern Zimbabwe. The data from here is even worse than that from other areas, and we also have an immediate problem in that gold was measured in terms of a unit called a matical, itself a word of Arabic origin. There are problems both with converting maticals (referred to also as meticals, miticals and mithqals) into weights, and into money of the time. Mudenge[55] accepts Godinho's calculation[56] that a matical weighed 4.25 grammes, giving a kilogram:matical ratio of about 1:235; thus 200,000 maticals make up 850 kgs. This is preferable to Chitticks's earlier and vaguer ratio of 1:200.[57] The ratio between the matical and the Portuguese money of account, reis, also varied considerably. Schurhammer[58] quotes 450 reis to the matical, while a document of 1506 gives 460 reis in Kilwa[59] and at the same time it was 500 reis in Sofala.[60] Other estimates are 467 and 480 reis.[61]

We have some amazing estimates of production before the arrival of the Portuguese. Duarte quotes Phimister as saying that the total pre-Portuguese gold production from the Zimbabwe plateau was between six and nine million ounces.[62] This estimate seems to be quite fabulous, for if we convert one ounce to 28.3 grammes then we have between 170 and 254 tonnes, though be it noted that this is over a very long period. Production began slowly at the start of the tenth century, or perhaps earlier, and was at its height in the eleventh to fifteenth centuries; it then declined drastically. At first placer mining, that is washing from alluvium, was most common, but later quite sophisticated reef mining techniques were also employed. This gold was exported through Sofala but marketed at Kilwa, up to 10 tonnes a year before the decline late in the fifteenth century.[63] A well informed Portuguese claimed in 1506 that when the land was at peace at least one million, and up to 1,300,000, maticals of gold were exported each year from Sofala, and maybe 50,000 from Angoche, this then totalling a maximum of 5,744 kgs.[64]

What data do we have for gold exports in the sixteenth century, once the Portuguese had arrived and we get slightly better figures? Mudenge's figures correlate more or less with those of Godinho. The latter quotes with some scepticism a figure for exports from Sofala and Kilwa of gold originating inland in Munhumutapa of 8,500 kgs a year. For later years he quotes the following figures for kilograms of gold from these mines being exported to Goa: 1585: 573 kgs; 1591: 716 kgs; 1610: 850 kgs; 1667: 1,487 kgs.[65] Lobato provides some confirmation for he finds about 830 kg coming to Goa around 1600.[66] A Portuguese calculation of 1614 said the trade was worth about 400,000 pardaus, in other words a little over 1,000 kgs.[67] Mudenge claims the following: 8,000 kgs at 1500, falling rapidly to 6,000 at c.1510, 3,500 at 1550, less than 1,000 in 1600, and then a slow rise to 1,500 kgs around 1670, and then a decline again.[68]

What is beyond doubt is that gold exports which came to the cognizance of the Portuguese fell very rapidly indeed soon after their arrival. Chittick claims that in 1512–15 the Portuguese got only 12,500 maticals (53 kgs) a year.[69] This fall was mostly a result of 'smuggling' and its prevalence in the sixteenth century means that official Portuguese figures need to be used with caution, as they are certainly too low to show total exports. There are three problems with the Portuguese official data, namely Portugal's own chimerical aspirations, the prevalence of smuggling, and the matter of adulteration. As to the first, the Portuguese records are full of wild claims of the wealth of the Mutapa state. They hoped to find their own Eldorado, or at least Potosí, there, and unscrupulous people tried to get support from Portugal for their inland ambitions by wildly exaggerating the dimensions of gold production in the interior. However, certainly the Portuguese attempt to control this trade, at first by sea and later in the interior, did produce our second statistical problem, for many local traders, and also Portuguese, refused to accept the official Crown monopoly.

C.R. Boxer[70] claims that three-quarters of the gold exported from Sofala evaded the purported royal monopoly in 1511. A year earlier a

Portuguese official noted that the king had got no gold from Sofala this year, but the unofficial and so illegal trade amounted to over 30,000 maticals (128 kgs).[71] Datoo noted copious smuggling by both local Portuguese and by Swahili traders. The Gujarati traders often paid for the gold with cloth. The pattern was the cloth was taken to the northern Swahili coast by Gujaratis, trading in ports not controlled by the Portuguese, and then taken south of Cape Dalgado by local craft, especially to Angoche.[72]

As noted, it was not only local traders who exported gold 'illegally', Portuguese did too. Similarly, the third serious problem, that of adulteration, was laid at the door of the Portuguese themselves. A letter from the city of Goa to the king in 1645 claimed that the householders of Mozambique falsified the gold with other base metals. They pointed out that the gold came from the mines very pure, but then was adulterated even up to 35 per cent, leading to great losses.[73] Some years later, in 1653, the king wrote to the viceroy saying he had had another complaint about this matter, and asked the viceroy to do something about it.[74] But the governors of Portuguese India replied in 1658 that they could do little about this. The gold was extremely pure while it was under the control of the 'cafres', but once it came into Portuguese hands, especially those of the captain of Mozambique's agent in Sena, it was falsified and adulterated. The governors could suggest no easy solution.[75]

Various factors may have affected production itself. In the seventeenth and eighteenth centuries unstable political conditions in the interior production areas no doubt diminished the amounts produced, as also possibly did Portuguese blockading efforts. Indeed, local producers apparently disguised the amounts of gold available in order to ward off Portuguese attacks. A letter from 1667 noted that in one rich gold area 'the Kaffirs who possess these lands will not allow more gold to be extracted than is necessary, that the Portuguese may not covet and obtain possession of their lands'.[76] The actual process of extraction was arduous and dangerous. When the Portuguese finally got to the gold-producing areas in the 1570s, 'they thought that they would immediately be able to fill sacks with it, and carry off as much as they chose; but when they had spent a few days near the mines, and saw the difficulty and labour of the Kaffirs, and with what risk and peril of their lives they extracted it from the bowels of the earth and from the stones, they found their hopes frustrated'.[77]

John Sutton has recently raised the matter of demand for this gold.[78] He claims that European demand for gold was at its height from about 1250 to 1350, as states transferred to a gold standard. Subsequently a slump in Europe, caused largely by the Black Death, reduced demand, which revived again only in the early fifteenth century. I would agree that demand, even for gold, can vary, as indeed fluctuations in its price show. However, Sutton's focus on European demand seems misplaced. Rather we should be looking for variations in demand, if any, in the Indian Ocean area, and especially in India itself.

What can we say generally about the size of these exports? Very little in fact, for the figures are so sparse, and the amount of smuggling so indeterminable that any broad trends are obscured. If we take a lower figure than Boxer's, say 50 per cent, for smuggling during the course of the sixteenth century, and if we estimate, with a huge margin of error, exports which the Portuguese knew about at 6,000 kgs in 1510 and 1,000 in 1600, we then would have perhaps 12,000 kgs a year being exported at the beginning of the sixteenth century, and 2,000 at the end. It must be noted that Godinho produces a much lower estimate[79] for he says that exports never fell below 500 kgs between 1500 and 1650, and were never more than 1,500 kgs. However, these are amounts which the Portuguese knew about, and take no account of 'smuggling'. My conclusion here is also fairly close to Mudenge's estimates noted above.

Finally, it is important for our purposes to note that this gold all stayed in the Indian Ocean area.[80] What was collected by the Portuguese was taken to Goa, and thence presumably flowed to other Asian areas. Given Goa's massive trade with Gujarat, most of it probably finished up there or was taken from there to North India. We have no records of the Portuguese taking any gold back to Portugal. Exports outside the Portuguese system similarly must have gone to Gujarat, or to the Red Sea area.

We can compare this very crude figure with other data from other areas to put it into some sort of perspective. In the peak years of West African gold production, from 1500 to 1520, the Portuguese got about 700 kgs a year.[81] Two centuries later, the Portuguese between 1712 and 1755, exported from Brazil to Portugal well over 10,000 kgs a year.[82] Spanish American exports in the sixteenth century were also large: about 900 kgs a year in the 1510s, 2,500 in the 1540s, and a high of 4,300 in the 1550s.[83] As we will see in a minute,

Japan in the later seventeenth century also exported large quantities of gold: 4,000 kgs a year in the 1660s, 11,500 in the next decade, and then a steady fall to 3,000 in the 1680s.[84] Kobata's figures for total world production of gold per year in the period 1521–1640 produces a rough average of about 7.75 tonnes a year.[85] The most we can hazard by way of conclusion is that exports from Munhumutapa were substantial, and so far have not been adequately discussed in the literature.

Turning now to Japan, Attman, in his most recent, and last, publication, still claimed that in an appraisal of the different routes which supplied precious metals to Asian markets, 'those which ran between Europe and Asia stand out as being by far the most important'.[86] Contrary to this, what was really happening, as Flynn puts it, was that 'Japan and Spain were major competitors in the world's first global market; China was the most important customer, followed by India'.[87]

Japanese production had risen greatly from the mid sixteenth century after a new smelting technique was developed. The silver ore was smelted with lead, and then the silver was isolated by blowing ash onto the molten mixture.[88] As a result copper coins, formerly the only currency in use in Japan, were replaced by gold and silver coins.[89] As usual our data for the sixteenth century is not good, and there is an additional problem in the case of Japan in that there were two degrees of fineness to be found in Japanese silver coins. The purer ones were called sooma-silver, as compared with what the Dutch called schuijtgeld, that is coins of only about 80 per cent purity.[90] Thirty years ago Kobata wrote that a 'bold conjecture' would put Japanese production at the start of the seventeenth century at 200,000 kgs a year.[91] Subsequent research shows this rough estimate is a little on the high side. Atwell provides some useful figures. He notes that China in the middle of the sixteenth century took about 20,000 kgs of silver a year from Japan, this being carried in East Asian ships, and by the end of the century up to 50,000. It is to be noted that these are exports to only one country. There was a further huge rise early in the seventeenth century, to over 150,000 kgs.[92] Flynn and Giráldez claim Japan shipped 'perhaps 200 tonnes per year at times', this being between 30 and 40 per cent of total world production.[93]

Glamman's figures[94] for Japanese gold and silver production in the later seventeenth century still have some validity. They show the effects of the ban, in 1668, on the export of silver from the country. For a time gold replaced silver after important finds in the late 1660s, but exports of gold later also fell off. In the six decades from the 1640s to the 1690s he finds for the first three silver production of 150, 130 and 105 tonnes. Silver then ends. Gold begins in the 1660s, and goes from 40 tonnes then to 115, 30 and finally 20 tonnes in the 1690s, these figures being for silver equivalent. When we compare these figures with those from Gaastra[95] for Dutch exports from Japan, which we quoted above, it seems that virtually all of total Japanese production of silver was taken by the Dutch in this closed country era after 1640, when they had almost monopoly access to Japanese supplies. However, as I will note in a minute, this is not necessarily a valid assumption.

A recent analysis finds the Portuguese took between 22 and 37 tonnes of silver a year from Japan from 1560 to 1600; if other exporters are added in the total becomes from 33 to 48 tonnes exported per year to China. In the first forty years of the next century, until the 'Closed Country' period, exports rose dramatically, to between 150 and 187 tonnes per annum to China. In the whole period from 1560 to 1640, Japan sent to China between 7,350 and 9,450 tonnes of silver, while the total from America to China in the same period was only about 1,320 tonnes.[96] The Portuguese retained a share of this trade. Souza finds that a minimum figure for Portuguese exports of silver from Japan to China in the period 1598 to 1638 is an annual average of 12.5 tonnes.[97] The Portuguese were expelled from Japan in this last year, and in the middle of this century, the VOC, enjoying a quasi-monopoly trade, took 130 tonnes per decade from Japan in the period 1640–80.[98] It will be remembered that after 1640 European trade with Japan was restricted to the Dutch, and even they traded on very restricted, not to say humiliating, terms. Nevertheless, their access to Japanese silver in the period 1640 to 1668, when silver exports were banned, was vitally important for them, as this was a period when, according to Furber, American production fell greatly.[99] However a drop in American production in the mid-seventeenth century is no longer universally accepted. Cross's figures do show this, with production per decade in Peru falling from 250 tonnes in the 1630s to 220, 170, 130 and 120 in the succeeding decades.[100] Braudel also notes this drop[101] but Barrett's twenty-five year annual averages for total American silver and silver equivalent show a rise from 340 tonnes per annum in the years 1601–25 to 395 in the next quarter century and 445 in the next.[102] It seems to be recognized now that what really happened was that Spanish imports of silver did not decline in the second quarter of the seventeenth century; rather they shifted from official to unofficial channels.[103]

There is in any case a major problem with all these estimates of Japanese production, for the assumption seems to be that Europeans, first Portuguese and later the Dutch, took it all and sent it mostly to China. But to equate Dutch exports with Japanese production seems to be perilous. We should note here that just as Ronald Toby's excellent book[104] found that Japanese 'isolation' in general applied only to cutting ties with Europeans, but not with its East Asian neighbours, similarly silver exports to China were allowed to continue for a time after 1668. Kobata[105] notes that at least until 1685 silver was exported to China, and we can assume that earlier there had also been a considerable 'unofficial' export trade from Japan not carried by Europeans, and indeed a large trade carried in *go-shuin-sen* (officially licensed) Japanese ships.[106]

Comparisons with Spain will put Japanese production in perspective. Cross, whom we have already quoted, noted that in the sixteenth century the New World produced 68.5 per cent of the world's silver, and in the seventeenth 84.4 per cent.[107] However, as I have already noted, using whole-century figures distorts the matter somewhat, for Japan had a period of expanded silver production which straddled these two centuries; a comparison for 1560–1640 finds that Japan's exports to China were 36 per cent of new world total production.[108] Another comparison is to note that in the seventeenth century America produced over 300 tonnes of silver a year, while in the early years of this century Japan's production was up to 200 tonnes.[109] A further useful comparison is to look at silver exports to China, the greatest sink of them all. Barrett[110] finds the following in tonnes per annum: silver from Japan to China in the period 1560–99 between 34 and 49 tonnes a year, and from 1600–40 150 to 187 tonnes; from America to China in the first period 10, and in the second 22.

Suffice to say then that this first truly global exchange of a particular commodity, bullion, needs to be put in a more correct perspective. Asia consumed much of the bullion available in the world in the early modern period. This applies not only to the contiguous sources of bullion, that is those in East Africa and in Japan, but also to the production of the Americas. Very recently Flynn and Giráldez have made this same point. Indeed in their commendable attempt to de-emphasize the role of Europe in world trade in silver they elevate China, as consumer, to a quite unrealistic pinnacle. It is strange indeed to find massive consumption of bullion in India and the Middle East totally ignored.[111]

We started this essay by noting that many scholars have noted that this worldwide flow of bullion created a true world economy for the first time, for it linked all the continents (except Australia). This however raises two final, related, more general questions. First, what were the effects of these flows on the economies of East Africa, India and China, and second, how does this creation of worldwide flows in this particular commodity relate to world-system theory?

We can sketch very quickly the effects of these flows of bullion on the economies of East Africa, India and China. Turning first to the Mutapa state in the area of modern Zimbabwe, in the early modern period the main exports from these states were ivory and gold (slaves came later). Imports were mostly Indian-made cloths and beads. Ostensibly then we are looking at the export of raw materials, and the import of manufactures, and this seems to show a clear first world/third world situation of exploitation. This perception is reinforced when we note the vast profits that foreign traders were making from this exchange. However, when we look at the relative values of these goods we find something different. Both gold and ivory were produced using discretionary, male, labour, and this was not extracted from more 'productive' activities such as embryonic manufactures or food cultivation. Nor was either product highly prized in the interior states. Gold is most valuable in a monetized economy, and these were not.

What production and export there was, was done on a part time basis by the Shona peasantry of the area in innumerable scattered riverside washings. As Beach says, it was 'the product of the secondary activities of an agricultural economy'.[112] The great contemporary Portuguese chroniclers both noted this. Barros said that 'As the land is rich in gold, if the people were covetous a great quantity would be obtained, but they are so lazy in seeking it, or rather covet it so little, that one of these negroes must be very hungry before he will dig for it',[113] and later Couto wrote 'As the Kaffirs are numerous, they always obtain a great quantity [of gold] although they are by nature so indolent that when they have found sufficient to buy two pieces of cloth to clothe themselves, they will not work any more'.[114] The important observer Padre dos Santos late in the sixteenth century wrote that there was plenty of gold, 'but the natives of the country do not trouble to seek it or dig for it, as they are at a distance from the Portuguese who might buy it; but they are much occupied with the breeding of cattle, of which there are great numbers in these lands'.[115] In short, it could be argued that gold production in the Mutapa state had almost no effect on the total economy, apart from providing some luxuries for the élite.

The effects on India and China of this vast influx of American silver have been much debated. Braudel put forward a strong case for this flow not being detrimental for Europe; rather it allowed Europeans to break into Asian trade (as indeed we quoted Furber as noting earlier in this essay), and on the other hand created what he seems to see as almost a situation of dependency in the receiving countries of China and India. He finds that the famous Mughal silver rupee was 'remote-controlled'. The advantage then was with Europe, which controlled American silver flows to Asia. One could see 'Europe, committed to Asia only by her passion for luxury goods, as having a stranglehold in the form of silver over the economies of the Far East, and thus being in a position of strength'.[116] It is of course a question of whether European demand for Asian goods was really so discretionary, and in any case this purported 'stranglehold' was never tested in practice.

The debate in the case of both China and India, by far the two largest and most integrated economies in Asia and the world in our period, centres around the matter of whether there was a European-style Price Revolution here also. It could be that this whole debate has a tinge of Eurocentrism about it. Just as historians once spent much time and effort trying to decide whether Asia had feudalism, now they take another European model or conjuncture and try to find this in Asia. Similarly, at one time scholars writing on the spice trade devoted most of their efforts to investigating the trade between the Indian Ocean and Europe. More recently we have remembered that only about 10 per cent of total Asian spice production went to Europe; we have begun to look at the much larger trade, that is the one within Asia. Maybe we will some day be able to write a more autonomous history of Asia which does not rely on Europe for models and ideas. But so far the literature has not really escaped these shackles.

To an outsider like myself the Chinese currency system appears to be a curious one. In the period from the seventh to the fifteenth centuries the empire had had a reasonably successful paper currency system. In our period the only coins were copper, but these were obviously low in value and so were unwieldy. Silver was the main medium of exchange. It was not coined, but was weighed and circulated as bullion. A piece would be cut off a lump of silver to make a payment.[117]

Nearly all of this silver was imported. Chinese domestic production had once been substantial, but had fallen in the fifteenth century. In the sixteenth century about 1,000 kgs a year were produced.[118] Braudel, to the contrary,[119] notes that China was the greatest importer of silver in our period in the world. We have already detailed the vast imports of silver into China from both America and Japan, and indeed some of the flow into the Indian Ocean area also finished up in Ming and Qing China. Silver flowed in because of the high value it held in China as compared with the rest of the world. Godinho says that in the first three decades of the seventeenth century the silver to gold ratio in China was between 5.5:1 and 8:1, with the mean about 7:1. In Japan the ratio was 10:1, in Mughal India 9:1, and in Spain 12.5:1 and going up.[120] Hence the vast shipments from Manila, and from Japan. The effect of these ratios was of course that Chinese goods could be paid for in cheap silver, and sold in Europe and elsewhere at comparatively high prices.

The reverse also was true: China desperately needed silver, given its expanding economy, the failure of the paper system, and the limitations of using copper. As a much-quoted aphorism had it, the Chinese said in broken Spanish that 'silver is blood'. ('*plata es sangre*')[121] The effect of the massive inflow was various. On the one hand it obviously helped the growth of the money supply, and so determined the pace of economic development for a huge population of around 100,000,000. In other words, the influx was vital for the expansion of the Ming Chinese economy. But this very influx also created problems, notably severe price inflation in the later Ming period from around 1600.

The Indian data seems to be rather fuller, though this may merely be a result of my greater familiarity with the historiography of this area. We could first remember that India had imported bullion long before American silver came on stream, for India had long been one of the most advanced economies in the world, and on the other hand had never had large supplies of domestic gold or silver. Shireen Moosvi has done some excellent work on flows in our period. Using mint data (remembering that nearly all silver imported was immediately minted at one of the many official mints, and remembering also that the Mughal emperors justifiably prided themselves on the purity of their rupees, which were standardized at about eleven grammes), she finds that between 1576 and 1705 Mughal mints each year coined over 150 tonnes of silver. French minting between 1631 and 1660 was only 75 tonnes.[122] She and her colleagues have also been able to give us more detailed information on diachronic flows. Habib has pointed out that the gold to silver ratio fluctuated in India as compared with Europe, and this influenced flows in and out of India. Around 1600 the silver price of gold in India was less than in Europe. By mid-century the two were the same. Later India rose a little above Europe, but by the end of this century the ratios were again the same.[123]

More interesting, there is strong evidence that flows into India correlated strongly with American production. Aziza Hasan shows there was a five to ten year lag. Thus in India between 1605 and 1630 there was a decline in mint outputs and in the inflow of bullion, the reason being a decline in Spanish imports between 1601 and 1605, and again from 1611 to 1615. The fall was also caused by the decline of the Portuguese *carreira* early in the seventeenth century, and by low imports by the Dutch and English, who in this early period of their activities in the Indian Ocean brought in only about 10 tonnes of silver a year.[124]

Another result of this influx of American silver was that through most of the seventeenth century, in India, the copper price of silver cheapened. The result was that silver coins, the rupee, from early in the century, replaced copper as the preferred coins in use in the empire. Up to the early seventeenth century copper *dams* retained their popularity. One of the great events of Indian currency history then was their displacement by silver from early in this century.[125]

The broader trend however was a vast expansion of coinage, mostly silver, in India in the first half of the seventeenth century. The number of rupees in circulation went up three times from 1591 to 1639, and then fell so that in 1684 there were only twice as many as in 1591. Overall between 1500 and 1650 India absorbed 6,000 tonnes of silver, coming via the Cape and the Levant, and this was more than one-third of the total amount of silver which came to Europe from America in this period.[126]

What were the effects of this influx on the Indian economy? There is a hoary, and covertly racist, claim that much of it was hoarded. This notion is now discredited. Some may have been hoarded, and some was used for ornamentation. But we need to remember first that there was sometimes a flow of gold out of India also, and second that before colonialism India historically always had a favourable balance of payments in its overseas trade. It may be noted that there have been almost no finds of Mughal coins outside India; rather silver always flowed in. Most of the influx then was a result of this, and it was used in an expanding Indian economy.[127] Chaudhuri notes that, contrary to the proponents of a wasteful Indian tendency to hoard, in fact the usual broad pattern was for American silver to flow either to Manila or India, and then go to China where it was exchanged either for gold or commodities. These then came back to India and were used to buy goods for Europe.[128] Prakash also denies the hoarding argument in the case of Bengal. The influx was used to increase the money supply.[129]

The two main debates today concern the matter of a Price Revolution in India as a result of the inflow, and the general effects of this inflow on the Indian economy. As to the first, the matter has of course been much discussed with relation to all the places where American silver flowed in: Europe, the Middle East, India and China. In the case of India, we must note that if we accept Habib's claim outlined earlier, that is that the silver age in Mughal India, based on American silver, begins only early in the seventeenth century, then a price revolution, if any, could have occurred only from this time. Chaudhuri opines, cautiously, that it is possible that the inflow did cause price rises.[130] Habib finds a price rise also, so that there was inflation in the seventeenth century, but the rate of increase came nowhere near to matching the rate of bullion inflow or the rate of increase in the money supply.[131] Brennig also agrees that there were price increases, but that these were not a result of the silver influx; price rises do not match the bullion flows. The real reason for what seems to be quite modest inflation was a fall in the value of silver.[132]

But the most recent work either denies, or is agnostic about, the very fact of a price rise. Moosvi finds no long term inflation, and Subrahmanyam agrees that given the existing state of our knowledge of price changes over time in Mughal India, we cannot yet talk of a general price rise.[133] Prakash in his detailed and very valuable regional study also thinks there was no general price rise in Bengal. He suggests that more money simply meant fewer barter transactions. There was also an increase in population in this area, and much of the bullion that came into Bengal flowed out again to other parts of the Mughal empire, and into the coffers of the state.[134]

But what of the general effects on the Indian economy? Chaudhuri claims that it made possible a general expansion of the Indian economy, and this is an unexceptionable statement. However, he then goes on to attribute most of this to the European trading companies, in a way reminiscent of Braudel's claim that the bullion influx made Asia dependent on Europe. Chaudhuri writes 'The industrial producers of India . . . were now drawn into an ever-expanding circle of market area through the intermediary of the European East India Companies, which supplied the working capital'. 'The two ends of the international chain of economic links now stretched from Asia to the New World with Europe providing the main force of expansion'. Later he notes that the inflow of bullion from Europe resulted in 'a general expansion in the economy of those areas of India that were most actively concerned with foreign trade'.[135]

This claim has been vigorously contested – not surprising, as our own data above shows that the primary role of the companies in importing bullion is a myth until at least well into the eighteenth century. Moosvi makes this same point[136] and then goes on to ask whether the inflow, regardless of where it came from, was in fact beneficial. She notes that the value of bullion depreciated constantly. It did increase the money supply of course, though this in turn may, as we have noted, have caused some inflation. Habib and Prakash find the inflow more positive. Prakash's study of Bengal notes first the huge imports of bullion by the VOC: in the 1660s the equivalent of 12.8 tonnes of silver each year, in the 1690s 20, and in the next two decades 24.3 and 28.7 tonnes on average per year. These figures look small when we compare them with the Chinese ones we quoted above, where perhaps in the first half of the seventeenth century some 250 tonnes entered China, from Japan and Manila, each year, but it must be remembered that the Bengal figures are for the VOC alone: the EIC imports were probably about the same. Also Bengal was only one, albeit a major one, of the provinces of Mughal India.

Between 1687 and 1717 87.5 per cent of VOC imports to Bengal were bullion. This influx was vital for the monetization of the economy, and of course it also made possible European trade with the area. More specifically, about 10 per cent of the textile workforce in Bengal was employed as a result of the demand of the Dutch and English, and this in turn was dependent on their imports of bullion to pay for the textiles.[137]

Asia and World Precious Metal Flows in the Early Modern Period   45

Over the whole of Mughal India, the increased supply of coinage was absorbed in an expanding market, and also made possible a large increase in the monetization of the whole economy. From this flowed the rise of great banking firms in India, and a vastly expanded *hundi*, or bill of exchange, system. The increase in money also made it possible for more and more land revenue to be collected in cash, not in kind. As Richards notes, the Mughal 'system encouraged all parties, from the producing peasants to the highest grandee, to support and facilitate the conversion of agricultural produce into money. This was indeed a commercialized agriculture'.[138] Land revenue was far and away the major source of government revenue in the Mughal Empire. The rate was high, from one-half to one-third of total production. Collecting in money then had far reaching effects, extending a market and cash economy well down into Indian rural society, and creating a host of intermediary towns and traders who made this system work. All this was made possible by American silver.[139]

Finally, does our data on bullion flows serve to modify, or confirm, recent trends in world-system research? Readers will remember that Wallerstein claims that the modern world-system, by definition a capitalist one, arose in western Europe during the sixteenth century. By the end of the century its core was in northwestern Europe. For world-system theory a crucial way to test whether an area was incorporated into the system is to examine the goods being exchanged. If only luxuries are exchanged between a particular area and the modern world-system, then the first area is to be considered as external to the world-system. However, if necessities are exchanged then this area has been incorporated as a periphery. The task then is to decide which items are necessities, and which luxuries. Many commentators have pointed out how difficult this is.[140] In the case of bullion, Wallerstein essentially claims that the flow of bullion from America to Europe was a trade in a necessity, for the expanding European economy needed these precious metals so that monetization could proceed. Hence this America-Europe flow created a periphery-core relationship between the two areas. However, this was not the case when the bullion flowed on to Asia, for here it was not 'used' but rather was hoarded or used in other unproductive ways. Hence the Indian Ocean area remained external to the evolving modern world-system.

We have just noted that the overwhelming consensus today is that the inflow to India was in fact not hoarded at all, but was used. Om Prakash has recently investigated this very point of how

Wallerstein's theories fit in this instance, and correctly finds them to be quite incorrect.[141]

Prakash does not go on to raise the implications of this finding for world-system theory, but in fact they are profound, for the flow of bullion from Europe to Asia must then be seen as a trade in a necessity, just as was the flow from the Americas to Europe. Thus the central claim that the Indian Ocean area remained external to the modern world-system until late in the eighteenth century seems to be unsustainable. In the present context I want merely to raise this matter; to discuss it further would take me outside the boundaries of this brief essay. However, the whole matter of flows of bullion also contributes to another area recently under discussion by world-system theorists. This is the matter of the nature of world-economies before capitalism.

Again readers will need no reminding of Wallerstein's notion that before capitalism there were both world-empires and world-economies. The Indian Ocean area is an example of the latter. Recently he and Ravi Palat have sketched this world-economy for the time around 1500.[142] They sketch the growth of trade, and the subsequent accumulation of riches in the two most commercialized areas, Coromandel and Gujarat, and in an innovative way tie this in to wet-rice cultivation. But this of itself does not have to mean there was 'an increasingly singular divisioning of labour to which we refer when we use the concept of a world-economy'. It could just show an exchange of preciosities between two autonomous systems, such as between India and Europe in 1500–1750. However, in fact this trade 'represented a transfer of the products of lowly-remunerated labourers located elsewhere along the Indian Ocean littoral to South Asia'. This was especially to be seen in the huge rise of coarse cotton cloth production in Gujarat and Coromandel, and the consequent 'deindustrialization' of other regions in the Middle East and Southeast Asia. The emerging core zones of Gujarat and Coromandel 'progressively drew upon sources of subsistence and raw materials for artisanal manufacture from increasingly distant regions – leading to the incorporation and subsequent peripheralization of the latter zones within an emerging world-economy centred around, and integrated by, transport across the Indian Ocean'.

Thus there was 'from the eastern coasts of Africa through the Arabian peninsula and the Indian subcontinent to the Malay archipelago . . . an evolving world-economy . . .' Yet this was not the same as a capitalist world-economy, in other words a modern world-system, partly because there was no ruthless drive to accumulate, but also because the basis lay in the nature of wet-rice cultivation. This then can hardly be unequal exchange as found in capitalism. Various things flowed from this, including different political structures. Thus what happened after 1400 in the Indian Ocean area was different from Europe, and the result was that in Europe a capitalist world-economy emerged, while in the Indian Ocean area it did not, especially as there was no real subsumption of labour to capital, which is a crucial part of the development of capitalism.[143]

It can be seen that the data already presented on bullion flows into India reinforces strongly this model. We have large amounts flowing into India (and of course China) from Europe, East Africa and the Americas. Yet we must remember that this flow, regardless of origin, was always a trade in a necessity. In terms of theory it can become quite complicated, for we seem to have flows into India from quite different areas, with then quite different systemic relationships being created depending on the origin of the bullion. Thus one could argue that the flow of gold from the Mutapa state to India created a periphery-core relationship in this pre-capitalist world-economy. What however of bullion from the Americas via the Pacific to China? This is a flow from an area, America, peripheral to the core of a capitalist Europe, to the core of a quite separate and non-capitalist world-economy, that is to China. But when the flow of American silver goes via Europe to India it is from the core of a capitalist world-economy, that is the modern world-system, to the core of a non-capitalist world-economy. If it could be claimed that India merely hoarded this bullion, then the theoretical difficulties I have just suggested fall away, but in fact as we have stressed it was used; the full implications of this for the theory must be left aside for now. I hope merely to have raised the matter. It is also for someone else to investigate a similar world-economy based on China at this same time; the structural parallels seem to be obvious.

If we leave aside neo-Marxist world-system theory this modest and largely empirical essay still raises very general questions to do with capital and capitalism.[144] Braudel found something he called capitalism developing from about the thirteenth century in Europe. Those of us who may be relatively unreconstructed Marxists would still like to maintain the vital distinction between capital and capitalism, the former implying merely the accumulation of capital, the latter of course signifying investment in and control over the productive process. The theoretical question, as I see it, is to do with the role of capital in economies such as that of India in our period. Most of the precious metals which flowed in to India were minted and became money. Equally important, in our period while some of the bullion came in European ships, once imported it entered internal Indian economies where Europeans had little role. A correct understanding of what this meant for the Indian economy, or more correctly economies, may help us to avoid the teleological and Europe-privileging implications of not only world-system writings but of most general works which seek to explain world history in the early modern period. The rise of capitalism, even in Europe, turns out to be a much more problematic matter than past authors, even Marx, realised. I hope that future studies of the uses of bullion-become-money in India will contribute to the elucidation of this central conundrum.

ENDNOTES

1. This paper is based on an earlier foray of mine into the field of monetary history, that is my contribution to the conference 'Silver Linings', held at the University of NSW in March, 1992. My paper, called 'The Flows and Effects of Precious Metals in India and China: 1500–1750', was subsequently published in *Annales*, II, 2, 1993, pp.51–69. The present paper, however, is based on considerable extra research, especially to do with East African gold, and the focus has been reoriented. It has also profited immensely from comments when it was read at Curtin University in July 1994.

2. While I will write about gold and silver, we need to remember that in many parts of the world large areas of most economies were not monetized through much of the eighteenth century. And in many areas humble currencies were used: in the case of India copper coins (very widely used of course in most areas), cowrie shells (used all over the Indian Ocean area), and even small bitter almonds. For copper and cowrie shells see Vitorino Magalhães Godinho, *Os descobrimentos e a economia mundial*, 2nd. ed., Lisbon, 1981–3, 4 vols., II, 7–49, and for cowries especially James Heimann, 'Small Change and Ballast: Cowry Trade and Usage as an Example of Indian Ocean Economic History', *South Asia*, n.s. III, 1, 1980, pp.48–69.

3. Eric R. Wolf, *Europe and the People without History*, Berkeley, 1982,

p.124; Fernand Braudel, *The Mediterranean and the Mediterranean World in the Age of Philip II,* London, 1972, 2 vols., p.477.

4. Godinho, *Descobrimentos*, I, 232, 242.

5. Vitorino Magalhães Godinho, *Mito e mercadoria, utopia e prática de navegar, séculos XIII-XVIII,* Lisbon, 1990, p.457.

6. Godinho, *Descobrimentos*, I, 237–8. Generally on bullion flows before European expansion see Ibid., I, 65–182; J.F. Richards (ed.), *Precious Metals in the later Medieval and Early Modern Worlds,* Durham, NC., 1983, part I, pp.29–227; John S. Deyell, *Living without Silver: The Monetary History of Early Medieval North India,* Delhi, 1990 for Indian monetary history to 1250.

7. Braudel, *Mediterranean*, p.464.

8. Ibid., pp.499–500.

9. Surendranath Sen (ed.), *Indian Travels of Thevenot and Careri,* New Delhi, 1949, pp.241–2.

10. Dennis O. Flynn and Arturo Giráldez, 'Born with a "Silver Spoon": The Origin of World Trade in 1571', *Journal of World History,* VI, 2, Fall 1995, p.203. They seem to be unaware that Europe always retained more precious metals than it exported. My thanks to Edmund Burke III of the University of California, Santa Cruz, for sending me a copy of this article before its publication.

11. See on this K.N. Chaudhuri, *The Trading World of Asia and the English East India Company, 1660–1760,* Cambridge, 1978 and Femme S. Gaastra, 'The Dutch East India Company and its intra-Asiatic trade in precious metals', in Wolfram Fischer, R. Marvin McInnis and Jurgen Schneider (eds), *The Emergence of a World Economy 1500–1914,* Wiesbaden, 1986, pp.97–112. This collection also includes an article by Dennis O. Flynn, 'The microeconomics of silver and East-West trade in the early modern period', in Fischer et al. (eds), pp.37–60, which does not treat precious metals as some 'monetary' sector different from the 'real' sector of goods. The end result is to support the Ricardian argument advanced in Chaudhuri, *Trading World,* pp.156–7.

12. Flynn and Giráldez, passim.

13. Holden Furber, *Rival Empires of Trade in the Orient, 1600–1800,* Minneapolis, 1976, p.232; see also Dennis O. Flynn in Fischer et al. (eds), pp.37–60; Chaudhuri, *Trading World,* pp.162–3 for ratios in London and in India between 1661 and 1720.

14. See A. Kobata, 'The Production and Uses of Gold and Silver in Sixteenth- and Seventeenth-Century Japan', *Economic History*

50

Review, XVIII, 1965, pp.252, 254. Other data on ratios are scattered throughout this article, pp.245–66. For East African ratios see Philip D. Curtin, 'Africa and the Wider Monetary World, 1250–1850', in Richards (ed.), *Precious Metals*, pp.259–68.

15. A.R. Disney, *Twilight of the Pepper Empire*, Cambridge, Mas., 1978, p.104.

16. Furber, *Rival Empires*, p.231.

17. Om Prakash, *Asia and the Pre-Modern World Economy*, Leiden, 1995, p.6.

18. Braudel, *Mediterranean*, p.452.

19. Ward Barrett, 'World Bullion Flows, 1450–1800', in James D. Tracy (ed.), *The Rise of Merchant Empires: Long-Distance Trade in the Early Modern World, 1350–1750*, Cambridge, 1990, pp.242–3, and passim, and for criticism of his estimates of retentions in Europe cf Dennis O. Flynn, 'Comparing the Tokagawa Shogunate with Hapsburg Spain: Two Silver-based Empires in a Global Setting', in James D. Tracy (ed.), *The Political Economy of Merchant Empires: State Power and World Trade, 1350–1750*, Cambridge, 1991, p.334.

20. Pierre Vilar, *A History of Gold and Money, 1450–1920*, London, 1976, p.104, and for early sixteenth-century American gold production see p.67.

21. Harry E. Cross, 'South American Bullion Production and Export 1550–1750', in Richards (ed.), *Precious Metals*, p.409.

22. Ibid., p.403.

23. Ibid., p.417.

24. Barrett, 'World Bullion Flows 1450–1800', pp.242–3.

25. Artur Attman, *American Bullion in the European World Trade, 1600–1800*, Goteborg, 1986 p.78 has also produced figures to show American production and Iberian imports.

26. Quoted in Furber, *Rival Empires of Trade*, p.231 and f.n.1.

27. Fernand Braudel, *Civilization and Capitalism, 15th to 18th Centuries*, London 1981–4, 3 vols., II, 198–9.

28. Ibid., III, 491.

29. Attman, *American Bullion*, p.78.

30. Artur Attman, 'Precious Metals and the Balance of Payments in International Trade, 1500–1800', in Fischer et al. (eds), *The Emergence of a World Economy*, p.115.

31. Barrett, 'World Bullion Flows, 1450–1800', p.251.

32. Godinho, *Descobrimentos*, I, 255. His figure for American production is much lower than Barrett's, who finds, op.cit. pp.242–3,

an average production of 265,000 kgs in the whole second half of the sixteenth century.

33. Shireen Moosvi, 'The Silver Influx, Money Supply, Prices and Revenue-extraction in Mughal India', *Journal of the Economic and Social History of the Orient,* XXX, 1987, pp.60–2. For a critique of her methodology see Sanjay Subrahmanyam's Introduction to his very valuable reprinting of several seminal articles in the field: Sanjay Subrahmanyam (ed.), *Money and the Market in India 1100–1700,* Delhi, 1994, pp.52–3.

34. Chaudhuri, *Trading World of Asia,* pp.512, 177.

35. Om Prakash, 'Foreign Merchants and Indian Mints in the Seventeenth and the Early Eighteenth Century', in Richards (ed.), *The Imperial Monetary System of Mughal India,* Delhi, 1987, p.172. Prakash's numerous articles on this and related topics have now been conveniently collected in *Precious Metals and Commerce: The Dutch East India Company in the Indian Ocean Trade,* Variorum, 1994.

36. Artur Attman, *The Bullion Flow between Europe and the East, 1000–1750,* Goteborg, 1981, p.52.

37. F.S. Gaastra, 'The Exports of Precious Metal from Europe to Asia by the Dutch East India Company, 1602–1795', in Richards (ed.), *Precious Metals,* p.451.

38. Ibid., p.474; see also Attman's comparable attempt: Attman, *American Bullion,* p.75.

39. Femme S. Gaastra, 'The Dutch East India Company and its intra-Asiatic Trade in Precious Metals', in Fischer et al. (eds), *The Emergence of a World Economy,* p.104.

40. Ivo Schoffer and F.S. Gaastra, 'The Import of Bullion and Coin into Asia by the Dutch East India Company in the Seventeenth and Eighteenth Centuries', in Maurice Aymard, (ed.), *Dutch Capitalism and World Capitalism,* Cambridge, 1982, pp.222–5.

41. Prakash, 'Foreign Merchants and Indian Mints', in Richards (ed.), *The Imperial Monetary System,* p.172.

42. Sanjay Subrahmanyam, 'Precious metal flows and prices in western and southern Asia, 1500–1750: some comparative and conjunctural aspects', *Studies in History,* VII, 1, 1991, pp.88–90.

43. Moosvi, 'The silver influx', pp.65–8, 70–3.

44. Joseph J. Brennig, 'Silver in seventeenth century Surat: monetary circulation and the price revolution in Mughal India', in Richards (ed.), *Precious Metals,* pp.479–80.

45. Ibid., p.481.
46. Schoffer and Gaastra, 'The Import of Bullion and Coin into Asia', p.230.
47. Moosvi, 'The Silver Influx', p.61.
48. Barrett, 'World Bullion Flows, 1450–1800', p.249.
49. Flynn, 'Comparing the Tokagawa Shogunate with Hapsburg Spain', in Tracy (ed.), *The Political Economy of Merchant Empires*, p.334.
50. William S. Atwell, 'International Bullion Flows and the Chinese Economy circa 1530–1650', *Past and Present*, no.95, 1982, p.74. For an up to date survey of flows across the Pacific see Flynn and Giráldez, p.204.
51. John J. TePaske, 'New World Silver, Castile and the Philippines, 1590–1800', in Richards (ed.), *Precious Metals*, pp.434, 444.
52. Chaudhuri, *Trading World*, p.181.
53. A.J.S. Reid, *Southeast Asia in the Age of Commerce: vol. I, The Lands Below the Winds*, New Haven, 1988, pp.96, 99; for Vietnam see John K. Whitmore, 'Vietnam and the Monetary Flow of Eastern Asia, thirteenth to eighteenth Centuries', in Richards (ed.), *Precious Metals*, pp.363–93; and for Southeast Asia generally S. Subrahmanyam, Introduction to *Money and the Market*, p.39.
54. Chaudhuri, *Trading World of Asia*, p.154.
55. S.I.G. Mudenge, *A Political History of Munhumutapa, c. 1400–1902*, Harare, 1988, p.382.
56. Godinho, *Descobrimentoes*, I, 205 and f.n.100; he notes quite important regional variations.
57. N. Chittick, 'The East Coast, Madagascar and the Indian Ocean', in Roland Oliver (ed.), *Cambridge History of Africa*, vol. III, Cambridge, 1977, pp.215–17.
58. Georg Schurhammer, *Francis Xavier: His Life, His Times*, vol. II, India, Rome, 1977, pp.46–7.
59. António da Silva Rego (ed.), *Documentos sobre os Portugueses em Moçambique e na Africa Central, 1497–1840*, Lisbon, 1962–89, 9 vols to date, account of Almeida's voyage of May 22, 1506, in I, 529.
60. Ibid., p.787.
61. Ibid., VII, 75; William Francis Rea, SJ, *The Economics of the Zambezi Missions, 1580–1759*, Rome, 1976, p.85, f.n.
62. Ricardo Teixeira Duarte, *Northern Mozambique in the Swahili World*, Stockholm, Maputo, Uppsala, 1993, p.43.
63. J. Devisse and S. Labib, 'Africa in inter-Continental Relations', in *General History of Africa*, Paris, 1984, vol.IV, p.655.
64. Diogo de Alcáçova to king, 20.11.1506, in da Silva Rego, (ed.),

Documentos, I, 395.

65. Godinho, *Descobrimentos*, I, 204–7. Unhappy to note that at least two later authors merely copy Godinho's figures: we could do with some new research! See W.G.L. Randles, *The Empire of Monomotapa*, Gwelo, 1981, p.79, and Sanjay Subrahmanyam, *The Portuguese Empire in Asia 1500–1700: A Political and Economic History*, London, 1993, p.99.

66. Manuel Lobato, 'Relações Comerciais Entre a India e a costa Africana nos Séculos XVI and XVII: O Papel do Guzerate no Comércio de Moçambique', International Seminar on Indo-Portuguese History VII, Goa, January 1994, typescript, p.26.

67. Treasury Council, Lisbon, to king, 4.4.1614, in da Silva Rego (ed.), *Documentos*, IX, 381.

68. Mudenge, *A Political History of Munhumutapa*, p.174.

69. Chittick, 'The East Coast, Madagascar and the Indian Ocean', pp.215–17.

70. C.R. Boxer, 'A Portuguese El Dorado: Monomotapa and Mozambique', *Geographical Magazine*, XXXIII, 3, June 1960, pp.279–86, 284.

71. Summary of letter to king of 20.12.1510, in da Silva Rego (ed.), *Documentos*, II, 513.

72. Bashir Ahmed Datoo, *Port Development in East Africa*, Nairobi, 1975, pp.82–3, 89–90. On 'smuggling' see also Godinho, *Descobrimentos*, I, 196.

73. Maria Manuela Sobral Blanco, 'O Estado Portugues da India: da Rendição de Ormuz à Perda de Cochim, (1622–1663)', University of Lisbon Ph.D. dissertation, 1992, 2 vols, text of city of Goa to king, 19.1.1645, II, 523.

74. Ibid., King to viceroy, 5.2.1656, in II, 700–2.

75. Ibid., governors to king, 24.8.1658.

76. F. Barretto letter of 1667 in G.M. Theal, *Records of South-Eastern Africa*, London, 1898–1903, 9 vols, III, 489–92.

77. João dos Santos, *Ethiopia Oriental*, Lisbon, 1891, 2 vols, I, i, 17.

78. J.E.G. Sutton, 'Kilwa', *Indian Ocean Review*, VII, 4, March 1995, pp.10–11.

79. Godinho, *Descobrimentos*, I, 207.

80. Godinho, *Descobrimentos*, I, 248; Vilar, *A History of Gold and Money*, p.94.

81. Vilar, p.56.

82. Cross, 'South American bullion', p.417.

54

83. Vilar, p.104.

84. Kristof Glamman, *Dutch-Asiatic Trade, 1620–1740*, Copenhagen, 1958, pp.58, 63.

85. A. Kobata, 'The Production and Uses of Gold and Silver in Sixteenth- and Seventeenth-Century Japan', *Economic History Review*, XVIII, 1965, p.247.

86. Artur Attman, 'The Flow of Precious Metals along the Trade Routes between Europe and Asia up to 1800', in Karl Reinhold Haellquist (ed.), *Asian Trade Routes*, London, 1991, p.20.

87. Flynn, 'Comparing the Tokagawa Shogunate with Hapsburg Spain', p.336.

88. Kozo Yamamura and Tetsuo Kamiki, 'Silver mines and Sung Coins – A Monetary History of Medieval and Modern Japan in International Perspective', in Richards (ed.), *Precious Metals*, p.347.

89. Kobata, 'The Production and Uses of Gold and Silver', p.245.

90. E. Kato, 'Unification and Adaptation: the Early Shogunate and Dutch Trade Policies', in L. Blussé and F. Gaastra (eds), *Companies and Trade*, Leiden, 1981, pp.227–8.

91. Kobata, p.248.

92. Atwell, 'International Bullion Flows', pp.69–72. We may note that Vilar's discussion of this matter is now totally outdated, for he finds Japan producing 2,000 kgs a year at the end of the sixteenth century! Vilar, *A History of Gold and Money*, p.95.

93. Flynn and Giráldez, 'Born With a Silver Spoon', p.202.

94. Glamman, *Dutch-Asiatic Trade*, pp.58, 63.

95. Femme S. Gaastra, 'The Dutch East India Company and its intra-Asiatic Trade in Precious Metals', in Fischer et al. (eds), p.104.

96. Yamamura and Kamiki, 'Silver Mines and Sung Coins', pp.344, 349, 351–3.

97. George Bryan Souza, *The Survival of Empire: Portuguese Trade and Society in China and the South China Seas, 1630–1754*, Cambridge, 1986, p.57, and generally 54–8.

98. Schoffer and Gaastra, 'The Import of Bullion and Coin into Asia', p.220.

99. Furber, *Rival Empires of Trade*, p.232.

100. Cross, 'South American Bullion Production and Export', p.409.

101. Braudel, *The Mediterranean*, p.477.

102. Barrett, 'World Bullion Flows, 1450–1800', pp.242–3.

103. Subrahmanyam, Introduction to *Money and the Market*, p.45, f.n.

104. *State and Diplomacy in Early Modern Japan: Asia in the Development of the Tokugawa Bakufu*, Princeton, 1984.

105. Kobata, 'The Production and Uses of Gold and Silver', p.256.
106. G.B. Souza, *The Survival of Empire*, pp.54–8.
107. Cross, 'South American Bullion Production and Export', p.403.
108. Based on Barrett, 'World Bullion Flows', pp.242–3 and Yamamura and Kamiki, 'Silver Mines and Sung Coins', pp.344, 349, 351–3, using an estimate of Japanese exports of 9,000 tonnes.
109. Flynn, 'Comparing the Tokagawa Shogunate with Hapsburg Spain', p.332.
110. Barrett, p.246. I have omitted his third column in this table as it seems to be meaningless.
111. Flynn and Giráldez, passim.
112. David Beach, *The Shona and Zimbabwe, 900–1850*, London, 1980, p.109.
113. João de Barros, *Da Asia*, Lisbon, 1778–88, I, x, 1.
114. Diogo do Couto, *Da Asia*, Lisbon, 1778–88, IX, cap. 22.
115. João dos Santos, I, ii, 10.
116. Braudel, *Civilization and Capitalism*, III, 491.
117. Chaudhuri, *The Trading World of Asia*, p.216.
118. Atwell, 'International Bullion Flows', *Past and Present*, no.95, 1982, pp.76–79.
119. Braudel, *Civilization and Capitalism*, I, 455. This point is made very strongly by Flynn and Giráldez, 'Born With a Silver Spoon'.
120. Godinho, *Descobrimentos*, II, 140.
121. C.R. Boxer, '*Plata es sangre*: sidelights on the drain of Spanish-American silver in the Far East, 1550–1700', *Philippines Studies*, XVIII, 3, 1970, pp.457–78.
122. Moosvi, 'The silver influx', p.58, and pp.53, 54, 56 also.
123. Irfan Habib, 'The Monetary System and Prices', in T. Raychaudhuri and Irfan Habib (eds), *The Cambridge Economic History of India*, vol. I, c. 1200 – c.1750, Cambridge, 1982, pp.366–7.
124. Aziza Hasan, 'The Silver Currency Output of the Mughal Empire and Prices in India during the Sixteenth and Seventeenth Centuries', *Indian Economic and Social History Review*, VI, 1, 1969; Sanjay Subrahmanyam criticizes her methodology in his Introduction to *Money and the Market in India*, pp.50–1; see also Moosvi, 'The Silver Influx', pp.63–4.
125. Irfan Habib, 'A System of Trimetallism in the Age of the "Price Revolution": Effects of the Silver Influx on the Mughal Monetary System', in Richards (ed.), *The Imperial Monetary System of Mughal India*, pp.137–70.

126. Habib, 'The Monetary system and prices', in *Cambridge Economic History of India*, I, 364; Moosvi, 'Silver Influx', pp.78–9.

127. J.F. Richards, 'Introduction', in Richards (ed.), *The Imperial Monetary System*, pp.1–12; Richards, 'Outflows of Precious Metals from Early Islamic India', in Richards (ed.), *Precious Metals*, pp.183–206.

128. Chaudhuri, *Trading World of Asia*, p.182.

129. Om Prakash, *The Dutch East India Company and the Economy of Bengal*, Princeton, 1985, p.250.

130. Chaudhuri, *Trading World of Asia*, pp.100–8.

131. Habib, 'The Monetary System and Prices', in *Cambridge Economic History of India*, I, pp.366, 372–6.

132. Brennig, 'Silver in Seventeenth Century Surat', in Richards (ed.), *Precious Metals*, pp.488–93.

133. Moosvi, 'The Silver Influx', pp.81–94; Subrahmanyam, 'Precious Metal Flows and Prices', pp.93–8.

134. Prakash, *The Dutch East India Company*, pp.251–6. See also a good discussion by the same author: 'Precious Metal Flows, Coinage and Prices in India in the 17th and Early 18th Century', in E. Van Cauwenberghe, *Money, Coins and Commerce: Essays in the Monetary History of Asia and Europe (From Antiquity to Modern Times)*, Leuven, 1991, pp.61–73. Also see Subrahmanyam, Introduction to *Money and the Market*, pp.43–54.

135. Chaudhuri, *Trading World of Asia*, pp.7, 159, 462.

136. Moosvi, 'Silver Influx', p.92; Shireen Moosvi, *The Economy of the Mughal Empire, c. 1595: A Statistical Study*, Delhi, 1987, pp.390–1.

137. Prakash, *The Dutch East India Company*, pp.234–5, 242, 249; cf Prakash, 'Foreign Merchants and Indian Mints', in Richards (ed.), *The Imperial Monetary System*, p.172.

138. Richards, 'Introduction', in Richards (ed.), *The Imperial Monetary System*, p.4; and for a case study of village-level monetary flows see Stephen P. Blake, 'The Structure of Monetary Exchanges in North India: The Provinces of Agra, Delhi and Lahore in 1600', in Richards (ed.), *The Imperial Monetary System*, pp.100–36.

139. Om Prakash, 'Precious Metal Flows in Asia and World Economic Integration in the Seventeenth Century', in Fischer et al. (eds), *Emergence of a World Economy*, pp.84–86; Habib, 'The monetary system and prices', in *Cambridge Economic History of India*, I, pp.362, 366; for European parallels see Braudel, *Civilization and Capitalism*, I, 436–57.

140. The literature is vast indeed. For a full statement of the model see Immanuel Wallerstein, *The Modern World-System*, 3 vols, New York,

1974–89, or for a synoptic view Terence K. Hopkins and Immanuel Wallerstein, 'Patterns of Development of the Modern World-System', *Review*, I, 2, 1977, pp.111–45. For other summaries see Thomas Richard Shannon, *An Introduction to the World-System Perspective*, Boulder, 1989 and M.N. Pearson, *Before Colonialism: Theories on Asian-European Relations, 1500–1750*, Delhi, 1988, chapter 1. For an early thorough going but sympathetic critique see Theda Skocpol, 'Wallerstein's World Capitalist System: a theoretical and historical critique', *American Journal of Sociology*, LXXXII, 5, 1977, pp.1075–90, and on the luxury-necessity dichotomy Jane Schneider, 'Was There a Pre-capitalist World-System', *Journal of Peasant Studies*, VI, 1, 1977, pp.20–29, reprinted in Christopher Chase-Dunn and Thomas D. Hall (eds), *Core/Periphery Relations in Precapitalist Worlds*, Boulder, 1991.

141. Prakash, *Asia and the Pre-Modern World Economy*.

142. Ravi Arvind Palat and Immanuel Wallerstein, 'Of What World-System was Pre-1500 "India" a Part?' in S. Chaudhuri and M. Morineau (eds), *Merchants, Companies and Trade* , forthcoming (my thanks to Dr. Palat for sending me a typescript). Other recent contributions, not to be discussed here for reasons of space, include André Gunder Frank and Barry K. Gills (eds), *The World System: Five Hundred Years or Five Thousand?*, London, 1993; Janet Abu-Lughod, *Before European Hegemony: The World System A.D. 1250–1350*, Oxford, 1989; Chase-Dunn and Hall (eds), *Core Periphery Relations*; and especially André Gunder Frank's recent iconoclastic *ReOrient: Global Economy in the Asian Age*, Berkeley, 1998. Dennis O. Flynn has recently published two very useful collections, one by him, one edited: Dennis O. Flynn, *World Silver and Monetary History in the 16th and 17the Centuries*, Variorum Collected Studies, 1996, and Dennis O. Flynn and Arturo Giraldez, (eds), *Metals and Monies in an Emerging Global Economy*, Variorum, An Expanding World, Vol.14, 1997.

143. Palat and Wallerstein, 'Of What World System was pre-1500 "India" a Part'.

144. This paragraph draws heavily on David Washbrook's stimulating and pugnacious overview, 'Progress and Problems: South Asian Economic and Social History c.1720–1860', *Modern Asian Studies*, XXII, 1, 1988, pp.57–96. Unfortunately a recent excellent article came to my notice too late for me to engage within the present piece. This is Najaf Haider, 'Precious Metal Flows and Currency Circulation in the Mughal Empire', *Journal of the Economic and Social History of the Orient*, XXXIX, 3, 1996, pp.298–364.

V

Indians in East Africa:
the Early Modern Period

Ashin Das Gupta in his many publications told us a lot about trade and other contacts between the west coast of India and West Asia. My objective in this short tribute is to extend the picture to the south a little, and sketch in the broadest terms contacts between western India and the Swahili coast in that early modern period which he made his own.

To set the scene, I will first raise a matter of terminology. The area of water separating the two areas under discussion is conventionally referred to as the 'Arabian Sea'. To my mind this privileges 'Arabia' in a quite unjustified way. By 1500, Arab navigation to India was sparse in the extreme; the thrust was much more of Indians trading to the Arab world. Similarly, as regards the Swahili coast it has long been accepted that any notion of Arab colonization of the area, or indeed of deep Arab influence, is wide of the mark. The trend today is entirely to see Swahili culture as inextricably African, one variant within many of a very rich and complex African mosaic. True, being coastal the Swahili were more open to foreign influences than were their interior fellow-Bantu speakers, yet this cannot take away from their essentially African character.

If we discard 'Arabian', what then should we call this body of water? My suggestion is that we use a neologism, that is the 'Afrasian Sea'. The advantage of this term is that it nicely captures the essential fact that it joined two separate continents and that both are represented in the name.[1]

I

Studies of Indian diasporas are of course legion. Indeed, for a time we were told that India had a long and glorious history of overseas expansion, mostly cultural but some even military. No doubt these older studies were in part produced as part of the effort to emphasize, or create, a glorious past for India as it suffered under British rule.

Indian influence, not only cultural and religious but even political, was claimed to be dominant in Southeast Asia, at least at the time of the Cholas. Now, however, scholars of Southeast Asia are trying to reclaim the autonomy of their area. They modestly do not aspire to show the influence of their region elsewhere, but there has been a pronounced nativism, a stress on autonomy and lack of foreign influence. Indeed, I have even heard the term 'southeast Asia' itself being questioned, for it seems to imply that the area is in some way merely part of south, and east, Asia, in a way a residual category with little new coming from indigenous sources. Today's trend very strongly emphasizes the autonomy of the area, and in particular the way it has absorbed and transformed many influences from both south and east Asia and turned them into something distinctively 'southeast Asian.'[2]

The historiography of Greater India influenced the west rather less than it did the east. Nevertheless, some earlier studies still found vast Indian influence on the east African coast, and even inland. My aim is to investigate these claims in a little detail, and then try to sketch a more accurate depiction of the Indian presence in east Africa in the early modern period.

Referring to the period before the arrival of Europeans in 1498, Serjeant found a very substantial Indian presence on the coast. Indians were financiers, bankers, moneylenders and merchants, and indeed 'much of the ocean-going shipping was Indian-owned and Indian manned.'[3] The eminent Mozambiquean historian Rita-Ferreira made similar claims, and found both Hindus and Muslims from Gujarat playing a very large role from the late fourteenth century. Indeed, referring to a much longer period, he claimed that one could write a book called 'How India underdeveloped East Africa'.[4] Quite recently Teotonio de Souza veered in a similar direction. Describing the martyrdom of the early Jesuit Gonçalo de Silveira at the Mutapa court in March 1561, he wrote:

The sudden change of attitude of the ruler of Monomotapa and the killing of the priest as a suspected agent of the Portuguese only confirms the close links that the Gujarati merchants of India maintained with the rulers of east Africa. It is not surprising therefore that the conversion and baptism of the ruler of Monomotapa at the hands of this Jesuit may have alarmed the bania merchants in the Rivers of Cuama [that is, the Zambezi valley].[5]

Unfortunately, the sources he cites to bolster this claim, one of them by me, do not support this statement, and indeed the copious documentation on this melancholy incident make it absolutely clear that it was Muslims, mostly African, whether from the coast or the interior, who instigated the murder.[6]

The thesis of a Greater India in east Africa found its fullest expression in an extraordinary American dissertation, two articles, and a book, all by Cyril A. Hromnik. The book, not surprisingly published in apartheid South Africa, was vigorously condemned as a racist tract at the time of its publication, and indeed Hromnik has not been heard from since.[7] To discuss all his lapses, exaggerations, unsubstantiated claims, and indeed his overt racism would be a tedious and unpleasant task. A few examples will suffice to give the flavour of his work.

The thesis, ostensibly a long, scholarly, well-documented study, in fact contains many problems. His focus is the role of Indian Christians, Canarins (that is, 'people from Kanara'), in the Zambezi valley and Zimbabwe plateau. This is an interesting and important topic; however he wildly exaggerates their role. For example, he claims that:

It is a well documented fact that at the end of the fifteenth century Christians from Malabar were able to navigate their boats along the coast from Cochin and Cranganur as far as Malindi, Kilwa, Angoche, Moçambique, and most probably Sofala also.[8]

As an example of his argumentation, he notes, when describing the journey of the ill-fated Fr. Silveira to the interior that,

He found Sena [on the lower Zambezi valley] to be a very large town where there are ten or fifteen Portuguese settlers, with some Christians from India. Since a very large town could not have been composed of the houses of fifteen Portuguese, there must have been many more Canarins than Portuguese.[9]

Soon after, he tells us that Indians had resided in Sena since the twelfth century, 'and in later centuries the town must have resembled a Goan village more than anything else as Canarins were its primary occupants.'[10]

The book is much worse. According to him, Great Zimbabwe is not African at all, while 'Africa owes its system of trade and currency, its metal technology and iron tools, and the terminology to express this entire complex of cultural development to India, Indonesia, China, with later contributions from the Muslim world and Europe.'[11] He claims that the famous carved doors of Lamu show Indian influence on the coast long before 1500, yet in fact none of the extant doors predate 1800. Indians began mining gold on the Zimbabwe plateau around the year 1000, and to cap it all, he proves that Indian trade was very extensive in earlier periods, else why was the Indian Ocean called 'Indian'?[12]

V

All of these accounts of Indian dominance of Africa, not just Hromnik's, are certainly stirring stuff, really hairy-chested claims of a vast Indian role far into the interior. Ashin Das Gupta from time to time chided me for my 'Indian-nativist' writings, for he considered them to be far too sympathetic to 'India' and far too derogatory of the Europeans, and especially the Portuguese. If this be true, then I should be thrilled to see, as de Souza claims, my favourite *bania* traders beating off an advance guard of European imperialism in the person of Fr. Silveira. Alas, the records cannot sustain these sorts of claims. It is time to turn to fact, not fancy, and attempt a broad-brush sketch of the role of Indians in east Africa in the early modern period.

II

One thing we certainly know is that Indian trade goods were overwhelmingly the main imports into east Africa over the whole of this period, regardless of who handled the actual exchange. In their early days the Portuguese built a fort at Sofala, and then tried to use trade goods from west Africa to buy gold, 'but the negroes of Sofala did not care for it, as they wanted articles which the Moors procured from India, especially from Cambay [a term used at this time for Gujarat in general].'[13] Among these goods, cotton cloths were overwhelmingly dominant, as indeed Albuquerque found as early as 1514 when he described to his king the vast and intricate network of trade in this item.[14] When the Portuguese sacked Mombasa for the first time in 1505 they found

in the city quantities of cotton cloth from Cambay because all this coast dresses in these cloths and has no others. In this way the captain-major gathered a great sum for the Sofala trade, finding a great number of very rich cloths, of silk and gold, carpets and saddle cloths, especially one carpet that cannot be bettered anywhere and which was sent to the king of Portugal with many other articles of great value.[15]

Other goods were also imported: wheat from Cambay, beads in enormous quantities, and also fine pieces of craft work, such as the 'bedstead of Cambay, wrought with gold and mother-of-pearl, a very beautiful thing...' which the ruler of Malindi gave to Vasco da Gama in 1502.[16]

The dominance of these goods is a rather strange phenomenon. It is unusual to find goods from one area so completely central in trade and exchange, regardless of who it was who brought them to the region. Whether it was Persians, Arabs, Indians or later Europeans, all of them depended on Indian goods, especially from Gujarat, for items which could find a market on the coast. We may note, however, that while Gujarati imports to the Swahili coast and parts of the interior were vital for the whole region, these goods did not make up a very substantial part of Gujarat's total exports. Edward Alpers has estimated the total at about 4 per cent only.[17] Tomé Pires' very well-known statement makes the same point, at least by omission: 'Cambay chiefly stretches out two arms, with her right arm she reaches out towards Aden and with the other towards Malacca, as the most important places to sail to, and the other places are held to be of less importance.'[18]

Indian, especially Gujarati, goods may have been central, but this is not to say that they came in only in Indian ships or were exchanged by Indian traders resident on the coast. We can now turn to a discussion of the role of Indian traders in east Africa.

It is very difficult to say anything very certain about the role of Indians before the arrival of the Portuguese, for the records are sparse. All we have are a few fragmentary mentions in Arabic sources, and some archaeological evidence. However, the accounts of the first Portuguese in the area, dating from 1498, can also be used to tell us what the situation was very late in the fifteenth century.

There are several problems with our sources before 1498. One is that trade between western India and the Swahili coast was often carried out with a stopover either in the Persian Gulf or Aden, or some other Hadramaut port. This raises the strong possibility that Indian goods may have been transhipped on the way, and thus taken to the Gulf or southern Arabia in Indian ships, and then transported onwards by west Asian traders, either Arabs or Persians. Further confusion comes from the fact that trade may have been handled by west Asian Muslims resident in western India, or alternatively by 'Indian Muslims', these being difficult to differentiate from Muslims from other areas. Perhaps this is the real point. The modern tendency to categorize people by nationality hardly applied in this early modern period; the distinction between say a Muslim who lived in India, one who visited India, one who traded in Indian goods, and one who was an agent for some other Muslim resident elsewhere is extremely nebulous. This was not, after all, a time when people had passports and citizenship of some particular country. Hindu merchants, if any, are of course much easier to identify, for they were certainly 'Indian'.

The dictatorship of the monsoons also complicates matters. Broadly speaking, the passage from India to the northern Swahili coast, that is down to Cape Delgado, can be done comfortably in one monsoon. However, south of there normally requires two. It seems that often the pattern was of trade goods being broken up on the north coast and taken further south in smaller, Swahili owned and operated, vessels.[19] Yet even this raises a problem. Foreign traders who arrived on one monsoon and left when the next started left themselves open to extortion, for the locals would simply raise their prices for the short time they were in port. In most other parts of monsoon Asia, traders solved this problem by staying over for a year, or more likely leaving an agent in place to buy when prices were low, and sell when they were high. This is to be seen in all the great port cities of the early modern Indian Ocean. It would be strange indeed if this was not done on the Swahili coast also.

So much for the difficulties. What we can say is that there is evidence of trade between India and east Africa from at least the beginning of the Common Era. It could well be that contact with the area north of Cape Delgado was much earlier than with the region to the south of this commonly-used dividing line. Mudenge finds Indian contact with the former area from at least the first century, but with the latter only from around the eighth century.[20] The Periplus from the first century, and Masudi from the tenth, find extensive Indian trade in East Africa. Al Biruni early in the eleventh century claimed that 'The reason why in particular Somanath has become so famous is that it was a harbour for seafaring people, and a station for those who went to and fro between Sufala in the country of Zanj and China.' This of course refers to a time well before Kathiawar was conquered by Muslims, yet the quotation does not necessarily mean that Hindus from Somnath travelled to Africa. Al Idrisi in the twelfth century found Indians trading as far south as Sofala.[21]

III

The archaeological evidence confirms extensive Indian contact with the area. There is, for example, evidence of many Asian plants being grown in east Africa before the Portuguese arrived.[22] Indian influence has been found even from the period before the rise of Islam, that is the sixth and seventh centuries, in local pottery, for there have been finds of pots made with local clay but using Indian motifs.[23] The extant Cutchi doors of the coast, found especially in Zanzibar and Lamu today, date only from the very late eighteenth century, but archaeologists have found Indian motifs in architecture dating from much earlier times.[24] Perhaps again we should remember not to categorize things too strictly. A little while ago a bronze lion statuette was found at Shanga. It dates from around 1100. It seems clear it was used in Hindu *puja*, and this means it would hardly be sold or used by a non-Hindu. However, mosques in Shanga date from around

800. The object is a real puzzle, though it could be that it was used as regalia. The more general point is that at least by this time coastal communities all over the Indian Ocean were linked by travel and trade. Thus 'The Shanga lion must therefore not be so much "Indian" or "African" but "Indian Ocean" in attribution.'[25]

This does raise one other matter, which is whether the Indians who travelled and traded on the coast also settled. Horton and Blurton speculate that their lion was made to order by local Hindu crafts people in Shanga. We have just noted Indian influence on local pottery and architecture in the period before the arrival of the Portuguese. However, it could be, as Wilding suggests, that these Indian crafts people came in on one monsoon, did their work, and then left again.[26] So also, perhaps, with the traders, who also came in, traded, and left again. Yet this really seems to be very unlikely. As we noted, this sort of schedule would gravely disadvantage traders, and also crafts people, who surely would prefer to stay and profit from their superior expertise. Here however we presumably also need to differentiate between Indian Muslims and Hindus. Some years ago I produced a body of evidence which seemed to show that Hindus travelled by sea much more in this period than has been generally recognized (and I must record here that this article had an early outing at Santiniketan, under the auspices of Ashin Das Gupta).[27] Nevertheless, as a rule of thumb there can be little doubt that Muslims did travel more than Hindus.

If we turn now to the accounts of the very first Portuguese on the coast we can make more progress on this matter of whether or not Indians settled, always of course in the context of the undisputed dominance of Indian trade goods in the area.[28] The senior Indian historian, Tirmizi wrote that

Unless more evidence is forthcoming, it is difficult to conjecture that there was a considerable Indian commercial community on the Swahili coast. The residence of Indian merchants on this coast was perhaps more seasonal than permanent before the nineteenth century.[29]

I will now accumulate the available evidence, which in sum seems to show that Indians, both Hindus and Muslims, certainly traded, and possibly settled, on the coast.

Most of our detailed information comes from Mombasa and Malindi, at that time the latter being much inferior to the former, let alone to Kilwa. We can briefly note what we know about three other Swahili port cities on the coast. In Mozambique, da Gama noted in 1498 'two captive Christian Indians', held by the local Muslims.[30] In Sofala, far to the south, we are merely told that there was a large trade in Gujarati products, carried there in small ships based at Kilwa, Mombasa and Melinde.[31] So also for Mogadishu in the far north, where Gujaratis themselves are described as having a direct large trade.[32]

Mombasa at 1500 was second only to Kilwa in its trade, or indeed, given the decline of the latter, may have been the premier port city of the coast at the time. Vasco da Gama was there in April 1498. One of the objectives of his voyage was to find the powerful Christian potentate Prester John. This meant he was keen to find Christians, and indeed he found some in Mombasa, or so he thought. Two fair-skinned Christians came on board the Portuguese ships, and later members of his expedition visited the houses of two Christian merchants, who 'showed them a paper, an object of their adoration, on which was a sketch of the Holy Ghost.' A footnote by none other than Richard Burton noted that this may have been a picture of an incarnation of Siva. Be that as it may, there is no doubt that these 'Christians' were in fact Hindus. As is well known, da Gama made the same mistake in Calicut next month, where he left still convinced that this port's Hindus were in fact somewhat schismatic Christians. However, these Hindu merchants, almost certainly Gujaratis, were mere sojourners, for the account of the voyage goes on to note that 'The Christian [sic. Hindu] merchants in the town are only temporary residents, and are held in much subjection, they not being allowed to do anything except by the order of the Moorish King.'[33]

The first viceroy, Francisco de Almeida, visited and sacked Mombasa in 1505. Several of the accounts of this early atrocity note the presence of three Gujarati ships in the port. They had already been unloaded, and run aground to be careened. They were well defended by their Muslim crew and the Portuguese withdrew. They did however acquire a vast booty in the town, and especially

there were in the city quantities of cotton cloth from Cambay because all this coast dresses in these cloths and has no others. In this way the captain-major gathered a great sum for the Sofala trade, finding a great number of very rich cloths, of silk and gold, carpets and saddle cloths, especially one carpet that cannot be bettered anywhere and which was sent to the king of Portugal with many other articles of great value.[34]

The Portuguese spent longer in Malindi, and had better relations with the ruler, so information from this port city is relatively voluminous. Barbosa and Castanheda noted a large trade between the locals and the Muslims and Hindus of Cambay.[35] The fullest account of da Gama's first visit in 1498 comes from an anonymous description by an eye-witness. He described how

We found here four vessels belonging to Indian Christians. When they came for the first time on board Paulo da Gama's ship, the captain-major being there at the time, they were shown an altar-piece representing Our Lady at the foot of the cross, with Jesus Christ in her arms and the apostles around her. When the Indians saw this picture they prostrated themselves, and as long as we were there they came to say their prayers in front of it, bringing offerings of cloves, pepper and other things. These Indian are tawny men; they wear little clothing and have long beards and long hair, which they braid. They told us they ate no beef. Their language differs from that of the Arabs, but some of them know a little of it, as they hold much intercourse with them.[36]

It seems clear that these Hindus came from Gujarat, for Gonçalves even calls them 'baneanes'.[37] Barros in his retrospective account, though one based on eye-witness testimony, noted both Muslims and Hindus from Cambay, and on the latter elaborated that these 'banians' were 'such devout followers of the teaching of Pythagoras that they will not even kill the insects by which they may be infested, and eat nothing which has life...' which may even lead one to identify them as Jains.[38] Castanheda has them variously coming from Cranganor and Cambay.[39] More to the point, he claims that they 'morão' in Malindi. This word means 'lived', and must be taken as quite strong evidence that these Hindus were resident; yet it could also mean they 'dwelt', not necessarily implying permanent residence. Castanheda also distinguishes between Arabian Muslims, whom he calls 'estrangeiros', or foreigners, and 'gente natural', or locals.

The next Portuguese visitor was Cabral in 1500. Accounts of his visit note the presence of three very rich Gujarati ships. Two different texts provide valuable descriptions of these ships. One put them at 200 tonnes each, and noted that

These naos have the superstructure built of cane and their hulls bound with ropes and caulked with pitch for the lack of nails; all the naos of these parts are fashioned so; they sail always with the wind astern for they cannot sail into the wind, and they have a quarter-deck.[40]

An anonymous account noted that 'Their hulls are well built of good wood, tied together with cord (for they have no nails), and they are covered with a mixture in which there is much incense. They have no castles except in the stern. These ships come to trade from parts of India.'[41] Finally, we have more evidence of Gujarati Hindus, possibly even Jains, in a description by a Spanish traveller from 1507. Figueroa told how

V

They went to Malindi, where the people live a frugal life. Called Gujarati, they are very withdrawn and sparing of conversation. Many of them will eat no living thing; by that I mean anything that must be killed and has blood. By another name they are known as Brahmans.[42]

There was at least one Hindu Gujarati still in Malindi in 1510, for in this year the Portuguese were selling the contents of a Gujarati ship which they had confiscated. Two items were sold to 'Gangua Guzurate'.[43]

It seems to be sound to use this early Portuguese documentation to also cast light on the situation for at least a little time before their arrival. What then can we say of the period around 1500? All the accounts note masssive trade by Gujaratis, as well as by Arabs and locals. Most of them say little about 'Indian' Muslims, presumably because they were indistinguishable from other visiting Muslims. The presence of Hindus, albeit often hopefully described as Christians, was much noted, and there is no doubt that these people were Hindus from Gujarat, though the extreme reverence for all forms of life may even point to Jains. What we do not know is whether or not these Gujaratis settled. The use of the word 'morão' may point to an affirmative answer, but on the other hand one account is definite that they were sojourners, and indeed were harshly treated.

IV

We have only scattered references to Indians trading on the coast in the sixteenth and seventeenth centuries. Portugal, of course, tried to impose its usual trade monopoly policies on the area. Their own records make it clear that there was much evasion, and indeed in the sixteenth century their power was limited to south of Cape Delgado. It was only with the acquisition of Mombasa in 1592, where they built Fort Jesus, that they had any sort of presence in the north. Consequently their records for the north are also scanty for the sixteenth century, and we must assume that Indians continued to trade there, along with Arabs and others. We do have one charming mention of their presence in the Lamu area in 1606. Fr. Gaspar de S. Bernadino arrived at Pate island, but none of the locals had had any experience with Christians or with Portuguese, and so had no idea how to treat this black-robed friar. Luckily, there were also present two Hindu merchants from Diu, who spoke good Portuguese. Diu of course had been under Portuguese rule for decades, so these two were able to act as intermediaries and tell the local ruler all about how priests behaved, such as their vows of poverty and chastity and their collection of alms.[44]

In the south the Portuguese established a strong base at Mozambique, and also the settlements of Sena and Tete, up the Zambezi river. Much evidence makes it clear that their trade control policies here also met with only limited success, for there was much evasion, especially by local and visiting Muslims. Gold from the Zimbabwe plateau was smuggled on a vast scale, as also were imports of Indian goods. And in any case the Portuguese, like everyone else, found the only trade items with any likelihood of finding a market were Indian products, especially cloths and beads. Thus to an extent Indian, Arab and other traders in the south were displaced by Portuguese, or ships licensed by the Portuguese, yet the products traded remained the same.

What is more interesting is to notice how Indians were able to operate within the entrails of the Portuguese quasi-empire in Mozambique. A sketch of how this operated will make up a contribution which has strong echoes in many other studies of indigenous assistance or cooperation in this somewhat ramshackle early modern empire.[45] When we look below the imperial Portuguese umbrella we find two distinct groups of Indians playing very different roles. By the eighteenth century, if not earlier, banias from Diu and elsewhere held a dominant position in the economy of the Portuguese area in the south, specializing especially in finance and money lending. The other Indian group were the Canarins, in other words Indian Christians, mostly from Goa, many of whom were *mestiços,* and who advanced far inland up the Zambezi valley and even to the Zimbabwe plateau. At first they operated in a subordinate position under the Portuguese, but by the later eighteenth century held dominant positions in those strange semi-feudal institutions, the *prazos* of the Zambezi valley. We will look at the Canarins first.

In broad terms the sequence is of Canarins coming in quite early in the sixteenth century and fulfilling subordinate roles in the Portuguese areas. However, through the seventeenth century they acquired a much larger role in trade, even on the plateau until they and the Portuguese were expelled by Changamire in 1693. In no way daunted, they then began to acquire prazos, and by the late eighteenth century it seems that most prazos were held by Goans, or people with some 'Indian' blood. The Portuguese complained from time to time about both their dominance of trade and then of the prazos, yet they also found that Canarins made much better and more willing settlers than did 'pure' Portuguese.

If we look first at the coast, in Sofala in the late 1580s there was a Christian settlement of some 600 souls, including Portuguese, mestiços, and 'gente da terra', which in this context means some

Indian Christians but mostly local African converts.[46] In the capital of Mozambique a Jesuit in 1568 found about 100 Portuguese householders, and about 200 Africans and mestiços.[47] This population seems to have grown rapidly, as late in the 1580s Fr. dos Santos found about 2000 Portuguese and other Christians.[48] We know little of the role of these Canarins, but the account of an English visitor from the mid-seventeenth century points to them being humble people who worked as lascars.[49] By the seventeenth century both Portuguese householders and also Canarins had occupied the mainland areas adjacent to Mozambique island, Mossuril and Cabeceiras. They married local Makua women, and created a distinctive hybrid littoral culture.[50]

As regards the interior, we again have some scattered evidence. Some of this comes as a consequence of what is perhaps the most famous event of the century for the Portuguese, the martyrdom of Fr. Silveira, and governor Barreto's subsequent punitive expedition. When the Father reached Sena, 260 km up the Zambezi in 1560, he found 10–15 Portuguese and also some Indian Christians.[51] He was accompanied on his journey by six Portuguese and a Canarin youth called Calisto.[52] Twelve years later the Portuguese sent off an ill-fated expedition to avenge Silveira's death. One of governor Barreto's five companies of troops consisted of 80 Canarins and locals, along with 60 Portuguese.[53] Further, the Portuguese also wanted to attack the ruler of Manica, in part at least because they claimed that he had on three separate occasions robbed Canarin traders.[54]

We have a few other indications of a sixteenth-century Canarin presence up the Zambezi. Fr. Santos in the late 1580s found 800 Christians in Sena, 50 of them Portuguese and the rest Indians and Africans. Further up river, at Tete, were 600 Christians, 40 Portuguese and the rest again Indian and African.[55] Early in the seventeenth century Fr. Avellar found 150 Portuguese in Sena, and 60–70 in Tete, in both cases along with 'many men of India'.[56] In 1633 we have news of the gardens of the Portuguese and natives of India at Sena, and indeed at this time, when the town was relatively prosperous, the population seems to have been very mixed indeed. At the school were sons of the Portuguese, but also children of Chinese, Javanese, Malabaris and Sinhalese, along with Africans and mulattoes.[57] At this same time António Bocarro noted both Portuguese and Indian Christians trading further inland.[58] Manuel de Costa, a Goan, was one of the wealthiest traders in the Zambezi valley in the mid-seventeenth century.[59] In the 1650s we even have a report of a Brahmin trading in ivory much further up river, though this could well be a misidentification.[60]

There is scattered evidence of Canarins trading in the interior in later times. Indeed, Newitt considers them to have been the dominant traders in the interior, as opposed to the Portuguese.[61] This role was facilitated by Portuguese policy, albeit inadvertently. In 1673 trade up the Zambezi was freed from the monopoly control of the governor of Mozambique, and became open to all. At the same time the Portuguese tried to restrict the opportunities this might open for the Canarins. All local ships leaving Mozambique for the Zambezi area were to be searched, and any Canarins found on board were to be thrown out, for they were considered to be very prejudicial to the commerce of the area. Similarly, the superintendent of the Portuguese factory at Sena was not to sell goods to them unless a Portuguese stood guarantor for them.[62] However, these racist and discriminatory policies met with little success. The Canarins moved in anyway. In 1690 the king complained bitterly about the effects of this opening. It was 'natives of this state', that is Canarins, who had moved in and quickly acquired a dominant role, very much to the detriment of the royal customs house. Their intense and expert competition had also led to a catastrophic fall in prices for cloth.[63] Finally, in 1690 the Portuguese decided to restrict trade again, this time to a state company.

Despite this, we have scattered evidence of Canarins continuing to trade in the interior. Fr. Conceição in 1696 noted some of them trading at what used to be a big fair. By 1696, however, Changamire had expelled all foreigners, including the Portuguese and the Canarins, from the interior. Even so some Canarins were able to make arrangements and stay. A place five-days journey inland from Tete had rich silver mines, in which Portuguese and Canarins stayed, among them one Domingos Carvalho. This enterprising trader made an agreement with the African now in charge of the area, to exchange cloth for silver, and for some time he did very well indeed.[64]

However, even from late in the sixteenth century some Portuguese had begun to acquire land on semi-feudal tenures in the Zambezi valley. The tendency for land control to replace trade (though of course the two were not totally mutually exclusive) accelerated through the next century, and perhaps reached its florescence once the Portuguese were expelled from the plateau in 1693. In the period before this the Portuguese in fact had actively promoted settlement, and increasingly looked to Goans to do this. Indeed, we have here an early version of planned settlement, a precursor of the famous Wakefield scheme which in the mid-nineteenth century resulted in colonies in several parts of New Zealand and Australia.

As early as 1679, the authorities in India were told that the ruler of Portugal had heard that there were Canarins and other natives in Portuguese India who could work in Mozambique and the Zambezi valley. They were told to look into this, for if it were true this would save the cost of populating the area with Portuguese from the metropolis.[65] Four years later the viceroy informed the king that 50 Canarins from Salcette and Ilhas, eight of them accompanied by their wives, were going off to the Zambezi area in a Portuguese ship.[66] A year later, in 1685, 18 Canarin couples, mostly farmers, arrived in Mozambique.[67] Fr. Conceição a decade later recommended bringing in more Goan families, as they were excellent traders. He also pointed out that the Portuguese women who arrived from time to time never had issue, except for one very young one. It would be best to bring in only very young Portuguese girls. The father also wanted to rebuild some of the ruined Portuguese forts in the area, for which task engineers, stone masons and carpenters were needed. However, it would be best if these workmen were Indians, for it was not suitable that Africans see Portuguese engaged in manual work.[68] In 1698 the king pointed out that it had always been difficult to get Portuguese to go to the Zambezi valley, and those who did usually died. It now became official policy that Canarins be encouraged, both men and women, merchants, craftsmen and farmers.[69]

These official schemes came to little, but informal settlement nevertheless proceeded. During the seventeenth and eighteenth centuries vast areas of land came to be controlled by Portuguese and Canarins. These were of course the famous prazos of the Zambezi valley. They have been much studied,[70] and in particular are now accepted as being essentially African institutions, rather than outposts of European imperialism. For our purposes, the point to note is that the prazos increasingly were controlled by Canarins, or by people with some Indian background. It is of course impossible, and undesirable, to be too specific about ethnicity at this time. Most of the *prazeiros* were probably mixtures of Indian, Portuguese and African ancestry.

Goan dominance seems to be a phenomenon of the later eighteenth century, and as this is really at the end of the early modern period with which I am concerned, I will only sketch this matter.[71] A census of Christians in the Zambezi valley from 1722[72] enumerated the following distribution: clearly Indians, that is Canarins, were far from dominant yet.

Table 1

Place	Portuguese and descendants		Indians		Natives
	Male	Female	Male	Female	
Sena	34	32	58	7	891
Gombe	8	7	4	1	101
Quelimane	10	9	10	6	16
Luabo	1	–	8	5	374
Manica	12	4	–	–	5
Sofala	13	13	9	1	279
Tete	24	36	16	8	768
Zumbo	67	27	23	–	300
Marave	3	–	11	11	180

But a half-century later this had changed. These new prazeiros dominated the province of Tete in Mozambique for most of the nineteenth century. They were heavily armed, and intermarried with locally powerful Africans. Indeed, the last of these independent feudatories was defeated and his territory incorporated into the Portuguese state of Mozambique only in 1888.[73]

It has been claimed that 'The Indian Ocean trade of 18th century Mozambique is essentially a story of the exploits of Banyan capitalism and Canarin backwoods traders.'[74] We can now turn to the activities of the other group of Indians who operated in Portuguese territory, the famous banias of Gujarat. They have of course been much studied in other regions.[75] Again I intend only a sketch to round off the story, for their dominance, like that of the Canarins in the prazos, lies later than my cut-off date of the end of the early modern period. We have scattered references to banias trading in the north, such as a petition from 'Amichande', the shahbandar of Massua, on the Ethiopian coast.[76] In 1671, the viceroy told the king he was not keen to stop the banias [*'gentios'*] of Diu from rebuilding their temples, and this favourable policy had been supported by D. Affonso Mendes, Patriarch of Ethiopia, as they had been helpful to him when he had been in Ethiopia.[77] Further south, in 1606 Fr. Gaspar de São Bernadino found two 'heathen merchants, natives of Diu' who knew Portuguese very well, at Siyu, on Pate Island.[78]

During most of the sixteenth and seventeenth centuries the Portuguese tried to regulate trade between their possessions in western India and Mozambique. There is evidence of extensive trade from Diu to Mozambique, done by banias from Diu and Surat. In 1639 a petition claimed that 1000 *bares* [240,000 kg] of cloth were

V

going from Diu to Mozambique, while another petition from the
next year found ivory worth 63,000 *pardaos* [Rs 113,400] coming in
to Diu in the single month of October 1639.[79] It was around this time
that there occurred a pronounced change in the priorities of the
Portuguese state. By the end of the 1660s they had lost to the Dutch
all of their possessions in Southeast Asia, and also Sri Lanka and the
Malabar coast. East Africa thus became, at least by process of
elimination, the most important trade area for the remaining
Portuguese possessions in western India. In 1686 the Portuguese,
having failed to make huge profits from their south-east African areas,
decided to end the monopoly of the captain of Mozambique over
the importation of Gujarati cloth into his port, and instead sell these
rights to a merchant group from Diu. This was the famous, and
ultimately unsuccessful, 'companhia de Mazanes de Dio', that is the
Company of Banias. This entity has been much studied.[80]

A recent account claims that it in fact merely recognized an existing
situation of bania dominance of Mozambique's trade.[81] It does,
however, seem to have changed one aspect, which is that more and
more banias now moved to this unhealthy island, and settled there
and in its neighbourhood.[82] By at least early in the eighteenth century
they held a stranglehold over the trade of the port and its neighbouring
settlements on the mainland. There was in fact an influx of banias
who controlled the wholesale and retail trade and also, so we are
told, engaged in such manual occupations as barbers, watchmakers,
and goldsmiths.[83] By the middle of the century banias owned 22 out
of 37 retail shops in Mozambique, Mossuril and Cabeceiras (these
two being on the mainland opposite the island). Banias dominated
the whole economy of Mozambique and the coast. Some had huge
incomes.[84] They had their own captain, who negotiated on their
behalf with the Portuguese authorities.[85] Indeed, their commercial
expertise and vast capital enabled them to out-compete the Portuguese
themselves, while petty Swahili traders were also unable to match
them. This of course led to considerable hostility from time to time,
yet the Portuguese state needed them and their financial resources,
so that official discrimination necessarily had usually to be moderated
by this stark economic reality.[86] Mbwiliza in fact claims that at least
in the first half of the eighteenth century Mozambique was 'in the
orbit of Indian merchant capital. The only challenge to the grasp that
the Banian merchants had, in alliance with Arab and Swahili
middlemen, over trade in Mozambique came from French slave
traders', who had entered the slave trade at Mozambique in the
1740s.[87] As a result, it has been claimed that 'National and religious

ideologies gave way to a multiracial class ideology, symbolically expressed under a new identity of *homens do chapeu* [hat-weavers].'[88]

Nor did the banias restrict themselves to the coastal area around the port city of Mozambique. They spread inland also, or at least their influence did, for they usually used intermediaries for the interior trade. These African agents, called *patamares,* were hired by the banias. They led the caravans which carried Indian trade goods into the interior, to the Makua people in Makuani, where they were exchanged for ivory. The banias also took part in the trade in foodstuffs, and extended credit to Portuguese and Swahili elites.[89] The extent of their influence was shown, *inter alia,* in an episode in the 1740s. In 1744, Diu's banias resident in Mozambique Island had been forbidden to trade in or own slaves, for fear that they would convert their African slaves to Hinduism. This ridiculous Portuguese suspicion was vigorously rejected by the banias. They pointed out that for them the slave trade was vital, and they also needed to own slaves to work in their houses and ships. They threatened, in a familiar way, to move elsewhere if the ban was enforced. They also promised not to sell slaves to Muslims. Two years later the king backed them up. Indeed, they needed to be able to sell and own slaves, and in any case they had never converted slaves to Hinduism; rather they had allowed them to become Christians.[90] This positive Portuguese response, after a fatuous attempt at discrimination, was par for the course.

The remainder of the story can be very quickly sketched. It seems that the banias moved north later in the eighteenth century. In the first half of this century the northern Swahili coast had undergone a period of instability thanks to attacks by the Omanis. However, as Omani power was solidified the banias moved in under this new umbrella, and participated vigorously in the slave trade. They even ran the state's customs service and treasury.[91] Their descendants can be seen in Zanzibar today. Later again, at the end of the nineteenth century, many Indians moved into the new British colony of Kenya, and after World War I to Tanganyika as well. Again banias were prominent in merchant and money-lending.

V

The conclusion from all this seems to be that we must be careful not to exaggerate the role of Indians in east Africa in the early modern period. The enthusiastic claims of dominance, of a massive impact of Indians in the area, are wide of the mark. What we can say is that Indian goods certainly were the main imports to the region, and that Indians, mostly Muslim but also a number of Hindus, participated in trade on the coast long before the arrival of Europeans. Their role in the next century or so is comparatively poorly documented, but we find them continuing to trade either within or without the Portuguese monopoly system, both on the coast and, in the case of the Canarins, far inland also. Two groups of Indians secured a major role for themselves under the Portuguese imperial umbrella in the eighteenth century. Canarins played a large role in interior trade, and especially became one of the dominant groups, if not the main one, of those who held prazos. However, to distinguish Canarins, or to see them as quite distinct from other prazeiros would be incorrect. Intermarriage or at least interbreeding was wide spread, so that most 'Portuguese' had some African or Indian blood, just as did the Canarins. Few of them would be pure-blooded Indians who had converted to Catholicism. The other group was much more distinct, these being the banias who here as elsewhere played a large role in finance, trade and commerce. The Canarins continued their role in the Zambezi valley until near the end of the nineteenth century. The banias moved in under other imperial umbrellas in this century, first that of the Omanis and then at the end that of the British in the northern sector of the Swahili coast.

NOTES

1. For a fuller discussion of this matter see my *Port Cities and Intruders: the Swahili Coast, India, and Portugal in the Early Modern Era*, Baltimore, The Johns Hopkins University Press, 1998, chapter 2.

2. See Lynda Norene Shaffer, *Maritime Southeast Asia to 1500*, Armonk, NY, 1996.

3. R.B. Serjeant, *The Portuguese off the South Arabian Coast*, Oxford, 1963, pp.3, 8–11.

4. A. Rita–Ferreira, 'Moçambique e os naturais da India Portuguesa', in Luis de Albuquerque and I. Guerreiro, eds, *II Seminário Internacional de história Indo-Portuguesa*, Lisbon, 1985, pp.617, 645. The late-fourteenth century date stems from the fact that Ibn Battuta in his account of 1331 did not mention Indians. The quotation of course is a parody on the title of Walter Rodney's well-known book *How Europe underdeveloped Africa*, Howard University Press, Washington D.C., revised edn. 1982. For similar wild claims of Indian presence, indeed dominance, see *inter alia*, R.R. Ramchandani, 'Indian Emigration to East African Countries from Ancient to Early Colonial Times, in *Mouvements de Populations dans l'Ocean Indian*, Paris, 1979, pp.309–29 and Prithvish Nag, 'The Indian Ocean, India and Africa: Historical and Geographical Perspectives,' in Satish Chandra, ed., *The*

Indian Ocean: Explorations in History, Commerce and Politics, New Delhi, 1987, pp.151–73.

5. T.R. de Souza, 'History of Mozambique: An Introduction to Bibliography', in *Purabhilekh–Puratatva,* VI, 1, 1988, p.66; T.R. de Souza, 'The Afro-Asian Church in the Portuguese Estado da India', in O.U. Kalu, ed., *African Church Historiography: An Ecumenical Perspective,* Bern, 1988, p.64.

6. Bertha Leite, *D. Gonçalo da Silveira,* Lisbon, 1946, pp.177–92; *Documenta Indica,* ed. J. Wicki et al., Rome, 1948, 20 vols to date, vol. V, *passim.*

7. Cyril Andrew Hromnik, 'Goa and Mozambique: the participation of Goans in Portuguese enterprise in the Rios de Cuama, 1501–1752', Ph.D. dissertation, Syracuse University, 1977; Cyril A. Hromnik, 'Background and content of the Historical Archives of Goa', *History in Africa,* V, 1978, pp.371–6; 'Canarins in the Rios de Cuama, 1501–76', *Journal of African Studies,* VI, 1, 1979, pp.27–37; Cyril A. Hromnik, *Indo-Africa: Toward a new understanding of the history of sub-Saharan Africa,* Cape Town, 1981. For reviews of the book see Martin Hall and C.H. Borland, 'The Indian Connection: An Assessment of Hromnik's "Indo–African",' *The South African Archaeological Bulletin,* vol. XXXVII, 1982, pp.75–80, and his response: Cyril A. Hromnik, 'African History and Africanist Orthodoxy: A Response to Hall and Borland', *The South African Archaeological Bulletin,* vol. XXXVIII, 1983, pp.36–9; see also reviews by C. Ehret, *International Journal of African Historical Studies,* XV, 3, 1982, pp.549–50, and C.P. Ownby, *Journal of African History,* XXIII, 1982, pp.415–6.

8. Hromnik, 'Goa and Mozambique', p.18.

9. Ibid.

10. Ibid.

11. Hromnik, *Indo-Africa,* p.81.

12. Ibid.

13. João de Barros, *Da Asia,* Lisbon, 1778–88, I, x, 3.

14. 'Albuquerque to king, Goa, 25 Oct 1514', in António da Silva Rego, et al., *Documentos sobre os Portugueses em Moçmbique e na Africa Central, 1497–1840,* Lisbon, 1962–89, 9 vols to date, III, 559–61 [hereafter DM].

15. Account of Almeida's voyage, DM, I, 533.

16. G.S.P. Freeman-Grenville, *The East African Coast: Select Documents from the first to the earlier nineteenth century,* London, 1962, p.75.

17. E.A. Alpers, 'Gujarat and the Trade of East Africa, *c.* 1500–1800', *International Journal of African Historical Studies,* IX, 1976, p.39. His estimate is based on Moreland's work from many years ago: we could do with a better attempt after all this time.

18. Tomé Pires, *The Suma Oriental of Tomé Pires,* ed. A. Cortesão, London, 1944, 2 vols, I, 42.

19. See, for example, Freeman-Grenville, *East African Coast,* pp.201–4; Bashir Ahmed Datoo, *Port Development in East Africa,* Nairobi, 1975, p.45; Neville Chittick, 'Indian Relations with East Africa before the arrival of the Portuguese', *Journal of the Royal Asiatic Society,* 1980, especially p.125.

20. Stanislaus I. Gorerazvo Mudenge, 'Afro-Indian Relations before 1900: a

246

Southeast African perspective', in Shanti Sadiq Ali and R.R. Ramchandani, eds *India and the Western Indian Ocean States*, New Delhi, 1981, pp.39–40.

21. James S. Kirkman, 'The Coast of Kenya as a Factor in the Trade and Culture of the Indian Ocean', in *Sociétés e compagnies de Commerce en Orient et dans l'Océan Indien*, ed. M. Mollat, Paris, 1970, *passim;* al-Biruni, *Alberuni's India*, ed. and trans. Edward Sachau, reprint, Delhi, 1964, II, 104; Gabriel Ferrand, ed. and trans., *Relations de voyages et textes géographiques Arabes, Persans et Turks relatifs a l'extréme-orient du VIIIe au XVIIIe siècles*, Paris, 1913, 2 vols, I, 173; Richard Wilding, *The Shorefolk: Aspects of the Early Development of Swahili Communities*, Fort Jesus Occasional Papers no. 2, mimeo, 1987, p.81.

22. A. Rita-Ferreira, *Fixação portuguesa e historia pre-colonial de Moçambique*, Lisbon, Instituto de investigação cientifica tropical, 1982, p.50.

23. Interview with Richard Wilding, Mombasa, 4 November 1991.

24. Interview with George Abungu, Mombasa, 4 November 1991; Wilding, *Shorefolk*, p.81; see also James de Vere Allen, *Swahili Origins: Swahili Culture and the Shungwaya Phenomenon*, ed. John Middleton, London, 1993, p.69 for a claim of very minor Indian influence.

25. M.C. Horton and T.R. Blurton, ' "Indian" Metal work in East Africa: the bronze lion statuette from Shanga', *Antiquity*, LXII, 1988, pp.21–2.

26. Wilding interview 4 Novmber 1991; Wilding, *Shorefolk*, p.81.

27. M.N. Pearson, 'Indian Seafarers in the Sixteenth Century', in *Coastal Western India: Studies from the Portuguese Records*, New Delhi, 1981, pp.116–47.

28. Many of these early Portuguese accounts are available in translation, especially in DM, and in G.M. Theal, *Records of South-Eastern Africa*, London, 1898–1903, 9 vols.

29. S.A.I. Tirmizi, *Indian Sources for African History*, vol. I, Delhi, 1988, p.17; for a good general overview see Wilding, *Shorefolk*, pp.81–9.

30. Account of da Gama's voyage in DM, I, 19.

31. Duarte Barbosa, *Livro*, London, 1918–21, 2 vols, I, 6–8.

32. Barbosa, *Livro*, I, 31.

33. Vasco da Gama, *A Journal of the First Voyage of Vasco da Gama*, London, 1898, pp.36, 39; Fernão Lopes de Castanheda, *História do descobrimento e conquista da India pelos Portugueses*, 3rd. ed., Coímbra, 1924–33, 9 vols, I, 9. For Calicut see M.N. Pearson, 'The Search for the Similar: Early Contacts between Portuguese and Indians,' in Jens Christian V. Johansen, Erling Ladewig Petersen and Henrik Stevnsborg, eds, *Clashes of Cultures: Essays in Honour of Niels Steensgaard*, Odense University Press, 1992, pp.144–59.

34. Castanheda, II, 6; account of Almeida's voyage in DM, I, 531–5; account of Almeida's voyage in Eric Axelson, *South East Africa, 1488–1530*, London, 1940, pp.235–6.

35. Barbosa, I, 21–2; Castanheda, I, x.

36. Da Gama, *Voyage*, pp.44–5; the same story in Luis de Albuquerque, *Crónica do descobrimento e conquista da India pelos Portugueses*, Coimbra, 1974, p.8.

37. Fr Sebastian Gonçalves, *Primeira Parte da Historia dos Religiosas da Companhia de Jesus,* ed. José Wicki, Coimbra, 1957–62, 3 vols, I, 83.

38. Barros, I, iv, 6.

39. Castanheda, I, 10, 12.

40. King of Portugal to king of Castile, Italian copy, printed in Rome 23 October 1505, DM, I, 47.

41. W.B. Greenlee, *The Voyage of Pedro Alvares Cabral to Brazil and India,* London, 1938, p.65.

42. James B. McKenna, *A Spaniard in the Portuguese Indies: The Narrative of Martín Fernández de Figueroa,* Cambridge, MA, 1967, p.73.

43. Register, Melinde, 20 March 1510, DM, II, 423.

44. Freeman-Grenville, *East African Coast,* pp.161–2.

45. See for example G.V. Scammell, 'Indigenous Assistance in the Establishment of Portuguese Power in the Indian Ocean', in John Correia–Afonso, ed., *Indo-Portuguese History: Sources and Problems,* Delhi, 1981, pp.163–73; G.V. Scammell, 'The Pillars of Empire: Indigenous Assistance and the Survival of the "Estado da India" c. 1600–1700', *Modern Asian Studies,* XXII, July 1988, pp.473–90; M.N. Pearson, 'Banyas and Brahmins: Their Role in the Portuguese Indian Economy', *Coastal Western India,* pp.93–115.

46. João dos Santos, *Ethiopia Oriental,* Lisbon, 1891, 2 vols, I, i, cap 2.

47. António da Silva, SJ, *Mentalidade missiológica dos Jesuítas em Moçambique antes de 1759,* Lisbon, 1967, 2 vols, I, 115; note that 'mestiço' refers to people of European and Indian blood, while an African and European mixture produced a mulatto.

48. Santos, I, iii, cap.4.

49. N. Buckeridge, *Journal and Letter Book of Nicholas Buckeridge, 1651–1654,* ed. J.R. Jenson, Minneapolis, 1973, pp.21. 65.

50. J.F. Mbwiliza, *A History of Commodity Production in Makuani, 1600–1900: Mercantilist Accumulation to Imperialist Domination,* Dar es Salaam, 1991, p.20.

51. Luis Frois, SJ, letter of 15 December 1561, Goa, DM, VIII, 41.

52. B. Leite, p.165; also Gonçalves, II, 400.

53. Monclaro's account of the Barreto expedition, DM, VIII, 399; also in *Documenta Indica,* VIII, 723; see also E.A. Axelson ed., 'Viagem que fez o Padre Antonio Gomes...ao Imperio de Manomotapa...', *Studia,* III, 1959, pp.155–242.

54. Alcantara Guerreiro, 'Inquerito em Mocambique no anno de 1573', *Studia,* 6, 1960, p.14.

55. Santos, I, ii, cap. 8.

56. Report on silver mines of Rios de Cuama by Fr Francisco de Avellar, 1617, in *Memoria dos documentos acerca dos Direitos de Portugal aos territórios de Machona e Nyassa,* Lisbon, 1890, p.95.

57. Axelson, 'Viagem...Gomes', pp.181, 220.

58. António Bocarro, 'Livro das plantas das fortalezas da India', *Arquivo Português Oriental,* ed. A.B. de Bragança Pereira, Bastorá, Goa, 1937–40, IV, 2, 1, pp.20–30.

59. Shanti Sadiq Ali, 'India and Mozambique: Past and Present', in *Purabhilekh–Puratatva*, VI, 1, 1988, p.12.

60. Eric Axelson, *Portuguese in Southeast Africa, 1600–1700*, Johannesburg, 1960, p.137. Newitt accepts this claim: M.D.D. Newitt, *A History of Mozambique*, London, 1994, p.182.

61. M.D.D. Newitt, *Portugal in Africa: the last hundred years*, London, 1981, p.10; M.D.D. Newitt, 'East Africa and the Indian Ocean Trade: 1500–1800', in Ashin Das Gupta and M.N. Pearson, eds, *India and the Indian Ocean, 1500–1800*, Calcutta, 1987, pp.213–4.

62. Oliveira Boleo, 'O "Regimento para o novo comercio de Mocambique" de 1673', *Studia*, III, 1959, pp.107–8.

63. King to viceroy, 20 March 1690, in P.S.S. Pissurlencar, ed., *Assentos do Conselho do Estado*, Bastorá, 1953–7, 5 vols, IV, 441–-2.

64. Fr. António da Conceição, 'Tratado dos Rio de Cuama, 1696', *O Chronista de Tissuary*, II, 1867, pp.64–5, 68; for a brief mention of the situation in 1693 see Maria Manuela Sobral Blanco, 'O Estado Português da India: da rendição de Ormuz à perda de Cochim, (1622–1663),' University of Lisbon, Ph.D. dissertation, 1992, 3 vols, II, 762–9, an account by 'Pe Frey Phelipe de Assumpção por andar nas ditas terras quatorze annos.'

65. Prince to governors of India, 27 March 1679, in *Assentos*, IV, 569–70.

66. Viceroy to king, 24 January 1683, in *Assentos*, IV, 570.

67. S.S. Ali, 'India and Mozambique', p.11.

68. Conceição, 'Tratado', pp.86–7.

69. King to viceroy, 28 February 1698, in *Memoria dos documentos*, p.129.

70. See M.D.D. Newitt, *Portuguese Settlement on the Zambezi: Exploration, Land Tenure and Colonial Rule in Eastern Africa*, Harlow, 1973; Allen Isaacman, *Mozambique: the Africanization of a European Institution*, Madison, 1972; S.I.G. Mudenge, 'The Goans in the Zambezi Valley before 1900: an Outline', *Purabhilekh–Puratatva*, II, 2, 1984, pp.1–7.

71. See especially the various works of Malyn Newitt cited above, and A. Rita-Ferreira, 'Moçambique e os naturais da India Portuguesa', in Luis de Albuquerque and I. Guerreiro, eds, *II Seminário internacional de história Indo-Portuguesa*, Lisbon, 1985.

72. 'Livros das Monções', Historical Archives of Goa, vol.87, ff.96–, and published in *Arquivo Português Oriental*, ed. A.B. de Bragança Pereira, Bastorá, Goa, 1937–40, IV, 2, 2, pp.88–9.

73. Henrik Ellert, *Rivers of Gold*, Gweru, 1993, p.167; Rita–Ferreira, 'Moçambique e os naturais', *passim;* Isaacman, *Mozambique,* e.g. pp.59, 76, 84.

74. S.S. Ali, 'India and Mozambique', p.12.

75. Most notably in Ashin Das Gupta, *Indian Merchants and the Decline of Surat, c. 1700–1750*, Wiesbaden, 1979; also in my *Merchants and Rulers in Gujarat*, Berkely, 1976, and *Coastal Western India*, citied above.

76. 'Cartas e Ordens', Historical Archives of Goa, III, f.73.

77. Viceroy to king, 3 October 1671, in 'Livros das Monções,' Historical Archives of Goa, vol. 36, f.258.

78. Freeman-Grenville, *The East African Coast,* pp.161–2.

79. Petition from B.S. Correa, rendeiro of Goa alfandega, December 1639, in 'Livros das Fianças', Historical Archives of Goa, II, ff.143–4; Ibid., f.174, petition of July 1640; other evidence of this trade in Buckeridge, *Journal,* 57, 65. For an enthusiastic account of bania trade generally in East Africa see Alpers, 'Gujarat and the Trade of East Africa', *passim.*

80. For documentation see J.H. da Cunha Rivara, 'A India no governo do Vice-Rei Conde de Villa Verde, 1693–1698', *O Chronista de Tissuary,* II–III, 1867–8; Newitt, *History of Mozambique,* pp.318–23; and especially Frederico Dias Antunes, 'A crise no Estado da India no Final do Século XVII e a Criação das Companhias de Comércio das Indias Orientais e dos Baneanes de Diu', in *Portuguese India and its Northern Province, Proceedings of the 7th International Seminar on Indo-Portuguese History,* in *Mare Liberum,* no. 9, Lisbon, July 1995, pp.19–29.

81. Manuel Lobato, 'Relações comerciais entre a India e a costa Africana nos séculos XVI and XVII: o papel do Guzerate no Comércio de Moçambique', in *Portuguese India and its Northern Province, Proceedings of the 7th International Seminar on Indo-Portuguese History,* in *Mare Liberum,* no. 9, Lisbon, July 1995, p.157.

82. A. Rita–Ferreira, 'História Pré-Colonial do Sul de Moçambique: Tentativa de Síntese', *Studia,* no.41–2, 1979, pp.137–64, and no. 43–4, 1980, 283–324; no.41–2, p.156.

83. History Department, Universidade Eduardo Mondlane, *História de Moçambique, vol. I, Primeiras sociedades sendantarias e impacto dos mercadores (200/300–1886),* Maputo, 1988, 2nd ed., pp.89–93.

84. Mbwiliza, p.28.

85. Letter from capitão-mor dos Baneanes, Narsy Ranuhor, to governor and captain-general, Moçambique, *Documentário Trimestral,* no. 72, p.115; no. 75, n.d. but presumably eighteenth century, p.172.

86. See Rita-Ferreira 'Naturais', *passim;* History Department, pp.89–93; Martin Hall, *The Changing Past: Farmers, Kings and Traders in Southern Africa,* Cape Town, 1987, p.124.

87. Mbwiliza, pp.13–14.

88. Mbwiliza, p.64.

89. History Department, pp.89–93; Mbwiliza, p.28.

90. King to viceroy, 12 March 1746 and 13 December 1746, in J.H. da Cunha Rivara, ed., *Archivo Português Oriental,* Nova Goa, 1857–77, 9 vols, IV, 467–9.

91. See Gervase Clarence-Smith, *The Third Portuguese Empire,* Manchester, 1985, ch. 2; and Alpers, 'Gujarat and the Trade of East Africa'.

VI

Littoral Society:
The Case for the Coast*

"If you wish to converse with me, define your terms." (Voltaire)
"I hate definitions." (Disraeli)

Maritime history, or the study of people at sea, has gained greatly in popularity in recent years. Symposia, books, societies, conferences and journals proliferate. A cognate field of endeavour, the history of port cities, often colonial, is also flourishing. Meanwhile, colonial and/or imperial history continue, with their implicit or explicit assumption that the arrival of the Europeans at some place "makes a difference".

There are problems with all three fields of study. Maritime history can all too easily degenerate into antiquarian discussions of particular ships or Old Salts, or dramatic tales of shipwrecks or naval campaigns. These often suffer from not being linked to general social, economic or political history. Thus the outcome of naval battles needs to be linked to the economic and political attributes of the home countries. The actions of people at sea are determined only in part by nautical influences; the land society from which they spring is usually much more important in governing their actions. Happily, wider dimensions are not ignored in *The Great Circle*, for the editor, in the journal's "Inaugural Newsletter", said that maritime history "includes all aspects of the human experience that have to do with the sea".[1]

The study of port cities similarly runs the danger of becoming too narrow. Existing studies usually do well in talking of the hinterland, in other words, describing the function of the port city as an outlet for the interior. What is often ignored is a more maritime dimension. There is no whiff of ozone in this work. Historians of port cities too seldom look up and down the coast on which their city is located, too seldom gaze out beyond the estuaries and the breakers to the open sea.[2]

As to the hoary old problem of Eurocentrism, one need only say that we still have some way to go to avoid an undue focus on European activities in Asia, to write a rounded and balanced history of the early European expansion.

One way forward could be for historians to focus on littoral society. Such a focus could help to overcome all the problems we noted above. A study of littoral society is much more holistic than that of port cities, and forces one to concentrate much more on the sea, thus avoiding the temptation to which many port city studies have succumbed, that is, the tendency to stray inland to distant markets and influences, and ignore the sea altogether. Obviously port cities are the largest population centres on coasts, but they need to be seen as part of coastal or littoral society at least as much as entrepots servicing an inland hinterland.

As regards maritime history, some problems can be avoided if the focus is on the littoral, for by definition it includes both land and sea; it is indeed land located on the sea shore, or that part of the land which is influenced by the sea. Thus the study of

---

* A first version of this article was presented at the Asian Studies Association of Australia meeting in Adelaide in May 1984. It gained immensely from the discussion there, notably from the comments of Ashin Das Gupta.

littoral societies must include an appreciation of landed society, and so avoid the tendency to see people at sea as *sui generis*.

Finally, the problems of perspective so often found in colonial history could be avoided if we focus more on the sea and the littoral. We would then, for example, see that 1498 is not really a watershed. (The reader will note that this metaphor is truly littoral, combining as it does land and water aspects!) Recent research on the history of the Indian Ocean finds many more continuities than radical changes in the whole period from the fifteenth century to the middle of the eighteenth. The degree and nature of the Portuguese impact in the sixteenth century is being played down, while recent studies stress how the Dutch and English in the seventeenth century fitted into existing trade patterns and practices. These new studies are especially revisionist because, we have always been told, it was precisely at sea that the early Europeans had their greatest impact. In fact, while the nature and quantity of the sources changes radically at 1500, the history of coastal western India does not. In this new, and to my mind more correct, perspective, littoral history will make a large contribution. If one's interest is the colonial and imperial history of the Europeans, one all to easily ignores basic continuities. But if one focuses on the sea, and the littoral, then on-going themes and trends become clear and one can escape the shackles of a largely European-derived documentation.

What follows is some rather general observations and comments designed to make the case for this sort of littoral focus. Many of my examples will be drawn from the coast of western India in the sixteenth and seventeenth centuries.

*   *   *

The basic question is whether one can distinguish a separate or distinctive littoral society around the Indian coast. Braudel's classic *Mediterranean* provides an entrée. One important theme is the unity of land and sea in the Mediterranean area:

> Its life is linked to the land, its poetry more than half-rural, its sailors may turn peasant with the seasons; it is the sea of vineyards and olive trees just as much as the sea of the long-oared galleys and the round-ships of merchants and its history can no more be separated from that of the lands surrounding it than the clay can be separated from the hands of the potter who shapes it.

Similarly, the region itself can be clearly defined; in this second edition he still stresses the "unity and coherence of the Mediterranean region . . . the whole sea shared a common destiny, a heavy one indeed, with identical problems and general trends if not identical consequences." Nevertheless, the sea as such is not only a uniter: "The sea is everything it is said to be: it provides unity, transport, the means of exchange and intercourse, if man is prepared to make an effort and pay a price. But it has also been the great divider, the obstacle that had to be overcome."

As to the problem of where the Mediterranean region ends, a crucial one for any study of littorals, it must be said at once that Braudel is more poetic than exact. Thus he notes that in times of great expansion "the historical Mediterranean seems to be a concept of infinite expansion. But how far in space are we justified in extending it? This is a difficult and controversial question; but if we are seeking to explain the history of the Mediterranean, it is perhaps the fundamental question we should be asking." Very promising, but do the following remarks, for all their flourish and insight, really lead us to a solution? The Mediterranean is a very wide zone. "We might compare it to an electric or magnetic field, or more simply to a radiant centre whose light grows less as one moves away from it, without one's being able to define the exact boundary between light and shade." And again, "The circulation of men and of goods, both material and intangible, formed concentric circles round the Mediterranean. We should imagine a hundred frontiers, not one, some political, some economic, and some cultural."[3]

It is interesting, though perhaps not surprising, that a later member of the *Annales* school, E. Le Roy Ladurie, finds a comparable situation in another littoral area at the same time, that is in mid sixteenth-century Normandy. The country gentleman whose diaries he is describing appears to be totally unaffected by the much-vaunted influx of bullion from Spanish America. He lives close to the great port of Cherbourg, yet his society "seems to be up to its knees in mud most of the time . . ." He is full of "self- sufficient parochialism". More important for the present discussion is Le Roy Ladurie's account of the peasant-fishermen of the coast, always in a hurry to get home from herring fishing "to get on with the more serious matters—looking after the cows, cutting the corn, laying down apple juice."[4]

There have recently been several contributions addressed to this problem of definition. Two of them are focussed on the characteristics of the Portuguese empire, but all implicitly help us to consider land-sea divisions and the nature of littoral society. First is A. R. Disney's very interesting article "The Portuguese Empire in India *c.* 1550–1650: Some Suggestions for a Less Seaborne, more Landbound Approach to its Socio-Economic History."[5] This article makes a strong case for research into the history of Portuguese land territories, in Goa and the North, instead of the current focus on the maritime history of the Portuguese empire. For his chosen period Disney sounds a useful caution, but certainly the early empire, in the first half of the sixteenth century, was oriented much more to the sea than to the land. In any case, while it is true that maritime history, being in vogue (and quite well financed) at present, has acquired a horde of camp-followers (if this be the appropriate metaphor), what we really need to see is a continuum. Land and sea intertwine in complex and various ways; they form integral parts of this continuum. Thus in the case of the Portuguese it is too distorting to see them as either purely land based or totally maritime. The two are inextricably connected.

An alternative, and preferable, way to look at the Portuguese empire was put forward some 45 years ago by A. B. de Bragança Pereira: "The Portuguese empire in the East, even at its height, was maritime rather than territorial. It spread along the coasts a network of factories, entrepots protected by forts, from Sofala to Timor and Solor. The armadas provided communications between these foci of the nervous system of the empire, which began at the Cape of Good Hope and ended in the islands of the Pacific."[6] The net, or network, notion was revived (probably unconsciously) by Denys Lombard, and founds its fullest expression in a study by L. F. Reis Thomaz: "The expression 'Estado da India' in the sixteenth century designates not a well-defined geographic space but an assemblage ('conjunto') of territories, establishments, goods, people, and administrative interests, created or protected by the Portuguese Crown in the Indian Ocean and adjacent seas or in the littoral territories from the Cape of Good Hope to Japan." Thus, "normally empires represent a political structure in a set geographic space, while the Estado da India is essentially a net, that is, a system of communication between various spaces."[7] At the least, this usefully avoids over-emphasis on either land or sea activities, and provides a new way to look at the empire. His scheme also helps to stress the links between various littoral societies. But we may find his qualitative assessment of the actions of this empire quite invalid. At times unfortunately he atavistically indulges in old-style patriotic Portuguese history.

C. R. Boxer has contributed to the discussion of littoral societies in a brief investigation of the received wisdom concerning fifteenth and sixteenth century Portugal. He

asks whether there is a division in Portugal between littoral and hinterland, and pro-
vocatively, whether the Portuguese are really a seafaring nation. He points to a
chronic scarcity of deep-sea sailors in Portugal, to a lack of good harbours, and to a
small percentage of the population engaged in fishing. Even for people near the coast,
the main economic activity was labour in the fields. The sea impinges only as gales
which destroy vines. He concludes that as a "race" the Portuguese were really more
earth-bound peasants than adventurous seafarers.[7]

On the crucial matter of the land limits of oceanic history, or of littoral society, a
recent contribution by J. C. Heesterman is of great interest.[9] He criticizes my
depiction[10] of a merchant-ruler axis or dichotomy in sixteenth-century Gujarat, and
points instead to a littoral-inland axis. Certainly, he says, the littoral and the interior
require very different sorts of government regimes, but there are also strong links.
Most obvious is trade, and especially the bullion imports which are essential for land
revenue transactions and general trade in the interior. Thus littoral and interior are
different, but complementary. "The littoral forms a frontier zone which is not there to
separate and close off, but which rather finds its *raison d'être* in its porosity." To be a
successful frontier, the littoral needs free exchange, as seen in merchant autonomy
and low customs duties, and so there is little government interference in its affairs.
Thus between hinterland and littoral there is both opposition and complementarity.
This is all very well, but one could suspect that Heesterman is being overly deter-
ministic. Is he saying that inland states *allow* littoral society more autonomy because
they know this is necessary for them to function and provide items needed in the interior? If he is, he seems to make Mughal policy far too deliberate and conscious,
overly-schematizing a much more organic evolution.

I would argue that while littoral *societies* are distinctive and can be described as different from inland areas, *government influence* is more or less the same all over such a
premodern state as the Mughal empire. For better or worse, the whole argument of my
book which he criticizes is that merchants were not in an unusual position in the political system. Rather they were one group among many who were able to operate most of
the time free of interference from the central government. The sum of all these groups
made up nearly the whole population of the empire. Thus there is a case for rejecting
Heesterman's depiction of the role of the central government. (This, however, is not to
say that smaller states, or states in decline, might not try to impinge much more
decisively on their populations, including merchants.) But two general points he
makes are well worth further thought and reflection. These are first the stimulating
notion of the porous coastal frontier, and second his stress on complementarity
between littoral and hinterland.

All this seems to be leading us towards a lack of definition, just like Braudel. There
is in fact no clear line of demarcation. Rather there is a continuum between land and
sea activities, with the strip of the littoral in the middle, acting as a hinge or mediator.
There is no dichotomy, the two are not discrete. Rather they merge and blend in the
littoral. Useful parallels can be drawn here with studies of rural-urban divisions.
Richard Fox writes of a "rurban" Indian town. Ira Lapidus and Susan Landay have
noted a mingling of urban and rural characteristics in Muslim society.[11] Similarly, E.
Le Roy Ladurie describes how in the late sixteenth century people living in Romans, in
southern France, a town of about 8,000, often worked all day in the fields and vine-
yards outside the walls of the town. One third of the town's inhabitants (by any definition then "urban" dwellers) were farmers.[12] To return to the coast and Heesterman,
our frontiers must necessarily be porous, flexible, unspecific.

One way forward could be to consider people actually on the sea shore. Can they be
seen as constituting a different society from people living inland? An historical recon-

struction may help here. Consider the Mughal emperors Akbar or Jahangir standing on the shore of the Gulf of Cambay. For them, and for the courtiers surrounding them, the sea is a marvel, a curiosity, but not something which impinged importantly on their consciousness, for these were intimately tied to the land, and people on it. Yet a few of the nobles with them were local governors, of Surat, Cambay, and of the whole province of Gujarat. The last named shared most of the emperor's attitudes, yet a quite large part of the revenue of the province was based on taxes on products destined to be exported by sea. The governors of the ports were of course much more tied to the littoral and the sea, yet they also were in this position only temporarily, subject as they were to transfer to inland positions. And even while governing their ports, they were responsible to, and subject to, the desires and orders of a totally land-oriented monarch, while their own salaries were often collected from inland areas.

Let us extend this recreation a little further, and imagine other people surrounding the great Mughal. Some Portuguese were present in 1572; indeed, Akbar spoke to them. They must be seen as perforce much more littoral—perhaps most purely of all, even if not by design, for the Portuguese were dependent on the sea for communications, for their livelihoods, as a means of escape even. Further away one can see various merchants, mostly Gujaratis, both Hindu and Muslim. These men are somewhat divided: some make most of their transactions by sea, and even travel on it themselves. Others supply goods to exporters, others again engage entirely in land commerce. And many fit in all three of these broad categories at different times.

This also applies to peasants and fishermen. As Braudel and Le Roy Ladurie noted, some would derive most of their livelihood from fishing and sailing, but perhaps most would do this and also cultivate a plot of land. Others could cultivate land on the water's edge yet have nothing to do with the sea. Similarly, most brahmins in the temples of coastal Gujarat and Saurashtra, although spatially located by the sea, in no sense can be considered to be influenced by maritime matters. Some however accompanied Hindu merchants overseas, to East Africa and the Red Sea especially.

This same point of variability, even among people actually on the coast, can be made with regard to the Orissan pilgrimage center of Puri. Most of the resident Oriya and Bengali pilgrims to the temple of Jaganath regard the ocean only as the edge of the land, or a wild fascinating backdrop, as also presumably do the brahmins and other resident in this temple complex. But for the fishing community, the Nuliyas, it is their life and being. For them the beach on which their modest huts are built is, virtually, the alien element.[13] The point, most simply, is that it is dangerous to talk of littoral society if one automatically includes in it all people near the sea. Even coastal residents may have very different perceptions and attitudes.

Religious affiliation provides a clear example of this, and demonstrates very well the influence of landed norms and prescriptions on people at sea. There were normative prohibitions and discouragements to maritime activity from the great traditions of both Islam and Hinduism. As is well known, for caste Hindus sea travel was considered to be ritually impure. From the Muslim side, consider the following two aphorisms reflecting the ethos of the land-oriented elite. "God save the land to the Muslims and the sea to the infidels." "Merchants who travel by sea are like silly worms clinging to logs." Yet despite these elite attitudes, we know very well that both Hindus and Muslims travelled and traded extensively by sea. Indeed, the first Muslim aphorism comes from the Ottoman empire, and hardly does justice to this empire's record of fearsome naval achievement. Nevertheless, religious norms evolved on land did have an influence on who went to sea, and how people behaved at sea. For Muslims there were no religious prohibitions. Indeed religious norms could encourage sea travel, for to the extent that travel by sea was necessary in order to make the pilgrimage to Mecca, this travel was meritorious. On the other hand, for high caste Hindus sea travel was best avoided: those brahmins who did travel by sea (including in the nineteenth century the vania M. K. Gandhi) were regarded with considerable suspicion by the orthodox. Narottam Morarjee, the later founder of Scindia Steam Navigation Company, on return from his travel to England in 1912/13 refused to undergo *Prayaschitta*, but he had taken his own Brahmin cook with him.[14] Also lower caste Hindus who travelled over water usually tried to avoid pollution by carrying and preparing their own food (as did Gandhi in 1888 on his way to England).[15]

We must also recognise here the influence of geography on littoral boundaries. This dictates that maritime influences, or perhaps the area we can call the littoral, are of very varying depth inland. Consider the western coast of India. For much of its length bordered and terminated by the dramatic and precipitous western Ghats, which even today cut off the coast from the interior, this means that maritime-inland interaction and trade is blocked, and it increases dramatically the independence of petty coastal states from influence from inland powerful states. The contrast is clear with Gujarat, and to a slightly lesser extent with Coromandel. In Gujarat the great ports were always subject to, even if not tightly controlled by, powerful inland states. This is primarily because of geography, and this also allowed their commercial success, for products from the fertile interior of Gujarat, and indeed even from further afield, could relatively easily be brought to the great ports.

What of the influence of politics on littoral societies? Here again the frontier varies. Two small examples will make this point. In 1623 the English had several complaints against the local authorities in Gujarat. To put pressure on them, they seized at sea some Gujarati ships. In retaliation their factors in Gujarat were imprisoned, to be released only on promise of better behaviour. This whole episode must then be seen as very littoral. But at times one has to go much further inland in order to understand events and trends at sea and on the littoral. Mughal-Safavid conflict over the great fort of Gandahar may appear to be a totally inland concern, yet this hindered the overland horse trade, and so increased the sea carriage of horses to India. The land-sea frontier is flexible, variable: *pace* Braudel, a thousand frontiers indeed!

*   *   *

A final answer must then stress the sea, but not separate it from the land. Our definition of the history of littoral societies is simply that it is a history focussing on people whose lives were connected with the sea, and who often travelled over salt water or were influenced by what occurred on it. The history of such people is not restricted to the sea. Influences on littoral society of which we must take note can come from far inland. It is always a matter of interaction between the affairs of land and sea. This interaction will never cease at sea, for no one lives totally on the water and completely uninfluenced by the land. The land frontier is porous, elastic; all we can say is that when a land activity is in no way influenced by the sea, then we are not interested. This then is the land frontier, the end of the littoral.

There is, however, a problem even with such a diffuse statement as this. If one stresses contact with the sea, then almost everywhere becomes littoral. The whole Malay world, for example, would have to be included. In the Indian case, the main import was bullion. This came by sea. Thus, to the extent that the Indian economy was monetized (as indeed it largely was by the seventeenth century) it was on our definition influenced by the sea, and so was littoral. This seems to be the place to revive the notion of a continuum, touched on above. Maritime influence varies greatly, and generally (though not universally) is stronger on the coast, and decreases as one moves inland. We could consider a cut-off somewhere near the middle of the continuum: at some, varying, point as we move inland land influence outweighs maritime. The exact specification of "influence" requires precise elaboration, but this may be some sort of way forward.

I am strongly convinced that this effort is well worth making. We need more precision, but there is no doubt that there *is* such a thing as a littoral society. It is, like an Indian village, a spatially defined social grouping which can be isolated, investigated, and defined. Several obvious characteristics, which set it off from the inland, can be noted here: elaborations and additions to these should be on our research agenda. Littoral society is more pluralistic than the inland, because of the diverse groups of foreign merchants in its ports. In littoral areas more fish is eaten than is the case inland. The monsoons affect all India, but in rather different ways in littoral areas, for here they dictate (much more so than inland) the times in which trade and travel is possible. (As a very mundane example, consider the traveller proceeding from Bombay to Goa. The voyage by sea is impossible, because of the monsoons, between June and August; by land, despite the monsoons, it is always possible.) In economic terms a littoral society both in trade and production is geared to much more distant and "foreign" markets than is an inland area. Finally, as noted above, there are important cultural and religious differences. Hindus who travel by sea have to make adjustments, and engage in rituals, festivals and ceremonies, unknown to their landed co-religionists. Often distinct castes have evolved among those who engage in maritime activity.[16] What is needed is empirical research to flesh out these distinctive elements.

*   *   *

Several historians have forcefully made the point that all this concern with definitions and categories is ultimately pointless: far better to write the history of traders, states, societies, and not waste time on tortuous speculation on the distinction between maritime and inland history, or the nature of littoral society. They quote particularly the matter of trade. Sea trade, where it duplicates land routes, is practically and functionally similar, and so cannot be seen to be distinct. Thus coastal trade on the western Indian coast, from say Bhatkal to Honavar, is "the same as" similar trade done by land: the same goods are carried by the same merchants and finish up fetching the same prices in the same place. Similarly with longer-distance trade. The horse trade from the Persian Gulf to India could go by land or sea indifferently. Europe could obtain spices by sea via the Cape of Good Hope, but also by the caravan route overland from Basra to Aleppo, or for that matter via the land-sea combined route up the Red Sea. All these routes are international, cosmopolitan, uncertain. No funotional difference is clear. Even some terminology is carried over: thus a *cafila* is both a land caravan and a convoy by sea.

One point can be quickly conceded. A concern with definitions, a rumination on the nature of a particular sort of history writing, is obviously not a substitute for writing "good" history. Rather it is a groundwork, a preliminary action before the real history is written. Yet I would insist that we need to be clear about what we are doing. Historians are too much inclined to write on, their assumptions and underpinnings unexplicated, their methods unexamined, their individual sociologies of knowledge unrevealed or even denied in a claim to objectivity. Beware especially of historians who claim only "to tell a story": their choice of *what* story, and *how* it is to be told, are very subjective decisions indeed.

A second point can also be accepted, at least in part. Doubtless all attempts at divisions and categories are ultimately artificial. History is really a seamless web, which we

7

cut up simply for our own convenience. But this is something all historians have to do, and where and how they do it is a matter of individual taste. Does one start a history of the Mughal empire in 1526, when the first emperor, Babur, established himself in Delhi and Agra? Or is Babur's birth year the best starting place, or does one write first of his ancestors, Timur or even Ghenghiz Khan? Indeed, is the Mughal empire really a category worthy of study at all? Does 1526 make any more difference than 1498?

Given then that all historians slice up a totality according to their taste or convenience, there seems no reason not to attempt to write of maritime or littoral societies. Indeed, it is arguable that their distinctiveness is greater than say "the Mughal empire". Further, the arguments made at the beginning of this article still seem to be convincing. The concept of littoral society has, I am sure, a "tin-opener" utility at the least. It can open for us a new and better series of categories, and help us to avoid the problems associated with maritime, port city and imperial history. Finally, the study of littoral society is by definition a study of a porous, transitional area, located somewhere near the middle of a continuum. Thus littoral history forces one to be comparative, to avoid an overly schematic and discrete writing of a part of total history.

Even such a laborious attempt at definition as the present one has some value. We all "know" what is good history, and what is bad. Thus K. M. Panikkar and hosts of others can be criticized for Eurocentrism, Auguste Toussaint's work can be faulted for both factual and methodological weaknesses. But if we are going to criticize others we need to have in mind some clear standard or definition and then fault them for not adhering to these. Unless we can say clearly what we are doing, and what we hope to achieve by writing either maritime or littoral history, we will continue shadow-boxing. Empirical research is of the essence, but should take place not in a vacuum, but as a means to test existing theory.

REFERENCES

1. Frank Broeze, 'Editorial', *The Great Circle*, Inaugural Newsletter (Oct. 1978), p. 7.
2. Dilip K. Basu, ed. *The Rise and Growth of the Colonial Port Cities in Asia* (Santa Cruz 1979), typifies these problems.
3. Fernand Braudel, *The Mediterranean and the Mediterranean World in the Age of Philip II*, 2 vols (London 1972-73), pp. 17, 14, 276, 167, 168 and 170.
4. E. Le Roy Ladurie, *The Territory of the Historian* (Chicago 1979), pp. 142-5.
5. In J. Correia-Afonso, ed. *Indo-Portuguese History: Sources and Problems* (Bombay 1981), pp. 148-62.
6. *História administrativa da India Portuguesa* (Bastorá n.d.), p. 67.
7. 'Estrutura politica and administrativa do Estado da India no século XVI', *Proceedings*, Second ' International Seminar on Indo-Portuguese History (Lisbon 1980), pp. 1-2.
8. C. R. Boxer, *The Portuguese Seaborne Empire, 1415-1825* (London 1969), pp. 13-14.
9. 'Littoral et intérieur de l'Inde,, *Itinerario*, 1980, pp. 87-92.
10. *Merchants and Rulers in Gujarat* (Berkeley and New Delhi, 1976), chs 5 and 6.
11. Richard Fox, *Urban India* (Durham 1970); Ira Lapidus, *Middle Eastern Cities* (Berkeley 1969); Susan Landay, *Economic Geography*, vol. 47, no. 2 (June 1971).
12. *Carnival at Romans* (New York 1980), pp. 8-9 and 98.
13. My thanks to John Broomfield for ideas in this paragraph.
14. N. J. Jog, ed. *Narottam Morarjee* (Bombay 1977), p. 11.
15. On some of these problems, see my 'Indian Seafarers in the Sixteenth Century', in *Coastal Western india* (New Delhi 1981).
16. The best research being done on this sort of problem is that by Dr Lotika Varadarajan: 'Traditions of Indigenous Navigation in Gujarat', *South Asia*, n.s. III, vol. 1 (June 1980), and 'Indian Seafaring: The Precept and Reality of Kalivarjya', *The Great Circle* vol. 5 (1983).

VII

GOA DURING THE FIRST CENTURY OF PORTUGUESE RULE*

"Goa has never been other than fundamentally Indian..." J.M. Richards, 1982.[1]

"The posteritie of the Portingales, both men and women being in the third degree, doe seeme to be naturall Indians, both in colour and fashion." J.H. van Linschoten, c. 1590.[2]

"Rich on trade and loot, Goa in the halcyon days of the sixteenth century was a handsome city of great houses and fine churches... In the eyes of stern moralists the city was another Babylon, but to men of the world it was a paradise where, with beautiful Eurasian girls readily available, life was a ceaseless round of amorous assignments and sexual delights". G.V. Scammell, 1981.[3]

"Twenty-nine years after the Portuguese conquest, the city of Adil Khan had grown and changed beyond all recognition. The glittering splendor of an oriental court was gone, but the horizon had been widened. Goa had been great in the past, as the chief port of the Deccan, the centre of the horse trade with Ormuz and Arabia; but it was now the capital of a seaborne empire stretching from Mocambique to the Moluccas". Elaine Sanceau, 1949.[4]

This paper will attempt to assess the degree of change in Goa during its first century of subjection to Portuguese rule. The period is an obvious one, for few historians today would follow the censorious nineteenth-century English historians who started the decline of Goa at the mid-sixteenth century and attributed it to such spurious and racist explanations as Catholic fanaticism, corruption, and "interbreeding." Rather they would follow C.R. Boxer and see Portuguese decline as a result of Dutch attacks, in other words an early seventeenth century phenomenon.

My concern is with the territory of Goa only, in other words Ilhas alone to 1543, and then, with the addition of Bardês and ˎSalcette, the Old Conquests. At present we know much more about changes in extra-Goan Portuguese fortunes, such as the decline of the trade to Europe, especially that in spices, and the consequent swing to country trade by both Portuguese individuals and the state itself. But I intend to ignore, by and large, Goa's position as the centre of an Asian trading network, the network noted above by Elaine Sanceau and stressed so often by C.R. Boxer.[5]

Nor will I follow Boxer in his emphasis on Portuguese India as a frontier society of conquest. This it no doubt was, but it was other things too. This paper will stress continuities in Goan history, and will conclude that Portuguese conquest and rule had little effect on most important aspects of Goan life in the sixteenth century.

Such a conclusion is not, given recent historiography, really very novel. G.V. Scammell's magisterial survey of the European maritime empires from 800 to 1650 explicitly draws out continuities in this period: da Gama and the later Portuguese are not, from a European perspective, very innovative. Similarly from an Asian angle, the recognition of the importance of the country trade to the Portuguese, which I noted above, was fostered by scholars like J.B. Harrison, C.R. Boxer, M.A.P. Meilink-Roelofsz, and V.M. Godinho. The implication was that the Portuguese in all Asia have to be seen as fitting into, rather than changing, existing trade networks. In the last few years we have learnt much more about the important role of the private trade done by Portuguese all over Asia, right outside (and sometimes in defiance of) official Portuguese control. Virgínia Rau, and again C.R.

Boxer and V.M. Godinho, pointed to this trend some years ago: G. Bouchon and F.R. Thomaz have now undertaken very important new researches. A forthcoming collaborative book will demonstrate conclusively how strong were elements of continuity in India's maritime history from the fifteenth century to around 1750.[6] This paper, while focussing on Goa, builds explicitly in these recent trends in research.

We know little enough about Goa before the Portuguese.[7] Ironically, it seems that Goa in the decades *before* the Portuguese conquest of 1510 was subject to *more* stress and change than at any time later in the century. We should first note changes in political control. Goa had been part of the Hindu empire of Vijayanagar until the area's conquest by the Muslim Bahmani sultanate in 1472. In the decade before 1500, as this sultanate fragmented, Goa was included in one of the five successor states, Bijapur. It was conquered by the Portuguese in 1510, and remained under their rule until 1961. Thus in the space of less than forty years Goa was part of four different states. The imposition of a Muslim ruling group in the 1470s must have caused major dislocation, especially as many of these Muslims were foreigners. As a concrete example, after the Bahmani conquest the rate of land revenue demand by the state was doubled. This is of course a cataclysmic change in an agrarian society. There appear to have been other changes in the all important land revenue system, during the brief period of Muslim rule. According to Baden-Powell, the Hindu system was *ryotwari*, with the state taking a proportion of the actual production of every cultivating family. Under the Muslims, and especially during the decade or so of rule by Bijapur before the Portuguese conquest, a major change occurred. Land revenue became payable in cash, and most important the unit of assessment was made not the family but the village as a whole. This increased dramatically the power of the village leader or leaders. It also seems that the method of assessment was changed under Bijapur. Finally, there is evidence that some of the Turkish auxiliaries of the sultan of Bijapur were allowed to seize lands from their Hindu customary holders.[8] It is not an over-statement to say that the imposition of Portuguese rule ushered in an eva of stability, a "Pax Portuguesa," after the shocks and upheavals of the previous forty years.

Given the continuing stress on sixteenth-century Golden
Goa as a large, wealthy and dissolute town we need to try
and work out in comparative terms just how big and wealthy
it really was, in the context of its sixteenth-century Indian setting. We have no figures for pre-Portuguese Goa's
population, not even an estimate, though it seems that Muslim harshness had made some Hindus flee. Our data for the
rest of the sixteenth century are only slightly better. De
Souza claims that the city grew in area by two-thirds during
this time, and seven or eight suburbs were added.[9] Despite
this, and also despite Boxer's claim that 2,400 Portuguese
left home each year in the century for overseas, mostly for
Goa, the city seems to have been rather small. In 1524 there
were 450 Portuguese householders in Goa city, and in 1540
about 1,800. The former figure refers to "pure" Portuguese,
while the latter includes descendents of Portuguese and local women, in other words mestiços.[10] In the 1540s at the
time of St. Francis Xavier, the city population included
10,000 Indian Christians, 3-4,000 Portuguese, and many non-
Christians, while outside the city the rest of Ilhas contained 50,000 inhabitants, 80 percent of them Hindu.[11] Recent estimates put the city population at 60,000 in the
1580s, and about 75,000 at 1600, the latter figure including
1,500 Portuguese and mestiços 20,000 Hindus, and the rest
local Christians, Africans, and others.[12] In the 1630s the
total population of the Old Conquests - Ilhas, Bardês and
Salcette - was perhaps a little more than a quarter of a
million.[13]

These figures point to two things: that the Hindu population remained large throughout the sixteenth century, a
point we will return to shortly, and that Goa was, in Indian
terms, a small city. H.K. Naqui and Irfan Habib have estimated the populations of Agra, Delhi and Lahore at 500,000
each early in the seventeenth century, and several other Mughal cities - Surat, Ahmadabad, Patna - contained at least
several hundred thousands each. European cities were much
smaller: around 1600 Naples was counting 200,000 inhabitants, Rome 110,000, London 170,000, Madrid 600,00, and
Lisbon in 1629 110,000.[14] One cannot regard these figures as
exact; nevertheless, it is clear that comparatively Goa was
only a small city. Of more interest and significance was the

change in the religious affiliation of the population. The Muslim ruling elite was replaced by a Christian one. Although there continued to be some Muslims in the city, among the general population, while Hindu numbers remained large, Christians made up an increasing proportion of the total over the course of the century.

Was it, however, a particularly distinctive or wealthy city? Physically it seems to have been of the same type as any other Indian (or medieval European) city, with bazars, quarters, a fort and a wall, and (with one exception, the Rua Direita) narrow winding streets.[15] Massive buildings devoted to the religion of the rulers dominated all else, just as did *jama masjids* in the Mughal empire and temples in South India. One should recall, however, that most of the colossal edifices that we see in Old Goa today are of the seventeenth-century: sixteenth-century Goan churches were comparatively humble.

This was, however, a "European" city ruled by Europeans; was the population of Goa then ethnically very distinctive? Obviously one can say nothing very definite here, but the data quoted earlier point to a comparatively small "pure European" component in the population of the city, while the countryside of course was almost totally Indian. Contemporary descriptions, notably those of Linschoten and Pyrard de Laval, give an overwhelming impression of an Indian city, with a small Portuguese population superimposed. Even this "Portuguese" population was, in racial terms, often more Indian than European, as again Linschoten noted. Nevertheless, the Portuguese stressed fairness of skin as an important part of female beauty. Albuquerque married his soldiers to "fair" Muslim women. Xavier, while urging the *casados* (settled Portuguese and *mestiços*) to marry their local concubines, drew the firmest of colour lines. "When the concubine was dark in colour and ugly featured, he employed all his eloquence to separate his host from her. He was even ready, if necessary, to find for him a more suitable mate."[16] Similarly, the most feared enemies of the Portuguese were the Rumes (Turks), the feared "white men" who fought so bravely and whose hostile presence in Goa was one motive for Albuquerque's decision to attack the town in 1510.

Thus most Portuguese saw "white" skin as preferable for both love and war. Yet many of them also seem to have had a passion for African women, nearly all of them slaves, while others had to make do with darker skinned Indians or *mestiças*. Hence Linschoten's comment quoted at the beginning of this paper. In this preference for fair women the Portuguese again were not unique. The Mughal elite stressed the desirability of a "wheat-coloured" complexion (as do marriage advertisements in the Indian press today). In both Goa and the Mughal empire the political elite tended to be fairer than the bulk of the population, but the latter were indistinguishable one from the other, regardless of whether ruled by Mughals or Portuguese.

Leaving behind the somewhat profitless matter of skin colour, what can be said of religious affiliation? Here we apparently have a major change during the sixteenth century. Religion, politics and trade were inextricably mixed right from the start of Portuguese expansion. As King Manuel wrote to the King and Queen of Castile in 1499 after da Gama's return, "for our forebears the basic principle of this enterprise was always the service of God our Lord and our own profit."[17] The effort to win converts, and to find existing Christian communities in Asia, was important right from 1498, though the conversion drive was more active from the 1540s as the Jesuits and the Counter Reformation reached Goa. In the 1540s, 300 temples were destroyed in each of Goa's three *talukas*. A series of ecclesiastical councils from 1567 laid down apparently rigid discrimination against Hindu weddings, cremations, and other ceremonies. Hindu orphans were forcibly converted, and many Brahmins fled away from Portuguese territory. In 1561 the Portuguese obtained a purported tooth of the Buddha from Ceylon. The King of Pegu offered up to 400,000 cruzados for it, and other inducements. But the Archbishop prevailed on the Viceroy, D. Constantino de Bragança (Boxer's "priest-ridden bigot" *par excellence*) and this symbol of idolatry was ground up and cast into the sea.[18] Such accounts of intolerance, bigotry, and forced conversions could be endlessly multiplied, and ostensibly these point to a major change in Goa in the sixteenth century.

Yet the reality was a little different. It may be true that the city of Goa by 1600 was about two-thirds Christian, yet one estimate claims a total Christian population in all Goa at 1600 of only about 50,000, or about 20 percent of the total.[19] Even if this is too low, the fact is that Christians were in a decisive minority.[20] As to the intolerance, this seems to have been more theory than practice. Linschoten noted how the numerous spice and grocery shops of the city were usually owned by brahmins, "which serve likewise for Priests and Indolatrous Ministers."[21] At the end of the century another traveller described a phenomenon often observed in Gujarat in the next century. Referring to Jains, he said that "in Goa I have seen them ransom from the hands of Portuguese boys birds, dogs, and cats that the boys, so as to extract money from them, had pretended to want to kill."[22] Such observations hardly fit with the fulminations of the Ecclesiastical Councils; rather they point to tolerance or laxness on the part of the Portuguese authtoties. More generally, Linschoten, describing the situation forty years after the arrival of the Church Militant, tells us what the real situation in Goa was:

"(The Portuguese) dwell in the towne among all sorts of nations, as Indians, Heathens, Moores, Iewes, Armenians, Gusarates, Benians, Bramenes, and of all Indian nations and people, which doe all dwell and traficke therein, everie man holding his owne religion, without constrayning any man to doe against his consciensce, only touching their ceremonies of burning the dead, and the living, of marrying and other superstitions and develish inventions, they are forbidden by the Archbishop to use them openly, or in the Island, but they may freelie use them upon the firme land, and secretly in their houses..." [23]

Here, rather than in the normative decrees, is to be found Goan reality in the sixteenth century.

Other particular aspects support this impression of slight social change resulting from the religious activities of the Portuguese. Consider, for example, the seminary set up in 1541 to train local clergy. At first sight an institution pointing to major social change, closer examination shows this to be less than important: the trainees became only secular, not regular, priests, and in any case the great majority of them were converted Brahmins. These men thus changed from being Hindu priests to being Catholic priests: their status position remained constant. Similarly, from the 1540s much land whose revenue had supported temples was now used for financing Christian institutions and the Orders.[24] But the sums involved were small, and the point in any case is surely that these lands continued to support religious activities: for their cultivators the move from Hindu to Christian can have made little difference.

We must consider the nature of the much-publicized conversions to Christianity. It is in no way to impugn the sincerity and fervour of Christianity in Goa either then or now to say that at least in the sixteenth century conversions, whether forced or not, were certainly done hastily and superficially. Even Mercês de Melo admits that many conversions were "much too hasty.... Anyone asking for Baptism was at once admitted, and once baptized was left very much to himself. The result was leakage and much ignorance in matters of religion."[25] According to both him and Fr. D'Costa this was a problem in the impulsive 1540s but from 1550 was remedied.[26] Yet in fact mass baptisms, preceded by little or no instruction and succeeded by no follow-up, continued. In twelve days in 1548, 912 people were baptized in only three of the parishes of the city of Goa. On 25 August 1559, after some persuasion, 450 people on Chorao Island suddenly decided to convert. They were baptized on the 29th. On Divar Island 1,535 people were baptized in three months. Even these feats appear minor when one considers Xavier's effort of baptizing over 10,000 villagers in Travancore in one month in 1544.[27]

The result, predictably enough, was less than "pure" Christian practice. Xavier's own biographer said that "The wives and male and female slaves of the casados were...often so ignorant of the faith that they lived almost like their Mohamedan or pagan relatives and neighbours and shared their superstitions."[28] Hindu processions continued despite prohibitions and Christians lent jewellery, finery and slaves to the participants, while Portuguese lent guns to fire salutes during the Muslim festival of Ramadan. No doubt Goan Christianity was fervent, and indeed the Church at this time stressed emotion and devotion over strict adherence to

norms. This was then for most a folk religion like any other, characterised by processions, festivals, fairs, plays,
dances, and attachment to such symbols as images, bells,
pictures and Crosses.[29] Caste, as we will see, continued to
be of crucial importance in social interaction. For Brahmin
become priest, let alone for Hindu peasant become Catholic
peasant, the transition, and the social dislocation, was minimal.

In several other areas Goa continued on as an Indian city, with the foreigners fitting in and doing very little to
modify existing patterns. Thus the Portuguese set aside fixed areas for various categories in the population -Muslims,
foreign Hindus, prostitutes - and similarly various occupational groups lived contiguously.[30] Such an arrangement was
of course familiar to the Portuguese from European practice,
and similarly to Indians, whose cities were also divided into quarters or occupationally-determined localities. In legal matters, the Portuguese were concerned at the propensity
to litigation of the local population, and appointed special
judges to try quickly minor cases without recourse to the
full panoply of Portuguese law. This however applied only to
the Christian minority: Hindus were left with their customary dispute-settling mechanisms.[31] The elite in Goa lived in
a very similar style to that of any elite in India at
the time, dressing ostentatiously in public, shielding themselves with umbrellas, accompanied by vast retinues of slaves and servants. Religious processions and festivals were
prominent and popular public events, whether for St. Catha-
rine's Day, or in other parts of India for Mohurram or Holi.
Even in the religious buildings one finds much interaction.
Church paintings were often done by Hindus, as were other
craft activities and later St. Francis Xavier's tomb. The
first thirteen of the famous portraits of the Viceroys, to
be seen today in the Archeological Museum in Old Goa, were
done by a Hindu.[32]

Social divisions were, of course, rigidly observed. Thus
the elite, especially those born in Portugal, shunned manual
labour as beneath their dignity, just as elites do everywhere. More important, a form of caste continued and continues
to be important in Goan society.[33] Generations after conversion, caste still determined many aspects of social beha-

viour: marriage, membership of Christian confraternities, acceptability for the priesthood, where one sat in church. Only in the taking of food was there some relaxation of the strict Hindu custom. Nor were even those born in Portugal really remote from the continuing system. Ribeiro quotes a distinguished Christian Brahmin saying "The Portuguese condemned the caste system, but they introduced one more into India."[34]

W.W. Hunter once noted, with typical Victorian aplomb, that "the Goanese became a byword as the type of an orientalised community, idle, haughty, and corrupt."[35] Leaving aside the racist overtones, it is true that a lack of differentiation between Portuguese and Indians can often be seen. Even a Viceroy and an Archbishop used Hindu doctors.[36] Linschoten and Pyard noted many aspects of this acculturation. Although bread was available, rice, eaten with the right hand, was the preferred food. In a clear continuance of caste pollution notions, Goans drank from a pot without letting it touch their mouths, and laughed at newly arrived Portuguese who had not yet mastered this difficult art. Goans chewed *pan*, rubbed themselves with "sweet sanders," drank *araq*, and washed frequently. All this, Linschoten pointed out, "they have learned and received of the Indian Heathens, which have had there costumes of long time."[37]

What of the exposure of Goans to a wider European world, and to the Portuguese language? As to the latter, certain Goans, by learning Portuguese early, became in demand as interpreters and go-betweens, and thus acquired or retained, wealth and position. The rural language however continued to be Konkani: only in later centuries were attempts made to spread Portuguese widely outside the cities. This language was thus in an analogous position to Persian in Muslim-ruled India at the same time.

As for the first point, it is tempting to see Goan isolation ended by its exposure to the Europe of the Renaissance, Reformation and Counter-Reformation. Here we must first make clear what "Goa" means, in other words we must again remember how remote Bardês and Salcette were in the sixteenth century, with few Portuguese there and the population still Hindu and little affected by Portuguese rule. Urban-rural, or Goa-hinterland, differences are well pointed up in the complaint of an official in 1566. He had complained of mal-administration in Goa, and for his pains was forced to flee the town and seek refuge "among the Hindus and lax Christians of Bardês."[38] Thus one can expect almost no "European impact" ouside of Goa city. But even here one may question the impact of these European intellectual trends. The Reformation was of course hardly allowed into Goa at all, while the Counter-Reformation, as seen in temple destruction, the Inquisition, and pressures to convert, was of dubious use or benefit. The impact of the Renaissance was more various. On the one hand one can see beneficial aspects of this broad intellectual movement in Goan church architecture, and in various literary works. The supreme manifestations are of course the works of Camoens and d'Orta, but the inquiring mind of a Renaissance man is also to be found in the navigational-geographic works of D. João de Castro. Yet one must set against these Castro's politico-military activities in the Gulf of Cambay in 1546-48, activities which can only be characterized as racist and barbarous.[39] But what then of that great disseminator of knowledge, the printing press? The first was introduced to Goa by the Jesuits in 1556, and was mostly used to spread a particular part of Renaissance knowledge, the Catholic faith. While it is true that one of the very first books printed in Goa was that great monument to Renaissance inquiry, Garcia d'Orta's *Colóquios dos simples e drogas* (1563), more typical was a virulent anti-Jewish tract published by the Archbishop in 1565.[40]

In any case, here and elsewhere it is a mistake to see pre-Portuguese Goa as static or isolated. On the contrary, it was a great trade centre and had contacts from this all around the vast and variegated Indian Ocean world. According to J.M. Richards it was also in the fifteenth century a great embarkation port for the *hajj*.[41] The point of course is that in the sixteenth century Goa was opened to different, but not necessarily more advanced, cultural influences: it had never been isolated.

With the conquest of 1510 Goa of course underwent a change of political control. Ostensibly this marks a major change. Goa's rulers changed from Indian Muslims to European Christians. From being a geographically isolated port city subject to an inland state it became the centre of a thalas-

socratic empire. Nevertheless, a consideration of two general points makes these changes appear rather less dramatic.
First, premodern states, whether Bijapur, Portugal or any
other, usuallly interfered very little in the everyday lives
of most of their subjects. Thus any change at the top political level made very little difference to the bulk of the
population: most of the data in this article support this
position.[42] Second, any upper level political authority is
going to be dependent for political effectiveness on the
help or at least acquiescence of local power figures. Thus
again continuity, rather than generic change, is ensured
despite the displacement of one ruling group (in this case
Bijapuri Muslims) by another (the Portuguese). Thus in the
actual conquest and early consolidation of Portuguese rule
in Goa a slightly dubious Hindu leader called Timmayya played an important role. Later other Hindus were of crucial
help to the Portuguese, so that Scammell's suggestion that
"the art of empire-building was to find the ally within"[43]
seems substantially correct.

On a more mundane level, we noted above the role of Lin-
goas, or interpreters of both language and custom.[44] Moving
up again to the top of the political system, it is a truism
that the Portuguese reserved to themselves the upper level
political positions, excluding as far as possible even In-
dian-born Portuguese, let alone mestiços. On ceremonial occasions, a notable one being the proclamation of Philip II
in 1581, only Portuguese took part.[45] Goa was subject to a
remote and foreign ruler who was so far away that local authorities had considerable autonomy. This, however, was also
the situation in the fifteenth century, even though the ruler was closer, in Vijayanagar or later Bijapur. Village administration was left strictly alone by the Portuguese. The
structure of government, with military, civil, legal and financial officials, was little different from common practice
in contemporary India. Nor apparently were the standards of
conduct of Portuguese officials very different from those
prevailing in the rest of the subcontinent. Artisan and
craft groups in Goa as elsewhere were governed by guild-like
organizations.

In two other related areas there seems to be more change.
The Municipal Council of Goa was, for India, a unique insti-

tution, and one whose decisions affected all levels of Goa's
population. At the least, it was more formalized than various caste or merchant organizations in Indian cities. Similarly, the Portuguese engaged in more public social service than did Indian ruling elites, whose charity was dispensed on a non-continuing, individual basis. The Misericórdia
of Goa, with its hospital and other benevolent activities,
has no exact equivalent in other parts of India.

The "Golden Goa" myth implies not only that Goa was a
large town, and a distinctively different one, but also that
it was remarkably wealthy. It is very difficult indeed to
test this claim quantitatively. No doubt in European terms
some Goans were fabulously wealthy, but there is an overrid-
ing impression that the Portuguese elite in Goa was considerably less rich than its Mughal equivalents. Given the sizes
of the two states, this is of course hardly surprising. Similarly, no Goan public building bears comparison with say
the Delhi and Agra fort complexes, or several of the great
Mughal tombs. We do have runs of figures for government revenues in Goa. These are worth at least a brief mention, but
it must be stressed that they give little impression of individual wealth. Sixteenth-century governments had rather
limited functions, with most areas of the economy being outside their control, or even cognizance. This said, what
sorts of revenues were available? Barros claimed that Bijapur got a revenue of 500,000 gold pardaos from the area of
Goa, or Rs: 9.00.000 This included Rs: 1.80.000 from Goa
itself, including taxes on the horse trade, Rs: 18.720 from
Ilhas, Rs: 3.960 from taxes on inland trade, and Rs 59.400
from other city taxes. The remaining Rs: 6.30.000 presumably
came from Bardês, Salcette, and other land.[46] Another account, of Goa city's rendas in the early 1540s, claimed that
Bijapur made Rs: 1.47.600 from a specified list of contracts, while the Portuguese now got about Rs: 18.000 only
from these.[47] A list of 1540 gives Goa's total revenue as a
little under Rs: 2.00.000, of which Rs: 1.51.200, or 75 percent, came from the horse trade alone.[48] Five years later we
have a total figure of Rs: 3.17.000, Rs: 1.47.000 of it from
the horse trade.[49] The 1545 figures exclude Bardês and Salcette, which after their conquest in 1543 raised Rs: 75.000
extra. It may be noted that the figures for horses are com-

parable, but the totals are not: I suspect that customs revenue, Rs: 1.05.750 in 1545, was excluded from the total given for 1540.

Later figures are roughly comparable. Goa's total revenue in 1586-87, by which time Golden Goa was meant to be at its height, was put at about Rs: 4.50.000.[50] In 1595 Goa alone contributed Rs: 4.45.000, while Bardês and Salcette together added another Rs: 1.23.000.[51] Around 1600 Goa's total revenue was claimed to be some Rs: 6.10.000.[52] The main changes in these figures reflect Goa's changing trade fortunes. Earlier the horse trade contributed an absolute majority of total revenue, while by 1586-87 the customs house, boosted by Goa's greatly expanded country trade, gave over half of total receipts.

Finally, we must remember that Goa was capital of a large seaborne empire, and, for example, received up to Rs: 2.00.000 a year in profits from Diu and Ormuz.[53] We do have figures for the total accounts of Portuguese Asia late in the sixteenth century, any profits presumably going to Goa. In 1586-87 the excess of receipts over expenses was close to Rs: 2.00.000.[54] while around 1600 it was claimed to be Rs: 6.00.000.[55]

What can we conclude from all this? If we accept a revenue of Rs: 9.00.000 under Bijapur, then under the Portuguese we have about Rs: 6.92.000 in 1545, Rs: 7.50.000 in 1586-87, and Rs: 9.10.000 around 1600, in all cases adding in Rs: 3.00.000 as profits from the rest of the empire.[56] The figures are certainly rough enough, but one conclusion can safely be ventured: Goa's government revenue under the Portuguese was not noticeably different from that realised by Bijapur, and indeed was probably smaller. This in turn presumably says something about just how wealthy Goa was, in Indian terms, in the sixteenth century.

We have noted that Bardês and Salcette continued throughout the sixteenth century to be somewhat remote and little affected by the Portuguese. They were little needed, except as a mission field, for the Portuguese were able to live from sea trade. Only as this declined under Dutch attack did presure on Goa's land increase from both casados and the Orders. Just after the conquest Albuquerque issued orders that local land holders and village authorities were not to be

disturbed - indeed, he remitted one-third of their land revenue. Muslim land, apparently a small amount, was confiscated in 1519, but generally the Portuguese continued a hands-
off policy, and this was extended to Bardês and Salcette
when these two *talukas* were finally acquired in 1543. This
policy was codified in Mexia's famous Charter of 1526,[57]
which aimed to preserve what Mexia took to be pre-Portuguese
practice. Decisions continued to be made by the *gancars* within the villages, or in *taluka*-wide assemblies of village
representatives. In Bardês and Salcette in the sixteenth
century, the Portuguese population was scanty indeed. It
could include soldiers in their forts and perhaps a few *casados* in the several small towns, but the main European representative was the parish priest: in Bardês a Franciscan,
and in Salcette a Jesuit. Sometimes these same priests had
been granted, in return for a quit rent (*aforamento*), rights
over particular villages. The main benefit was the right to
collect tribute from the villages concerned. This, of course, is not a matter of a transfer of land ownership; village rights and customs were not affected. The same applies
to the lands which had supported Hindu temples which were,
as already noted, transferred to support Christian activities. New people were skimming off the tribute, but rural
society was little affected. The situation certainly changed
in the seventeenth century for the reasons noted above: thus
in 1628 the King forbade Portuguese obtaining *gancar* rights
in Goa;[58] one assumes some Portuguese had started to do this
as their trade by sea declined.

In the sixteenth century Portugal's main impact on Goan
rural society was, first, the beginning of the conversion
drive, by no means completely successsful at the year 1600,
and second, the introduction of new flora, many of which today are firmly part of Goa. The list includes tobacco, pineapples, papaya, cashews, and red peppers.[59] These crops acculturated quickly; the same can be said of improved technology introduced by the Portuguese. Their ships and cannon
were in some respects better than those available in Asia
though not to a large degree. Whatever superiority they
had here was soon lost as skilled Asian craftsmen, sometimes
aided by "renegade" Europeans, copied Portuguese techni-

ques. For that matter, the Portuguese often used local ships
and guns.[60]

Nor does it appear that the Portuguese made large amounts
of money from the *foros*, or land revenue, paid by Goa's villages. Under Bijapur thirty villages in Tissuari, or Goa Island, paid Rs: 11.7000, while Divar, Chorao, and Jua Islands
paid Rs: 7.020.[61] In 1586-87 the Portuguese reveived Rs11.
550 and Rs: 5.370 respectively.[62] Bardês and Salcette, being
larger, contributed more: Rs: 1.02.600 in 1586-87, about
two-thirds of this coming from Salcette.[63] The overall impression is of continuity and very little Portuguese impact.

This in fact holds true for the total Portuguese impact
on Goa's economy. Goa had been an important trade centre in
the fifteenth century, and continued to be so in the sixteenth. The volume of trade probably increased in the second half of the century, but, taking into account price rises, not by a really huge amount. The Portuguese lived by
this trade, as did other foreigners in Goa, especially Hindus and Jains from Gujarat. Retail trade, and artisan activities, continued to be handled by local people, whether
Hindu or Christian.[64] Goa's trade with the interior seems to
have decreased, but in any case the port city had always
lived as an entrepot, not as an outlet for local products.
Apparently the only Goan products to be exported were coconuts, areca, and salt. Goa developed an export capacity only
with the iron ore mining boom of the twentieth century. The
major change in Goa's trade in the sixteenth century was a
political one: her fifteenth-century trade had been acquired
freely, while under the Portuguese she became the centre of
their system of compulsion and forced trade.

As will be clear from all the above, the Portuguese impact on Goa (let alone on the rest of Asia) was minimal. In
many activities they acculturated and were merged into Indian life, while in other areas they deliberately kept
aloof. Yet one does not want to go on from this to a Giberto
Freyre style paeon to cordial race relations and general
harmony based on sexual interaction, a myth which Scammell
at times comes close to reinforcing.[65] As C.R. Boxer has so
often reminded us, the Portuguese did have very definite
aims and prejudices, designed in sum to make a major impact
on Indian society: one thinks of trade control, of the In-

quistion, of forced conversions, of denial of opportunity to Indian priests, of virulent anti-Muslim feeling and actions. An obvious solution to this apparent contradiction is to say that the Portuguese were not very efficient: their aims may have been large but their ability to achieve them was limited.

Such an argument has frequently been made, but I think one can go beyond this. In several areas the Portuguese were really not trying to affect generic change: rather, whether tacitly or not, they were simply altering or redirecting existing patterns. This certainly applies to their trade control system, as has often been noted, but if our argument above about Goan Christianity is accepted, then it is relevant here also. Medieval Hindu devotionalism was diverted into an initially rather superficial Catholicism which used many of the same folk techniques, and which was propagated by a Church which at this time stressed emotion and passion over strict formal adherence to dogma. There was also a negative factor which contributed to the lack of impact. Previously isolated areas like South America and the Pacific Islands were hit by European diseases. This of course did not apply to Goa, or indeed Asia generally.

One final and even more general point may be made to explain this lack of impact. Western Europe in the sixteenth century was at the beginning of scientific and agricultural revolutions - Marshall Hodgson's "technicalistic" revolution [66] - which were to transform relations between Europe and Asia. Asian countries stood still or even declined. This relative shift was plain to see in the second half of the eighteenth century in India. Before this, while in Europe the seeds of change certainly were planted, only later did they begin to sprout. Meanwhile the relative positions were much more equal. Historians have often looked to military conquest to explain western impact, but in a more general sense it seems that it was rather this relative shift which was crucial. While the balance was roughly equal, as applies to the overtly imperialistic Portuguese in the sixteenth century and to the trading Dutch and English in the seventeenth, the impact of Europe was minimal, for they were, like Indians at the same time, essentially "preindustrial," in the sense in which this term has been used recently by Fernand Braudel in

Civilization and Capitalism. Hence their lack of a decisive impact on Goa. It was not so much a case of the Portuguese inability to put into effect major social change, as one of there being little qualitative difference between the society they represented and implanted, and the one already in existence in Goa when they arrived.

NOTES

* This article was prepared for the Admiral A. Teixeira da Mota memorial volume and is reprinted through the kindness of Prof. Luís de Albuquerque, its editor.

1. J.M. Richards, *Goa* (Delhi, 1982), p. 131.
2. J.H. van Linschoten, *The Voyage of J.H. van Linschoten to the East Indies*, 2 vols (London, 1885), I, 184.
3. G.V. Scammell, *The World Encompassed* (London, 1981), p. 243.
4. Elaine Sanceau, *Knight of the Renaissance: D. João de Castro* (London, 1949), p. 59.
5. See, for example, C.R. Boxer, *The Portuguese Seaborne Empire* (London, 1969), and my *Merchants and Rulers in Gujarat* (Berkeley, 1976), and *Coastal Western India* (New Delhi, 1981).
6. Ashin Das Gupta and M.N. Pearson (eds), *India and the Indian Ocean, 1500-1800.* Forthcoming.
7. See João Manuel Pacheco de Figueiredo, 'Goa Pré-Portuguesa', *Studia* 12, 13-14 (1963, 1964); P.S.S. Pissurlencar, *Goa Pré-Portuguesa através dos Escritores Lusitános dos séculos XVI e XVII* (Bastorá, 1962).
8. B.S. Shastry, *Studies in Indo-Portuguese History* (Bangalore, 1981), p. 123. B.G. D'Souza says from one-sixth to one-quarter: *Goan Society in Transition* (Bombay, 1975), pp. 25-26. See also T.R. de Souza, *Medieval Goa* (New Delhi, 1979), p. 78; B.H. Baden-Powell, "The Villages of Goa in the Early Sixteenth Century", *Journal of the Royal Asiatic Society*, 1900, pp. 275-7, 285; a letter

from Albuquerque to the King, quoted in A.B. de Bragança Pereira, *História Administratíva da India Portuguesa* (Bastorá, n.d.), p. 127.

9. T.R. de Souza, *Medieval Goa*, p. 112; cf. Linschoten, I, 179.

10. C.R. Boxer, *Portuguese Society in the Tropics* (Madison, 1965), pp. 28-29.

11. Georg Schurhammer, *Francis Xavier, His Life, His Times*, *vol. II. India, 1541-1545* (Rome, 1977), pp. 180-1.

12. T.R. de Souza, *Medieval Goa*, p. 115; Scammell, p. 242.

13. T.R. de Souza, "Glimpses of Hindu Dominance of Goan Economy in the 17th Century", *Indica* XII (1975), pp. 29-30.

14. H.K. Naqui, *Urban Centres and Industries in Upper India 1556-1803* (New York, 1968), pp. 81-82; K.S. Lal, *Growth of the Muslim Population on Medieval India (A. D. 1000-1800)* (Delhi, 1973), pp. 61-62, 218-20; Irfan Habib in *Cambridge Economic History of India* (Cambridge, 1982), pp. 170-1.

15. For scenes and views of the city, see the Dutch edition of Linschoten, 3 vols (s'Gravenhage, 1955-57), and Schurhammer, p. 147 for a city plan, and pp. 148-281 for an extended description of the city in the 1540s.

16. Schurhammer, p. 228.

17. Arquívo nacional da Torre do Tombo, Lisbon ('ANTT'), "Colecçao de São Vicente", III, ƒ.513. It should be noted that this phrase was something of a formula. Portuguese Kings justified most activities as being *"muito a serviço de Deus e ao meu e aproveitamento da minha terra"*.

18. Diogo do Couto, *Da Asia*, 15 vols (Lisbon, 1778-88), VII, ix, 17.

19. De Souza, *Medieval Goa*, p. 115; Boxer, *Seaborne Empire*, p. 79.

20. See de Souza, "Hindu Dominance", *Passim;* this seems to show Boxer's 50.000 to be too low, and also points to massive conversions in the seventeenth century.

21. Linschoten, I, 229-30.

22. Francisco Carletti, *My Voyage around the World* (London, 1964), p. 204.

23. Linschoten, I, 181-2.

VII

55

24. De Souza, *Medieval Goa*, pp. 93-94; Carlos Mercês de Melo, *The Recruitment and Formation of the Native Clergy in India (16th-19th Century): An Historico-Canonical Study* (Lisbon, 1955), p. 86.
25. Mercês de Melo, pp. 21-22.
26. *Ibid.*, pp. 22-23. 26; Anthony D'Costa. *The Cristianization of the Goa Islands* (Bombay, 1965), pp. 173-4.
27. Schurhammer, pp. 470-1; D'Costa, pp. 49, 97-99, 100, and see generally H. Heras, *The Conversion Policy of the Jesuits in India* (Bombay, 1933).
28. Schurhammer, p. 213.
29. See D'Costa, pp. 182-7; C.R. Boxer, *Race Relations in the Portuguese Colonial Empire, 1415-1825* (Oxford, 1963), p. 124; J.B. Harrison, "The Portuguese", in A.L. Basham, ed., *A Cultural History of India* (Oxford, 1975), pp. 346-7.
30. J.H. da Cunha Rivara, ed., *Archivo Português Oriental*, 6 vols (Nova Goa, 1857-77), III, 412-3. IV, 23, 52.
31. Historical Archives of Goa ("HAG"), "Livro Verde", I, ff. 71-73r; "Provisões a favor da Cristandade", ff. 75r-76, 99r-100.
32. Pissurlencar, pp. 42-43; see generally Mulk Raj Anand et al., *Golden Goa* (Bombay, 1980), for Indo-Portuguese interaction in architecture and decoration.
33. Richards, *Goa*, p. 27; B.G. D'Souza, pp. 150, 242-55; Boxer, *Race Relations*, pp. 75-76; Orlando Ribeiro, "Originalidade de Goa", III Coloquio Internacional de Estudos Luso-Brasileiros, *Actas*, I (Lisbon, 1957), pp. 175-7.
34. Ribeiro, p. 177.
35. W.W. Hunter, *A History of British India*, vol. I (London, 1899), p. 157.
36. Pissurlencar, pp. 42-43.
37. Linschoten, I, 207-8, 212-3; Francois Pyrard de Laval, *The Voyage of Francois Pyrard de Laval*, 2 vols (London, 1887-90), II, *passim*.
38. ANTT, "Corpo Chronologico", 1-108-12.
39. Sanceau, *Knight of the Renaissance*: see also *Merchants and Rulers in Gujarat*, pp. 95-96.
40. C.R. Boxer, *The Church Militant and Iberian Expansion, 1440-1770* (Baltimore, 1978), pp. 41, 45.

41. Richards, p. 18; I have been unable to verify this yet.
42. This claim is spelt out in more detail in my *Merchants and Rulers in Gujarat*, especially chapters 5 and 6, and in my "Pre-Modern Muslim Political Systems," *Journal of the American Oriental Society*, CII (1982). If one were to extend this argument to later times, one could say that major change occurred in Goa (as a result of a change in the aspirations and nature of the ruling group) only under Pombal, or perhaps even not until the Indian conquest of 1961.
43. For Timmayya see B.S. Shastry, pp. 92-127; G.V. Scammell, "Indigenous Assistance in the Establishment of Portuguese Power in the Indian Ocean", John Correia-Alfonso, ed., *Indo-Portuguese History: Sources and Problems* (Bombay, 1981), p. 172.
44. See A.R. Disney, "The Portuguese Empire in India, c. 1550-1650", in Correia-Alfonso, ed., p. 156.
45. Couto, X, i. 4.
46. João de Barros, *Asia.* 4 vols (Lisbon, 1945-46), II, p. 2, *The Commentaries of the Great Alfonso Dalbuquerque*, 4 vols (London, 1875-84), II, 95, claims a revenue of only 200,000 pardaos. The sources on which the following paragraphs are based use several different monetary units. To facilitate comparisons I needed a common unit; finally I decided on standard Mughal rupees, and their division into lakhs (100,000) and crores (10,000,000). I used the following conversion ratios: one rupee = 200 reis; one xerafim = 300 reis; one pardao d'ouro = 360 reis; one pardao em tangas = 300 reis; one cruzado = 400 reis. My readers will be as aware as I am of how arbitrary at times this is.
47. ANTT, "Cartas de Vice Reis", no. 134; see also another, largely illegible, list in ANTT, "Corpo Chronológico", 3-10-75.
48. *As Gavetas da Torre do Tombo*, 10 vols (Lisbon, 1960-74), V, 244-248.
49. *Ibid.*, III, 213. The scribe noted resignedly at the end of this account "This is what Goa raised last year, leaving aside what the officials stole".
50. Arquívo Histórico Ultramarino, Lisbon ("AHU"), Codice 500, *passim.*

51. F. Paes, "Goa," *O Oriente Português*, no. 66, p. 97.
52. Luis de Figueiredo Falcão, *Livro em que se contém toda a Fazenda e real património dos Reinos de Portugal, India e Ilhas adjacentes* (Lisbon, 1859), pp. 75-78.
53. Pearson, *Merchants and Rulers*, pp. 97, 109.
54. AHU, Codice 500, *passim*.
55. Figueiredo Falcão, *loc cit*.
56. This apparent increase was no doubty largely vitiated by the price rise of the sixteenth century, felt in coastal India as much as in Europe. See V.M. Godinho, *Ensaios*, II (Lisbon, 1968), pp. 157-74.
57. See de Souza, *Medieval Goa*, pp. 64-65; D'Costa, pp. 20-25; Baden-Powell, pp. 261-91.
58. HAG, '*Livro Verde*', I, f. 225; cf. prices paid by the Convent of Santa Monica for three villages in Bassein in ANTT, *Documentos Remetídos da India*, XVI, ff. 164-5.
59. Harrison in Basham, p. 341.
60. Scammell, *World Encompassed*, p. 265; see also C.R. Boxer, "Asian Potentates and European Artillery in the 16th-18th Centuries", *Journal of the Malay Branch of the Royal Asiatic Society*, XXXVIII (1965).
61. Barros, II, v, 2.
62. AHU, Codice 500, *passim*, and almost exactly the same figures for 1600 in Figueiredo Falcão, pp. 75-78, and for the mid 1620s in AHU, Codice 219.
63. Paes, p. 97; AHU, Codice 500, *passim*.
64. On this see *Coastal Western India*, chapters 4 and 5.
65. For another article stressing mutual influence and synthesis, see Mariano José Dias, "The Hindu-Christian Society of Goa", *Indica*, XVII (1980), pp. 109-16.
66. See Marshall Hodgson, *The Venture of Islam* (Chicago, 1974, 3 vols) and Immanuel Wallerstein, *The Modern World-System: Capitalist Agriculture and the Origins of the European World-Economy in the Sixteenth Century* (New York, 1974).

VIII

Conversions in South-east Asia: Evidence from the Portuguese Records

Studies of conversion and proselytization in South-east Asia in the sixteenth and seventeenth centuries have usually relied on fragmentary sources in local languages, and on occasional references in Dutch and English accounts. An important source which has been strangely neglected is the accounts of Christian missionaries, both Portuguese and Spanish, belonging to various religious orders. John Villiers, writing on a subject rather different from mine, and with reference only to the Jesuits, recently put this matter well when he wrote:

Because the Jesuits were often in close touch with local rulers and notables, whether or not they succeeded in converting them to Christianity, and because they lived among their subjects for long periods, depending on them for the necessities of life and sharing their hardships, their letters and reports often show a deeper understanding of the social, economic and political conditions of the indigenous societies and, one suspects, give a more accurate and measured account of events and personalities than do the official chroniclers and historians of the time.[1]

It is true that Christian records cannot be used in isolation. To write this article I also used the standard Portuguese secular chronicles, and other sources. Yet the missionary records are, as I hope this article will make clear, of particular interest for several reasons. First, the Christian missionaries were themselves professional proselytizers, trained specifically for this purpose and engaging in this activity on a full-time basis. As such, their comments on their rivals, that is, Muslim religious specialists, are of particular interest; it is a matter of one team of experts describing, and evaluating, the success of the competition. The records of the Dutch and English are different and inferior, for they are nearly always written by lay people who had no particular interest in religion. This is not to say, however, that the Catholic evaluation of their rivals was a friendly one; of course it was not. The standard phrases include 'the accursed sect of Muhammad',· and the 'false law of Muhammad'. Nevertheless, there is a sense of lingering respect in the Christian accounts, as well there might be, for, as we know,

---

[1] John Villiers, 'Las Yslas de Esperar en Dios: The Jesuit Mission in Moro, 1546–1571', *Modern Asian Studies*, 22, no. 3 (1988), 593.

54

many more people in island South-east Asia converted to Islam than to Christianity, as indeed is also the case in Africa today. This is not to say that these records are 'objective'. Far from it; the authors were obviously committed Christians, and also the letters were written for two quite worldly purposes: to recruit more missionaries in Europe, and to encourage the faithful to contribute to the missions.

This then leads to the second general point, which is that the theme in this documentation is very much one of competition. It is no flight of fancy to talk of a race between the Cross and the Crescent, but one where the Cross was handicapped by a late start. Both groups of religious specialists found much of the area to be a *tabula rasa* in religious terms, and realized that the first exemplars of a more sophisticated and all-encompassing religion to reach a particular area had an excellent chance of making mass conversions. The example of the Philippines is well known. Here, the present division between Christianity and Islam is a result of events in the sixteenth century. There is little doubt that had the Spanish arrived a few decades later than 1565, they would have found the whole area firmly Muslim; conversely, had they arrived a century earlier, Mindanao and possibly even the Sulu islands (where Islam had arrived perhaps late in the fifteenth century), as well as the rest of the Philippines, would probably be Catholic today. We will note below several other examples of these 'races' between the two great traditions of Islam and Christianity.

Two other general points about the data which follows can be made. We mostly have evidence of the *process* of conversion rather than actual dates and specific numbers of converts. As we would expect, the Muslim proselytizers succeeded in part because they did not press too hard, but rather were prepared to tolerate 'deviations', and a rather syncretic form of Islam. Again, this is not in any way unusual, and nor was this tolerance to be seen only in those who converted to Islam. Christianity, as found in the Spanish Philippines and in Portuguese Goa, was and is basically syncretic, including many pre-Christian practices and beliefs under a veneer of great tradition Catholicism which at times is superficial in the extreme. A final advantage of these Christian records is that, thanks to the labours of generations of clerical historians and archivists, especially members of the Society of Jesus, most of them are published, though not translated.

On the whole matter of religious change, the influential theory of Robin Horton, who has studied conversions in Africa, is important. He finds a two-tier cosmology, and describes how the focus of many people shifts from the lower or second tier (that of lesser spirits) to the higher or first (that of the supreme being). This shift in focus and emphasis occurs because the latter, higher, level was better able to help people cope with a wider world, and with more specific social changes and disruption. The task for the missionary was to get such people to identify the higher level of their cosmology with the missionary's own supreme being, be it Allah or God.[2] In the South-east Asian context, it seems that the pre-Muslim and Christian social context included some areas which were close to vacuums; in other words, only the lower tier was present. Religious practice in many parts of the Philippines seems to have been still basically animist, with only a very vague notion of any supreme being. In other areas of island South-east Asia, the missionaries, whether Muslim or Christian, were operating in a social context of a population which owed partial allegiance to rather corrupt forms of Buddhism or Hinduism. Thus, following Horton, in remote parts of the Philippines and some other areas, conversion implied the *creation* of an upper tier in the cosmology, while in most places the task was to replace not very well entrenched notions of some ultimate being with their much firmer concepts of either God or Allah. In both cases, however, the lower tier of lesser spirits continued to be important, to varying degrees, in the lives of the converts.

A. H. Johns has given us an excellent general statement about conversions to Islam in South-east Asia. He writes:

Islam came to Southeast Asia in the pre-Indonesia period. The story of its coming is a very complex one, and its records are fragmentary, scattered among different regions, each with its own history and character. It is a region full of stops and starts, periods of confusion and new beginnings.

Islam makes its début in the port cities of the island archipelago, with their communities having their roots in the hinterland, but looking out to and across the sea. Port cities have been part of the life of the region for at least two thousand years. Their rise and fall, their rivalries, their disappearance from one point and re-appearance at another is one of the fascinations of Southeast Asian history. This being so, the beginnings of Islam must be seen in the same way. We take it as axiomatic, then, that there is no room for a single big-bang explanation that sees Islam as a fall-out from events at a single place or in a single period, no bold generalisation such as 'Java was converted from Malacca' that can provide a key to the problem. Instead we must look for a variety of starting points and numerous modalities for its diffusion, and above all realise that we are studying a process that waxed and waned, and took its strength from an irregular pattern of pulses over the centuries, wherever these were articulated: whether Haru Pidir, Pasai, Malacca, Acheh, Banten, Tuban or Makassar.

Having stated this general principle however, it is an abnegation of responsibility not to recognise the limits of such a statement, for historical processes depend in large measure on the drive of individuals, whether in their time they are accounted as successes or failures. In the history of Islam as in that of Christianity, one must see as crucial to the growth and stature of the religion, men aglow with the love of learning and the desire for God. It is this basic yearning which lies at the heart of every intellectual and spiritual movement within Islam wherever it occurs and throughout its history. Every event and every movement in one place has a counterpart and relevance to events, ideas, and

---

[2] See Robin Horton, 'African Conversions', *Africa*, 41, no. 1 (1971), 85–108, and 'On the Rationality of Conversion', *Africa*, 45, no. 3 (1975), 219–35, and no. 4 (1975), 373–99. My thanks go to Geoff Oddie for bringing the work of Horton to my attention. For excellent comparative and theoretical discussions of conversions to Islam in India, see Richard M. Eaton, 'Approaches to the Study of Conversion to Islam in India', in *Approaches to Islam in Religious Studies*, edited by Richard C. Martin (Tucson, 1985), pp. 106–23, and P. Hardy, 'Modern European and Muslim Explanations of Conversions to Islam in South Asia: A Preliminary Survey of the Literature', in *Conversion to Islam*, edited by Nehemia Levtzion (New York, 1979), pp. 68–99.

56

individuals in another. The individual is central. For the love of learning and the desire for God can only be recognised and experienced in individuals.[3]

What our Christian sources are describing is the continuing major Islamic 'push' for conversions. As is well known, Islam began to make converts in South-east Asia from the late thirteenth century (pride of place is usually given to Samudra in north Sumatra), and in this process *sufis*, often affiliated with and travelling with groups of Muslim merchants, were the spearhead of the effort; this is not to say that coercion did not also occur at times. Conversions *en masse* happened mostly from the later fourteenth century; in the second half of this century east Java was won over. Islamic states appeared during the fourteenth century, first in north Sumatra and then in coastal Java. From the mid-fifteenth century Melaka was the focus of the conversion effort. When the Portuguese arrived in the area, Islam was well entrenched in coastal, central and east Java, the Malay peninsula, the southern Philippines, and Sumatra. In these areas, then, the Christians were too late to hope for success. Converts to Islam were beginning to be made in Maluku, but in general Indonesia east of Java was still open. This, then, was the area where Muslim and Portuguese missionaries came into conflict and competition.[4]

Neither Islam nor Christianity were indigenous to South-east Asia. Ties with the centre, respectively Mecca and Rome, were important for both,[5] and as has been noted recently in the case of Islam, this contact was mediated through the port cities: 'The city in Southeast Asia furnished the crucial link

[3] A. H. Johns, 'Friends in Grace: Ibrahim al-Kurani and 'Abd al-Ra'uf al-Singkeli', in *Spectrum: Essays Presented to Sutan Takdir Alisjahbana on his Seventieth Birthday*, edited by S. Udin (Jakarta, 1978), pp. 470–71.

[4] The classic account of all this is in B. Schrieke, *Indonesian Sociological Studies* (The Hague, 1955–57), 2 vols. The best modern overviews are by Anthony Reid, 'The Islamization of Southeast Asia', in *Historia: Essays in Commemoration of the 25th Anniversary of the Department of History, University of Malaya*, edited by Muhammad Abu Bakar et al. (Kuala Lumpur, 1984), pp. 13–33, which is excellent on disentangling motivations; M. C. Ricklefs, *A History of Modern Indonesia* (London, 1981), pp. 3–13; by the same author, specifically on Java, 'Six Centuries of Islamization in Java', in *Conversion to Islam*, edited by Levtzion, pp. 100–28; and A. H. Johns, 'Islam in Southeast Asia: Reflections and New Directions', *Indonesia*, 19 (1975), 33–56. Johns has argued for the important role of *sufis*: see, for example, 'Sufism as a Category in Indonesian Literature and History', *Journal of Southeast Asian History*, 2, no. 2 (1961), 10–23. Several other studies are overly concerned with the rather unimportant questions of when Islam first arrived, and where did the missionaries come from: see, for example, G. W. J. Drewes, 'New Light on the Coming of Islam to Indonesia?', *Bijdragen tot de Taal-, Land-, en Volkenkunde van Nederlandsch-Indie*, 124 (1968), 433–59; K. R. Hall, 'The Coming of Islam to the Archipelago: A Reassessment', in *Economic Change and Social Interaction in Southeast Asia*, edited by Karl L. Hutterer (Ann Arbor, 1977), pp. 213–31; G. R. Tibbetts, 'Early Muslim Traders in Southeast Asia', *Journal of the Malay Branch of the Royal Asiatic Society*, 30, no. 1 (1957). My thanks go to Ben Kiernan for help with these references.

[5] It is worth stressing these ties, as some scholars have seen Indonesian Islam as isolated until the nineteenth century. Paul Toomey in a recent major work of reference claims, quite erroneously, that 'the opening of sea travel in the nineteenth century broke down the isolation of Indonesian Muslims from the sources of their tradition in the Middle East. Pilgrims who returned to Java and established Qur'anic schools there are credited with strengthening orthodox Islam in that country', in *Encyclopedia of Asian History*, edited by Ainslie T. Embree (New York, 1988), 4 vols, III, 257, *s.v.* 'Pilgrimage'.

between international Islam and the local Muslim community whose bonds stretched far into the rural interior.'[6] We have evidence of quite extensive contact with Mecca in the sixteenth and seventeenth centuries, and indeed with other centres of Islamic power.[7] In 1561 a Portuguese fleet saw a great ship, which they considered to be as large and well-equipped as the huge *naus* they themselves used on the Lisbon–Goa *carreira*. It was based at Aceh and bound for the Red Sea, but had stopped in Tenassarim. On board were 'over a million in gold', fifty bronze artillery pieces, five hundred men-at-arms, and a palanquin that the king of Aceh was sending to the Sultan of Turkey ('o Turco') which was decorated with gold and precious stones worth two hundred thousand *cruzados*.[8] Political ties between these two Islamic powers of course continued and grew during this century.[9] Kathirithamby-Wells makes a distinction between political and military ties between Aceh and the Middle East, and the links Banten maintained with Mecca; these were for religious guidance and patronage. In 1638 the title of sultan was bestowed on the ruler of Banten, and his son twice made the *hajj*.[10] In 1581 the Portuguese noted another ship which, apart from a very rich cargo, had on board one hundred and fifty women, these being among the most noble of the kingdom of Pegu, who were going with very rich presents to offer them to 'their false prophet and legislator Muhammad' ('o seu falso propheta e legislador Mafoma').[11]

These women were presumably going on pilgrimage, or *hajj*, to Mecca. This subject has been much studied for nineteenth-century Indonesia, but there is occasional evidence of this journey being made in the period of this study also. Thus in the 1560s we hear of 'a *caciz* of the area [Maluku] who went to Mecca on pilgrimage'.[12] We can assume that even in our period

[6] J. Kathirithamby-Wells, 'The Islamic City: Melaka to Jogjakarta, c. 1500–1800', *Modern Asian Studies*, 20, no. 2 (1986), 342 and passim.
[7] On this, see Schrieke, II, 125, 187, 238–53.
[8] Diogo do Couto, *Da Ásia* (Lisbon, 1778–88), Década VII, Book 10, Chapter 3.
[9] See especially for an overview of Ottoman-Aceh relations, Anthony Reid, 'Sixteenth Century Turkish Influence in Western Indonesia', *Journal of Southeast Asian History*, 10, no. 3 (1969), 395–414, now supplemented by Naim R. Farooqi, 'Moguls, Ottomans, and Pilgrims: Protecting the Routes to Mecca in the Sixteenth and Seventeenth Century', *International History Review*, 10, no. 2 (May 1988), 215–16.
[10] See her article, 'The Islamic City', pp. 343–44.
[11] A. de S. S. Costa Lobo, *Memórias de um Soldado da Índia* (Lisbon, 1877), p. 27.
[12] *Documentação para a História das Missões do Padroado Português do Oriente: Insulindia*, edited by Artur Basílio de Sá (Lisbon, 1954–58), 5 vols, III, 406. This source will henceforth be referred to as Sá, *Documentação*. The denomination *caciz* will be frequently met in this article. The role of these people has often been obscured by attempts to describe them as 'Muslim priests', which of course they could not be precisely. Thus, a nineteenth-century English scholar defined them as 'Cacizes, priests whose duty was to recount with dramatic vehemence in high places, and public concourses, the circumstances of the death of the Prophet.' (Walter de Gray Birch, in *Commentaries of the great Afonso Albuquerque* (London: Hakluyt, 1875–84), 4 vols, III, 69, note). A modern Portuguese Jesuit defined them as 'Mussulman religious heads; Muslim priests' (Sá, *Documentação*, II, 648) and the standard Portuguese-Asian glossary similarly defines them simply as 'Muslim priests' (S. R. Dalgado, *Glossário Luso-Asiático* (Coímbra, 1919–21), 2 vols, *s.v.* 'caciz'). Hubert Jacobs, the editor of the important series of documents *Documenta Malucensia* (Rome, 1974–84), 3 vols, does much better: 'Caciz is a word of Syrian origins, used by the Portuguese to indicate a

58

many local Muslims made the long and dangerous voyage to the Red Sea, in order to fulfil this religious obligation. Then as now, considerable prestige accrued to those who had made the *hajj*, and especially to those who had actually sojourned and studied in the Holy City, as Snouck Hurgronje noted in the late nineteenth century. In the 1580s an Indian Gujarati scholar visited Aceh but had little success. So he went off and did the *hajj*, and then returned to Aceh. Now he had more success, in part because of his new status as a *hajji*. Later, his nephew, who had already done the *hajj*, arrived in Aceh and was very influential at court in the 1630s.[13] English and Dutch records from the seventeenth century also point to a considerable amount of contact between Indonesia and the Red Sea. In 1642 the English let the Sultan of Mataram send a number of Javanese on an English ship to Surat, and so to Mecca. Similarly, in 1664 the English gave passages to four servants of the Sultan of Makassar, who had been on a pilgrimage to Mecca.[14] The Dutch, though not themselves vitally interested in converting their increasing number of Indonesian subjects, were dubious about the effects of the *hajj* and tended to discourage it. While in 1667 they gave passage to some pilgrims, three years earlier they had decided not to allow three Buginese *hajjis* coming from Mecca to land in their territory; instead, they were expelled to the Cape of Good Hope, 'as their arrival among the here living superstitious Mahometan nations would have very serious consequences'.[15]

It is debatable whether these Muslims who were responsible for converting large numbers of people in South-east Asia can be described precisely as 'missionaries'. Few Muslims who spread their faith in the area were religious specialists engaged in full-time proselytization, in the way the members of the Christian orders were. Most conversions to Islam apparently were made by people who were traders or travellers, pious no doubt but engaged in worldly activities also. Many traders were members of *sufi* orders, and indeed it is a matter of degree, for while most were primarily traders, a few

Muslim religious teacher, that is, a scholar of Islamic law, or a scribe, or even any mosque official. Here it rather means a Muslim apostle and saint, called in Indonesia a *wali* (I, 11, note 36; hereafter referred to as D. *Malucensia*). For a typically lucid discussion, see Henry Yule and A. C. Burnell, *Hobson-Jobson* (New Delhi, 1968), *s.v.* 'casis'. For the career of a Portuguese *caciz*, see a fascinating account of the life of Fernão Dias in Gaspar Correia, *Lendas da India* (Coimbra, 1921–31; Lisbon, 1969), 4 vols, II, 348.

[13] See C. Snouck Hurgronje, *Mekka in the Latter Part of the Nineteenth Century* (Leiden, 1931), pp. 6, 243, 258, and S. A. A. Rizvi, *A History of Sufism in India* (New Delhi, 1978–83), 2 vols, II, 334–35.

[14] *The English Factories in India, 1618–1669*, edited by William Foster (Oxford, 1906–27), 13 vols, 1642–5, 36–37; 1661–4, 317.

[15] Jacob Vredenbregt, 'The Haddj, some of its Features and Functions in Indonesia', *Bijdragen tot de Taal-, Land-, en Volkenkunde van Nederlandsch-Indie*, 118 (1962), 95–96. For nineteenth- and twentieth-century parallels, see Vredenbregt, *passim*; W. R. Roff, 'Sanitation and Security: The Imperial Powers and the Nineteenth Century Hajj', *Arabian Studies*, 6 (1982), 143–60; W. R. Roff, 'The Meccan Pilgrimage: Its Meaning for Southeast Asian Islam', in *Islam in Asia*, edited by Raphael Israeli and Anthony H. Johns, II, *Southeast and East Asia* (Boulder, Colorado, 1984), 238–45; B. Schrieke, *Sociological Studies*, *passim*; and Harry J. Benda, *The Crescent and the Rising Sun* (The Hague, 1958).

were primarily religious guides for their fellow Muslims and also people interested in spreading the faith.

In any case, not all of these 'missionaries' came from the Red Sea area. In fact we have evidence of them coming from a very wide range of countries. Many of them were, in a sense, second generation, in that they came from relatively recently converted areas in India rather than from the older-established areas of the heartland in the Middle East. But there appears to be very little evidence to back up claims by Wink and other recent scholars[16] that Islam spread in South-east Asia via Muslims from South India. Most of them are described as coming from the Middle East, and from Gujarat and Bengal. It could well be of course that earlier some missionaries had come from South India, for we must remember that the conversion process in Indonesia spread over several centuries. In any case, it hardly seems to be of major importance to work out where in India they came from, for the end result was the same, that is that Indonesia finished up Muslim.[17] What is more important to note is that these people were more 'local' than the Christian priests, and learnt local languages more readily and easily. These two advantages contributed powerfully to the success of Islam.

In our period missionaries from the Middle East may well have stopped off in Malabar ports en route to South-east Asia, but their homes were not there, as the following accounts show. The ruler of Melaka was converted by a *caciz* from 'Arabia',[18] while maritime Sumatra had missionaries from Persia, Arabia, Gujarat and Bengal.[19] Francis Xavier claimed that Amboina was subjected to the attentions of three *cacizes* who came from Mecca, adding, in a mistake often found in the records, that this was where Muhammad's body was to be found.[20] Fernão Mendes Pinto found Turkish and Arab missionaries working in Siam in the 1550s.[21] A detailed account of 1556 found all over South-east Asia *cacizes* from Mecca, Cairo, Constantinople and other very remote places, spreading their faith.[22] Late in the decade, Solor was being worked on by 'three or four *cacizes*, two from Calicut and three from Bengal [*sic*]'.[23] In the 1570s we find 'Arabs' in Maluku.[24] A more

---

[16] André Wink, 'Al-Hind: India and Indonesia in the Islamic World-Economy, *c.* 700–1800 A.D.', *Itinerario* (1988), no. 1, 49. Drewes, as cited in note 4, quotes among others Snouck Hurgronje to support his cautious claim that most missionaries came from South India; Hall, also cited in note 4, supports this, again with some reservations.

[17] There has also been some discussion recently over the role of Chinese in spreading Islam in South-east Asia, a debate which unfortunately has got caught up in current Indonesian politics. For an overview, see Ann L. Kumar, 'Islam, the Chinese, and Indonesian Historiography — A Review Article', *Journal of Asian Studies*, 46, no. 3 (1987), 603–16.

[18] Couto, *Da Ásia, Década* IV, Book 2, Chapter 1.

[19] João de Barros, *Da Ásia* (Lisbon, 1778–88), *Década* III, Book 8, Chapter 1.

[20] *Documentação para a História das Missões do Padroado Português do Oriente: India*, edited by António da Silva Rego (Lisbon, 1947–58), 12 vols, III, 345.

[21] Silva Rego, *Documentação . . . India*, V, 372.

[22] *Documenta Indica*, edited by J. Wicki (Rome, 1948–), 16 vols to date, III, 537.

[23] Sá, *Documentação*, II, 345, and also printed in *D. Malucensia*, I, 302–03.

[24] *D. Malucensia*, I, 687.

60

detailed account from the same decade talks of missionaries from Mecca and Aceh and Malaya working in Tidore, while the editor of this collection notes that many Turks came to Borneo, Sumatra and Ternate after Dom João of Austria won the battle of Lepanto, in 1571.[25] Finally, we have a record, already cited, of a Gujarati Muslim, and later his nephew, being influential in Aceh.[26]

It was also noted that this Gujarati's influence increased greatly once he had made the *hajj* to Mecca. The above accounts show clearly that missionaries from the Red Sea and Middle East were most important, followed by those from North India, while few came from South India. It is likely that most of those who did not come from the Islamic heartland would have done the *hajj* at some time, and probably would have studied in Mecca too. Falatehan, a native of Pacem (Pasai) in Sumatra, was probably typical. Around 1520 he went off to the Red Sea, and he stayed in the Holy Cities for two or three years studying Islam. He then came back to South-east Asia and was a successful missionary for some years and later a powerful ruler.[27] A. H. Johns has given us excellent information on a comparable personage, called 'Abd al-Ra'uf of Singkel. His career shows very well the cosmopolitan nature of Islam at this time, and the very many links and connections over the whole wide Muslim world. Born in north Sumatra in about 1615, around 1640 he went to study in Medina with the Kurdish-born scholar Ibrahim al-Kurani. But he spent most of his time in Mecca, nineteen years in all. There he acquired very considerable prestige, and taught hundreds, or even thousands, of Indonesians there, and also initiated many of them into the Shattariyya *sufi* Order. When he returned to Aceh in 1661 he functioned as a revered and prestigious teacher for nearly thirty years. He kept in touch with his former teacher in Medina, and spent much time teaching pilgrims, who usually stopped for some time in Aceh on the way to the Red Sea.[28] In short, there is no doubt that, then as now, any Muslim who came from, or made the voyage to the Holy Cities acquired considerable prestige and respect.

The theme of competition, of personal face-to-face confrontation between representatives of the two religions, and even of races between the two to fill

---

[25] D. *Malucensia*, II, 39 and note.
[26] Rizvi, *Sufism in India*, II, 334–35. See also K. A. Steenbrink, 'Indian Teachers and their Indonesian Pupils: On Intellectual Relations between India and Indonesia, 1600–1800', *Itinerario* (1988), no. 1, 129–41. He finds declining Indian influence on Indonesian Islam in this period.
[27] Barros, *Da Ásia*, Década IV, Book 1, Chapter 13; for Indian comparisons of this theme of the centrality of Mecca, see my 'The Hajj (Pilgrimage) from Mughal India: Some Preliminary Observations', *Indica*, 23 (1986), pp. 143–58.
[28] See Johns, 'Friends in Grace', pp. 471–72, and another account of 'Abd al-Ra'uf in his *The Gift Addressed to the Spirit of the Prophet* (Canberra, 1964), pp. 8–11. Indeed, this latter work also shows other connections, for it consists of a study of a Javanese text on *sufism*, which in turn was based on a seventeenth-century Arabic text from Gujarat concerning orthodox *sufism*.

vacuums, is writ large in our records.[29] This whole matter of competition between exemplars of the two faiths was recently well summed up by a modern-day member of the Society of Jesus, who noted that many of the Muslim preachers were from outside the area of island South-east Asia: 'This points to the fact that, beside the Christian mission among these people, there was a more or less organized Muslim mission which drew preachers from Arabia, Turkey, and Egypt. Inconspicuously but repeatedly they occur in the Portuguese and Spanish sources on Maluku. In order to outline a realistic picture of the Christian apostolate in 16th and 17th century Indonesia, a study of this counter-attack should be undertaken'.[30] In a sense, the next few paragraphs are a contribution towards the attainment of this very worthwhile aim. We may note first the case of the King of Ternate, who in 1566 was described as being such a committed Muslim that 'as soon as he heard that "*gentios*" ['gentiles': here meaning either Hindus, Buddhists or people belonging to no major religion; I will use the term gentiles to refer to all who were neither Muslim nor Christian, as does the contemporary documentation, but of course with no pejorative implication] wanted to convert to Christianity he would order off *cacizes* to make them Muslim, as now one sees in the conversion of Sulawesi, and of the nephew of the King of Bengai and Lucebatas, who, as soon as he knew they desired to become Christian, he gave them all the favours they wanted in order that they not become Christian but rather adopt his faith'.[31]

Poaching of each other's converts was widespread in this fluid religious environment. In 1563 a Jesuit mentioned the arrival in the port of 'Rocanive' in Ambon (Amboina) of two ships from Hito (or Hitu), also in Ambon. Hitu was a Javanese settlement on the island, and a stronghold of Islam.[32] Among the passengers was a *caciz* who was the son of an important man in the area, and who immediately set about preaching Islam. The local Christians were newly converted and not yet well instructed in their new faith; this, plus threats of retaliation against Christians, and the status of the *caciz* made up a powerful threat to Christianity; nevertheless, on this occasion, helped by the Jesuits of the area, the new converts held firm.[33] But not all new converts resisted this pressure. In Makassar in the 1660s a Spanish priest noted, 'There were abundance of Slaves to the Portugueses there, who had renounced their Religion; upon any little Domestic Quarrel these Slaves would go away to the Moors. When they had abjured Christianity, they would come to scoff at their Master. I understand another thing there which is

---

[29] See Schrieke, II, 232–37. John Villiers' article, cited in footnote 1, gives an excellent account of competition in the area of Moro.
[30] Jacobs in *D. Malucensia*, I, 40, note 38.
[31] *D. Malucensia*, I, 484. Bengai is probably Bacan. According to Schrieke, II, 236, the King of Ternate was called Bab, more correctly Baab Ullah. But in fact the Sultan of Ternate until 1570 was the strongly Muslim Hairun, for whom see Villiers, passim.
[32] Schrieke, I, 33, 35, 47, 73.
[33] Sá, *Documentação*, III, 23.

62

deplorable, viz. that Christian Men kept Mahometan Women, and Mahometan Men, Christian Women. Where have sprung these and many other spiritual Calamities?' Where indeed, for later the same author claimed that more than four thousand Christians in Makassar had converted to Islam.[34]

Not that success was all one way. In an area of Ambon in the 1570s a group of Muslims had been converted to Christianity, and had become zealous in their new faith. They competed with each other to destroy things associated with their old faith, that is 'nitos' (spirit symbols or sanctuaries) and tombs. But the delicate balance between the two faiths was well revealed in the way in which none of them dared to destroy a tomb in which was buried two *cacizes*, 'whom they considered to be holy men', for they feared anyone who desecrated it would meet with some great harm. Finally a Portuguese Jesuit brother gave them the example, literally throwing the first stone, and then the newly converted joined in with much vigour.[35]

The Christians claimed that their success, such as it was, was at least in part due to their probity. They performed religious duties without charge while, according to them, the *cacizes* always charged. A Jesuit letter from Ambon (Amboina) in 1563 noted the solemnity and reverence with which the Christians went about their work, while apparently the Muslims were less formal. Also, everything that the Padres did was without any interest, and done only for the love of God, while the *cacizes* did everything not for love, but always for 'interest', that is, for payment.[36] A few years later, another letter referred explicitly to the situation in Tidore. Many locals came to talk to the Jesuits, 'and they were very edified from these things, knowing and seeing how superior are our priests to their *cacizes*; that the king himself said many times that his *cacizes* did nothing except for profit and interest. And when these Muslims saw that everything that we did was free, only for the love of God, and that theirs did it for money, for this reason and for others that they saw in us, they very much desired to become Christians'.[37] One final example makes the same, admittedly probably self-serving, point. In 1608 the Jesuits buried the bones of a relative of the King of 'Labuh' (Labuha), in Maluku, in a church. The King was impressed with the service, and especially by the fact that there was no charge, while the *cacizes* certainly would have charged for the same service.[38]

Apart from this sort of poaching and direct competition, both sides were anxious to be first on the spot in order to fill any newly-discovered religious vacuum. In 1564 the Portuguese decided to investigate Sulawesi, about which they knew little, and they sent in the ship a Padre, 'for we have heard

[34] Friar Domingo Navarrete, *The Travels and Controversies of Friar Domingo*   8–
1686, edited by J. S. Cummins (Cambridge, 1962), 2 vols, I, 122–23; II, 268.
[35] D. *Malucensia*, I, 606.
[36] D. *Malucensia*, I, 394.
[37] D. *Malucensia*, II, 92.
[38] D. *Malucensia*, III, 103.

that they are gentiles and we feared that there might be there a *caciz* converting them to Islam'. This, however, turned out to be a false alarm, and many locals were converted to Christianity.[39] But in a famous 'ecclesiastical boat race' Islam won out. Around 1600 the inhabitants of Makassar were all gentiles, but then they decided that they either should become Christian, via the Portuguese in Melaka, or Muslim, via Siam (or possibly Aceh).

> So they resolved to make use of an extravagant Expedient, which was at one and the same time to send away a Vessel to Siam for Mahometans, and another for Religious to Malacca, resolving to admit the Religion of those that should come first. This was their decision to give a true Solution to that Question, and not to err in so essential a Matter! The Mahometans came first through the fault of those at Malacca ... so the People of Macasar received them and their Law, which they have since observed most strictly, and it has obstructed the Conversion to Christianity of those People.

This story may sound apocryphal, but the modern-day editor of the above account cites several other references to this race.[40]

While sometimes rulers converted after many of their subjects, more often political control facilitated conversion. Both sides were well aware of the advantages of an elite convert, for the possibility of a trickle-down conversion process, sometimes backed up by force, was strong. I noted above the threat represented by a *caciz* who came from an important family in Rocanive. In 1561 the Portuguese noted sourly that the King of Ternate had enormous influence in the surrounding areas, as far as Banda, so that he was widely known as 'the great king' ('o rey grande'), which name had formerly been applied to the Portuguese. Conversion in the face of this was very difficult.[41] Yet earlier a predecessor of this Sultan Hairun had so antagonized people in his area that they, led by their leaders, turned to the Portuguese for help and converted from the top down in order to get protection.[42] In the 1530s a Portuguese captain in Maluku, António Galvão, pursued a conscious policy of converting the elite, sending local kings presents and weapons if they converted. As the chronicler noted, priests sponsored by him first converted various kings, and then their families, and then 'many nobles, and common folk'. They even managed to convert a Muslim Arab, a descendant of Muhammad himself (presumably then a *sayyid*), who had very great prestige among the local kings and lords. This was a very important catch indeed for Christianity. Galvão treated him with great

---

[39] D. *Malucensia*, III, 103.
[40] Navarrete, *Travels*, I, 113 and note. This race, if it ever did occur, must have been at least two decades before the 1620s, the date given by Navarrete, as Reid cites evidence of conversions among the elite from 1603. See Anthony Reid, 'The Islamization of Southeast Asia', in *Historia* (Kuala Lumpur, 1984), 22–23, and sources there cited.
[41] Sá, *Documentação*, III, 269.
[42] See Villiers, pp. 595–96.

64

honour, and stood himself as his sponsor when he was baptized.[43] The result was that many Muslims and gentiles came forward to be baptized too. The *cacizes* and kings who stayed firm in their Muslim faith fought back as best they could, but with only limited success.[44]

Galvão may, however, have been something of an exception in his concern to help the missionaries, for letters home to Europe from the religious often complain of the lack of support they received from the secular authorities. Most Spanish and Portuguese governors and captains put political, and especially economic matters before conversions. As one example, in the 1650s a report on Maluku noted despairingly that in the villages in Ternate *cacizes* openly preached every week 'the Koran of Muhammad', even in villages where Spanish troops were stationed.[45] In a more general sense, the efforts of the missionaries were often hindered and obstructed, rather than facilitated, by their fellow-Christians. In many areas of seaborne Asia the Portuguese in the sixteenth and seventeenth centuries had unenviable reputations. This was both at an official and individual level. As is well known, the Portuguese tried forcibly to monopolize trade in spices and some other products, and direct other Asian trade, forcing all sea trade to pay customs duties to them at their forts. Most sea trade in the Arabian Sea, and increasingly also in island South-east Asia, was handled by Muslims; thus this political and economic conflict spilled over into religious hostility, indeed the two were symbiotic and fed on each other.

In terms of conversions, the result was that the Muslims were often able to say, with considerable justice, that the Portuguese were merely brigands and outlaws. Why convert to the religion practised by people who went around sinking peaceful trading ships and massacring their crews? An early example of this occurred in Melaka in 1511, when Albuquerque arrived to avenge the failure of an earlier Portuguese mission. All the various Muslim trading communities there (showing considerable prescience, for of course the Portuguese did conquer the port city) advised the ruler of Melaka not to negotiate with the Portuguese, 'and they had also on their side the Cacizes, who made long harangues to him, declaring that the Portuguese were renegades and thieves, desirous of lording over the whole world, and that he would be sorry for it if he allowed them to come into the city'.[46] In 1548 a Jesuit letter from Melaka to the head of the new Order, Loyola, noted the same reputation for the Portuguese. It said that Muslims from Arabia, Persia and Turkey came to the area 'to preach the accursed law of Muhammad'.

[43] Similarly in Goa in 1548, when an important Hindu agreed to convert, the bishop performed the service, and the governor stood as godfather in a lavish public ceremony. F. X. Gomes Catão, 'Subsídios para a História de Chorão', *Studia*, 15 (1965), 54–63. For another Goan comparison, and generally for religion and the Portuguese in Goa, see M. N. Pearson, *The Portuguese in India* (Cambridge, 1987), pp. 116–30.
[44] Barros, *Da Ásia, Década* IV, Book 9, Chapter 21; Couto, *Da Ásia, Década* V, Book 7, Chapter 2.
[45] D. *Malucensia*, III, 584–85.
[46] Birch, *Commentaries of Albuquerque*, III, 69–70.

These people were very detrimental to the Portuguese: 'They are very prejudicial and our great enemies, because they say to the gentiles that we are thieves and men without law.'[47]

It was not only the official policies of the Portuguese state which contributed to their unsavoury reputation. The conduct of private Portuguese traders also at times lowered the reputation of them all. It is true that these private traders simply operated in Indian Ocean waters on a basis of equality with any other petty traders, but even so their moral reputation seems to have been a low one; again, this must have exacerbated the difficulties of their compatriots who were trying to make conversions, and must have made the task of the competition, the *cacizes*, that much easier. A longish account, admittedly by a hostile Spanish priest, makes clear precisely this problem. Writing in the later seventeenth century, he noted of Cochinchina that:

The Women there being too free and immodest, as soon as any Ship arrives, they presently go aboard to invite the Men; nay, they even make it an Article of Marriage with their own Countrymen, that when Ships come in, they shall be left to their own Will, and have liberty to do what they please . . . A Vessel from Macao came to that Kingdom, and during its stay there, the Portugueses had so openly to do with those Infidel Harlots, that when they were ready to sail, the Women complained to the King, that they did not pay them what they owed them for the use of their Bodys. So the King ordered the Vessel should not stir till that debt was paid. A rare Example given by Christians, and a great help to the conversion of those Infidels! Another time they were so lewd in that Kingdom, that one about the King said to him, 'Sir, we know not how to deal with these people, the Dutch are satisfied with one Women, but the People of [Portuguese] Macao are not satisfied with many.[48]

The Portuguese in effect hindered their own efforts in another way too. We have good evidence of *cacizes* travelling on Portuguese ships, and disembarking in a port of their choice to go about their conversion activities. In 1556 a long letter noted, 'There was another thing here in which God Our Lord is much disserved, and I consider this to be one of the worst things imaginable; it was, that in our own Portuguese ships Muslims, *cacizes* in the sect of Muhammad, embark, and, under the pretext of being merchants, and that they are carrying goods, they stay in gentile areas' and that they successfully engaged in conversions. These *cacizes* were so keen that they came from all over the Muslim world. On one occasion, a particularly flagrant one, in the very ship in which a Jesuit father was travelling, a Muslim boarded in Baticala, near Goa, along with his entourage. He claimed to be a relation of Muhammad, in other words a *sayyid*, and thus was greatly

---

[47] Sá, *Documentação*, I, 586. We may note in passing that Ming Chinese accounts of the Portuguese were even more unflattering. They were described as inveterate eaters of Chinese children, and malignant goblins. See K. C. Fok, 'Early Ming Images of the Portuguese', in *Portuguese Asia: Aspects of History and Economic History (Sixteenth and Seventeenth Centuries)*, edited by R. Ptak (Stuttgart, 1987), pp. 143–55.
[48] Navarrete, *Travels*, II, 268.

66

respected by all Muslims. He travelled to Borneo, where there were already some of his fellows, and they had enormous success in their conversion efforts, so much so that a local king paid obeisance to this sheikh three times a day ('tres vezes no dia lhe faz o rey da terra a sumbaia'). When the ship ran into bad weather, alms for the (Christian) saints were solicited to avoid shipwreck, and to avoid detection this Muslim was one of the first to contribute.

It was not as though he was the only offender; the practice of Portuguese ships carrying proselytizing Muslims was widespread. One intrepid *caciz* had got as far as Japan in this way, but had met with no success in his efforts.[49] Another account noted that Islam was spreading rapidly in South-east Asia, and 'the cause of its increase are the Muslim Arabs, who travel as sailors in the Portuguese ships which sail to the south, many of which remain there and spread their faith, and they have converted many kings and kingdoms'. The King of Portugal was asked to forbid the use of Muslim sailors (an unlikely prospect given that most sailors at this time were Muslim) and instead use Hindus. Thus the King of Portugal's subjects would no longer 'for the sake of temporal profits foster the increase in the sect of Muhammad'.[50] A similar Jesuit complaint from Maluku in the 1570s claimed that the main proselytizers were Arabs who had come to the area as sailors on Portuguese ships engaged in the clove trade.[51]

The second major area of interest illuminated by these missionary records is their descriptions of the actual process of conversion to Islam in South-east Asia. They very usefully flesh out and amplify our knowledge of this important topic. And they are especially useful for a particular reason. These sources, when they talk of conversion to Christianity, tend to explain this, both implicitly and explicitly, by reference to the obvious superiority of the Christian faith; a Christian missionary would of course really feel no need to explain why people converted, for this was only to be expected. The same applies, as we will see shortly, to normative Muslim accounts of conversion to Islam. But when the Christians describe conversion to the competition they go into more detail, and are much more explicit about what actually happened, for obviously they could not describe conversions to Islam as being merely predictable, and to be explained as God's will manifest.

Two Muslim accounts of conversion to Islam will serve as examples of the sorts of explanations which both sides recounted to explain their own successes. A. H. Johns quoted a Malay chronicle: 'On one occasion there came to Ampel a holy man named Molana Usalam. After remaining there for some time he proceeded on his travels. A calm forced him to land at Balambangan. The daughter of the Regent of Balambangan was at that time

[49] *Documenta Indica*, ed. Wicki, III, 537–38.
[50] *Archivo Português Oriental*, edited by J. H. da Cunha Rivara, 6 vols (Nova Goa, 1857–77), IV, 26.
[51] D. *Malucensia*, I, 687 and note.

very ill, and the saint was requested to help her. He gave her a *pinang* fruit, and on eating it she was cured. As promised, she was given in marriage to her deliverer', and thus Islam gained an entrée.[52] An account from the Malabar coast of India is remarkably similar in style and content. A group of Muslims arrived at Cranganore,

and intelligence of their arrival having reached the King, sending for them into his presence, he manifested towards them much kindness, conversing with them without reserve: and enquiring of them their circumstances and condition, the Sheikh, encouraged by the King's condescension, related to him the history of our prophet Mahomed (upon whom may the divine favour and blessing ever rest!), explaining also to the monarch the tenets of Islamism; whilst, for a confirmation of their truth, he narrated to him the miracle of the division of the moon [which purportedly the Prophet had done]. Now, conviction of the Prophet's divine mission, under the blessing of Almighty God, having followed this relation, the heart of the King became warmed with a holy affection towards Mahomet (on whom be peace!).

He and later many others converted to Islam.[53]

Christian accounts of their successes are rather similar. A description of the Siau mission, in northern Sulawesi, of 1676, describes local spirit customs, and then goes on to note 'the brutal law of Muhammad', the 'depravity' of Dutch Calvinism, and contrasts these three with Catholicism, which is characterized by 'the grandeur of its mysteries, the clarity of its doctrine, so conformable to reason, and the solemnity of its ceremonies'.[54] In other words, for the faithful on both sides, conversion really needed no explanation: gentiles exposed to the truth would accept it automatically.

It should be noted that Christian accounts naturally tend to play down Muslim successes and exaggerate their own. Indeed, one could get the impression that South-east Asia would soon be totally Christianized if one took these records at face value. With hindsight, of course, we know that quite the reverse happened. In this context, how did the Christians account for the successes of their rivals? The important conversion of the ruler of Melaka was briefly described by a Portuguese chronicler in an account which makes clear the merger of trade and religion: 'Some ships arrived at Melaka from the ports of Arabia, and one year there came a *caciz* to preach the law of Muhammad in these parts.' He was successful in becoming influential with the King, and impressed on him the grandeur ('largueza') of Islam. Conversion followed, and the King was honoured by being given the name of the Prophet himself.[55] A little later in the fifteenth century, just

---

[52] A. H. Johns, 'Sufism as a Category in Indonesian Literature and History', *Journal of Southeast Asian History*, 2 (1961), 16. For an excellent survey of comparable indigenous accounts of conversion in South-east Asia, see Russell Jones, 'Ten Conversion Myths from Indonesia', in *Conversion to Islam*, edited by Levtzion, pp. 129–58.
[53] Zain-ud-din, *Tohfut-ul-Mujahideen*, translated by M. J. Rowlandson (London, 1833), pp. 48–50.
[54] D. *Malucensia*, III, 701–02.
[55] Couto, *Da Asia, Década* IV, Book 2, Chapter 1.

before the arrival of the Portuguese, another chronicle described well the evolving situation in Sumatra, and again demonstrated the close link between trade and religion. The people of the interior were described as brutal, savage, cruel and warlike, and some of them were cannibals. But in the littoral areas people were Muslim. These people had been converted by Muslims who came to the area for commerce. They noted the size of the area, and the existence of a religious vacuum ('o Gentio sem lei'), and were able to make many conversions because the locals wanted the goods of the foreign Muslims, and also because of the marriages with local girls made by the Muslims.[56]

Another account describes well the role of the Red Sea area as a centre for the whole faith, the connection of trade and religion, the importance of elite conversions, and the role of intermarriage with local women. Around 1520 a Muslim called Falatehan, a native of Pasai in Sumatra, went off to the Red Sea in a ship carrying spices. He stayed two or three years according to his plan, learning more of the Muslim religion. But when he returned to Pasai he found that the Portuguese had established a fort there, and this acted to hinder his intention of converting more of his neighbours to Islam. So, instead, he took ship to Japara in Java and with his new-found status as one who had studied in Mecca ('com o nome de Caciz de Mafamede') he was able to convert the King, and then, with his permission, many gentiles. So impressed was the newly-converted King that he gave Falatehan his sister in marriage, and he then sought permission to go off to Banten to carry on the good work. There he met and converted an important local figure. Finding that the local king was off in the interior, Falatehan sent a message to his brother-in-law, the King of Japara, asking that his wife, and some people, be sent to help him. The King sent off the woman, and also 2,000 men. With their help, Falatehan became lord of the city of Banten.[57]

The preceding account is very much one of conversion from the top, the trickle-down phenomenon, but Islam did not always need to start at the top and rely on actual or implied political sanctions to make mass converts. The situation in Siam in the middle of the sixteenth century was well described in a letter by the adventurer-turned-religious Fernão Mendes Pinto. He told his Jesuit fellows that there were various religious beliefs followed in Siam, but the Muslims were doing very well. Already in the capital there were seven mosques, with foreign *cacizes*, and 30,000 Muslim hearths. Proselytization proceeded apace ('estes mouros pregão continuamente o alcorão de

---

[56] Barros, *Da Ásia, Década* III, Book 8, Chapter 1.
[57] Barros, *Da Ásia, Década* IV, Book 1, Chapter 13. Barros says he became ruler of 'Bintam Cidade de Sunda' but it seems clear that he is mistaken and that Banten is meant: see Anthony Reid, 'Sixteenth Century Turkish Influence', p. 409. Notice, however, that Ricklefs, basing his account on indigenous sources, has a quite different version. Banten rose thanks to Sunan Gunungjati (d. *c.* 1570), who was born in Pasai, went to Mecca, returned in 1524 and married a sister of the ruler of Demak, and with their help conquered Banten. At the least, this illustrates the difficulties of reconciling Portuguese and local sources! (M. C. Ricklefs, *A History of Modern Indonesia* (London, 1981), pp. 34–35).

Mafoma'). The King, however, maintained a hands-off attitude to the whole matter: 'The King lets everyone do what they want; they can be Muslim or gentile, for he says he is king of nothing more than their bodies.'[58]

We can even begin to reconstruct some more precise dates concerning the process of conversion in one area, Maluku, though this is of course a rather large area, and some of the evidence is conflicting. Writing in 1515 Tomé Pires claimed that seventy-five per cent of the inhabitants were still pagan, and that the conversion process had begun fifty years ago, that is, in the 1460s.[59] Francis Xavier worked in the area thirty years later, and in a letter of 1546 from Amboina he claimed that there were still more gentiles than Muslims in the area. He claimed that the Muslim conversion drive had started seventy years ago, that is, in the 1470s. According to him most of the gentiles really wanted to become Christians, not Muslims.[60] Nevertheless, after another thirty years a Jesuit letter of 1576 said that almost all the inhabitants were Muslim by now.[61] However, some confusion over the date of conversion appears from other letters, which interestingly use the consumption of pork as the litmus test of conversion to Islam. A letter of 1559 claimed that in Makassar at least 'Islam has still not entered, because they still eat nothing but pork ...'. But in the 1640s another visitor noticed that 'there are ... no hogs at all because the natives, who were Mohamedans, have exterminated them entirely from the country' (and the women now wore all-enveloping veils).[62] Similarly, in 1570 in Ambon (Amboina) an optimistic account claimed that many influential Muslims gave the ultimate sign of their desire to convert to Christianity by publicly eating pork.[63]

An account from 1556 will serve to close this sketch of the process of conversion. The writer claimed the Muslim missionaries also traded, and this indeed would often be the case; I noted earlier that it is difficult, and indeed unnecessary, to try and differentiate too closely between traders and missionaries. Similarly, the Jesuits mixed service to God and to Mammon. The usual situation was that *sufis* and other religious specialists travelled alongside merchant groups to whom they were attached, and themselves traded at times. There was a strong link between trade and conversion in South-east Asia. The writer claimed that these Muslim missionaries were doing far too well all over the area. Their new converts were especially devout. In Siam, when these *cacizes* speak, the locals stand listening with their mouths open and fanning with their hands (?'avanando com a mão'),

---

[58] Silva Rego, *Documentação ... India*, V, 372.
[59] Tomé Pires, *The Suma Oriental of Tomé Pires*, edited by A. Cortesão (London, 1944), 2 vols, p. 213.
[60] Silva Rego, *Documentação ... India*, III, 345.
[61] D. *Malucensia*, I, 687 and note.
[62] Sá, *Documentação*, II, 348; Reid, 'Islamization of Southeast Asia', p. 22.
[63] D. *Malucensia*, I, 604.

saying that the air of the words, that enters via the mouth, sanctifies in their hearts.[64]

This curious practice is an example of a well-known phenomenon, that is of partial or superficial conversions. Full conformity with the tenets of orthodox Islam normally took generations to achieve, if indeed it ever was. This was also, of course, the case with new converts to Christianity, as indeed the missionaries noted. Successful missionaries were usually those who tolerated a fair degree of diversity, at least at first. 'Purer' observance was achieved only slowly. Xavier even claimed that the new converts to Islam in Amboina really knew nothing of their religion.[65] An account from the 1570s in Amboina noted how local converts to Islam retained their reverence for spirits and tombs of pre-Islamic saints.[66] In 1588 a Jesuit account of Maluku, a rather confused one, noted that all four of the kings in the area, and their nobles, were Muslim, but they were much inferior to the Turks as Muslims because they had no teachers, except for some ignorant ones. Nevertheless, they were very firm in their faith, and observed closely the rules and ceremonies that the *cacizes* taught them, except for the nobility and kings, who were more lax.[67] A Spanish missionary described a practice which has very little to do with great tradition Islam but which shows the survival of earlier folk practice: 'In Funerals, the Moors of Macasar usually have four Boys very well clad at the four corners of the Bier, which is very large. Every one of them carries a Fan and fans the dead Body which goes in the middle, which is to cool the Soul, because of the great heat it endures in the other world. This I myself have seen.'[68]

It seems to me that these Portuguese and Spanish records, mostly written by professional missionaries, have a great value for any studies of conversions to either Islam or Christianity in South-east Asia. They provide informed and valuable comments on the whole matter. It is a pity that so far they have not been used coherently. This short sketch will at least, I hope, make clear the sort of information they contain. I have used only published, though of course untranslated, sources in this article; possibly archives in Seville, Rome and Lisbon contain much extra data, though the modern-day religious historians and archivists who compiled the series I have used are very thorough indeed, and it could be that the most useful information has already been published.

[64] *Documenta Indica*, III, 537–38.
[65] Silva Rego, *Documentação ... India*, III, 345.
[66] D. *Malucensia*, I, 606.
[67] Sá, *Documentação*, V, 91.
[68] Navarrete, *Travels*, I, 118.

The Search for the Similar: Early Contacts between Portuguese and Indians

Niels Steensgaard's work has been concerned to identify when a qualitative and quantitative difference appeared between Asia and Europe. His first, and perhaps still most influential, book saw a broad similarity between the activities of the Portuguese and the peddlers in the sixteenth century. He claimed that the northern European trading companies, the English EIC, and especially the Dutch VOC, from their inception represented a new and superior organizational form which right from the start was at least potentially superior to the peddlers and the Portuguese. This superiority played itself out over the next century or so. All his later work in this area has been concerned to flesh out, and sometimes modify, this basic scenario.

The present short essay is also concerned with the problem of the emergence of "difference" between Asia and Europe, but it is about perceptions rather than economics. I must also say at once that this is in many ways a very preliminary piece, which ignores several important areas. I have no space to consider differing perceptions based on skin colour, though I should note that while the Portuguese did differentiate in this way, this is not to be seen as an example of the "scientific" racism of the nineteenth century. More important, I have not included here any analysis of Asian perceptions of Europeans. Such a complementary study would have to draw on very difficult and scattered sources, and in any case limitations of space dictated that this reverse angle be left for some future occasion. The present study then may raise more questions than it answers. I feel comfortable with this, for Niels Steensgaard also is an historian who raises questions, who can be speculative and controversial. I hope that what follows will at least begin to help us think about the problems of perceptions, and the creation of differences. Trade and commerce have for too long dominated studies of initial contacts between Europeans and Asians, and for that matter works dealing with the Indian Ocean as an historical area of study.[1] Cultural and social matters have been strangely neglected.

145

Recent work, including later pieces by Steensgaard, makes it clear that the whole nature of the European presence in Asia changed dramatically some time after the middle of the eighteenth century. Up to this time, Asians and Europeans traded with each other on a basis of more or less equality. There was no pronounced advantage to either side, or more correctly sides for both Asia and Europe are far too gross terms; I am aware of this but will use these terms, "Asia" and "Europe," simply for convenience. It is true that we can see the beginnings of European advantage in some areas even late in the seventeenth century, and more clearly quite early in the eighteenth. Nevertheless, the major dichotomy, a clear economic and technological advantage for the Europeans, appeared only from the middle of the eighteenth century. This dramatic change was a result of the beginnings of the vast and cumulative historical conjuncture conventionally called the Industrial Revolution. Many major historians have followed this sort of division, Fernand Braudel for one, and Immanuel Wallerstein for another. In terms of the World System model, the Indian Ocean area moved from being an area external to the Modern World-System to being incorporated as a periphery. In the specific case of India, this is considered to have occurred over the very long period of 1750 to 1850.[2]

Michael Adas has recently produced a very fine book which discusses the way in which European perceptions of Asia and Asians were affected by technological change. His findings are congruent with the above discussion, for he says that technological and scientific advance in Europe in the eighteenth century changed profoundly the way Europeans viewed Asians. Asians were now seen as backward and primitive because they had, it was thought, fallen so far behind Europe in these areas.[3] This change in the relationship between Asia and Europe was built on economic change in Europe, but this in turn had antecedents which were not solely mundane. I am thinking here of a change in the whole character of European thought over these centuries. We are told that in the fifteenth and sixteenth centuries Europeans tended to see society and history in static terms. There were changes to be sure, but these were cyclical, and did not, it was thought, lead to progress and fundamental novelty. It was in the eighteenth century that thinkers began to see long-term secular trends, and ideas of progress and development began to hold sway.[4] Thus even in the realm of thought a gap began to open between Europe and Asia.

In the earlier period there was much more congruence between the most basic views of the world in these two areas. As Adas notes, in the sixteenth and seventeenth centuries "virtually all European travelers, including the best educated, viewed the world in ways that fundamentally resembled the outlook of the peoples they encountered overseas".[5] For both, belief systems were grounded in religion, and this then made religion the prime method of distinction. For the

IX

uropeans, and especially the Portuguese in the sixteenth century, the Christian faith was seen as "the key source of their distinctiveness from and superiority to non-Western peoples".[6]

My concern then is to discuss Portuguese views of Indians in the sixteenth and seventeenth centuries, before economic and technological disparities had begun to be perceived.[7] My main guide will not be Adas's book, excellent though it is, for he is most concerned to delineate perceptions of economic similarity and later difference. Rather I have found most useful Edward Said's well known discussion of Orientalism. His time frame fits very well with what I have said above, for he also finds the most ominous and objectionable form of Orientalism appearing in the late eighteenth century. It is perhaps worthwhile to remind the reader that Said finds three different sorts of Orientalism.[8] First is the academic discipline, represented at one time by the School of Oriental and African Studies at the University of London. Second is the basic distinction made between "the Orient" and "the Occident," one which has a very long history and which is an example of the common human need to define oneself by reference to a perceived different "Other". The third type, Said's main concern, developed since the late eighteenth century. This is "Orientalism as a Western style for dominating, restructuring, and having authority over the Orient". "The relationship between Occident and Orient is a relationship of power, of domination, of varying degrees of a complex hegemony". For the purposes of this essay, it is Said's second category which is most instructive, for it relates to the period before European hegemony.

We need first to establish how new India was for the Europeans. How much did da Gama and his crew know when they arrived in Malabar in 1498? The best way to start this discussion is to remember Braudel's notion of a Mediterranean world encompassing both northern and southern shores. This is still suggestive, even if his application of it was flawed. "Africa" and "Europe" had certain commonalities. Similarly, one of Niels Steensgaard's most fruitful notions was that of Eurasia. Following on implicitly from Marshall Hodgson's work, he told us that we should not be deceived by modern maps and perceptions of something called Asia which is different and separate from something else conventionally called Europe. At least in the area of the eastern Mediterranean (what used to be called the Levant) and the Red Sea, there were intricate connections, sufficient to make this a viable area of study even if it does straddle two "continents" which we call Europe and Asia.

There had been considerable contact between the Mediterranean area and the Indian Ocean long before 1498, going back at least to Roman times.[9] In later centuries we have records of groups of merchants, often Venetians, travelling and trading in the Indian Ocean. Similarly, people from outside Europe had experience of the Mediterranean. Da Gama was met in Calicut by two Tunisian

Muslims who spoke Castilian and Genoese. A little later he came across a Polish Jew who spoke Hebrew, Venetian, Arabic, German and a little Spanish. These people of course moved goods: Asian products, notably the famous spices, had been readily available in the Mediterranean for centuries before the Portuguese got to India, and European bullion had flowed, in fits and starts to be sure, into Asia since Roman times.

A concrete example which shows there was already some knowledge is the melancholy matter of da Gama's contacts with Muslims in east Africa. Pero de Covilham found that the east African coast as far south as Sofala was Islamic, and that Muslim traders linked these areas with the Muslim heartland further north, and indeed with other areas all over the Indian Ocean. The first Muslim ruler da Gama met was the sultan of Mozambique Island. Immediately age-old prejudice appeared on both sides, fuelled by remembrances of the Crusades, endemic warfare for decades in north Africa, and the Portuguese reconquest of their homeland from Muslims. When they met Muslims, the Portuguese knew exactly what they thought: they hated them and were hated in return. This certainly was not a new and unfamiliar world.

Once they got to India, what did they find? We noted that Adas claimed to find certain similarities between the world views of Europeans and Asians, while other literature already quoted notes broad commonality in the economic lives of human kind before the Industrial Revolution. This certainly applies well enough when we look particularly at Portugal and India. The material condition of the respective populations shows no decisive advantage for either. Braudel has produced some very broad comparisons which seem to confirm this picture.[10] In both, the vast bulk of the populations were peasants, subjected to what Eric Wolf has called a tributary mode of production[11] where a considerable part of the surplus from agricultural production was skimmed off by lords and kings: as much as a third or even a half. In both areas kin ties were crucial in self-definition, followed probably by locality and occupation. The notion of belonging to a particular state was not one commonly found. For the peasant, the state was merely an annual imposition of an arbitrary collection of part of one's production, the collection usually being mediated through a local power figure. In both areas life was hard, poor, and short.

Many Portuguese who got to India came from coastal areas; indeed the bulk of Portugal's population has always lived close to the coast. In India they also spent most of their time on the littoral, few of them penetrating to the great production and population centres inland. Here again we can find broad similarities. Lisbon as a port was not markedly different from many of the great Indian ports on the west coast, as we will show later when we note the innumerable comparisons the Portuguese made between Indian cities and their own. Cities at this time were usually divided into various occupationally-defined quarters which had a considerable amount of autonomy in governing themselves. Cities of course meant trade and merchants, cosmopolitanism, a more open society than the masses stuck on the land. In both, seasons for sailing constrained economic activity. Portuguese ships had to leave for India at set times in order to make the voyage expeditiously, and similarly shipping within the Indian Ocean was governed tightly by the pattern of the monsoons.

It was at sea that one of the most important differences appeared, namely sea power. As is well known, Portuguese ships had a pronounced advantage in that they had better artillery on board, and this was decisive in their early successes. Nevertheless, this was an isolated instance, at this time, of a European advantage in a technological area. It hardly seems necessary to elaborate on this, for the notion of a broad similarity in economic life in Europe and Asia before the eighteenth century is widely accepted.

In the most general sense, the Portuguese when they came across people they had not met before were aware of corporeal similarities, that is that human bodies had a certain commonality regardless of skin colour. As the modern editor of Ramusio's *Travels* noted, he tried to put forward "the view of one single world consisting of homogenous [sic] regions inhabited by men".[12] But as one would expect from the preceding discussion they also found a sense of similarity and commonality in material matters. This found expression in the many statements the Portuguese made about how various Indian cities were "the same as" or "like" cities they knew back home. What they were doing when they made these comparisons was to define themselves against an "Other". As Said noted, like all other humans they used the device of comparison to make intelligible what they found. In material matters they usually found similarities.

One could make a long list of such statements.[13] Manuel Godinho, travelling in the Middle East in 1663, noted that Baghdad "is as big as Santarem, including Ribeira", while a square in the town "is where the horse fairs are held, and is about the size of our Rossio". North of Baghdad he found an island in the middle of the Euphrates river "as big as the Lisbon castle". In Aleppo "The roads are paved from wall to wall as in our Oporto"[14]

Fernão Mendes Pinto also constantly referred back to the familiar to describe the new. In China he saw a shrine "which was about the size of the Church of São Domingos in Lisbon," and one Chinese city he noted, "compared to many other cities [in China], was of far less importance than in Portugal Oeiras is, compared to Lisbon". In Peking he found two streets "all decorated with stone archways covered on top like those of the hospital of Lisbon, only much nicer. . ." Of the city in general he wrote that "One should not imagine for a moment that it is anything like Rome, Constantinople, Venice, Paris, London, Seville, Lisbon, or any of the great cities of Europe, no matter how famous or populous". Nor was it like a list of eighteen great cities of Asia: it was far bigger and grander than any of these.[15]

Turning specifically to India, we could multiply endlessly similar examples. In Gujarat similarities between their women and Portuguese ones were noted,[16] and Barbosa found in Cambay "many fair houses, very lofty with windows and roofed with tiles in our manner",[17] an opinion echoed by the chronicler Goes, who found "very large houses made in our manner".[18] Cambay's artisans were as good as those of Flanders.[19] Other Gujarati cities have "high houses of stone and mortar like those of Spain".[20] In 1508 Malik Ayaz, governor of Diu, was making ships as good as those of the Portuguese,[21] while later in the century the third Jesuit Mission found Cambay to be "not dissimilar to Evora in Portugal" including gates like those of cities in Europe.[22] Before the Muslim conquest of Gujarat the Rajputs acted as "knights and wardens" to control the area.[23]

So also with other areas of India. In Malabar Gujarati merchants lived in houses in their own streets, just as "the Jews are wont to dwell in our land".[24] The inhabitants of Vijayanagar have "facial features like our own".[25] Donald Lach's compilation gives us a convenient impression of more searches for the familiar. In Goa they produced oil from sesame "in presses as we do ours", while the auction in the town is like "the meeting upon the burse in Andwarpe".[26] Chittagong is like Venice, Cochin is like Rome, Mandu is like ancient Rome, and Mughal cities generally are as large as Lisbon. The Ravi river in the north "is almost the same size as the Tagus".[27] Varthema even gives us an example of a sort of reverse comparison when he describes what is to be found in Chaul by reference to what is not, of familiar European plants, present. Chaul thus abounds in everything "excepting grapes, nuts and chestnuts".[28]

So far we have been describing attempts to find similarities, to make the unfamiliar explicable. This is related to, but not the same as, the phenomenon of acculturation, one which was notoriously found in Goa and other Portuguese areas. In Goa rice was the staple food even though bread was available, and it was eaten with the hands, just as the Indians did, "for there they eate nothing with spoones, and if they should see any man doe so, they would laugh at him". Similarly with drinking, where it seems the influence of Hindu pollution notions meant that the Portuguese also drank water from a pot without the pot touching the lips. When a new arrival attempted this and spilt any water the locals laughed at him, "calling him Reynol, which is a name given in iest to such as newlie come from Portingall, and know not how to behave themselves in such grave manner, and with such ceremonies as the Portugales use in India; so that at the first they are much whooped and cried at in the streets, untill by use [and practice] they have learned the Indian manner, which they quicklie doe". Portuguese Goans rubbed their bodies with "sweet sanders", chewed betel, washed frequently, and drank araq, and all this "they have learned and received of the Indian Heathens, which have had those costumes of long time".[29]

Acculturation seemed to have particularly pronounced in the medical field. Here again we find no qualitative difference between India and Portugal, and as a result the Portuguese learnt from the local practitioners. The related notions of a lack of qualitative difference, and that Indian diseases were "different", meant that even governors and clerics used Hindu doctors because of their supposed better local knowledge. In 1548 an Indian brahmin doctor was practicing in the Jesuit College of St. Paul, and another *vaidya* (Hindu doctor, also sometimes called pandit) was doctor to Governor Barreto in 1574.[30] Linschoten in the 1580s noted that "there are in Goa many Heathen phisitions which observe their gravities with hats carried over them for the sunne, like the Portingales, which no other heathens doe, but [onely] Ambassadors, or some rich Marchants. These Heathen phisitions doe not onely cure there owne nations [and countriemen] but the Portingales also, for the Viceroy himselfe, the Archbishop, and all the Monkes and Friers doe put more trust in them than in their own countrimen, whereby they get great [store of] money, and are much honoured and esteemed".[31]

Portuguese racism sometimes tried to limit the prestige of these Hindu doctors; in 1572 the governor decreed that Hindu teachers and doctors were not to go about on horseback or in palanquins, but the doctor who served the governor's own household was exempt from this. The reverse of this sensible arrangement was that most governors brought their own doctors out with them from Lisbon as part of their vast retinues of relatives and hangers-on, all of them hoping to make a fortune in India during the three-year term of their patron. These newly arrived Portuguese doctors were nearly always rewarded by being made the chief doctor of the important Royal Hospital, but several contemporaries noted that this was a prime cause of mortality, for they knew nothing of Indian diseases, and just as they began to acculturate they returned to Portugal with their gubernatorial patron.[32] In 1610 the king ordered that this practice cease and that the doctors and surgeons who went out with the viceroys not be allowed to practice in the Royal Hospital, "because they have no experience of the region and its medical methods". This order seems to have provoked a storm of complaints from Goa, and three years later it was lifted.[33]

Despite this, what we find overwhelmingly in Goa is a mixture of European and Hindu practice. Goans seem to have had a quite ad hoc and experimental attitude to health, and tried different systems quite freely. An Augustinian friar with a very painful swelling in the testicles was cured by a poultice of stewed leaves applied by an old woman. A Hindu doctor was considered to know a perfect cure for scrofula, a swelling of the glands which was probably a form of tuberculosis. In the Portuguese settlement of Daman in the 1690s a French visitor found a young Portuguese girl with fever, whose "Indian physician, instead of letting her blood, had covered her head with pepper". The European insisted on bleeding her with leeches, and perhaps surprisingly she recovered quickly.[34]

The incident points to the major divergence between European and Hindu medicine, which was the routine use of bleeding by Europeans. As Pyrard noted, Indians, that is Hindus, did not use bleeding at all.[35] In the 1670s the Abbé Carré fell ill with a fever, and insisted on being bled. Great quantities were hacked out of him by enthusiastic but amateur bleeders, and "This made me so feeble that I cannot bear to speak of it. Yet, though I felt very weak, I was not surprised that the fever grew less, as it no longer had the cause [that is, excess of blood] which had kept it up; and I further reduced it by refusing for eight days to eat many little delicacies that I would have liked – sometimes one thing, sometimes another, though I must confess I refrained with very great difficulty. For eight or ten days I still had my sight, my memory, and my senses, but so feebly that I did not remember anything that happened to me".[36] There were clearly problems with this method of dealing with fevers, especially when it was used so often; patients in the Royal Hospital of Goa could be bled thirty or even forty times.

Yet more often we find acculturation and intermingling. Ovington late in the seventeenth century in Surat noted a treatment for fever which is still used in India today, and did not comment adversely on it: "Cooling Herbs and Congy [Hindi, kanji, rice gruel], that is, Water with Rice boil'd in it, and Abstinence, are the best Receipts they prescribe for mitigating Intestinal Fervors of the Spirits, and al-laying the Heat of the Blood, which they think is better preserv'd and cool'd within the Veins than let out, if it boils too fast".[37] In the 1750s in Malabar Grose noted what seems to be a variant on this method, or at least the rice was apparently boiled drier than was the case in the just quoted instance. "For bloody fluxes, the Bramins suggest a very simple, and as they pretend a most infalliable remedy, consisting in a strict abstinence from everything but rice stewed dry; to which they allow no sauce of any kind whatever, and attribute to it an absorbent quality, that is excellent against that acrimony which preys on the entrails and breeds the disorder. For drink they give nothing but water, corrected by a very moderate amount of cinnamon".[38]

My findings of similarities and acculturation seem to run counter to what some other authorities have said. Cohn claims that right from the start the British in India separated themselves from India in "their dress and demeanour". They always "dressed in their own fashion",[39] a statement contradicted by much contemporary evidence. For example, Mandelslo in 1638 found that the English and the Dutch in Gujarat usually wore native dress.[40] Donald Lach more generally seems to deny his own evidence, which I have been quoting extensively, and stresses differences, and European perceptions of India as a strange and foreign place.[41] Similarly with Braudel, who wrote a typically evocative passage which is more poetic than sound. In the sixteenth century "Asia was still a *terra incognita*, another planet; even the plants and animals were different here in this whole continent of different peoples, different civilizations, religions, forms of society or types of land tenure. Everything was strange and new: even the rivers were not like European waterways. What was large in the West was multiplied immeasurably here. The towns of the East were vast ant hills teeming with people. How strange the westerners found these civilizations, societies and cities!"[42] All I can say is that this passage runs contrary to both the limited evidence I have quoted above, and a vast bulk of other data which space precludes my noting, as well as the general consensus in the recent literature, of which Adas is the best example.

So much for the material world. We find a search for the similar, and resulting from this and no doubt also from practical considerations, a strong degree of acculturation. Nevertheless, as Adas says, the early Europeans did see a strong difference in religion. He notes that "Virtually all European travelers, including the best educated, viewed the world in ways that fundamentally resembled the outlook of the peoples they encountered overseas". In both cases belief systems were grounded in religion, and this in turn meant that it was here that difference was perceived. For the early Europeans then the Christian faith was seen as "the key source of their distinctiveness from and superiority to non-Western peoples".[43] As one would expect, this was especially strong among religious specialists: thus Lach stresses Jesuit contempt and hostility to all Indian religions.[44] This sort of attitude is completely predictable, but what of lay opinion?

There is little to say about Portuguese attitudes to Islam, for they were inveterately hostile. The Portuguese knew about Islam, and knew they disliked it and were afraid of it and its practitioners. Said claimed that Europeans found Islam threatening, while India "never provided an indigenous threat to Europe...[so it never had] the sense of danger reserved for Islam".[45] Lach notes this also,[46] and similarly Adas says that Portugal had had long contact with Islam, and so never had to "discover" it. The two were more closely linked, and Islam had been much more influential in Europe than were Hinduism or Buddhism.[47] Godinho in a recent work does not, I feel, differentiate enough between Islam and Hinduism, but he does see Islam as being hostile and threatening to the Portuguese.[48]

It does seem, however, that greater familiarity could bring a more nuanced approach. This is not to say that the Portuguese ever approved of Islam, but they possibly became a little more discriminating and even positive. Graça's excellent account of ten European travellers who went overland through the Middle East between 1560 and 1670 claims that these travellers were aware of corporeal similarities, but were bothered by social, and especially religious, differences. It was always religious difference which stuck in the throat of the Portuguese. One of the travellers, Frei Pantaleão de Aveiro, described favourably a local ruler: "he is a type of perfect prince, except that he is not Christian". Another, Rebelo, noted of some Muslims that they were so inclined to good works that all they lacked to be part of the Faith was baptism. Their accounts then are always filtered through their belief in the superiority of Christianity.[49]

Nevertheless, there were attempts to equate Muslim practice with that of Christians. A small but revealing example concerns an implicit assumption that Islam must have dates and calenders like the Christians did. Many Europeans claimed that the great Muslim festival, that is the ceremonies of the *hajj* or pilgrimage to Mecca, took place on a certain day each year. The normally careful Pires wrote of "the time of the Jubilee, which is held every year on the first day of February", while nearly two hundred years later Daniel noted that "They solemnize a festival here [at Mecca] once a year, being on the three and twentieth of May".[50] So also for the usually well-informed Jesuit traveller Manuel Godinho, who noted "Mecca, where Muhammad was born, and world famous on this account, and also for the universal fair held there each year during August and September, at which gather by land and sea goods from all over the world".[51] A slightly earlier account, by Sanson, "geographe ordinaire du Roy" of France, in 1652 made a very similar mistake as to the date: "La Ville [Mecca] est belle, remplie de six mille maisons, bien basties, à son Temple fort sumptueux... Sur la fin de May, qui est le grand Jubilé des Mahomedans, il se tient icy une foire, oI il se trouve souvent plus de cinquante mille hommes estrangers, & prés de cinquante mille Chameaux".[52]

The problem is that the Islamic year, being based on the moon, "loses" eleven days each year compared with the western solar calendar; in other words the time of the jubilee or festival, that is the *hajj*, "moves" through the western calendar and so cannot be on the same western day each year. We could see these claims as early examples of a western failure to appreciate different cultures and different customs, but this can also constitute another example of a search for the familiar, the similar. These observers presumably were simply assuming that Muslims were like Christians, and held their festivals at set times each year, failing to recognize that the Muslim year is calculated on a different basis. Others appear to have thought the *hajj* was some ritual that could be done at any time, just as they could go to church whenever it suited them.

The attitude to Hinduism was much more complex, and a discussion of this will close this short essay. I want to stress two things. First, most of what follows is Portuguese responses to Great Tradition Hinduism, that is the more literate and refined, as opposed to folk, version of the religion. The Portuguese commented surprisingly little on popular Hinduism. Second, especially at this upper level there are objectively very few similarities between Christianity and Hinduism. The former is monotheistic, the latter monistic, and at the popular level polytheistic. Christians believe in one life and then judgement, Hindus believe in multiple rebirths. The role of Jesus and the Virgin Mary in Christianity has no exact parallel in Hinduism. Such Hindu practices as cremation, sati, and the caste system were unknown in Christianity. The list could go on and on.

Before I quote cases, I want to introduce a notion from Said which may help us to understand the data which follows. "Something patently foreign and distant acquires, for one reason or another, a status more rather than less familiar. One tends to stop judging things either as completely novel or as completely well known; a new median category emerges, a category that allows one to see new things, things seen for the first time, as versions of a previously known thing. In essence such a category is not so much a way of receiving new information as it is a method of controlling what seems to be a threat to some established view of things. If the mind must suddenly deal with what it takes to be a radically new form of life... the response on the whole is conservative and defensive".[53]

In the light of this, and given the pronounced objective differences between Hinduism and Christianity, what can we make of comments such as the following? Tomé Pires, who lived in Malabar for at least a year, wrote in his famous *Suma Oriental* that "The whole of Malabar believes, as we do, in the Trinity of Father, Son and Holy Ghost, three in one, the only true God. From Cambay to Bengal all the people hold this [faith]". D. João de Castro said of Cambay that it "is inhabited by a people called Guzarates... among whom there are some men, like philosophers and religious men, who are called Bramenes, who believe in the Holy Trinity, Father, Son, Holy Ghost, and many other things of our very sacred law".[54] Castanheda, who was in India for ten years and was, Donald Lach to the contrary, well educated, could still write in the mid sixteenth century that Konkani brahmins "have hints of the birth of our lord and his sufferings," they venerate the picture of Our Lady, and on festival occasions wash themselves "as a kind of baptismal rite".[55] And the following from Barbosa on Gujarat: "These *Bramenes* and Heathen have in their creed many resemblances to the Holy Trinity, and hold in great honour the relation of the Triune Three, and always make their prayers to God, whom they confess and adore as the true God, Creator and maker of all things, who is three persons and one God, and they say that there are many other gods who are rulers under him, in whom also they believe. These *Bramenes* and Heathen wheresoever they find our churches enter them and make prayers and adorations to our Images, always asking for Santa Maria, like men who have some knowledge and understanding of these matters:

and they honour the Church as is our manner, saying that between them and us there is little difference".[56]

The most famous example of an attempt to equate Christianity and Hinduism concerns Vasco da Gama in Calicut. The account of his voyage is quite firm that "The city of Calicut is inhabited by Christians". As is well known, he and his party were taken to a "church", in the centre of which was a sanctuary "all built of hewn stone, with a bronze door sufficiently wide for a man to pass, and stone steps leading up to it. Within this sanctuary stood a small image which they said represented Our Lady... In this church the captain-major said his prayers, and we with him". The temple was full of images: "this made da Gama and the rest take it for a Christian church. Entering it, they were met by certain men, naked from the waist upwards, and from thence to the knees covered with calico. They wore pieces of calico also under the armpits, with certain threads, which were hung over their left shoulder, and passed under the right arm, just as the Catholic priests used to wear their stoles formerly". (These of course were brahmins, wearing *dhotis* and the sacred thread, and attached to the service of this temple.) On seeing a female deity, "da Gama and the rest, taking it for an image of the Virgin, fell on their knees and prayed".[57] Dom Manuel, the king, was delighted at this news and in his instructions to the next expedition, led by Cabral, he said concerning the ruler of Calicut, the Zamorin, that "since we have information that he and his subjects and the dwellers in his kingdom are Christians and of our faith" he was sending ships "in order that they might more completely have instruction in our faith and might be indoctrinated and taught in matters pertaining to it".[58]

The end of this passage shows that the king was a little bit dubious about the quality of Christianity in Calicut, even if he thought it had some similarities with his own beliefs, and indeed one of da Gama's party in the temple also had his doubts. João de Sala in making his genuflections said, "If this be the devil, I worship God". Da Gama brought back with him the Jewish convert Gaspar da Gama, and Sernigi wrote from Lisbon to a correspondent in Florence that "he says in those countries there are many gentiles, that is idolators [Hindus or Buddhists], and only a few Christians; that the supposed churches and belfries are in reality temples of idolators, and that the pictures within them are those of idols and not of Saints".[59] Two accounts from Cabral's time in Calicut show that others also soon worked out there were differences. One noted that the Gujaratis in Calicut, and the locals, were "idolators, who worship the sun, the moon and cows" and another account noted that "The king is an idolator, although others have believed that they are Christians. These have not learned so much about their customs as we who have had considerable trade relations with Calicut".[60]

Later Barros referred to the Brahmin trinity, and noted that it was very different from the Christian one, and was also rejected by the local Muslims.[61] The change was well encapsulated in Luis de Camoens account of da Gama and the temple. He was in India from 1553 to 1567, and the *Lusiads* were first published in 1572. He distorts the whole matter to make it fit with Counter Reformation intolerance and opposition to Hinduism. For Camoens the images in the temple were "so many imaginings prompted by the devil. The statues were abominable... Here the barbarous heathen performed his superstitious devotions".[62] Fernão Mendes Pinto in his *Travels*, a satire on the Portuguese empire, remained a voice of reason and tolerance, always stressing the closeness of Asian and Western religions, and seeing all as being capable of ethical action. He is critical, to be sure, but there is no hint of automatic western superiority in any sphere, including the religious.[63]

Some of this data may have reminded readers of the activities of the famous seventeenth-century Jesuit Roberto de Nobili. It is important to be aware of the differences between what he was doing and the search for the similar we have described above. De Nobili was from a good Italian family, and is well-known for his attempt to win converts by argumentation. His idea was to study Hindu scripture, and then argue with Hindus on the basis of logic that Christianity was a much more "correct" system of belief than was Hinduism. Part of his effort was to demonstrate, at least to his own satisfaction, similarities between the two religions. Most of this is quite different from the phenomenon we have described above. De Nobili was finding the familiar in order to bore from within Hinduism and so undermine it. His finding of the Same was not an agreeable and humane notice of similarity, but rather a tactic to subvert. As is well known, his efforts were not appreciated by his ecclesiastical superiors, and in any case they were unsuccessful.[64]

What can we make of all this? One could say that the early accounts of similarities between Hinduism and Christianity, such as da Gama's, merely show ignorance. Very quickly the Portuguese became well aware of the profound differences between their faith and that of the Hindus. Religious specialists had never had any doubts about this, and their solidity, and total rejection of idolatry, was powerfully reinforced once the Counter Reformation came on stream in mid century. The problem here is that the search for the same continues for a surprisingly long time. Tomé Pires and Duarte Barbosa were writing fifteen years after most Portuguese knew that the Hindus were not Christians, not even very lapsed ones. Fernão Lopes de Castanheda published his work in the 1550s, after ten years in India. How could they get it so wrong? It is possible that those who continued, despite the evidence, to find the Same were simply more humane, less intolerant than most of their fellows who launched vicious attacks on Hinduism.

For most Portuguese, the point presumably is that Hinduism during the sixteenth century obviously became less and less (in Said's terms) "radically new," and so could be evaluated more correctly, that is as near enough to totally different. Material matters could be evaluated neutrally, and objectively correctly, with no perception of European superiority. Counter-Reformation Portuguese could not do this in matters concerning religion.

Notes

1. For a recent excellent discussion see S. Arasaratnam, "Recent Trends in the Historiography of the Indian Ocean, 1500 to 1800". *Journal of World History*, I: 2 (Fall 1990), pp. 225–48.
2. Immanuel Wallerstein, "Incorporation of Indian Subcontinent into Capitalist World-Economy". *Economic and Political Weekly*, XXI, 4 Jan 1986, pp. 28–39; also published in *The Indian Ocean, Explorations in History, Commerce and Politics*, ed. Satish Chandra. New Delhi, 1987, pp. 222–53. Wallerstein, *The Modern World-System*, 3 vols. New York, 1974–89 [*The Modern World-System: Capitalist Agriculture and the Origins of the European World-Economy in the Sixteenth Century*, 1974; *The Modern World-System II: Mercantalism and the Consolidation of the European World-Economy, 1600–1750*, 1980; *The Modern World-System III: The Second Era of Great Expansion of the Capitalist World-Economy, 1730–1840s*, 1989].
3. Michael Adas, *Machines as the Measure of Men: Science, Technology and Ideologies of Western Dominance*. Cornell UP, 1989.
4. William Outhwaite, "Social Thought and Social Science". *New Cambridge Modern History*, vol. XIII. "Companion Volume," ed. Peter Burke. CUP, 1979, pp. 275–6. For an excellent discussion concerning how European travel became more "methodised," this culminating in a "truly modern scientific outlook" late in the eighteenth century, see Justin Stagl, "The Methodising of Travel in the 16th Century: A Tale of Three Cities". *History and Anthropology*, IV, (1990), pp. 303–38, especially p. 326.
5. Adas, *Machines*, p. 31.
6. Ibid. pp. 22, 31.
7. For earlier examples of similar work to do with the Pacific, see Bernard Smith's classic *European Vision and the South Pacific*, 2nd. ed. Yale UP, 1985, and the section "Mapping Mankind". *European Voyaging towards Australia*, eds. John Hardy and Alan Frost. Canberra, 1990.
8. Edward Said, *Orientalism*. London, 1978, pp. 2–3, 5, and passim. A good critique is Lata Mani and Ruth Frankenberg, "The Challenge of Orientalism". *Economy and Society*, 14:2 (May 1985), pp.174–191. See also Bryan Turner, "From Orientalism to Global Sociology". *Sociology*, XXIII:4 (1989), pp. 629–38. It is curious that Adas, working on a similar theme, makes so little use of Said's insights. See also Rana Kabbani, *Europe's Myths of Orient: Devise and Rule*. London, 1986, though she does not really differentiate power very well and she is not consistent on the relative power positions of her travellers. Most of the book is about the nineteenth-century use of the perceived sensuality and violence of the Orient to justify domination.
9. The following discussion draws on my *The Portuguese in India*. CUP, 1987, pp. 11–29, 81–115.

10. Fernand Braudel, *Civilization and Capitalism, 15th to 18th centuries.* London, 1981–84. 3 vols., III, pp. 534–5.
11. Eric R. Wolf, *Europe and the People without History.* Berkeley, 1982, pp. 79–88.
12. Quoted in Stagl, "Methodising", p. 310.
13. See a short but interesting article: Maria Emilia Madeira Santos, "A procura do semelhante e do familiar nas novas terras descobertas" in *Vice-Almirante A. Teixeira da Mota: In Memoriam*, Vol. II. Lisbon, 1989, pp. 57–60. The author provides a brief list of geographical similarities in Africa, such as that Melinde is physically very like Alcochete, on the Tagus near Lisbon.
14. *Intrepid Itinerant: Manuel Godinho and his Journey from India to Portugal in 1663*, ed. John Correia-Afonso. Bombay, 1990, pp. 161, 162, 177, 199.
15. Fernão Mendes Pinto, *The Travels of Mendes Pinto*, ed. and trans. Rebecca Catz. Chicago UP, 1989, pp. 173, 128, 223, 218.
16. "Descrição das terras da India Oriental, e dos seus usos, costumes, ritoes e leis". Biblioteca Nacional, Lisbon, f. 15 v.
17. Duarte Barbosa, *The Book of Duarte Barbosa*, ed. M.L. Dames. London, Hakluyt, 1918–21, 2 vols. I, p. 140.
18. Damião de Goes, *Crónica do felicíssimo Rei D. Manuel.* Coímbra, 1949–55. 4 vols, III, p. 241.
19. Barbosa, *Book*. I, p. 141.
20. Fernão Lopes de Castanheda, quoted in Donald F. Lach, *Asia in the Making of Europe*, vol. I. "The Century of Discovery", Chicago UP, 1965, p. 40.
21. "Livro de Varios Papeis," Biblioteca da Academia das Ciencias, Lisbon, A 64, f. 292 v.
22. Quoted in Lach, *Asia*. I, p. 458. Evora was the great favourite for comparison; apparently few Asian cities were *not* like Evora.
23. Barbosa, *Book*. I, p. 110.
24. Barbosa, *Book*. II, p. 73.
25. Barbosa, *Book*. I, p. 205.
26. Lach, *Asia*. I, pp. 390, 482.
27. ibid, pp. 417, 433, 454, 463.
28. Ludovico di Varthema, *The Itinerary of Ludovico di Varthema of Bologna from 1502–1508*, ed. Sir Richard Carnac Temple. London, 1928, p. 47.
29. J.H. van Linschoten, *The Voyage of John Huyghen van Linschoten to the East Indies.* 2 vols, London, 1885, I, pp. 207–8, 212–3; and all this is confirmed by François Pyrard de Laval, *The Voyage of François Pyrard of Laval to the East Indies*, vol. II. London, 1888, passim.
30. J.M. Pacheco de Figueiredo, "The Practice of Indian Medicine in Goa during the Portuguese Rule, 1510–1699". *Luso-Brazilian Review*, IV:1 (1967), pp. 52–3.
31. Linschoten, *Voyage*. I, p. 230.
32. See Alberto C. Germano da Silva Correia, *La Vieille-Goa.* Bastorá, 1931, p. 275, and Pyrard, *Voyage*, intro. p. xii, and II, 14. For the career of one such *fisico-mor*, Dimas Bosque, who was attached to the viceroy D. Constantino de Bragana, 1558–61, see Jaime Walter, "Dimas Bosque, fisico-mor da India a as sereias," *Studia*, XII (1963), pp. 261–71.
33. King to viceroy, Jan. 23, 1610, *Documentos remettidos da India, ou Livros das Monções*, ed. R.A. de Bulhão Pato. Lisbon, 1880–1935, 5 vols. I, p. 304, and king to viceroy, Jan. 30, 1613 *ibid.*, II, p. 300.
34. A.K. Priolkar, *The Goa Inquisition.* Bombay, 1961, p. 14 of Dr. Dellon's account.
35. Pyrard, *Voyage*. II, p. 13.
36. Abbé Carré, *The Travels of the Abbé Carré in India and the Near East, 1672–1674.* London, Hakluyt, 1947–48. 3 vols., pp. 284–5.
37. John Ovington, *A Voyage to Surat in the Year 1689*, ed. H.G. Rawlinson. London, 1929, p. 206.

38. John Henry Grose, *A Voyage to the East Indies...to which is added A Journey from Aleppo to Busserah, over the Desert, by Mr. Charmichael* [lst French ed, 1758, lst English ed 1766, 2nd Eng ed 1772, which adds Charmichael] 2nd ed., 2 vols. London, 1772. I, p. 250.

39. Bernard S. Cohn, "Cloth, Clothes and Colonialism: India in the Nineteenth Century". *Cloth and Human Experience*, eds. A. B. Weiner and J. Schneider. New York, 1989, p. 309.

40. *Mandelslo's Travels in Western India, A.D. 1638–9*, ed. M.S. Commissariat. Bombay, 1931, pp. 13–20.

41. Lach, *Asia*, pp. 822–35.

42. Braudel, *Civilisation and Capitalism*. III, p. 488.

43. Adas, *Machines*, pp. 22, 31.

44. Lach, *Asia*. I, pp. 431–46.

45. Said, *Orientalism*, pp. 59–63, 75.

46. Lach, *Asia*. I, p. 831.

47. Adas, *Machines*, p. 11–12.

48. Vitorino Magalhães Godinho, *Mito e mercadoria, utopia e prêtica de navegar, séculos XIII–XVIII*. Lisbon, 1990, p. 115, and generally 106–18.

49. Luís Graça, *A visão do oriente na literatura portuguesa de viagens: os viagantes portugueses e os itinerários terrestres (1560–1670)*. Lisbon, 1983, pp. 217–24, 260–80.

50. Tomé Pires, *The Suma Oriental of Tomé Pires and the Book of Francisco Rodrigues*, ed. Armando Cortesão. London, Hakluyt, 1944, I, 12–13; Daniel in *The Red Sea and Adjacent Countries at the Close of the Seventeenth Century as described by Joseph Pitts [c.1685], William Daniel [1700], and Charles Jacques Poncet [1698–1700]*, ed. William Foster. London, Hakluyt, 1949, p. 78.

51. *Intrepid Itinerant*, p. 81.

52. Nicolas Sanson, *L'Asie en plvsievrs cartes novvelles, et exactes; en divers traittes de geographie, et d'histoire...* Paris, 1652, p. 27. Interesting to note that a very recent study of Islam and India makes the same mistake: André Wink, *Al-Hind: The Making of the Indo-Islamic World. Vol. I. Early Medieval India and the Expansion of Islam, 7th–11th Centuries*. Leiden, 1990, p. 33, where it is claimed that the *hajj* "usually coincided with the south-west monsoon".

53. Said, *Orientalism*, pp. 58–9. He is in fact writing about European views of Islam, but to my mind what he is saying applies much better, at least in my period, to Hinduism, for Islam was perfectly familiar to Europeans.

54. Tomé Pires, *The Suma Oriental*, I, p. 66. Pinto, *Travels*, p. 345, notes similarities between the behaviour of Buddhist pilgrims and Christians going to Santiago de Compostela.

55. Quoted in Lach, *Asia*. I, p. 387 and f.n. Lach himself, p. 187, shows that Castanheda had a good education.

56. Barbosa, *Book*. I, pp. 115–6.

57. Vasco da Gama, *A Journal of the First Voyage of Vasco da Gama, 1497–99*. Hakluyt, 1898, pp. 49, 52–5.

58. Pedro Cabral, *The Voyage of Pedro Alvares Cabral to Brazil and India*. Hakluyt, 1937, p. 170, and cf. 188–90.

59. Da Gama, *Journal*, pp. 137–8.

60. Cabral, *Voyage*, p. 79.

61. João de Barros, *Da Asia*. Lisbon, 1778–88. I, iv, 9; II, v, 1.

62. Luis Vaz de Camoens, *The Lusiads*, trans. W.C. Atkinson. Penguin, 1952, p. 170.

63. See Rebecca Catz's excellent edition and introduction, passim, cf. note 15.

64. For an agreeable account of de Nobili see Vincent Cronin, *A Pearl to India: The Life of Robert de Nobili*. London, 1959.

X

The Indian Ocean and the Red Sea

This chapter describes the role of the Indian Ocean, and more specifically the western corridor or sector of this ocean, the Arabian Sea, in the spread and continuance of Islam in eastern Africa. It will begin by sketching some salient characteristics of this vast entity, looking first at "deep structure" matters like winds and currents and topography.[1] The account moves on to consider connections across these waters, looking at matters like trade and the dissemination of crops and disease. It then focuses on the circulation, via the ocean, of religion, with particular reference to the role of seaborne Muslim religious specialists and ideas. However, in what follows I will aim only to write about external matters in the wider Muslim world that affected Islam in eastern Africa. What happened when these influences arrived in our area is the concern of several other chapters in part 3 of this book.

At first glance, it may seem that one would expect few connections across and around the Indian Ocean before our modern era. We are often told that the world today is far more integrated than ever before—that we live in a global village. Yet there was, as we will see, copious interaction over long distances across the Indian Ocean for at least the last two millennia. A matter that may seem to hinder communication is the sheer extent of the Indian Ocean. This is an ocean that stretches from 28 degrees north latitude in the far north at the head of the Red Sea to around 26 degrees south latitude in the far south of Mozambique. Indonesia is in longitude 95 to 140 east, as compared with about longitude 38 east for Mozambique. By comparison, the continental United States occupies only from 50 to 30 degrees north latitude, and from longitude 125 to 75 east. The coast with which this chapter is most concerned, that is the west coast from the head of the Red Sea to southern Mozambique, stretches for more than five thousand miles. A direct passage from east Africa to Indonesia is more than four thousand miles. Again by comparison, the United States at its greatest extent is fewer than three thousand miles from east

X

coast to west coast. Consequently, travel times in this ocean area were very large: often some months to go from one major entrepôt to another. Yet people were able to overcome these difficulties, helped in part by particular deep-structural factors.

The pattern of winds in the Arabian Sea is familiar enough. Many authorities stress the divide of the coast at Cape Delgado. As a rule of thumb, down to Cape Delgado is the region of one monsoon, from Arabia and India; south of there is the region of two. The northeast monsoon starts in November, and one can leave the Arabian coast at this time and reach at least Mogadishu. However, the eastern Arabian sea has violent tropical storms in October and November, so for a voyage from India to the coast it was best to leave in December. By March, the northeast monsoon was beginning to break up in the south, and by April thè prevailing wind was from the southwest. This was the season for sailing from the coast to the north and east. At its height, in June and July, the weather was too stormy, so departures were normally either as this monsoon, the southwest monsoon, built up in May, or at its tail end in August.[2] Ocean currents also affected travel by sea.

The third geographical matter that affects the influence of the ocean on travel and the land is coastal topography. Broadly speaking, no matter how favorable the winds and currents may be, no one is going to want to travel to an uninhabited desert shore. Equally unattractive would be an unproductive coastal fringe cut off from a productive interior by impenetrable mountains. But in fact, most of the shores of the Arabian Sea are not quite as inhospitable as these examples. In India, a fertile coastal fringe, especially in the south, the area of Kerala, is backed by the high mountain range called the western Ghats, but these are nowhere completely impenetrable. So also on the Swahili coast, where again behind a productive coastal zone is the *nyika,* a mostly barren area difficult, but not impossible, to travel through on the way to more fertile land farther inland. On the northern shores of the Arabian Sea, the coastal fringe is mostly much less productive, and leads to inland areas that often are hostile deserts. This may help to explain a long history of out-migration from such areas as the Hadhramaut and Oman.

Who are some of the people who traveled around and across the Indian Ocean? We will deal in detail with people transporting religious ideas later. For now, we can note merchant groups from very diverse areas indeed. Armenians traveled from their homeland in Iran all over the littoral of the ocean, and far inland. Everywhere they traveled they found hospitality from fellow Armenians. Jews were to be found all around the shores of the ocean, and especially on the west coast of India. Muslim merchants traveled and traded far and wide. From bases in Egypt or southern Arabia, their reach extended all around the shores of the ocean, and as far as China: indeed, Patricia Risso considers that their fortunes in faraway China influenced importantly their activities in the ocean.[3] Hindu merchants were to be found in little colonies or merely as sojourners in every major port city all around the ocean's shores, including the so-called exclusive Muslim heartland of the Red Sea. More recently, various other communities have traveled and settled very extensively. The Goan Christian population are to be found in other Portuguese colonies, especially

Mozambique, and more recently in the Gulf oil states. Nor did people travel only for trade or to find employment. About fifteen hundred years ago, a vast, and as yet poorly understood, movement of people from what is now known as Indonesia resulted in the population of the huge island of Madagascar. This influence is plain to see today in many areas of life. Many questions remain unanswered: Was this a more or less individual, or even accidental, enterprise, or was there some directing hand? Was any contact maintained with their homeland far to the east?

Other people who traveled and sometimes settled are legion. One example, giving a glimpse of very diverse connections indeed, is the actual people on the ships. Merchants, or their agents, traveled far and wide in search of profit. The famous Asian peddlers, an important part of Asian sea trade for centuries, were pure itinerants, who often had no home at all. Skilled navigators seem to have been a group of their own, their skills being recognized internationally. The pilot who fatefully guided Vasco da Gama from Malindi to Calicut in 1498 is one example; da Gama was so impressed with him that he took him back to Portugal, where he was quizzed on his knowledge by, among others, Italian merchants.[4]

The most discussed, and the most notorious, of all human movements was trade in humans themselves. This topic is hardly germane to a discussion of the Indian Ocean and Islam in eastern Africa; just because many of the traders were Muslim, and some slaves were sold into Muslim areas, does not mean this was an "Islamic" trade. Similarly, as western Europe industrialized, the slave mode of production became outmoded and inefficient. This did not happen in the Indian Ocean world, and hence, for Arab traders and producers, the trade continued; this however was not a function of their being Muslim but of their not yet having made the transition to capitalism. There was an extensive trade to 'Abbasid Iraq from eastern Africa, primarily from the northern areas of Ethiopia and Somalia, from at least the eighth century. Severe oppression and backbreaking work in the marshlands of southern Iraq led to numerous revolts, the largest being the Zanj revolt of 868–83. This revolt may well have contributed to the weakening of the 'Abbasid empire, while in turn this weakening led to economic decline in the Middle East and hence a smaller demand for slaves. Later we find African slaves serving on board ships, and as military elites, in India; indeed, even some Indian Muslim rulers were technically slaves. From the late eighteenth century, this trade expanded enormously, with slaves from eastern Africa being destined for date plantations in Oman, plantation agriculture on the Swahili coast and in Zanzibar, and European plantations on the French islands, especially Madagascar, and in the Americas, notably in Brazil.[5]

Early contacts around and across the ocean were primarily for trade. We know, for example, of a quite extensive trade between Mesopotamia and the Indus Valley civilization some five thousand years ago. Romans traded with India, and from this same time of about two thousand years ago, Indians, and possibly Arabs, were active on the east coast of Africa. By the early modern period, trade had increased, and linked together very far-flung areas.

The general point here is that eastern Africa was solidly geared into the Indian

Ocean world long before the rise of Islam. Arabs certainly had come down from the Red Sea and so along the coast; in the seventh century, these traders converted to Islam, and kept on trading. Indians had been in the area for centuries before Islam. Pre-Islamic Sassanian pottery testifies to ties with the Gulf before Islam, while Chinese porcelain fragments again point to very early contacts. It is not, then, a matter of newly converted Muslims "opening up" the Swahili coast. Trade patterns continued, relatively unchanged at first.

This was a very long-distance trade, and one where a vast variety of products were traded—both humble items like cloths and food and luxuries like gold and ivory. High-cost luxuries made up a considerable, and glamorous, part of the trade. Some came from outside the ocean, such as silks and porcelains from China. Others originated in the ocean area. Spices—mace, nutmeg, cloves, cinnamon, and pepper—came mostly from Indonesia, with some pepper from India and cinnamon from Sri Lanka, and were universally valued to flavor food. Spices thus flowed all around the ocean, and far beyond. China was a huge market for pepper, as was Europe.

Precious metals also were in demand everywhere, at first for hoarding and ornamentation, but increasingly to be used for money. The Indian Ocean area produced little here. The exception was gold from the Zimbabwe plateau, which reached a peak of production before 1500. Soon after this, precious metals flowed in from the Americas in a complicated pattern. Some came across the Pacific to Spanish Manila, and then on to China. From about 1550 to 1700, Japan produced much gold and silver, most of which ended up in China. The bulk of the supply for our area came across the Atlantic from South America to Spain. From there some came via the Cape of Good Hope to the Indian Ocean in Portuguese ships, and later with the Dutch, but much more flowed through the Mediterranean and to the ocean via the Red Sea and the Gulf. Other luxury products were legion: for example, ivory from eastern Africa was much in demand as being far superior to Indian and Southeast Asian equivalents. This product was to be found all along the shores of the ocean, and indeed far away in China.

Probably the greatest bulk of trade items were cotton cloths from India. Some of these were very fine things indeed, with gold and silver woven into the diaphanous material, but much of it was cheap stuff for poor people's everyday wear. Huge amounts of such cloths were exported from the three main Indian production zones of Gujarat, Coromandel, and Bengal. It was only in the nineteenth century, when English machine-production undercut Indian handicrafts, that India ceased to be the region that clothed virtually the whole littoral and far inland in the Indian Ocean. Today this trade has again reverted to the control of countries around the ocean: India again, and also many countries in Southeast Asia, not to mention vast production in China. *Kanga,* long strips of colorfully dyed cloth very widely worn on the coast, provide a specific modern example. In the nineteenth century, these were imported from England. Later in the century, India was allowed to develop a modern textile industry, and kanga came from there. Now some are made locally, some in India, and some in China.

Most cloths must be considered to be necessities, not luxuries. Another necessity is food, and basic foodstuffs like rice and wheat were carried very long distances in the early modern Indian Ocean. Several of the great port cities—Melaka in the sixteenth century, Zanzibar in the nineteenth—imported most of their food. Another item was lumber. Mangrove poles from the Swahili coast, and teak from India, were valued for house building and ship construction.

Products were not only traded across the ocean; sometimes they were transplanted to grow in new places. One famous modern example is cloves, which in the nineteenth century were taken from their major production area in the Malukus in eastern Indonesia and grown, very successfully, in Zanzibar. They thus moved from the far east of the ocean to the far west. As one would expect in an oceanic zone so open to exchange and contact, many other plants have moved, and indeed they have become so indigenized that today we think of them as native. Hot chili peppers, for example, are often thought of as typifying Indian curries, yet they were introduced only in the sixteenth century, from the Americas by the Portuguese.

Some products and styles that today are spread all around the ocean originated in the distant past in one particular area. The best example is bananas, which came from Indonesia with the migrants to Madagascar, and subsequently were much modified and improved in Africa. The areca nut, a mild stimulant that originated in Southeast Asia, again is ubiquitous around the ocean. Ibn Battuta was offered some in Mogadishu as a gesture of respect for his learning. Newitt and Middleton provide quite long lists of products, techniques, and crops imported into, and indigenized in, East Africa: cotton, rice, bananas, coconuts, mangoes, outrigger canoes, looms, square houses, and the use of coral cement in construction.[6] Many other products apart from chili peppers were introduced to the Indian Ocean from America by the Portuguese: pineapples, maize, cassava, cashew trees, cucumbers, avocados, guava, and tobacco.

Another importation from American to the Indian Ocean was apparently a much more virulent version of syphilis. It is believed that someone on Columbus's second voyage was responsible for bringing the infection into Europe, where it spread with remarkable rapidity to Asia. There is a case reported from Canton as early as 1502, and in 1505 the Italian Varthema in Calicut claimed that the ruler had "the French disease ['Frangi'] and had it in the throat."[7]

David Arnold has written more generally about the Indian Ocean as a "disease zone." Bubonic plague, for example, may well have spread to Europe not only by land but also by sea via the Indian Ocean, and of course this fearsome disease was to be found also around the shores of the Indian Ocean. Cholera and smallpox also spread out from India all over the ocean. In the early eighteenth century, leprosy spread in South Africa. Its origins may well lie on the other extreme of the ocean, with the Malay servants and slaves recently introduced to this Dutch colony. A century later, as communications became more frequent and intense, a series of cholera epidemics spread out from India all over the ocean. In 1821, cholera reached Java, where it killed 125,000 people, and at the other end of the ocean, in eastern Africa, there was a particularly serious outbreak in 1865. The *hajj* was a great transmitter of this disease, and mortality at Mecca itself was often fearsome. In 1865, fifteen thousand out of a total of ninety thousand pilgrims died. In the 1880s, rinderpest was introduced into Ethiopia, probably again from India, and in the next decade spread, with devastating effects, down the east coast of Africa.[8]

A recent trend in history writing has been the effort of "world historians" to transcend state boundaries. The Indian Ocean is a particularly suitable area for this sort of analysis, for states, and more generally politics, played little role for most of its history. It is in fact precisely five hundred years since politics was introduced into the ocean. Before the arrival of the Portuguese, there is very little evidence of landed states attempting to extend their power to control over the ocean. By and large, the seas were, in contemporary Western juridical terms, mare liberum, where all might travel freely.[9] To be sure, the controllers of port cities levied taxes on those who called to trade, but on the other hand they made no attempt to force seafarers to call at their ports. And even if they had wanted to do this, two major limitations would have rendered their efforts nugatory. First, none of them had armadas effective enough to roam over the vast ocean and force people to call at a particular port. Second, in areas such as the eastern African coast and the western Indian coast, these port cities competed with each other. Sea traders were looking for entrepôts where the products they wanted were available; they also expected taxes to be reasonable, and they wanted no arbitrary confiscation of their goods or other abuses. If they were ill-treated in one port city, they had the option to turn to another; hence, the ocean's long list of port cities that rose and declined.

This is not the place to describe in detail the impact of western European powers on the Indian Ocean. Suffice it here to note that it was them, and the Portuguese first of all, who introduced politics and naval power into the ocean. The Portuguese tried to monopolize trade in some products, and direct and tax other trade. From the seventeenth century, they were imitated by the Dutch and the British, and later by the Omanis, and indeed the British in the nineteenth century were able to monopolize and limit to themselves the use of force in the ocean. As we will see, this had little effect on the subject of this chapter—the role of the Indian Ocean in the spread and changing nature of Islam in east Africa. The point for now is merely that naval power and "politics" played a small role in integrating the ocean—really none before the arrival of Europeans, and even then, very little.

We can now turn to cultural connections and so lead into our main concern; that is, Islam in the ocean and its shores. The aspect of culture that most concerns us is religion, more specifically Islam, but it is best to look more generally at cultural connections first. The key concept here is littoral society. The subject is far from fully studied yet, but the general notion is that there is a certain commonalty about all societies located on the shores of the Indian Ocean. We may note here that the very term *Swahili* means "shore folk," those who live on the edge of the ocean. It is argued that such societies, whether they be in eastern Africa or western or eastern India, around the shores of the Gulf and the Red Sea, on the southern Arabian shore, or in insular Southeast Asia, share certain characteristics. Heesterman stresses that it is transitional, permeable: "The littoral forms a frontier zone that is not there to separate or enclose, but which rather finds its meaning in its permeability."[10] In an earlier discussion, I sketched the case for identifying such a society, which has certain links and a commonalty to do with society, religion, and economy.[11]

East African specialists have contributed to this discussion. Chittick argued that the monsoons made the Indian Ocean a united entity. "This has resulted in its constituting what is arguably the largest cultural continuum in the world during the first millennium and a half C.E. In the western part of the basin, at least, the coasts had a greater community of culture with each other and with the islands than they had with the land masses of which they form the littorals."[12] Or, as Pouwels has it, by 1500 Swahili culture was "a child of its human and physical environment, being neither wholly African nor 'Arab,' but distinctly 'coastal,' the whole being greater than the sum of its parts."[13] A useful new concept here, which seems to get the essential relationships of coastal people very well, is resac. This refers to "the three-fold violent movement of the waves, turning back on themselves as they crash against the shore, [which] seeks to elucidate the way in which [like] the to-and-fro movements of the Indian Ocean, coastal and inland influences keep coming back at each other in wavelike fashion."[14]

The precise elements of commonalty of littoral society have not yet been adequately worked out. We could look at food, obviously largely derived from the sea. Houses may well be different from those inland, as they often use materials, especially coral, available on the shore. The whole rhythm of life is geared to the monsoons. Ship architecture historically may have been similar, characterized by the use of lateen sails. Certainly, littoral society was much more cosmopolitan than that of inland groups, for at the great ports, traders and travelers from all over the ocean, and far beyond, were to be found. There seem also to have been certain languages that achieved wide currency, such as Arabic in the earlier centuries. Jan Knappert finds that there are some five thousand words of Arabic influence in Malay, and more than that in Swahili, and about 80 percent of these are the same (that is, in Malay and Swahili) so that we have a "corpus of traveling Arabic words."[15] Freeman-Grenville tried to find links and commonalties between Swahili and the language of the Sidis of Sind.[16] Later, a sort of nautical Portuguese, and today variants of English, have achieved a similar, quasi-universal status.

Folk religion on the littoral similarly is to be distinguished from inland manifestations. On the coast, religion had to do with customs to ensure safe voyages, or a favorable monsoon. Particular gods were propitiated for these purposes. Specifically maritime ceremonies marked the beginning and end of voyages. Thus, folk religions on the littoral were functionally quite different from those found inland, precisely because the concerns of coastal people were usually quite different from those of peasants and pastoralists inland. It was the increasingly cosmopolitan aspect of the Swahili coast that contributed to its conversion to Islam.

James de Vere Allen, in one of his provocative but frustratingly erratic overviews, claimed that among the elements that contributed to an Indian Ocean world was indeed the Muslim religion. This means that he excludes from this world Sri Lanka, Burma, and Thailand, as they were not Muslim, but he includes South India, since this region, while not Muslim, is too important to be left out of the Indian Ocean world.[17] Despite these inconsistencies, Allen's central point is valid: Islam indeed provided a crucial link around most parts of the Indian Ocean, while on the other hand, any consideration of Islam in eastern Africa must include a maritime dimension, one focused on the Arabian Sea and the Red Sea. I will now turn to this central task.

The central thesis is that the Indian Ocean tied in eastern Africa to a vast, diverse, and cosmopolitan Muslim world. We have shown how the Indian Ocean has always been a place of movement, circulation, contacts, and travel over great distances. It could be that Islam fits well into this sort of environment. The Quran itself has positive things to say about travel by sea: "It is He who subjected to you the sea that you may eat of it fresh fish, and bring forth out of it ornaments for you to wear; and thou mayest see the ships cleaving through it; and that you may seek of His bounty, and so haply you will be thankful."[18] Islam has spread over very great distances. The travels of the famous scholar-traveler Ibn Battuta illustrate this very well, for in the fourteenth century he traveled about seventy-two thousand miles in nearly thirty years, and all the time virtually was in a Muslim world, from West Africa to China. It could be that Islam is more peripatetic than the other great world religions. Famous scholars and saints attracted, and continue to attract, the faithful from very wide areas.

In particular, Islam involves travel and movement because of the central role of the hajj, where historically hundreds of thousands, and today millions, gather together in one place at one time for one purpose. No other world religion has anything exactly similar. The role of Mecca and the hajj has been much studied. It is here that Muslims for the last thirteen hundred years and more have been brought face-to-face with the numbers and diversity of their fellow Muslims. The hajj then is a remarkably efficient method of integrating the worldwide community.[19]

A few more or less random case studies will demonstrate these far-flung ties of Islam over the Indian Ocean, before we turn to a more chronological description of the various Muslim influences coming into the eastern coast of Africa. Here are a few from Southeast Asia. A. H. Johns has investigated the career of Abd al-Rauf of Singkel, and this gives us a clear picture of the many ties and networks and connections established in seventeenth-century Islam, as well as of the centrality of the holy places in this process. Abd al-Rauf was born in North Sumatra around 1615. In about 1640, he moved to the Hijaz and Yemen to study. In Medina, his main teacher was the Kurdish-born Ibrahim al-Kurani. Abd al-Rauf spent a total of nineteen years in Mecca and gained very considerable prestige. In particular, he taught hundreds, even thousands, of Indonesians there, and initiated many of them into the order of which he was a distinguished member, the Shattariyya. He returned to Sumatra, to Aceh, in 1661, and was a revered teacher there for nearly thirty years. He kept in touch with Ibrahim in Medina and taught what he had learned from him to the many Indonesian, especially Javanese, pilgrims who stopped for a time in Aceh on the way to the Red Sea.[20]

Another Asian example stresses the role of Medina; it, too, shows the extreme cosmopolitanism of Islam, in this case in the eighteenth century. Muhammad Hayya, the teacher of Ibn 'Abd al-Wahhab, founder of the Wahhabiyya movement, studied in Medina with scholars from India, Persia, Algiers, and Morocco. His students came from Turkey, India, Yemen, Jerusalem, Baghdad, Damascus, and other Muslim cities. As Voll notes, "The Medinese scholarly community in general was able to contact people from throughout the world of Islam because of the Pilgrimage."[21]

Now two examples from India. Hajji Ibrahim Muhaddis Qadiri was born near Allahabad in northern India. He did the hajj and then studied in Cairo, Mecca, and Syria. He was away twenty-four years, but then returned to India, settled in Agra, and was a prestigious teacher until his death in 1593.[22] The international character of Islam at this time, and the pattern of a career for a Muslim religious specialist, is well illustrated in the history of a founder of the Suhrawardiyya sufi order in India. Shaykh Bahaud-Din Zakariyya was born late in the twelfth century, near Multan. He memorized the Quran, and undertook further study in Khorasan for seven years. Then he traveled to Bukhara, did a hajj, and subsequently studied hadith for five years in Medina. Later he traveled and studied and taught in Jerusalem and Baghdad, the latter place being where he joined his order.[23]

The career of Sayyid Fadl, a Hadrami sayyid very influential in the Mappilah community of Malabar in the nineteenth century, provides yet another example. Early in his career, he spent four years visiting Mecca and the Hijaz. It may have been during this time that he became an authority in Shafi'i law and a member of the 'Alawi *tariqa,* a sufi brotherhood. Later, his political activities in Kerala annoyed the British rulers, who after some time, in 1852, made him emigrate to Arabia. Subsequently he spent time in Istanbul and became one of the most important theoreticians of the Pan-Islamic movement, along with Jamal al-Din al-Afghani. When he was resident in Mecca, he influenced the some two thousand *hajjis* from Kerala who each year made the pilgrimage.[24]

Finally we turn to eastern Africa for a sketch of the career and travels of Sayyid Ahmad bin Sumeyt. His father Abubakar was a Hadrami sharif, born in Shiban, who was a trader and scholar and was made *qadi* (judge) of Zanzibar in the time of Majid (1856–70). Ahmad, too, grew up to be a trader and scholar. He interrupted his trading to study religion in Grand Comoro under the supervision of two scholars, one of them his father, who had retired there. Then Ahmad studied under an Iraqi scholar in Zanzibar, where he was made qadi in the 1880s. Even so, he later visited the

Hadhramaut three times to study yet more under famous scholars and get their *ijaza*—that is, a certification, license, or permit. While away between 1883 and 1886, he spent time in Istanbul and studied with Sayyid Fadhi Basha bin Alwi bin Sahi, a famous Hadhrami scholar, and through his influence received an Ottoman order from Sultan Abdul Hamid. In 1887, he studied in Al-Azhar and Mecca, and in 1888 returned to Zanzibar. From then until his death in 1925, he was famed as a scholar and teacher; students came from all over the coast. Indeed, he had an international reputation, for he was asked by the mufti of Mecca himself to settle a quarrel between two Zanzibari *ulama* (religious specialists). Even prestigious scholars in Egypt sometimes sought his opinion, such was his reputation.[25]

We now turn to a more chronological analysis of Islamic influences flowing into eastern Africa. These began even during the time of the Prophet, for there were Africans in Mecca at the time of the Prophet, and some became his Companions, such as Bilal, the freed Ethiopian slave. Close ties with Ethiopia, just across the Red Sea, are also demonstrated by the way before the *hijra*, Muhammad's migration from Mecca to Medina, some members of the new faith fled there. Islam spread across the Red Sea to the Dahlak Islands very early on, maybe by 700. Another important beachhead was Zayla, in the Gulf of Aden, from whence Islam was disseminated to southern Ethiopia. Moving farther south, Islam also spread to the Horn very early on. Even the interior was converted in perhaps the twelfth century C.E., or even earlier. Shaykh Barkhandle, whose religious name was Shakh Yusuf al-Kawneyn, is given much credit for this. His tomb is in the north of Somalia.[26]

As we would expect, Islam first spread into Somalia from the coast. By the tenth century at least, there were Arab merchants from Aden, Yemen, and the Hadhramaut in Mogadishu, Brava, and Marka, but while the local Somali population converted, it was not "Arabized," there being no large-scale Arab settlement in the area; rather, there evolved a mixture of local and Arab influences. Later there also was extensive contact with the Gulf.

What we have just noted about a mixture of Arab and Somali elements applies even more strongly farther south, in the Swahili coast proper. It used to be claimed that Arab colonies were established, and that these colonies owed nothing to the interior; they looked out, to the Indian Ocean and the Red Sea, never inland to the interior. Today we know that this is far from the case. The earliest mosques so far excavated, possibly dating from the eighth century, were for the use of visiting Arab merchants, or merchants who even had already settled. Wholesale conversions of the existing Swahili indigenes came later, in the twelfth century and a few decades on either side of this. In this context, an observation by two outstanding younger African scholars, F. T. Masao and H. W. Mutoro, is apposite: "The role of outsiders in the early history of the East African coast cannot be denied, but it is one thing to be part of a process of change and completely another to claim responsibility for the process."[27]

Muslims from the heartland of Islam, Hadhramaut especially, moved south for various reasons. Often they were traders, for the strong nexus between trade and the spread of Islam has been much noted all over the Indian Ocean world. Some moved as a result of push factors; in other words, they exchanged a life of poverty in the inhospitable regions of southern Arabia for the more benign region of eastern Africa. It used to be claimed that many of these migrant Hadhramis established or took over city-states on the coast. In seeing how this can square with the current rejection of any notion of Arab colonization, it is important to note two things. First, while many were no doubt from the Hadhramaut or Oman originally, they rapidly became merged into the Swahili world; that is to say, through acculturation and intermarriage they became another element, albeit a politically important one, in the Swahili world. Second, historically, and especially during the Omani period, a claim to an ancestry deriving from the heartland of Islam was a matter of prestige, and clearly many genealogies were manufactured, or at least embroidered, in order to support such claims. A detailed analysis of this matter may be found in chapters 12 and 14 of this book.

To continue on the topic of Arab colonization, it used to be thought that some of the early settlers and rulers were Shirazis, from the eastern shores of the Gulf. This also is now generally discounted. We noted some settlement from the Gulf on the Benadir coast of Somalia, and it seems that some people claiming Shirazi ancestry moved on south from there. Indeed, it could be that the (perhaps mythical) place of origin of the Swahili people, called Shungwaya, probably located somewhere around the Tana River area in the north of modern Kenya, may be linked to the Shirazi origins myth. Anyway, whether these purported Shirazis came from there or somewhat further north, they certainly succeeded in establishing ruling dynasties in several of the major port cities, whose rulers then proudly proclaimed their Shirazi ancestry. These rulers shared a common myth of origin, and had lineage ties with each other. But the claim of a direct link with Shiraz, or the Gulf in general, can be discounted. There was, however, extensive trade with that region during the period that the 'Abbasid caliphate, centered in Baghdad, was at its height, from the ninth to the thirteenth centuries. This was also a time of very extensive trade with China. Baghdad was very thoroughly sacked by the Mongols in 1258 and the focus of trade on the eastern African coast then shifted to southern Arabia, and especially the Red Sea and Hadhramaut area.[28]

What we see here are very extensive connections across the Indian Ocean, with rulers claiming origins in very distant, but still maritime, locations. These rulers, regardless of origins, interacted closely with religious specialists, and indeed in terms of Islam in Africa it is these people who are most important for our purposes. We can, then, now turn to the role of Hadhrami religious specialists on the coast.

We must first note that while contact between these two areas is most important for our purposes, in fact this was all part of a much wider flow, by which Muslims from the heartland, in this case southern Arabia, spread far and wide across the Indian Ocean. It seems that push factors at several times led to an outflow of men from the Hadhramaut, and indeed also from Oman to the east and Yemen to the west. Thus they moved to India after about 1200, and even today the "Arab" community in Gujarat preserves stories of their Hadhrami origins. They also, unlike other Muslims of northern India, belong to the Shafii *madhhab*. In Hyderabad in the Deccan, Hadhramis arrived in the eighteenth century to serve as soldiers for the Nizam, the ruler of this state. They also retain their Shafii allegiance despite being surrounded by Hanafi Muslims.

The flow to eastern Africa began after about 1250, and to Malaysia, Indonesia, and then the Philippines after about 1300. Thus were created vast, far-flung lineages, merchants and scholars mixed together, who had connections for both piety and pelf all over the ocean. Stephen Dale's exemplary work on the Mapillas of Malabar provides further detail. He notes that in this area, today called Kerala, Islam is of the Shafii madhhab, as compared with the Hanafi school of the Turkic-Persian rulers of the great inland empires. Scholars came to Kerala from Yemen, Oman, Bahrain, and Baghdad. From Kerala, Islam flowed on, to Southeast Asia, especially to the north Sumatran state of Aceh in the sixteenth century, and even to the Philippines. Indeed, in their wars against the Portuguese in the sixteenth and early seventeenth centuries, the Acehnese were helped by Muslims from southern Arabia and by Mapillas from Kerala. Further to demonstrate wide ties, some military support was supplied by the Ottoman Turks, whose sultan the Acehnese recognized as caliph.[29] Given this, there is a question about whether the Shafii madhhab is peculiarly suited to maritime locations. Certainly it is the dominant school in eastern Africa, the Comoro and Maldive Islands, the west coast of India, and Indonesia. The Shafii madhhab expanded to all those lands that surround the Indian Ocean, from the port towns of southern Arabia and the Gulf, through the work of itinerant merchants, scholars as well as migrants. They crossed the ocean or made their way from one port to the other.

While contact, and migration, was more or less continuous between other Muslim areas around the Arabian Sea and the African coast, a particular area, the Hadhramaut, and two particular times, the thirteenth to the fifteenth centuries and the later nineteenth century, are when there seems to have been most extensive contact between the coast and southern Arabia. If we think of the whole Indian Ocean, or even just the Arabian Sea, as a cultural corridor, then we have what may be called a subcorridor linking these two areas, that is coastal towns in the Hadhramaut such as al-Shihr and al-Mukalla, and also inland towns, connected to the Swahili coast.

In the fourteenth century, the Swahili city-states were at their most flourishing, and contact with the Hadhramaut was at its height. Large numbers of prestigious Muslims came to the area. These migrants brought with them the Shafii madhhab and, if they were sharifs or sayyids, very considerable *baraka,* or prestige, based on their claim to be direct descendants of the Prophet.

In the north, in Ethiopia and Somalia, these contacts seem to have been close throughout, given their location, so that there were continuing and extensive contacts with Hadhrami, Yemeni, and Hijazi migrants. But this northern area is also subject to other influences from the north, so that while the Shafii madhhab predominates on the Swahili coast, on the west bank of the Red Sea and further inland, the situation is more diverse, no doubt a result of location, and also of the continuing Coptic Christian presence in the area. In Ethiopia and the Horn, we find the

Shafi'i school, which clearly demonstrates influences from Arabia, but also the Maliki, from the Sudan, and the Hanafi, which comes in with the Ottomans.

On the Swahili coast, as we would expect, contact was especially close in the north, in the Lamu archipelago. A Portuguese observer noted of Pate, about 1570, that it "has considerable trade with Mecca and other parts. The town is very large and has many buildings. It was here that a Moorish caciz, the greatest in the entire coast, resided."[30] Late in the sixteenth century, a new group of Arab settlers, called Hatimi, arrived in Pate from Brava, a little way to the north, but who claimed to have originated in far-distant Andalusia.

This first wave of Hadhrami influence was succeeded by a more negative presence from across the sea—that is, the Portuguese, who came up from the Cape of Good Hope after 1498. Certainly they aimed to combat Islam wherever they found it, and here again we can see very wide connections indeed. The visceral hatred of the Portuguese for Muslims derived from their own experience in conquering their homeland from Muslims. Even after this, the Portuguese experience in fighting Muslims in Morocco all through the fifteenth century continued their tradition of a curious mixture of hatred and fear toward Muslims. The impact of the Portuguese on the coast is traced in chapter 12.

If it can be said that the Portuguese presence had mixed effects on Islam in the region, what can we say of the next major political change—that is, the Omani hegemony of the nineteenth century? The connection between Oman and the Swahili coast provides yet another example of close ties and connections all across the Arabian Sea, albeit a political rather than a religious one.

The major port of Oman, Muscat, had been ruled by the Portuguese until 1650, when they were expelled by the Ya'rubi dynasty. Soon after, Muslims in Mombasa, at this time ruled by the Portuguese, wrote to the Omanis asking for help to expel the foreign rulers. Oman responded and sacked Mombasa in 1661, raided Mozambique in 1670, and in 1689 destroyed the Portuguese settlement at Pate. In 1698, they captured Mombasa. In the second half of the seventeenth century, there was extensive Omani naval activity in the Hadhramaut area, near the Bab al-Mandab, and at Mocha and al-Shihr.

Early in the eighteenth century, Omani interest in and activity on the coast declined due to instability at home, but around the middle of the century, a new and much more mercantile dynasty, the Busaidi, gained control and increasingly focused on eastern Africa, especially as their activities in India were curtailed by the beginning of the establishment of British rule there. Zanzibar became the center of Omani power in East Africa, and in 1840 replaced Muscat as the capital of the Omani empire. Contact, both in terms of movements of people and trade, continued to be intense throughout the century, with especially large numbers of slaves being taken off to work on the date plantations of Oman.

On the face of it, one could predict quite major changes in religion on the coast. The Omani rulers, after all, belonged to the Ibadi group within Islam, and thus apparently had quite different religious practice than did the Swahili, with their adherence to the Shafi'i madhhab. Further, the Omanis established a powerful state in Zanzibar, one that had profound political and economic effects on the coast. For the first time, and the last, most people whom we call Swahili were being ruled under one authority and by fellow Muslims. Yet in fact the Omani state neither achieved, nor wanted to achieve, deep penetration into the lives of its more or less nominal subjects on the coast. Ibadi Islam is one of the more moderate tendencies among the Khawarij schism within Islam. In theory, the leader of the Ibadis was to be the one with military and religious knowledge, rather than the more usual emphasis on tribe or family or race. This was greatly diluted under the Busaidi dynasty, who indeed even took the title of sultan. But even at its purest, Ibadi Islam differs from Sunni or Shi'a mostly in terms of "theology," not in, say, ritual, taxation, marriage, or inheritance.[31] Hence, as other chapters show, the Omani impact on Islam in eastern Africa was again a mixed one, and appears to have been no more major, whether for better or worse, than was the Portuguese.

Wider connections were also in evidence in more social matters, and again we see the importance of the Hadhrami connection, which had a recrudescence under the Omanis in the nineteenth century. Family registers were kept to maintain linkages and the legitimacy of descent claims, especially for the dominant lineages, that is *shurafa'*, or sharifs. Hadhrami sharifs keep family registers, the central one being in the place of origin of the lineage in the Hadhramaut. Lineage members, wherever they are, must report births and deaths to this center—that is, to the *munsib*, the lineage head. Thus the sharif of the Jamal-al-Layl sharif lineage keeps a genealogy of the eastern African branch in Mombasa. He keeps it up-to-date by corresponding with other lineage members on the coast, the Comoros, and Madagascar, and periodically he also sends it to the head of the Jamal-al-Layl in the Hadhramaut.[32]

Just as these scholars and merchants, and their lineages, were cosmopolitan in the extreme, so also were the sufi tariqas, arguably the most vibrant and important part of Islam in the nineteenth century, if only because it impacted much more on common Swahili than did the learned work of the scholars. Different brotherhoods were dominant at different times and places. In the north, Ethiopia, the Horn, and Somalia, the Qadiri order had long been important. During the nineteenth century, it was challenged by the reformist Idrisi strand from the north. Later in the nineteenth century, a new brotherhood founded in Mecca found its way over the Red Sea. This was the Salihiyya brotherhood, named after its leading shaykh, Muhammad ibn Salih al-Rashidi, who died around 1919. He was from the Sudan, but settled in Mecca and acted in a way typical of sufi orders in that he initiated men into his order as khalifas (deputies) who then went home to spread his doctrine. Sayyid Muhammad, as one would expect, had spent five or six years in Mecca, Medina, and Yemen studying, undertaking the hajj, and getting initiated into the order.

The most influential brotherhood on the coast was the 'Alawi order, a very austere one, with its main shrine at Inat. Late in the nineteenth century, a branch of the main 'Alawi order, the Shadhiliyya, won much support on the coast, even as far south as Mozambique. The founder of this branch, Shaykh Ma'ruf, was from the

Comoro Islands; a sharif, he did the hajj. Here we see another example of widespread connections: one of the areas where he was most influential was southern Somalia. Shaykh Ma'ruf died in 1905 and his tomb in the Comoros is a place of pilgrimage for all the Shadhilis of eastern Africa.

The Qadiri brotherhood, followers of Abdul Qadir Gilani, were at least as far-flung across the ocean as were the 'Alawi. The legends of the founder have been translated into Swahili as well as Malay and Javanese. During the colonial period, the Qadiri network reached from Mecca and southern Arabia along the Somali coast past Brava, Kisimaiu, and Lamu to Mombasa, and then via Voi, Nairobi, and Kampala into the Belgian Congo. Other lines went to German East Africa, others west through the Sudan to Nigeria and Mali. Their teachings spread from the Hadhramaut ports to Indonesia. Not surprisingly, then, some textbooks found in the Belgian Congo were identical to those in use in Indonesia. This was a very rich and important network.

Several other interlocking strands from outside the area have been important during the last two centuries. Among them are the reformist Wahhabi movement, Pan-Islam, the Islamic reform movement associated with Muhammad Abduh, the influence of colonialism, and the impact of the so-called Islamic revival of recent times. As to the first, the Salihiyya order in the north was a strictly observant movement not unlike the reformist Wahhabi tendency that had arisen in Arabia late in the eighteenth century. It is interesting, however, that Wahhabism, while influential in inland Arabia, and to an extent in Ethiopia, and a source of continuing problems for the rulers of Oman, never gained much support in the Hadhramaut, and hence had little impact on the Swahili coast.

Pan-Islam, promoted by Abdul Hamid II, the Ottoman sultan, after 1880, had a wide impact on the Muslim world and frequently was tied in with anticolonial movements. Notions of Islamic unity and the centrality of the caliph in Istanbul were widely dispersed in our area. These ideas were given greater currency by the rulers of Zanzibar, as Pouwels notes in chapter 12.

This was a reciprocal matter, for some scholars from eastern Africa spent time in, and were influential in, Istanbul itself. So, for example, an important Zanzibar scholar, Ibn Sumayt, spent a year in Istanbul and studied with his fellow Hadhrami scholar Fadl b. Alawi, who was one of the theoreticians of the Pan-Islam movement. Yet when World War I broke out, the flimsiness of the ties to Turkey were revealed, as indeed they were also in India and in the Hijaz. In the former, the khalifat movement met with little success, while in the latter the sharifian dynasty in Mecca and Medina opted for the Arab Revolt and the Allies rather than the Ottomans and their German allies.

The broad impulse to moderate Islamic reform, associated with Muhammad Abduh in Cairo and his successors, met some response on the coast. However, this may have been tempered by the orthodoxy of the Shafii school and the Qadiri brotherhood, so that many Swahili desiring to study in the heartland went not to Cairo and al Azhar but to the traditional *ribat* (sufi lodge) at Tarim. Nevertheless, there was some influence, such as *Al-Islah* ("Reform"), a Mombasa paper established in 1932 that spread Islamic antiimperialist and nationalistic messages from Cairo.

Colonial rule from the late nineteenth century interacted with these various tendencies and influences from outside. A new wave of very confrontational prose-lytizers—in this case, Christian missionaries—were tolerated, sometimes supported, by the European colonial states. Their activities did much to produce a reaction that favored Islam as the more indigenous, and locally older established, religion. Colonial rule also involved speedier communications, and the widespread dissemination of ideas via the printing press. Knappert notes that textbooks for prayer sessions printed in Egypt, Bombay, Singapore, and Penang have been found in Jakarta, Mombasa, and Dar es Salaam. Texts for Shafi'i law were published in Swahili, Malay, Javanese, and Amharic.[33]

The end of colonialism, and the Islamic revival, have produced new trends in the Islam of eastern Africa, some positive and some negative. In Kenya, and to an extent Tanzania, the Swahili are now marginalized, considered to be collaborators with the slave-trading Omanis and then with the Western colonial rulers. In the face of this, some lineages "are now picking up on their Yamani or Umani patrilines where they can and going to Jeddah, Mecca, Muscat, Dubai and Abu Dhabi."[34] Others, no doubt the less prestigious, with no kin ties to the outside, have turned to Islam as a positive force and reaffirmation of a Swahili identity. Some have even converted to Shi'i Islam, this being considered to be more militant. Here for perhaps the first time in history we may see an influence from Iran, especially Iran since the revolution of 1979. In Zanzibar, the anti-Arab revolution of 1964 led to a period of downplaying of any foreign influences, but more recently, in 1985, an Omani consulate was set up, significantly not in the capital of Tanzania, Dar es Salaam, but in Zanzibar. Around the same time, discontent with what was perceived to be an anti-Islamic mainland regime led the island to join the Organization of Islamic Countries. Following a great outcry from mainland Christian politicians, this decision was reversed in 1993.

I want finally to locate all this material in a wider historiographical context. During the colonial period, Western authors presented Africa as a tabula rasa, on which European influence had a positive effect. Two tendencies have responded to these slights, but there is a tension between them. On the one hand, is a commendable effort to see Africa in its own terms—in fact, to indigenize African history. On the other hand, historians influenced by once-fashionable political-economy notions have written of African history as a long story of dispossession, and of deleterious foreign impacts.

Where, then, in a wider historiographical context, can we locate our data on religious flows and influences? We are not here dealing with the matter of the "quality" of the Islam of eastern Africa; other chapters deal with that in detail. All that need be said is that coastal Islam is a significant regional variant within the broad rubric of "Islam." The key point is reciprocity. It is not just a matter of Arabs and other foreigners impacting on the Swahili; nor is it merely the Swahili Africanizing the Arabs. Rather, it is a matter of to and fro, with input from both. Nor is this an unusual finding, for the same could be said about most other Islamic areas in the world, where local cultures have influenced profoundly what happens, and produced many regional variants—all of them, however, Islamic.

My concern is with external influences. Was eastern Africa merely a passive recipient of religious norms and practices from overseas, especially from Arabia? More than twenty years ago, the above-cited Allen noted with some despair that the received wisdom, which he hoped was not true, was that everything came from Asia, nothing from Africa.[35] We need to consider the extent to which the Islam of eastern Africa has merely drawn on, and modified, trends from the wider Islamic world around the Indian Ocean, as opposed to what it has contributed to the wider Islamic world.

The balance is heavily weighted toward the former. This is not to belittle Islam on the coast, for to an extent this applies to all Muslim areas around the ocean. Yet it seems to apply especially strongly to this area. This chapter has constantly stressed the centrality of the heartland. Local boys are sent off to study in Mecca, or Medina, or in the case of eastern Africa more likely in Tarim, and then come back with the prestige of an ijaza from these centers. Thousands, today even hundreds of thousands, of people from around the ocean go on hajj each year. This chapter has constantly noted the prestige, the baraka, of people who can trace their lineages back to the Prophet, or to some other acclaimed lineage from the Hadhramaut. Similarly, *madrasas* (Islamic schools) were set up in most of the major towns of the coast, but their founders, their inspiration, and their most prestigious teachers all came from outside.

In this regard, an Indian comparison may reinforce the point. The great madrasa of Deoband, in northern India, is generally considered to be second only to al Azhar in prestige for a traditional Sunni education. During its first one hundred (Islamic) years, it produced more than 7,000 graduates. Of these, 431 worked outside the subcontinent, with the greatest number in Afghanistan, Russia, Burma, China, Malaysia, and South Africa. There were even two who worked in Saudi Arabia and Kuwait, and one in Yemen.[36] Eastern Africa can boast no such prestigious college. To be sure, Muslims from outside eastern Africa attend some of the major festivals, but significantly these are considered to be in a way poor people's substitutes for the hajj itself.

In short, just as Swahili ships seldom left the coast, and very few Swahili traveled from the coast, so also we can say that norms and ideas came to the coast, but few went out. Possible exceptions are the occasional prestigious scholar from the coast who found a wider, Islam-wide audience (though most of these would claim to be Hadhrami, Meccan, or whatever by origin), the Mawlidi festival at Lamu, and the Ukitani Institute in Zanzibar, which have over the last century attracted people from many parts of Africa; these seem to be unique, and so atypical, examples. There never was, nor is, on the coast an Islamic center that attracts people from the wider Muslim world; obviously there is no Mecca or Medina, but also no shrine of a great sufi *pir*, no pilgrimage to the tomb of an imam, no influential variant, such as Shïi Islam in Iran since 1500, no educational institution such as Deoband or al Azhar, all of which cater to a worldwide Muslim constituency. The evidence, then—so far admittedly inconclusive—seems to be that, while the Indian Ocean network has operated to spread, and then influence, Islam on the coast, there has been little flow in the other direction, from the coast to the wider Muslim world.

Notes

1. For general accounts of the Indian Ocean, see Das Gupta and Pearson 1987, Arasaratnam 1994, Chandra 1987, McPherson 1993, Mathew 1990, 1995. For Southeast Asia, see Reid 1988–93. For a "popular" overview, see Hall 1996.

2. For details and references, see Pearson 1998, 51–54.

3. Risso 1995.

4. Subrahmanyam 1997, 121–28.

5. For a recent discussion and extensive references, see Alpers 1997.

6. Newitt 1994, 127; Middleton 1992, 202 fn. 8.

7. Varthema 1928, 63; Carmichael 1991.

8. Arnold 1991. On rinderpest, see Dahl 1979.

9. Subrahmanyam 1997, 109–12.

10. Heesterman 1980.

11. Pearson 1985.

12. Chittick 1980, 13.

13. Pouwels 1987, 31.

14. Caplan 1996. She is referring to the contribution of Jean-Claude Penrad in the book under review.

15. Knappert 1985, 125.

16. Freeman-Grenville 1988.

17. Allen 1980.

18. Arberry 1955, sura 16: verse 14; see also 2:164; 30:46.

19. Pearson 1994; Peters 1994; for the flavor of the hajj, by a participant, see Wolfe 1993, 1997.

20. Johns 1978, 471–72; Johns 1964, 8–11. The discussion here draws on Pearson 1990.

21. Voll 1975, 32–39.

22. For many other examples, see Rizvi 1978–83, 2:146–47, 294, 167, passim.

23. Rizvi 1978–83, 1:190.

24. Dale 1980, 6–7, 116–18, 128, 134–35, 167.

25. Salim 1973, 141–43; Pouwels 1987, 152–58.

26. Galaal 1980, 24.

27. Masao and Mutoro 1988, 586.

28. On the Shirazi matter, see Middleton 1992, 186–87; Spear and Nurse 1984, 74–79; Allen 1982.

29. Martin 1975. On Gujarat, see Misra 1964, esp. 78; for Malabar, Dale 1980, 26, 56–60.

30. Fr. Monclaro's account printed in Silva Rego, 1962–89, 8:355. A *caciz* is a Muslim religious specialist. For details, see Pearson 1994, 71–72.

31. See Risso 1986, 5, 22–33, for a concise introduction to the doctrine.

32. Shepherd 1984, 152–77; see esp. 157, 159.
33. Knappert 1985, 129.
34. Shepherd 1984, 172.
35. Allen 1980, 149.
36. Metcalf 1982, 110–11.

Bibliography

Abungu, George H. Okello. 1994. "Islam on the Kenyan Coast: An Overview of Kenyan Coastal Sacred Sites." In *Sacred Sites, Sacred Places,* ed. David Carmichael et al., 152–62. London: Routledge.

Adas, Michael, ed. 1993. *Islamic and European Expansion: The Forging of a Global Order.* Philadelphia: Temple University Press.

Allen, J. de Vere. 1980. "A Proposal for Indian Ocean Studies." In *Historical Relations across the Indian Ocean,* ed. C. Menaud, 137–51. Paris: UNESCO.

———. 1982. "The 'Shirazi' Problem in East African Coastal History." In *From Zinj to Zanzibar: Studies in History, Trade, and Society on the Eastern Coast of Africa (in Honour of James Kirkman),* ed. J. de Vere Allen and T. Wilson, 9–27. Wiesbaden: Steiner.

Alpers, Edward. 1997. "The African Diaspora in the Northwestern Indian Ocean: Reconsideration of an Old Problem, New Directions for Research." Paper presented at the conference on the Northwest Indian Ocean as Cultural Corridor, Stockholm, Jan. 1997.

Arasaratnam, Sinnappah. 1994. *Maritime India in the Seventeenth Century.* Delhi: Oxford University Press.

Arberry, A. J. 1955. *The Koran Interpreted,* ed. C. Mehaud. New York: Macmillan.

Arnold, David. 1991. "The Indian Ocean as a Disease Zone (1500–1950)," *South Asia* 14:1–21.

Bang, Anne. 1997. "The Hadramis of East Africa (ca. 1860–1910): A Diaspora Community in Context." Paper presented at the conference on the Northwest Indian Ocean as Cultural Corridor, Stockholm, Jan. 1997.

Barbosa, Duarte. 1918–21. *Livro.* 2 vols. Ed. M. L. Dames. London: Hakluyt.

Bouchon, Geneviève. 1973. "Les musulmans du Kerala à l'époque de la découverte portugaise," *Mare Luso-Indicum,* vol. 2, 3–59.

Braudel, Fernand. 1972. *The Mediterranean and the Mediterranean World in the Age of Philip II.* London: Collins.

———. 1981–84. *Civilization and Capitalism, Fifteenth to Eighteenth Centuries.* 3 vols. London: Collins.

Caplan, Patricia. 1996. Review of *Continuity and Autonomy in Swahili Communities,* ed. David Parkin (London: School of Oriental and African Studies, 1994) in *Journal of the Royal Anthropological Institute* 2:764.

Carmichael, Ann G. 1991. "Syphilis and the Columbian Exchange: Was the New Disease Really New?" In *The Great Maritime Discoveries and World Health,* ed. Mario Gomes Marques and John Cule, 187–200. Lisbon: Escola Nacional de Saude Pública.

X

Chandra, Satish, ed. 1987. *The Indian Ocean: Explorations in History, Commerce, and Politics.* New Delhi: Sage.

Chaudhuri, K. N. 1985. *Trade and Civilisation in the Indian Ocean: An Economic History from the Rise of Islam to 1750.* Cambridge: Cambridge University Press.

Chaudhuri, K. N. 1990. *Asia before Europe: Economy and Civilisation of the Indian Ocean from the Rise of Islam to 1750.* Cambridge: Cambridge University Press.

Chittick, H. Neville. 1980. "East Africa and the Orient: Ports and Trade before the Arrival of the Portuguese." In *Historical Relations across the Indian Ocean,* 13–22. Paris: UNESCO.

Dahl, Gudrun 1979. *Suffering Grass: Subsistence and Society of Waso Borana.* Stockholm: University of Stockholm Studies in Social Anthropology.

Dale, Stephen F. 1980. *Islamic Society on the South Asian Frontier: The Mappilas of Malabar (1498–1922).* Oxford: Oxford University Press.

Das Gupta, Ashin. 1979. *Indian Merchants and the Decline of Surat, c. 1700–1750.* Wiesbaden: Steiner.

————, and M. N. Pearson, eds. 1987. *India and the Indian Ocean (1500–1800).* Calcutta: Oxford University Press.

Dunn, Ross E. 1986. *The Adventures of Ibn Battuta, a Muslim Traveler of the Fourteenth Century.* London: Croom Helm.

Esmail, Aziz. 1975. "Towards a History of Islam in East Africa," *Kenya Historical Review* 3:147–58.

Freeman-Grenville, G. S. P. 1988. "The Sidi and Swahili." In *The Swahili Coast, Second to Nineteenth Centuries: Islam, Christianity, and Commerce in Eastern Africa.* London: Variorum.

Galaal, Musa H. I. 1980. "Historical Relations between the Horn of Africa and the Persian Gulf and the Indian Ocean Islands through Islam." In *Historical Relations across the Indian Ocean,* ed. C. Mehaud, 23–30. Paris: UNESCO.

Godinho, Vitorino Magalhães. 1981–83. *Os descobrimentos e a economia mundial.* 2nd. ed., 4 vols. Lisbon: Editorial Presença.

Goitein, S. D. 1954. "From the Mediterranean to India: Documents on the Trade to India, South Arabia, and East Africa, from the eleventh and twelfth centuries," *Speculum* 29:181–97.

Gonçalves, Fr. Sebastian. 1957–62. *Primeira Parte da História dos Religiosas da Compánhia de Jesus.* Ed. José Wicki. 3 vols. Coìmbra: Atlântida.

Hall, Richard. 1996. *Empires of the Monsoon: A History of the Indian Ocean and Its Invaders.* London: Harper Collins.

Heesterman, J. C. 1980. "Littoral et Intérieur de l'Inde," *Itinerario,* no. 1:87–92.

Horton, M. C. 1986. "Asiatic Colonisation of the East African Coastline: The Manda Evidence," *Journal of the Royal Asiatic Society:* 201–13.

Hourani, George. 1995. *Arab Seafaring in the Indian Ocean in Ancient and Early Medieval Times.* Rev. and exp. ed. Princeton: Princeton University Press.

Ibn Battuta. 1962. *The Travels of Ibn Battuta.* vol. 2. Trans. H. A. R. Gibb. Cambridge, U.K.: Hakluyt.

Johns, A. H. 1964. *The Gift Addressed to the Spirit of the Prophet.* Canberra: Australian National University Centre of Oriental Studies.

———. 1978. "Friends in Grace: Ibrahim al-Kurani and `Abd al-Rauf al-Singkeli." In *Spectrum: Essays Presented to Sutan Takdir Alisjahbana on his Seventieth Birthday,* ed. S. Udin. Jakarta: Dian Rakyat.

Kelly, J. B. 1972. "A Prevalence of Furies: Tribes, Politics, and Religion in Oman and Trucial Oman." In *The Arabian Peninsula: Society and Politics,* ed. Derek Hopwood. London: Allen & Unwin.

Khoury, Ibrahim. 1983. *As-Sufaliyya, "The Poem of Sofala," by Ahmed ibn Magid, Translated and Explained.* Coimbra: Centro de Estudos da Cartográfia Antiga, Seção de Coìmbra, Série Separatas 148, Junta de Investigações Científicas do Ultramar.

Kirkman, James S. 1970. "The Coast of Kenya as a Factor in the Trade and Culture of the Indian Ocean." In *Sociétés et compagnies de Commerce en Orient et dans l'Océan Indien,* ed. M. Mollat. Paris: SEVPEN.

Knappert, Jan. 1985. "East Africa and the Indian Ocean." In Stone 1985.

Le Guennec-Coppens, Françoise, and Pat Caplan, eds. 1991. *Les Swahili entre Afrique et Arabie.* Nairobi: CREDU/Karthala.

Levtzion, Nehemia, ed. 1979. *Conversion to Islam.* New York: Holmes & Meier.

Martin, B. G. 1975. "Arab Migration to East Africa in Medieval Times," *International Journal of African Historical Studies* 7:367–90.

———. 1976. *Muslim Brotherhoods in Nineteenth-Century Africa.* Cambridge: Cambridge University Press.

Masao, F. T., and H. W. Mutoro. 1988. "The East African Coast and the Comoro Islands." In *General History of Africa,* ed. M. El Fasi, vol. 3. Paris: UNESCO, 586–615.

Mathew, K. S., ed. 1990. *Studies in Maritime History.* Pondicherry: Pondicherry University.

———. 1995. *Mariners, Merchants, and Oceans: Studies in Maritime History.* New Delhi: Manohar.

Mazrui, Alamin M., and I. N. Shariff. 1994. *The Swahili: Idiom and Identity of an African People.* Trenton, N.J.: Africa World History.

Mazrui, Ali A. 1985. "Towards Abolishing the Red Sea and Re-Africanizing the Arabian Peninsula." In Stone 1984.

McPherson, Kenneth. 1993. *The Indian Ocean: A History of People and the Sea.* Delhi: Oxford University Press.

Menaud, C., ed. 1980. *Historical Relations across the Indian Ocean.* Paris: UNESCO.

Metcalf, Barbara Daly. 1982. *Islamic Revival in British India: Deoband (1860–1900).* Princeton: Princeton University Press.

Middleton, John. 1992. *The World of the Swahili, an African Mercantile Civilisation.* New Haven: Yale University Press.

Misra, S. C. 1964. *Muslim Communities in Gujarat.* London: Asia Publishing.

Newitt, M. D. D. 1994. *History of Mozambique.* London: Hurst.

Pearson, M. N. 1985. "Littoral Society: The Case for the Coast," *Great Circle* 7:1–8.

———. 1990. "Conversions in Southeast Asia: Evidence from the Portuguese Records," *Portuguese Studies* 6:53–70.

———. 1994. *Pious Passengers: The Hajj in Earlier Times*. Delhi: Sterling/Hurst.

———. 1998. *Port Cities and Intruders: The Swahili Coast, India, and Portugal in the Early Modern Era*. Baltimore: Johns Hopkins University Press.

Peters, F. E. 1994. *The Hajj: The Muslim Pilgrimage to Mecca and the Holy Places*. Princeton: Princeton University Press.

Pouwels, Randall L. 1987. *Horn and Crescent: Cultural Change and Traditional Islam on the East African Coast (800–1900)*. Cambridge: Cambridge University Press.

Purchas, Samuel. 1905. *Hakluytus Posthumus or Purchas His Pilgrimes*. 20 vols. Glasgow: Hakluyt.

Reid, Anthony. 1988–93. *Southeast Asia in the Age of Commerce*. 2 vols. New Haven: Yale University Press.

Risso, Patricia. 1986. *Oman and Muscat: An Early Modern History*. New York: St. Martin's.

———. 1995. *Merchants and Faith: Muslim Commerce and Culture in the Indian Ocean*. Boulder, Colo.: Westview.

Rizvi, S. A. A. 1973–83. *A History of Sufism in India*. 2 vols. New Delhi: Manoharlal.

Russell-Wood, A. J. R. 1992. *A World on the Move: The Portuguese in Africa, Asia, and America (1415–1808)*. New York: St. Martin's.

Salim, A. I. 1973. *The Swahili-speaking Peoples of Kenya's Coast (1895–1965)*. Nairobi: East African Publishing.

———. 1992. "East Africa: the Coast." In *General History of Africa*, ed. B. A. Ogot, vol. 5. Paris: UNESCO, 750–775.

Schimmel, Annemarie. 1980. *Islam in the Indian Subcontinent*. Leiden: Brill.

Serjeant, R. B. 1963. *The Portuguese off the South Arabian Coast*. London: Oxford University Press.

Shepherd, Gill. 1985. "Trading Lineages in Historical Perspective." In Stone 1984.

Silva Rego, António da, ed. 1962–89. *Documentos sobre os Portugueses em Moçambique e na Africa Central (1497–1840)*. 9 vols. Lisbon: National Archives of Rhodesia and Nyasaland, Centro de Estudos Historicos Ultramarinos.

Spear, T. T., and D. Nurse. 1984. *The Swahili: Reconstructing the History and Language of an African Society (A.D. 500–1500)*. Philadelphia: University of Pennsylvania Press.

Stone, J. C., ed. 1985. *Africa and the Sea: Colloquium at the University of Aberdeen* (March 1984), proceedings. Aberdeen: Aberdeen University African Studies Group.

Subrahmanyam, Sanjay. 1997. *The Career and Legend of Vasco da Gama*. New York: Cambridge University Press.

Tibbetts, G. R. 1971. *Arab Navigation in the Indian Ocean before the Coming of the Portuguese*. London: Royal Asiatic Society.

Tolmacheva, Marina. 1993. *The Pate Chronicle*. East Lansing: Michigan State University Press.

Trimingham, J. Spencer. 1964. *Islam in East Africa*. London: Oxford University Press.

Van Leur, J. C. 1955. *Indonesian Trade and Society.* The Hague: Hoeve.

Varthema, Ludovico di. 1928. *The Itinerary of Ludovico di Varthema of Bologna from 1502 to 1508.* Ed. R. C. Temple. London: Argonaut.

Voll, John. 1975. "Muhammad Hayya al-Sindi and Muhammad ibn ʾAbd al-Wahhab: An Analysis of an Intellectual Group in Eighteenth-Century Madina," *Bulletin of the School of Oriental and African Studies* 37:32–39.

———. 1994. "Islam as a Special World-System," *Journal of World History* 5:213–26.

Wilding, Richard. 1987. *The Shorefolk: Aspects of the Early Development of Swahili Communities.* Mombasa: Fort Jesus Occasional Papers no. 2. Mimeo.

Wilkinson, J. C. 1981. "Oman and East Africa: New Light on Early Kilwan History from the Omani Sources," *International Journal of African Historical Studies* 14:272–305.

Wink, Andre. 1990. *Al-Hind: the Making of the Indo-Islamic World.* Delhi: Oxford University Press.

Wolf, Eric R. 1982. *Europe and the People without History.* Berkeley: University of California Press.

Wolfe, Michael. 1993. *The Hadj: An American's Pilgrimage to Mecca.* New York: Grove.

———. 1997. *One Thousand Roads to Mecca: Ten Centuries of Travelers' Writing about the Muslim Pilgrimage.* New York: Grove.

Wright, H. T. 1993. "Trade and Politics on the Eastern Littoral of Africa (A.D. 800–1300)." In *The Archeology of Africa: Food, Metals, and Towns,* ed. Thurstan Shaw et al., 658–72. London: Routledge.

Zain al-Din. 1899. *História dos Portugueses no Malavar por Zinadim.* Trans. David Lopes. Lisbon: Imprensa Nacional.

The East African Coast in 1498:
A Synchronic Study

The present article is an attempt at a fairly synchronic depiction of what the Swahili coast looked like when Vasco da Gama arrived in March of 1498. It is presumably essential to have as clear an idea as possible of the context into which the Portuguese sailed in 1498, in Africa no less than in India, just as any study of Portuguese activities in the Indian Ocean area needs to be based on as profound a knowledge as possible not only of the Asian context, but also of the Portuguese mind frame.

While this will not be a history of the Swahili coast up to 1498, obviously I will draw on history from time to time to explain how the situation at 1498 had evolved. Yet in an important way this whole effort may be dubious. If we sketch the coast at 1498 then we are implicitly saying that this was a turning point, a watershed, a 'significant' date in the history of the area. Such an assumption may not be valid. If we try, we may find more momentous dates in the history of the coast than the arrival of the Portuguese: maybe the arrival of Islam; the more successful thalassocracy established by the Omanis from the late eighteenth century; the British and German move to formal colonialism a century later. To answer these questions would be to undertake a huge project; sketching some salient features of life on the coast at the close of the fifteenth century is task enough. The sources for the coast at this time are few indeed. By and large we have to rely on the accounts of the newly-arrived Portuguese, and make due allowances for their Eurocentric perceptions and prejudices. We are indeed making bricks without straw, yet even so an attempt to establish a benchmark has a certain heuristic utility, or so I hope.

Who were these coastal inhabitants, the Swahili? A portentous and difficult question indeed to answer for any time in history! Let us first acknowledge that the term itself is of rather recent derivation, and that there are major regional variations in culture and language over this huge coastal strip, stretching for over 3000 km from Mogadishu to Maputo. Further, who the Swahili people are, what they practice, what language they speak, all of these matters change over time; to be a member of the Swahili community in 1498 was a very different matter to being a member of what was ostensibly the same community at the height of Omani power in the mid-nineteenth century, or today. Let us also make clear that their relationship with their Bantu kin in the interior is a matter of controversy. Early colonial writers saw them as at least partially civilized, and so to be clearly differentiated from their barbarous neighbours inland. During the high colonial period, and indeed before this under the Omanis, the Swahili themselves emphasized their distinctiveness, the better to win privileges from their masters. Since independence chickens have come home to roost, and the Swahili have been commonly depicted as insufficiently 'African.' Some authorities in Kenya have even threatened to send them all back to Arabia. Yet the whole thrust of scholarship (as compared with the 'majimboism' or ethnic cleansing pursued by the Kenyan government recently) over the last twenty years or so, has been to depict the Swahili as inextricably African, having much more to do with the interior than with the maritime foreland. To be sure, as coastal people they were more exposed to influences from across the sea than were their interior kinfolk, yet overwhelmingly they are to be seen as African, as one variant in the rich mosaic of all the inhabitants of East Africa.

Inland and Maritime Influences

It is appropriate, then, to start by investigating the orientation of the Swahili port cities in 1498, and their ties with both the sea and the interior. We know that the Swahili did not travel far by sea, restricting themselves to coastal trade designed to provide goods for the larger Middle Eastern and Indian ships which undertook the oceanic voyages. Some Swahili people may have travelled, but not in the ships. Early in the sixteenth century in the great port city of Melaka, Tomé Pires found, among many others, men of Kilwa, Mombasa, Mogadishu and Malindi, but he implies that these people in fact were foreigners from the Swahili coast, not themselves Swahili, and in any case it is clear that these people did not travel in East-African-based ships.[1]

The relative orientation to the land is also shown in the very location of these port cities. Recent studies have suggested that the port cities were located so as to give access to the land rather than the sea. Wilson has investigated 116 Swahili sites from Mogadishu to the Tanzanian border, and finds that of these sixteen had no anchorages at all. Of the one hundred which did, thirteen could be classified as good, forty-seven as fair, and forty as poor.[2] The location of the major town of Gedi is apposite here. From the fourteenth to sixteenth centuries this town covered some eighteen hectares within its outer walls, which were three metres high. The largest building, dubbed the 'palace,' was about 25 metres by 35 metres. Yet this town was 6 km from the sea, and 3 km from the nearest creek.[3] No convincing explanation for its location has been put forward, to my knowledge. It is likely that it is simply an extreme example of Wilson's analysis, that is, that its concerns and connections were much more with the land than with the sea. If this were the case, it would tend to support Brown who, on the basis of his work on Siyu, also finds that the port cities were much more oriented to the land than to the sea. He even claims that the coastal locations of these port cities is not really anything to do with the sea, but rather with fresher well water on the coast, and the availability of the best building material, coral, there. Coral is too heavy to carry inland, hence they built on the coast.[4]

It is clear that there were copious social interactions between the Muslim Swahili and their immediate neighbours in the umland.[5] Influences in fact went both ways, though it must be stressed that one of the prime differentiators, Islam, remained urban. Wilding, in a powerful reinforcement of the land-oriented argument, stresses that Swahili merchants were much more likely to marry their daughters or sons to influential interior families than to sea-borne foreigners, whether Arab or Persian, let alone Indian or Portuguese.[6] Other Swahili people intermarried with the people they lived amongst, that is the slave populations who cultivated Swahili farms on the coast.[7] More social connections, and often conversion, resulted from the shifting power patterns of the interior. Groups who were displaced took refuge with people they already knew, the townspeople, and over the years merged into their society. Thus Swahili Islam and its wider society evolved, with powerful influences from the Bantu people of which they were part.

Economic relations with the umland were similarly reciprocal. Indeed, it is impossible to imagine a society as urban-oriented and specialized as the Swahili not having close relations with the surrounding countryside; they were essential. Two sorts of goods were being traded. In the countryside the main thing seems to have been foodstuffs to feed the towns, but some production was also destined for export, while the manufactures of the towns, especially cloth, were seldom exported but rather went to local markets.

Several recent studies have elaborated a little on these connections. In the case of Pate, Lamu, and Siyu we find very close ties between the port cities, in these cases located on islands, and the umland. Indeed, many of the mainland plantations were owned by Swahili from the towns, and used slave labour. In the early sixteenth century, Barbosa noted the usual mixture of war and economic symbiosis which characterized relations between Pate and Lamu and the coastal people: 'These carry on trade with the inland country, and are well walled with stone and mortar, inasmuch as they are often at war with the Heathen of the mainland,[8] Brown's thesis elaborates on Siyu, on Pate island. This stress on a land rather than sea orientation may be excessive, perhaps because Siyu fits this notion much better than some of its neighbours. He stresses that the port city was inaccessible to large *dhows*, but it was located in a rich agricultural area. Its residents cultivated land on the mainland, returning to their island home in the off-season.

On the mainland the Siyu people interacted with the Boni from Somalia, who once were pastoralists and now were hunters and gatherers. Siyu's mainland cultivation area overlapped with the traditional hunting grounds of the Boni, so there was mutual interaction. The Boni got food and cloth in exchange for ivory, timber and honey. They helped to plant and cultivate crops, and married with the rural Swahili slave population, and sometimes with the Swahili themselves.[9] So also in the region around the mouth of the Tana river, where at least today several different groups interact. In the wetlands areas the land is used by the Pokomo and Swahili for agriculture, by the Orma for grazing, and by the hunter-gatherers for exploiting wild resources, including animals.[10] Similarly with Lamu, where in fact, due to the infertility of Lamu island, most food seems to have come from the mainland, and here again the townspeople interacted with various mainland non-Muslim people.[11]

Further south we have excellent information on the situation in the immediate interior behind Malindi and Mombasa. Duarte Barbosa described Mombasa in the early sixteenth century.

This Mombaça is a land very full of food. Here are found many very fine sheep with round tails, cows and other cattle in great plenty, and many fowls, all of which are exceeding fat. There is much millet and rice, sweet and bitter oranges, lemons, pomegranates, Indian figs, vegetables of diverse kinds, and much sweet water. The men thereof are oft-times at war and but seldom at peace with those

120

of the mainland, and they carry on trade with them, bringing thence great store of honey, wax and ivory.[12]

Mutoro provides a fuller list of exchanges between Mombasa and the Mijikenda, the people living just inland from the port city. The Swahili got grain and other food from the Mijikenda, and the Mijikenda in return got cloth, beads, fish, cowrie shells, porcelain, glass and wire.[13] Connections at least in this area around Mombasa were facilitated by creeks which linked several coastal towns, including Mombasa itself, with what Willis calls the 'immediate hinterland'. These creeks could be navigated by small craft up to the foot of the main ridge.[14]

Richard Wilding provides a broad statement which will serve to sum up the matter of connections between the Swahili port cities and the close interior:

The Mijikenda obtained cattle from the Oromo of the hinterland, and used these animals not only for subsistence but also for trade with the Swahili settlements of the coastline. This function of commercial middlemen is visible in several other important trade commodities. Mijikenda also passed to the Swahili from the plains behind the coast incense, ivory, rhinohorn, rockcrystal, carnelian and small stock, in return for metal goods, cloth, beads and wire. They also traded their own hunted and gathered goods into the Swahili settlements, including gum copal, honey and hardwoods. The grain surpluses which they were able to produce on the fertile hills were also traded into the coastal towns. This commercial symbiosis was recorded physically by the spread through the Mijikenda settlements of the coconut palms, used for copra, wine, nut flesh, cooking oil and frond roofing tiles.[15]

Politics

The major Swahili port cities in 1498 were autonomous, subject to no inland or maritime power. All that we can find is a theoretical acknow-ledgement on one occasion of the claims of the Khalif of Islam, at this time the ruler of Egypt, the Mamluk sultan. In 1507 the Portuguese tried to communicate with the ruler of Oja, in the Tana river area, but he refused communication with those who cruelly persecuted peaceful Muslim traders going about their lawful business. His only overlord, he defiantly proclaimed, was the Khalif in Cairo.[16]

Nor indeed does it seem that any one city tried to dominate any of the others.[17] Our information on this matter is fragmentary enough, and it could be for example that towns closely clustered together, such as Siyu, Pate and Lamu, were opposed from time to time. In the absence of more information, it seems that dominance was a result of economic success rather than military attack. This applies particularly to Kilwa, the dominant Swahili port city in the fourteenth century. Sofala, much further south, was dominated by Kilwa, and channelled all its exports, of which gold was by far the most important, to it. It could be that as gold exports from the Zimbabwe plateau declined, so also did Sofala and by extension Kilwa. We do not, however, have any indication that this dominance was achieved by force. Indeed, the great distance, some 1600 km, between the two ports renders such a possibility *prima facie* unlikely. Kilwa's dominance may have been to do with the monsoon wind pattern, for ships from the north and east could reach Cape Delgado on one monsoon. Thus Kilwa, north of the Cape, could be reached, but not Sofala in the extreme south. Hence geography dictated that Kilwa was the great centre for receiving exports from the south, and breaking up and redistributing imports from the north. At the time of the arrival of the Portuguese it was Mombasa which had become dominant, at least on the northern coast, but it seems that openly hostile relations with its neighbour, Malindi, were a product of the sixteenth century and had something to do with the Portuguese presence in a way analogous to relations between Cochin and Calicut on the southwest coast of India.[18]

An important authority, Richard Wilding, has written of 'the kaleidoscopic political mayhem of Swahili life.'[19] We have evidence of considerable factionalism among the élite of some of these towns, most notably Mombasa, whose Swahili inhabitants were divided into twelve communities.[20] More open tension, to the point of violence, came from the ports' immediate neighbours inland. The political context is one where the port cities controlled neither land nor sea, and from time to time were threatened from both directions. We know much more about this once the Portuguese arrive and we have quite well documented accounts of such tensions, but it is clear that these were to be found in 1498 also. For example, it was a traditional obligation of the ruler of Mombasa to pay a tribute or more accurately protection money to an interior group, the Mozungullos, who lived around Mombasa. They were described by the Portuguese, referring to a continuing situation, as having 'neither law nor king nor any other interest in life except theft, robbery and murder.' There were about three or four thousand of them. Although described as timid, they were formidable users of poisoned arrows, so that Mombasa was always afraid of them. In theory they were vassals of the ruler of Mombasa, but 'their submission was mainly obtained by giving them cloths. They were in reality quite different from vassals.' Indeed, the Swahili inhabitants of the coast north and south of Mombasa are described as being 'like prisoners of the Mozungullos Caffres, because they have to pay them a large tribute in cloth in order to be allowed to live in security.'[21] The total picture then is an unusual one, of a city being held in thrall by the rural inhabitants of its own interior.

A very similar political nexus between town and country prevailed on the mainland opposite Lamu. The Swahili inhabitants had close relations with the various groups who controlled the mainland over the years. Indeed, when a mainland controlling group was expelled by newly arrived peoples, they often would take refuge on the islands with the Swahili people they had known for so long, and in time would merge into Swahili society.[22]

On the other hand, it seems that Kilwa at its height had much more domineering relations with its immediate inland. Ibn Battuta in 1331 noted that Kilwa was a very substantial town. Its inhabitants were mostly 'Zinj', jet black in colour. Its people undertook *jihad* against the heathen Zinj people who were contiguous with them. Its Sultan often raided the Zinj and took booty, one-fifth of which was used for pious purposes.[23] In sum, the port cities had complex political relations with their immediate neighbours, varying at different times between cooperation, uneasy alliances based on payments from the towns, and occasional hostility.

Finally in this section on politics, we must address the vexed question of whether these port cities tried to interfere in the conduct of sea trade, for example by forcing ships to call in, or even patrolling the ocean to control trade. We have no evidence at all of either of these activities in what does seem genuinely to have been a *mare liberum*. However, we do have some curious and conflicting information about the collection of customs duties in these port cities, and there seem here to be hints of some element of coercion being involved.

One would expect these fortunately located port cities to levy high taxes, and indeed they did. It has been generally assumed that the wealth of Kilwa, seen in the vast 'palace' and mosque, was derived by rulers from the profits of taxing trade. Yet there is considerable confusion in the sources over the role of these mini-states in trade, and especially how and if they taxed it. Barros presents a version of a state of nature in Mozambique when da Gama arrived. The Portuguese admiral was greeted by a native of Fez, this in itself indicating how international the trade was. This person told da Gama that the custom of the sultan 'was when strange ships arrived to send and enquire what they sought; and if they were merchants they might trade in that country, and if navigators bound to other parts he provided them with whatever was to be had there.'[24] This happy situation, if indeed it existed, was soon to be disrupted by the Portuguese.

Other evidence seems to show that some Swahili rulers had never even thought of taxing trade. Tolmacheva, in her analysis of various versions of a Pate chronicle, notes that the chronicle says that the Portuguese said to the local ruler, "'Your kingdom is very great, but there is no profit. Why do you not make taxes?" So they made a customs house at a place in Pate harbour called *Fandikani;* in the language of the Portuguese it means "customs."' She points out in a footnote that *-ni* is only a locative postfix, so the word is in fact *fandikan,* that is the Portuguese word for a customs house, *alfandega.* Another version of the chronicle says that the word is *fundika.*[25] We are thus asked to believe that the whole idea of levying customs duties came from the Portuguese. One thing to consider is that it could well be that the wealth of the rulers, as well as the local merchants, came from participation in trade rather than in controlling and taxing it. However, an account of customs payments in Mombasa, Kilwa and Sofala, dating from 1506, seems to show rulers doing very well indeed both from customs payments and from their own trade.[26] The account is detailed, but if it is taken at face value it seems to mean that if a merchant started off with 1000 pieces of cloth, he would be left with only about twenty-five by the time he got to Sofala and was able to start trading, and he would have paid other levies also. True the merchants' profits were very high, but this account seems to be wildly exaggerated.

Trade

The role of the Swahili ports and their inhabitants in trade varied from place to place. By and large the ports produced little of their own, apart from some cloth production in the north. The ports of the northern coast mostly acted as transhipment centres, funnelling exports from further south and imports from across the sea. There have been claims of a larger trade with the interior in the north than was previously suspected, but so far these claims have not been adequately proven. However, the ports in the south certainly collected and exported products from the interior, as well as channelling imports.

The trading network in which these Swahili port cities participated was a complex one. Some idea of the seaward connections, and of the major role played by Gujarat, can be gained from the descriptions by several Portuguese from early in the sixteenth century. Duarte Barbosa wrote of Zanzibar and Pemba that the élite 'are clad in very fine silk and cotton garments which they purchase at Mombaça from the Cambaya merchants.' Mombasa had a very large trade, 'and also great ships both of those which come from Çofala and those which go thither and others which come from the great kingdom of Cambaya and from Melynde ...'.[27] When Almeida sacked Mombasa he found 'a great number of very rich cloths, of silk and gold, carpets and saddle-cloths, especially one carpet that cannot be bettered anywhere and which was sent to the king of Portugal ...'.[28] In Malindi Barbosa claimed that the Muslim inhabitants

...are great barterers, and deal in cloth, gold, ivory, and divers other wares with the Moors and Heathen of the great kingdom of Cambay; and to their haven come every year many ships with cargoes of merchandise, from which they get great store of gold, ivory and wax. In this traffic, the Cambay merchants make great profits and thus, on one side and the other, they earn much money. There is great plenty of food in this city

including even wheat imported from Cambay.[29]

Barbosa is hinting here at a trade in necessities. In this category we have wheat from India, lumber taken to the Red Sea, and rice grown locally but not for local consumption but to sell to the Portuguese.[30] Nor was wheat eaten by these coastal Africans. When da Gama was in Malindi he asked for wheat, but the king told him this was not a trade item. The Gujarati merchants imported it, but only for their own consumption. When Cabral reached Malindi in 1500 he found that the helpful sultan had imported wheat from Gujarat especially for them.[31] Perhaps the best example of long-distance trade in an essential product was the lumber trade from the northern Swahili coast to the lumber-deficit Red Sea and Hadramaut areas. This humble trade has been ignored by most historians, yet the economic and political consequences of it were profound.[32]

Most trade in necessities was not long distance. As one would expect there was a large trade in foodstuffs and necessities all up and down the coast. Many of the port cities were food deficit areas and so relied on supplies brought either by land or sea. Ibn Battuta noted that Mombasa was a large island, with no mainland territory. No grain came from the island; supplies had to come from the neighbouring coastal lands.[33] Generally this humble, and essential, trade has been submerged in the records by the more glamorous long-distance items, to which we will now turn.

In this period before massive slave trading, ivory ranked with gold as the main export. African ivory was considered by consumers in both India and China to be especially workable and well patterned, much to be preferred to Indian or Sri Lankan. The trade was large indeed. Goa's great savant Garcia da Orta claimed a total importation to India of 330,000 kg,[34] a figure which at first glance seems extraordinary. However, it may be that he was trying to include illegal, unofficial, imports as well as that quantity counted by the officials; in other words, he was trying to estimate the total trade done by locals and by Portuguese, rather than just that done under the auspices of the Portuguese state. This later sixteenth-century data needs to be used with some caution anyway, for it could be that the Portuguese increased ivory exports from the southern coast.

Comparatively vast quantities of cloths were taken into East Africa from Gujarat. When Almeida sacked the greatest city on the coast, Mombasa, in 1505, 'great wealth was burned, for it was from here that the trade with Sofala and Cambay was carried on by sea ... And there were in the city quantities of cotton cloth from Cambay because all this coast dresses in these cloths and has no others.'[35]

Cloth was vital in the trade all up and down the coast, and far inland too. In this non-monetized world it, along with weights of gold, often served as currency. However the relativities are also important. These imports were vital for East Africa, but in their place of origin, Gujarat, the trade to East Africa was a rather minor one. Tomé Pires noted, in a much-quoted passage, that 'Cambay chiefly stretches out two arms, with her right arm she reaches out towards Aden and with the other towards Malacca, as the most important places to sail to, and the other places are held to be of less importance.'[36] Alpers has estimated that only four per cent of the total export trade of western India was with East Africa.[37]

We have some amazing estimates of gold production before the arrival of the Portuguese. Duarte quotes Phimister as saying that the total pre-Portuguese gold production from the Zimbabwe plateau was between six and nine million ounces.[38] This estimate seems to be quite fabulous, for if we convert at one ounce to 28.3 grams then we have between 170 and 254 tonnes, though be it noted that this is over a very long period. Production began slowly at the start of the tenth century, or perhaps earlier, and was at its height in the eleventh to fifteenth centuries; it then declined drastically. At first placer mining, that is washing from alluvium, was most common, but later quite sophisticated reef-mining techniques were also employed. This gold was exported through Sofala but marketed at Kilwa, up to 10 tons a year before the decline late in the fifteenth century.[39] A well-informed Portuguese claimed in 1506 that when the land was at peace at least 1,000,000 and up to 1,300,000, *maticals* of gold were exported each year from Sofala, and maybe 50,000 from Angoche, this then totalling a maximum of 5,744 kg.[40] Godinho quotes with some scepticism a figure for exports from Sofala and Kilwa of gold originating inland in the Mutapa state of 8,500 kg a year.[41]

126

Mudenge claims exports of 8,000 kg in 1500,[42] but my own feeling is that this is a rather large estimate.

Religion and Language

Many scholars have seen Islam as a defining characteristic of the Swahili. Traders from the Middle East had voyaged to the coast long before the appearance of Islam, and after their conversion in the seventh century they continued to trade. The early Muslim accounts of East Africa reflect very clearly that the locals had not converted. The tenth century 'Wonders of India', a collection of Arab stories, describes 'Zanj' as a strange wild place, with sorcerers, cannibals, strange birds and fishes.[43] Al-Biruni in the early eleventh century still seems to find East Africa a wild, strange, and largely un-Islamic place.[44] It was from the later eleventh century that the locals were converted, and we can talk for the first time of a Swahili civilization, that is if we follow Middleton and see a defining characteristic of the Swahili being that they are Muslims.[45] In this century earlier wooden mosques at Kilwa were enlarged and constructed in stone. By around 1300 the main mosque at Kilwa was some 12 metres by 30 metres, implying a very large Muslim resident population.[46] Wright has pointed out that all the larger communities seem to have accepted Islam at roughly the same time, that is primarily in the twelfth century and a few years on either side of this. He thinks that this suggests that Islam was not spread by settlers from the Middle East, nor by missionaries, but rather that the origins of Swahili Islam are endogenous to the coast, the result of some common factor in the larger Swahili communities.[47]

One could speculate that Islam on the coast was more influenced by norms from the heartland in the period before the arrival of the Portuguese, and then by the Omanis once they had established themselves in the late eighteenth century. I am of course making no value judgements about 'pure' or 'localized' Islam; I have no intention of judging Swahili Islam against some normative text-based standard, and then condemning it for its lapses and local influences. But I am saying that Portuguese activities, and their hostility to Islam, may have acted to make more difficult connections between the Red Sea and the coast than was the case before their arrival, or after their power had diminished. The effects on coastal Islam of the Omani hegemony cannot detain us here, but we do have evidence of quite close ties between the coast and the centre around 1500, and these may contrast with Portuguese depictions of a rather indigenized Islam later in the sixteenth century, this being a result of their making it more difficult for scholars and teachers to travel from the Red Sea to the coast. It is surely interesting that I have found no evidence of Swahili undertaking the *hajj* in the sixteenth century; no doubt many in fact did, yet we can also speculate that this pious obligation was made more difficult by the presence of the Portuguese.

We have several pieces of evidence which tend to show considerable ties between the coast and the Red Sea and the heartland around 1500 and earlier. One we have already quoted: the claim of the ruler of Oja that his only overlord was the Khalif in Cairo. In the fourteenth and fifteenth centuries Hadrami *sayyids* were influential, which meant that Muslims on the coast were predominantly influenced by the *shafi'i* school of law, and this continued despite the influence of the Omani rulers from the eighteenth century.[48] Martin has made an excellent study of flows and interaction and movement back and forth of holy men and others between East Africa on the one hand and Yemen and the Hadramaut on the other.[49] The much-travelled Ibn Battuta found patronage and respect on the coast in the 1330s. Nor was he alone: in 1331 in Kilwa he found that *sharifs*, religious specialists, came from Iraq and the Hijaz to profit from the pious generosity of the sultan.[50] Da Gama was disconcerted to find many 'foreign' Muslims as he travelled up the coast in March to May 1498. This was especially the case in Mozambique, where they came from as far afield as Fez.[51] Such men knew the Portuguese well, and both sides instinctively mistrusted each other as a result of a long history of antipathy in the Mediterranean and North Africa. In short, at 1500 it could well be that the coast was more tied in to Middle Eastern Islam, and more influenced by these more 'orthodox' norms, than was the case subsequently.

Finally, what of the Swahili language at this time? Historical linguistics is a slippery field indeed, but there is some reason to say that, just like Islam, the Swahili language at 1500 was 'purer', more clearly Bantu, than was the case later. There was an identifiable Swahili language before Islam arrived. The language spread from north to south in the ninth and tenth centuries, a century or so before mass conversions. The vast majority of the later borrowings were from Arabic, though the original words were often greatly modified as they acculturated. In any case, most of these borrowings from Arabic occurred during the last two centuries, as a result of the period of Omani rule.[52] There are some Hindi-derived words, though these also are probably of recent origin. Some European words have also been acquired, as one would expect, though studies of words of Portuguese origin show surprisingly few examples. Prata has a list of about 110 words, but in fact many of even these are dubious. What he misses is that the Portuguese picked up many Sanskrit-based terms in India, and took them to Africa, and some

128

of them then passed into Swahili.[53] In any case, the point is that obviously all borrowings from European language occurred after 1498, while at this time borrowings from either Arabic or Indian languages seem to have been minimal. The people with whom the Portuguese spoke Arabic were either 'foreign' traders, or the Swahili élite who spoke Swahili in everyday life, but had enough Arabic to be able to communicate with these foreigners.

This was then a rich and variegated society in 1498. We do not need to see this nostalgically as some Golden Age before the arrival of Europeans, but we can note that trade appeared to be flourishing; indeed, the port cities seem to have done well even if their native inhabitants did not themselves travel away from the coast. These ports clearly had much closer ties with their immediate hinterlands than with lands over the sea, as is to be expected given that the Swahili were and are inextricably part of the Bantu world. While nearly all exports came from the inland rather than the coast, the coast on the other hand broke up and distributed imports to the area. While no inland power, such as the Mutapa state, made any effort to dominate the coast, relations between the close interior and the ports were often tense; yet at the same time the two areas were closely tied both economically and socially. We have no evidence of any port trying to dominate another by force. Finally, it is at least possible that coastal Islam at this time had closer ties to the centre than was the case in later centuries, while the language also may have been 'purer', more clearly a Bantu tongue, than was later the case. It was into this world that Vasco da Gama sailed in 1498.

Notes

[1] Tomé Pires, *The Suma Oriental of Tomé Pires*, A. Cortesão (ed.), 2 vols, London, 1944, vol. 1, p. 46; vol. 2, p. 268.

[2] See T.H. Wilson, 'Settlement Patterns of the Coast of Southern Somalia and Kenya', unpublished paper for first international congress of Somali studies, July 1980, Mogadishu.

[3] U. Ghaidan, *Lamu: A Study of the Swahili Town*, Nairobi, 1975, p. 80; J. Kirkman, *Gedi*, 8th ed., Nairobi, 1975, p. 3.

[4] W.H. Brown, 'History of Siyu: The Development and Decline of a Swahili Town on the Northern Kenya Coast', PhD dissertation, Indiana University, 1985, pp. 100–2; for a directly contrary position, possibly reflective of majority opinion, see R. Wilding, *The Shorefolk: Aspects of the Early Development of Swahili Communities*, Fort Jesus Occasional Papers no. 2, mimeo, 1987, p. 57. As Om Prakash judiciously pointed out at the conference where this paper was first presented, such a finding calls into question the terminology of 'port city' as it applies to the East African coast, for these seem hardly to be ports. We still have a way to go to develop useful categories for habitations located on coasts.

[5] Umland is defined as: 'formerly applied in a general way to surroundings, and included in hinterland; now more precisely applied to an area which is culturally, economically and politically related to a particular town or city'. See A.N. Clark, *Longman Dictionary of Geography*, Essex, 1985, s.v. 'umland'.

[6] Wilding, *Shorefolk*, p. 57; yet Wilding's main thrust is to see the Swahili as coastal, sea-oriented.

[7] Brown, 'History of Siyu', pp. 43–4.

[8] Durate Barbosa, *Livro*, 2 vols, London, 1918–21, vol. 1, p. 29.

[9] Brown, 'History of Siyu', pp. 43–4, 100–2, 148–51.

[10] G.H.O. Abungu, 'The Mid to Lower Tana', *Mvita*, no. 6, 1995, pp. 3–6.

[11] T. Spear, *Kenya's Past: An Introduction to Historical Method in Africa*, London, 1981, p. 93.

[12] Barbosa, *Livro*, vol. 1, pp. 20–1.

[13] H.W. Mutoro, 'An Archeological Study of the Mijikenda 'Kaya' Settlements on Hinterland Kenya Coast', PhD dissertation, UCLA, 1987, p. 67; also Spear, *Kenya's Past*, pp. 94–5. There is however some dispute as to when the Mijikenda first became involved in this sort of exchange. Compare D.C. Sperling, *The Growth of Islam among the Mijikenda of the Kenya Coast, 1826–1933*, SOAS, PhD dissertation, University of London, 1988, pp. 34–8; and W.R. Ochieng', 'The Interior of East Africa: The Peoples of Kenya and Tanzania, 1500–1800', in *General History of Africa*, vol. 5, *Africa from the Sixteenth to the Eighteenth Century*, Paris, 1992, pp. 839–40.

[14] J. Willis, *Mombasa, the Swahili, and the Making of the Mijikenda*, Oxford, 1992, pp. 22–3.

[15] Wilding, *Shorefolk*, p. 47.

[16] E. Axelson, *Portuguese in Southeast Africa, 1488–1600*, Johannesburg, 1973, p. 68.

[17] R. Austen, *African Economic History: Internal Development and External Dependency*, London, 1987, p. 60. A new edition is now being prepared.

[18] We know far too little about relations between Mombasa and Malindi before 1498. Mombasa clearly was the more important port, and Serjeant writes of antagonism between the two, yet they also traded with each other extensively. See for example R.B. Serjeant, *The Portuguese off the South Arabian Coast*, Oxford, 1963, pp. 9–10; Barbosa, *Livro*, vol. 1, p. 20.

[19] Wilding, *Shorefolk*, p. 112.

[20] Spear, *Kenya's Past*, p. 95, and also pp. 85–8; for the quite comparable situation of the Vumba, around the mouth of the Umba river, and their relations with the Segeju and Digo see Spear, *Kenya's Past*, pp. 95–6.

[21] J.M. Gray, 'Rezende's Description of East Africa in 1634', *Tanganyika Notes and Records*, vol. 23, 1947, pp. 7–12. Parts of this translation are not to be relied on.

[22] Spear, *Kenya's Past*, p. 93.

[23] Ibn Battuta, *The Travels of Ibn Battuta*, H.A.R. Gibb, (trans.), Cambridge, 1962, vol. 2, p. 380.

[24] João de Barros, *Decadas*, 9 vols, Lisbon, 1778–88, 1, iv, 3.

[25] M. Tolmacheva, *The Pate Chronicle*, East Lansing, 1993, pp. 62, 175.

[26] Diogo de Alcaçova to king, 20 November 1506, in António da Silva Rego et al, *Documentos sobre os Portugueses em Moçambique e na Africa Central, 1497–1840*, Lisbon, 1962–89, 9 vols to date, vol. 1, pp. 397–9 (hereafter 'DM').

[27] Barbosa, *Livro*, vol. 1, pp. 20, 28.

[28] Account of Almeida's voyage to India, 22 May 1506 in DM, vol. 1, p. 533.

[29] Barbosa, *Livro*, vol. 1, pp. 22–3.

[30] João dos Santos, *Ethiopia Oriental*, Lisbon, 1891, 2 vols, 1, i, 13.

[31] Gaspar Correa, *Lendas de India*, 4 vols, Coímbra, 1921–31, Lisbon, 1969, vol. 1, pp. 58, 166.

[32] See P.D. Curtin, 'African Enterprise in the Mangrove Trade: The Case of Lamu', *African Economic History*, vol. 10, 1981, pp. 23–33 for the modern trade.

[33] Battuta, *Travels*, p. 379.

[34] C. Markham, *Colloquies on the Simples and Drugs of India by Garcia da Orta*, London, 1913, chapter 21.

[35] Account of Almeida's voyage to India, 22 May 1506 in DM, vol. 1, pp. 531–3.

[36] Pires, *Suma Oriental*, vol. 1, p. 42.

[37] E.A. Alpers, 'Gujarat and the Trade of East Africa, c. 1500–1800', *International Journal of African Historical Studies*, vol. 9. 1976, p. 39.

[38] R.T. Duarte, *Northern Mozambique in the Swahili World*, Stockholm, 1993, p. 43.

[39] J. Devisse and S. Labib, 'Africa in Inter-continental Relations', in *General History of Africa*, vol. 4, Paris, 1984, p. 655.

[40] Diogo de Alcáçova to king, 20 November 1506, in DM, vol. 1, p. 395.

[41] V.M. Godinho, *Os descobrimentos e a economia mundial*, 2nd. ed., 4 vols, Lisbon, 1981–83, vol. 1, pp. 204–7.

[42] S.I.G. Mudenge, *A Political History of Munhumutapa, c, 1400–1902*, Harare, 1988, p. 174.

[43] Buzurg ibn Shahriyar, G.S.P. Freeman-Grenville, (trans. and ed.), *The Book of the Wonders of India* [Kitab al Ajaid al Hind], London, 1981, pp. 10, 31–6, 38, 102, 105.

[44] E. Sachau (trans. and ed.), *Alberuni's India*, 2 vols, Delhi, 1964, vol. 1, p. 270.

[45] J. Middleton, *The World of the Swahili: An African Mercantile Civilisation*, New Haven, 1992, passim, e.g. p. 37.

[46] J. Sutton, *A Thousand Years of East Africa*, British Institute in Eastern Africa, Nairobi, 1990, pp. 67–8.

[47] H.T. Wright, 'Trade and Politics on the Eastern Littoral of Africa, AD 800–1300', in Thurstan Shaw et al (eds), *The Archeology of Africa: Food, Metals and Towns*, London, New York, 1993, pp. 669–71.

[48] *Encyclopedia of Islam*, 2nd ed., 8 vols to date, Leiden, 1954–, s.v. Kenya. Scholars have often claimed that the version of Islam dominant in Oman, that is Ibadi Islam, was quite different from the more orthodox *shafi'i sunni* Islam of the Swahili. Risso however claims that while there were theological differences, in most matters there is a large degree of commonality between Ibadi Islam and the various sunni schools: P. Risso, *Oman and Muscat: An Early Modern History*, London, 1986, pp. 22–3.

[49] B.G. Martin, 'Arab Migration to East Africa in Medieval Times', *International Journal of African Historical Studies*, vol. 7, 1975, pp. 367–90.

[50] Battuta, *Travels*, p. 380.

[51] Barros, *Decadas*, 1, iv, 3–4; Vasco da Gama, *A Journal of the First Voyage of Vasco da Gama*, London, 1898, pp. 23, 29.

[52] Sutton, *A Thousand Years*, pp. 59–60.

[53] See A.P. Prata, *A influência da língua Portuguesa sobre o Suahíli e quatro línguas de Moçambique*, Lisbon, 1983, especially pp. 29–46 for a list of about 110 words; also G.S.P. Freeman-Grenville, 'The Portuguese of the Swahili Coast: Buildings and Language', *Studia*, vol. 49, 1989, pp. 235–54.

XII

Hindu Medical Practice in Sixteenth-Century Western India: Evidence from Portuguese Sources

There are many studies of *ayurvedic* medical practice in India in the period before the arrival of Europeans, but most of these are based on normative texts, such as those of Susruta and Caraka.[1] These tell us quite a lot about what healers in the *ayurvedic* system were meant to do, and the sorts of information they received from their texts, but they give almost no information on actual practice; in other words, did healers follow the texts, or was there rather a mixture of information from the texts and folk knowledge, with these two in turn being influenced by empirical observation? A. L. Basham provides a cautious summary of this: 'The instructions of the textbooks can only be taken as normative, and not as having been universally applied'.[2]

Turning to western India, we know very little about health care in Goa before the Portuguese conquest. Figueiredo claims that long before the Portuguese all branches of knowledge, including medicine, were taught in institutions of higher learning, and in settlements of brahmins. These attracted students from far and wide.[3] His information is so fragmentary as to be of little use, for we cannot distinguish between medicine and other scholarly disciplines. We can assume that healers in Goa were often brahmins, and their more book-based practice was supplemented by locally proven recipes and nostrums dispensed by village women healers. We have almost no evidence of hospitals, or of state involvement in health care, before the coming of the Portuguese. All we have is one reference (from the eleventh century) to a house of mercy, which provided relief for the poor,

---

[1] See, for example, O. P. Jaggi's numerous works in the series 'History of Science and Technology in India', especially *Medicine in Medieval India* (Delhi: Atma Ram, 1977), on *yunani* medicine, and *Indian System of Medicine* (Delhi: Atma Ram, 1974), on *ayurvedic* medicine. The best modern summary is by A. L. Basham, 'The Practice of Medicine in Ancient and Medieval India', in *Asian Medical Systems: A Comparative Study*, ed. by Charles Leslie (Berkeley: University of California Press, 1976), pp. 18–43. Two older, classic, accounts of *ayurvedic* medicine by western orientalists still have detail of great value: Jean Filliozat, *The Classical Doctrine of Indian Medicine: Its Origins and its Greek Parallels* (Delhi: Munshiram Manoharlal, 1964); Heinrich Robert Zimmer, *Hindu Medicine* (Baltimore: Johns Hopkins University Press, 1948). For the state of research today on traditional Indian medicine see *Studies on Indian Medical History*, ed. by G. Jan Meulenbeld and Dominik Wujastyk (Groningen: Forsten, 1987); most relevant to this study is T. J. S. Patterson, 'The Relationship of Indian and European Practitioners of Medicine from the Sixteenth Century', pp. 119–29.
[2] Basham, p. 25.
[3] John M. de Figueiredo, 'Ayurvedic Medicine in Goa according to European Sources in the Sixteenth and Seventeenth Centuries', *Bulletin of the History of Medicine*, 58 (1984), 225–32 (p. 226).

XII

sick and pilgrims, established by a chief minister of a local king in Goa Velha.[4]

We do have considerable information about practice as opposed to theory as regards *yunani* or Muslim medicine. Such information is quite copious in the *Memoirs* of both Babur and Jahangir, in Abul Fazl's *Ain-i Akbari*, and in many other Persian texts such as the *Tibbi-Sikandari*, written under the patronage of Sikandar Lodi. Our concern however is with Hindu practice, and here it seems that Portuguese records from the sixteenth century provide us with accounts which are comparable to those from the Mughal emperors and other Mughal sources, but which relate to Hindu practice. So far these Portuguese sources have been little studied, but it is my contention, which I hope will be confirmed by the material later in this article, that they are extremely valuable as eye witness accounts of actual medical practice.

This is not to say that Portuguese sources can be used as 'objective' and 'neutral' accounts. There is first the obvious and generally acknowledged difficulty of using the records of a colonial power to describe the society which it dominated. In particular, Norman Owen has reminded us of the difficulties of historical accounts of illness. All of these are of course transmitted through culture, in our case Portuguese. Also, diseases themselves are mutable, so that the sources might be describing a syndrome which no longer exists, such as the mysterious English sweating sickness which came and went in the sixteenth century.[5] Further, each account is based on assumptions about what illness meant, something very different in sixteenth-century Goa as compared with today. Finally, some diseases are more dramatic (cholera especially) than others. Owen distinguishes between crisis mortality and background mortality. The former, the dramatic and much described causes of mortality, include cholera, smallpox, influenza and various 'fevers', such as malaria and typhoid. However, perhaps three-quarters of deaths were in fact caused by the less glamorous background category of ailments, such as tuberculosis, dysentery and infantile diarrhoea.[6]

There is another whole category of minefields in the area of medical history in general. It is too easy to be overly influenced by what we think are modern medical methods, and to test the past in accordance with what we, social historians with only a spotty expertise in medicine anyway,

---

[4] João Manuel Pacheco Figueiredo, 'Goa Pré-Portuguesa', *Studia*, 12 (1963), 139–259; and 13/14 (1965), 105–225 (p. 160).

[5] Fernand Braudel, *The Structures of Everyday Life, The Limits of the Possible*, Civilization and Capitalism, 15th–18th Century, 1 (London: Collins, 1981), pp. 78–88; E. L. Jones, *The European Miracle* (Cambridge: Cambridge University Press, 1981), pp. 140–41.

[6] 'Introduction', in *Death and Disease in Southeast Asia: Explorations in Social, Medical and Demographic History*, ed. by Norman G. Owen (Singapore: Oxford University Press, 1987), pp. 4 and 12.

think is 'correct' and 'scientific' practice today. Andrew Wear claims that in his edited collection of studies:

> The nineteenth- and twentieth-century values of the medical profession which in past history of medicine had been applied to earlier periods to condemn empirics, quacks, magical and religious practitioners have been discarded. In the process a much richer medical world has been uncovered.[7]

All this said, it is still my contention that several Portuguese accounts of Hindu medicine in western India in the sixteenth century have considerable value. I am not, of course, venturing to write a history of Hindu medical practice at this time; my much more modest aim is merely to demonstrate the value of Portuguese records, in the absence of indigenous ones, for knowledge about certain diseases in certain areas at this time. Nor indeed is 'Hindu' quite appropriate, for in fact we are dealing with sources which implicitly are describing not a unity but rather health care which varied in two ways. First, our sources often differentiate between different regions, so that we have Hindu healers in Malabar dealing quite differently with disease as compared with Canarins from the area around Goa, as compared again with Gujarati practice. Second, we are sometimes informed of 'brahmin' practice, and this presumably refers to more book-based healing methods; the 'Great Tradition' of Hindu medicine if one likes, as compared with a host of locally-derived techniques and drugs which could be considered to be regionally-specific folk traditions.

We have an excellent description of this latter, and by far the most important, sort of healing in Tavernier's account of his travels in southern India in the mid-seventeenth century. We can assume that this would also stand for an accurate description of Goan practice.

> As for the commonalty, when the rains have fallen and it is the season for collecting plants, mothers of families may be seen going in the mornings from the towns and villages to collect the simples which they know to be specifics for domestic diseases. It is true that in good towns there are generally one or two men who have some knowledge of medicine, who seat themselves each morning in the market-place or at a corner of the street and administer remedies, either potions or plasters, to those who come to ask for them. They first feel the pulse, and when giving the medicine, for which they take only the value of two farthings, they mumble some words between their teeth.[8]

---

[7] 'Introduction', in *Medicine in Society: Historical Essays*, ed. by Andrew Wear (Cambridge: Cambridge University Press, 1992), p. 2. Basham wrote disparagingly of 'untrained quacks and charlatans' (p. 25) in ancient India, but today we would be reluctant to use such judgmental terms. For a general account of village practice in Goa during the whole period of Portuguese rule see Fátima da Silva Gracias, *Health and Hygiene in Colonial Goa: 1510–1961* (New Delhi: Concept, 1994), pp. 157–72.
[8] Jean-Baptiste Tavernier, *Travels in India of Jean-Baptiste Tavernier*, trans. by V. Ball and W. Crooke, 2nd edn, 2 vols (New Delhi: Munshiram Manoharlal, 1977), I, 240.

Turning now specifically to western India, two early lists of drugs and plants can be noted briefly, for they are purely botanical. First is a list dating from 1516 of twenty-seven drugs, and where they grew, compiled by the important early observer of coastal India, Tomé Pires. Second is a shorter list of drugs by Simão Alvares from the mid-sixteenth century. Neither includes anything on the uses of these plants in medical practice.[9] There is also a later (1738) list of nearly fifty Indian plants used for medicinal and food purposes written by a well-informed Jesuit.[10] Our two main sources for Hindu medical practice are works by Garcia d'Orta and Christavão da Costa. These books consist of lists of simples and drugs and medicinal plants found in western India, but they both also include data much more relevant to our concerns, for they describe how these *materia medica* were used in treatment, both by themselves, that is the Portuguese, and also by *yunani* and *ayurvedic* practitioners.

Some background on d'Orta and Costa will help us to evaluate the usefulness of their information. The New Christian Garcia d'Orta (1501–68) is generally considered to be the greatest scholar of sixteenth-century Portuguese Goa. D'Orta was the first major naturalist to study the main medicinal plants and other therapeutic substances used in coastal Asia, and was also a doctor and historian of medicine, a pharmacist and a wide-ranging savant interested in history and anthropology. His famous work, *Coloquios dos simples, e drogas he cousas mediçinais de India*, was one of the first books, and one of the very few secular books, to be published in Goa in the sixteenth and seventeenth centuries. The rare (only twenty-four copies are known) first edition is dated 1563.[11]

It is divided into fifty-seven chapters, each of them in the form of a dialogue or colloquy. This literary conceit means that the usual pattern is that in each colloquy d'Orta's interlocutor, Dr Ruano, asked him a

---

[9] Tomé Pires, *The Suma Oriental of Tomé Pires and the Book of Francisco Rodrigues*, trans. and ed. by Armando Cortesão (London: Hakluyt Society, 1944), pp. 512–18; Jaime Walter, 'Simão Alvares e o seu rol das drogas da India', *Studia* 10 (1962), 117–49.

[10] This list has been thoroughly analysed by Dr Arion Rosu, 'Les missionnaires dans l'histoire des sciences et des techniques indiennes (I). Un inédit jésuite sur la phytothérapie indienne au XVIIIe siècle', *Journal of the European Ayurvedic Society*, 3 (1993), 174–228. My thanks to Professor Rahul Peter Das for sending me a copy of this article, and to Dr Rosu for providing useful comments on an earlier version of the present study.

[11] For d'Orta (and not Horta, da Orta, or Orta) see Garcia d'Orta, *Coloquios dos simples e drogas e cousas mediçinais da India: reprodução facsimilada da edição impressa em Goa em 10 de abril de 1563, comemorando o quarto centenário da edição original, obra dada a estampa pela Académia das Ciencias de Lisboa* (Lisbon : Académia das Ciencias de Lisboa, 1963); Garcia da Orta, *Coloquios dos simples, e drogas he cousas mediçinais de India*, ed. by Conde de Ficalho, 2 vols (Lisbon: Imprensa Nacional, 1891–95); *Colloquies on the Simples and Drugs of India by Garcia da Orta*, trans. by Clements Markham (London, Sotheran, 1913). Especially important is C. R. Boxer, *Two Pioneers of Tropical Medicine: Garcia d'Orta and Nicolas Monarde* (London: Hispanic & Luso-Brazilian Councils, 1963). See also Daya de Silva's excellent *The Portuguese in Asia: An annotated bibliography of studies on Portuguese colonial history in Asia, 1498–c.1800* (Zug: IDC, 1987), entry no. 2336, pp. 252–53.

question, such as 'Do Hindu doctors use Portuguese methods?'. D'Orta then provided the answer. Other characters also appear from time to time, such as a servant girl and a Hindu doctor who is introduced for the sole purpose of singing the praises of d'Orta. Each colloquy dealt with one drug or simple. In each case he described the drug, said where it grew, and commented on its therapeutic use. Most of them were vegetable, but he also dealt with ivory and diamonds. It is an excellent comprehensive empirical study of Indian *materia medica* and botany in general, not just medicine, although he was a famous doctor in sixteenth-century Goa, serving as the physician of the Royal Hospital at the time of St Francis Xavier's stay in Goa in the early 1540s, and ministering to the Portuguese elite of the town.

Even in terms of European practice of the time, d'Orta's medical knowledge was not advanced. This can be seen in his description of cholera. Goa was hit by a major cholera epidemic in 1543; all classes and ages were struck by it that winter, that is the monsoon period. The Portuguese doctors could do nothing, and of every hundred who were affected, only ten survived. Twelve, fifteen, even twenty victims were buried each day. The governor, Martim Afonso de Sousa, even ordered an autopsy in a fruitless attempt to find the cause of the affliction.[12] D'Orta was the first European to describe cholera in India; in the *Coloquios* he mentions the Hindu and Arabic names for it, and compares what he saw in Goa with what he knew of Europe. He considered there was a toxic humour which had to be expelled. It was caused by overeating, or by too much sexual intercourse. He noted that the local *vaidyas* used rice with pepper and cardamom, cauterized the feet of the patient, tied up the patient's limbs and applied long peppers to the eyes.[13] As to fevers, d'Orta followed European practice and treated fevers with bleeding and purging, and rich foods. Of opium he noted that its long term use produced impotence, despite its popular use as an aphrodisiac. But he also claimed that the use of opium could help conception. This was because its use delayed ejaculation by the male by 'slowing down his imagination'. As women are slower in 'the act of Venus' this meant 'they both complete the act at one time. [. . .] The opium also opens the channels by which the genital seed comes from the brain, by reason of its coldness, so that they complete the act simultaneously.'[14]

Clearly we must not make too much of d'Orta's medical expertise. He seems to have been thoroughly grounded in European practice of the first

---

[12] For a dramatic description see Gaspar Correa, *Lendas da India*, 4 vols (Lisbon: Académia real das sciencias, 1858–66), IV, 288–89.

[13] See d'Orta, *Coloquios*, no. 17 for a description of 'mordexim' in 1543 (references to *Coloquios* in the text are to the translation by Markham).

[14] *Coloquios*, no. 41.

XII

half of the sixteenth century. The main influences on his medical thinking were the thoroughly predictable ones: Galen, Aristotle, Hippocrates and Ibn Sina. The basis was what may be called humoural pathology. His book goes into very elaborate detail to work out whether various simples and drugs were warm or cold or hot, moist or dry or wet. Concerning the plant 'anarcardo' ('semecarpus anarcardium') he was asked, 'In what degree do you place it — warm and dry?' to which he responded that some

place it in the fourth, warm and dry; others in the second part of the third; but neither of these satisfy me, for when green it is clearly not so warm and dry. It therefore does not appear reasonable to make it as warm and dry as some other spices, such as pepper, which is placed in the third degree.[15]

D'Orta never went beyond the standard authorities of his time. He did correct and criticize these authorities on occasion, once for example writing 'let not any text of any author deny what my own eyes have observed [. . .] Frighten me not with Dioscorides or Galen, for I do not say but the truth and what I know.' A similar empirical rigour is seen when his interlocutor, Dr Ruano, quoted to him the opinion of some Italian friars. D'Orta replied: 'I do not want Friars as reprehenders except in the pulpit'.[16] However, he never questioned the fundamental paradigms governing premodern European medical practice.

A possible reason for this conservatism was the constraining fact that d'Orta was a New Christian, and indeed apparently a far from convinced convert. Born in 1501, he studied at the Spanish universities of Salamanca and Alcalá de Henares, where his medical training consisted of memorizing Hippocrates, Galen and Ibn Sina. Subsequently d'Orta taught at Lisbon from 1526 until he left for India. It seems very likely that his departure for Goa in 1534, as the personal physician of the later governor, Martim Afonso de Sousa, was a result of increasing intolerance in Portugal. Two years after he left the Inquisition was set up in Lisbon, and was in full swing four years later. As a New Christian he was forced to step carefully as this new age of intolerance began in Portugal. As a result, the massive compilation that was the Coloquios was generally ignored in Portugal, though it was widely used in other parts of Europe in the late-sixteenth century and subsequently, thanks to a Latin translation which went

---

[15] *Coloquios*, no. 5; compare no. 12 for a similar learned and somewhat circular (to modern eyes) discussion.
[16] *Coloquios*, nos. 9 and 30. See especially Boxer, *Two Pioneers*, pp. 7–13; Georg Schurhammer, *Francis Xavier: His Life, His Times*, 3 vols (Rome: Jesuit Historical Institute, 1977), II, 203; and M. B. Barbosa and J. Caria Mendes, 'Garcia d'Orta, pioneer of tropical medicine and his descriptions of cholera in his Coloquios (1563)', in *Proceedings of the XXIII International Congress of the History of Medicine*, 2 vols (London: Wellcome Institute of the History of Medicine, 1974), II, 1258–59.

through five editions, the first one being published in 1567 in Antwerp.[17] D'Orta himself suffered posthumously from this intolerance. He died in 1568, but in 1580 he was condemned as a Jew by the Inquisition, and his remains were dug up and burnt at an *auto de fé*. A sister had actually been burnt by the Inquisition in Goa in the year after his death.

For us d'Orta's main value is his accounts of indigenous medical practice. He knew of *yunani* medicine from its local practitioners, or *hakims*, and had a cordial relationship with these people at the court of the Nizam Shahs in Ahmadnagar. D'Orta in fact claims that his cures were often more efficacious than those of the Muslims. The general point is that he was much more attuned to *yunani* methods than to *ayurvedic*, and this for the obvious reason that many of the authorities he quotes, such as Galen, Ibn Sina and al-Rhazi, are also prime texts for *yunani* medicine; indeed Ibn Sina and al-Rhazi were of course Muslim healers. There was then a large degree of commonality between his European knowledge and that of the *yunani* practitioners. He had much more to learn from Hindu healers for their system, while not totally discrete from his own, was more different than the *yunani* one. He usually appreciated the abilities of the local *vaidyas* with whom he had contact, considering their cures as often superior to those he knew. However, he had no inkling of the vast and ancient body of *ayurvedic* theory. Great names such as Susruta and Caraka were unknown to him. All he knew of Hindu medicine was the actual practice of possibly not very well informed healers in Goa. He knew no Sanskrit; indeed Sassetti (see below), was the only European in the sixteenth century to attempt to learn this language. He claimed that the Hindu doctors 'are men who cure according to experience and custom' but in fact this merely shows that he was unaware of the very great *ayurvedic* scholarly tradition which was passed on through the generations by its followers.[18]

D'Orta had a quite objective attitude to other medical systems. In a general passage which describes particularly well his attitude to diverse medical knowledge, he noted how his patient, the King of Ahmadnagar, 'taught me the names of illnesses and medicines in Arabic, and I taught him the same in Latin, which pleased him very much'. The Hindu doctors often used Portuguese methods too,

But most of them not correctly. For they say there is bleeding, and they never bled before we were in the land; but they used cupping-glasses, sawing and leeches [. . .]

---

[17] On the spread of d'Orta's book see Donald F. Lach, *Asia in the Making of Europe*, 3 vols (Chicago: University of Chicago Press, 1965–93), I, 192–95, and III, 457, where it is noted that the first Dutch book on tropical medicine, by Bontius, published posthumously in 1642, is closely modelled on d'Orta. For an excellent account of medical scholarship in Portugal in the sixteenth century see Ligia Bellini, 'Notes on Medical Scholarship and the Broad Intellectual Milieu in Sixteenth-century Portugal', *Portuguese Studies*, 15 (1999), 11–41.

[18] *Coloquios*, no. 36. On Sassetti see Lach, I, 477, and II, Book 3, 541.

they were never accustomed to look at waters [i.e. do urinalysis]. I can tell you that they cure dysentery very well, can tell you whether there is fever or not from the pulse, and whether it is weak or strong, and what is the humour that offends, whether it is blood or heat or phlegm, or melancholy; and they give a good remedy for obstruction.

Sometimes they classify things incorrectly, he says, such as getting the heat or dryness of particular drugs wrong. It must be remembered here that Hindu medicine also depended on the notion of humours, albeit slightly different ones from those of the European and Muslim traditions, which are remarkably similar.[19] He considered that their knowledge of anatomy was very weak. However, d'Orta himself took many things from both *ayurvedic* and *yunani* healers. In general he would try European methods first, but if these failed he would then use 'brahmin' ones.[20] Indeed he modestly claimed that he was the best informed healer in Goa, for in the *Coloquios* he has a Hindu doctor say 'Dr Orta knows better than all of us; for we only know the Gentios [sc. Hindu], but he knows Christians, Moors [sc. Muslim], and Gentios better than us all.'[21]

We know much less about our other authority, Christavão da Costa. He arrived in Goa in the year of d'Orta's death, and in 1569 was a doctor in the Royal Hospital in Cochin.[22] Modern libraries often list him as 'Cristobal Acosta, ca. 1515–ca. 1592'. His book in English was called *Treatises on Drugs and Medicines of East India* (1578). In some ways his work is more useful to us than is d'Orta's. Costa has more on Hindu medicine, though less on Muslim, where d'Orta profited from his long association with the court of the Nizam Shahs. Costa, on the other hand, notes in a typical passage that he asked a brahmin doctor in Cochin about some local cures. This brahmin was a friend of Costa's, and very popular among both the local inhabitants of Cochin and also the many Portuguese who lived there.[23] He says more about the healing properties of the drugs he describes, while d'Orta is more botanical. He also, unlike d'Orta most of the time, differentiates between different Hindu systems in different areas. Thus brahmin, Canarin and Malabar treatments are specified.[24] However, Costa's general background was similar to d'Orta's. He also

---

[19] *Coloquios*, no. 36; Figueiredo, 'Ayurvedic Medicine', p. 231.
[20] *Coloquios*, no. 36. See my fuller study of acculturation and mixing: 'First Contacts between Indian and European Medical Systems: Goa in the Sixteenth Century', in *Warm Climates and Western Medicine: the Emergence of Tropical Medicine, 1500–1900*, ed. by David Arnold, The Wellcome Institute Series in the History of Medicine (Amsterdam: Editions Rodopi, 1996), pp. 20–41. On d'Orta ministering to the ruler of Ahmadnagar see *Coloquios*, nos 11 and 24. It is not really my brief to pronounce on the 'objective' truth of d'Orta's work, but I should note here that while bleeding, the great staple of European practice, was indeed not done in the ayurvedic tradition, there is evidence of Hindu doctors using urinalysis for diagnostic purposes.
[21] *Coloquios*, no. 54.
[22] *Tratado das drogas e mediçinas das India Orientais, por Christovão da Costa*, ed. by Jaime Walter (Lisbon: Junta de Investigações do Ultramar, 1964), p. 125 (hereafter 'Costa').
[23] Costa, p. 28.
[24] Costa, pp. 23 and 28.

relied essentially on humoural pathology, and the classical authorities. Thus *canafistula* ('cassia fistula') he thought was between hot and cold as regards temperature in the first degree in terms of humidity, while tamarinds were cold and dry in the second degree.[25]

Earlier scholars dismissed his work by claiming that all he did was summarize d'Orta, though his book did include numerous illustrations. However, Donald Lach has shown that while he knew of and used d'Orta, the two books do differ widely. For example, Costa describes forty-seven plants, and of these fourteen are not mentioned by d'Orta, while nine of d'Orta's are not in Costa.[26] His modern editor, Jaime Walter, provides a good discussion of this matter. As noted above, he does include material based on his own experience, which differs from d'Orta, and supplements him in other ways, yet much of his work is indeed merely a copy, with additions or deletions, of d'Orta. For example, the discussion on opium quoted above is reproduced by Costa, but the notion of opium delaying ejaculation and so fostering conception is left out.[27] Not that Costa tries to hide his sources. In his discussion on 'turbito' ('ipomoea turpethium') he specifically says that he has not seen this plant, so he is relying on d'Orta, who had.[28] Of all the authors he quotes, d'Orta leads with ninety-seven citations, followed by Ibn Sina with fifty-five, Dioscorides with forty-five, Serapião with forty-one, and Galen with thirty-eight.

When we turn to their specific information about Hindu practice, we find most useful material on fevers, dysentery and especially cholera. There is, however, much other curious and obscure information, which is noted briefly. One general matter that Costa pointed out was that Hindus, brahmins, vanias, all of them, never started the day without bathing the whole body. Muslims did this at least every three days, while Europeans notoriously would have been much more parsimonious in their ablutions. In 1569 the King of Cochin was ill, but he told Costa that even if it cost him his life he still had to take his bath every morning.[29]

The two authors generally find some differences and some similarities between European and Hindu practice. Thus for 'fevers' (a very general category indeed, which could include malaria, typhoid, and even it seems cholera), d'Orta liked to feed people up, and combine this with bleeding and purging, but Indians starved their patients for ten or even fifteen days, and then fed them mango juice, and later whole mangoes. On the other hand, Gujarati healers 'did not cure in any other way than to give nothing

---

[25] Costa, pp. 44, 86, 127. On tamarinds see also Rosu, p. 203, n. 111.
[26] See Lach, II, Book 3, 436–37.
[27] Costa, p. 279.
[28] Costa, p. 199.
[29] Costa, pp. 125–26.

XII

to eat'.[30] However, Albuquerque early in the century described quite a different treatment in Malabar. Those who had a fever were given meat to eat, and fish, then were purged, and then given liquids.[31] Pires, writing at almost the same time as Albuquerque, said 'if they have fever they eat fish and keep washing themselves.[. . .] Our people when they have fevers eat fat chickens and drink wine and are cured.'[32]

Costa noted the use of nutmeg by both Portuguese and Indians. He said that both 'Indian' and 'brahmin' doctors used it for all cold illnesses of the brain and paralysis, and other nervous problems, and also for infirmities of the womb ('enfermidades da madre').[33] Here we may be approaching folk medicine as compared with *ayurvedic*, though to say this assumes the superiority of the latter, and relegates the former to the now abandoned margins of medical practice. If however such a differentiation has any value, then the famous bezoar stone must belong to folk medicine. This stone, widely described in the popular lore of many cultures, was thought to be the result of incrustations building up around a foreign body in the stomach of ruminant animals. Wild goats from Persia were especially fecund in producing these invaluable stones. They were believed to be an excellent antidote to poison, a purgative, a means of preserving one's youth and virility, and also a cure for the plague, bladder complaints, and so on. The Jesuits jealously guarded the recipe for their cordial stone, a bezoar stone with an amazing list of other added ingredients. It was used for heart problems, and was a good example of the blend of Indian and European practice. Taken back to Portugal, these bezoar stones were widely used by the elite for their medicinal and amulet qualities.[34]

Aloes provide another example. Hindu healers used it as a purgative, and also for kidney diseases, colics, and for healing wounds. When mixed with myrrh it was called 'mocebar', and was used to cure horses and to kill maggots in human wounds.[35] To cure wounds in general one Malabar method was to wash the wound in warm coconut oil for an hour or so twice a day.[36] Tabashir, or the bark milk from within the stems of bamboos, was used by Hindus to deal with over-heating, either external or internal, and also for fevers and dysentery.[37] Turpethin, the gummy part of

---

[30] *Coloquios*, no. 36.

[31] Afonso de Albuquerque, quoted in Figueiredo, 'Goa Pré-Portuguesa', *Studia*, 13/14 (1965), 161–62.

[32] Tomé Pires, p. 69.

[33] Costa, p. 23.

[34] *Coloquios*, no. 45; Costa, p. 103; Ann Maria Amaro, 'Goa's Famous Cordial Stone', *Review of Culture*, 7/8 (1988–89), 82–103. My thanks to Fr Charles Borges for this reference. For their use in Europe see Lach, II, Book 1, 12.

[35] *Coloquios*, no. 2; and see *Coloquios* for a detailed account of Muslim purging practice, following Ibn Sina's advice, also described in Costa, p. 125.

[36] Pires, p. 69; Afonso de Albuquerque, quoted in Figueiredo, 'Goa Pré-Portuguesa', p. 162.

[37] *Coloquios*, no. 51.

a creeping plant, was used to reduce inflammation, and as one of the ingredients to produce a purgative.[38] Another useful plant was 'anarcardo,' ('semecarpus anarcardium'). The juice of this 'dry' fruit was widely used in all of Malabar in place of caustic. It was applied to external ulcers and to rotten teeth, and was also used as a fixative when dyeing cloth.[39]

According to Figueiredo, dysentery was the great killer in Goa for at least two centuries.[40] We have noted several nostrums to produce purging, and it seems that these were routinely used when dysentery was diagnosed. Apparently not all healers did the purging first, but regardless of this there were then several methods to cure patients and build them up. Some used a type of dog-bane, others a more complicated mixture. Neither Indians nor Portuguese prescribed any wine. Rather kanji, rice broth, was provided, with chicken pieces soaked in it.[41] Costa said all doctors, brahmin, Canarin and Malabari, used the skin or husk of nutmeg mixed with buttermilk ('leite azedo'), for all kinds of dysentery. This was given twice a day, in the morning and at night, and then the patient was given boiled rice without salt or butter (that is, *kanji*) again mixed with chicken. If the attack was severe opium was also administered, though this was done more by Muslims than by Hindus.[42]

D'Orta, however, differentiates between various Hindu practices on this. The Portuguese method was different from Malabari, and it differed from the Malayalam. (I am not sure what this distinction is based on as Malayalam is of course the language of the Malabar, now Kerala, region.) The Malabar treatment was much more rigorous than the Portuguese one, while the Malayalis mixed opium with the nutmeg. On this matter d'Orta thought that the native methods had much to commend them compared with Portuguese treatments.[43] Here again however there seem to be major differences in our sources, for two early-sixteenth-century accounts both say that in Malabar dysentery was treated with fresh young coconut milk, which points to a much milder treatment.[44]

The great killer in Goa and western India in the sixteenth century was cholera. Early modern accounts are united in their presentation of a feared and usually fatal disease. I offer just two examples: Fr Godinho said it was 'so fatal that the end comes in a matter of hours', while Linschoten noted that 'the sicknesse is very common, and killeth many a man, whereof they

---

[38] *Coloquios*, no. 54.
[39] Costa, p. 143.
[40] Figueiredo, 'Goa Pré-Portuguesa', p. 176.
[41] *Coloquios*, no. 27.
[42] Costa, p. 28.
[43] *Coloquios*, no. 27.
[44] Pires, p. 69; Afonso de Albuquerque, quoted in Figueiredo, 'Goa Pré-Portuguesa', p. 162.

hardly or never escape'.[45] Ovington, an educated man and a clergyman, reflected a European consensus concerning cause and cure when he wrote that cholera ('mordechine') is 'violent Vomiting and Looseness, and which is caus'd most frequently by an Excess of Eating particularly of Fish and Flesh together. It has been Cur'd by a Red-hot Iron clapt to the Heal of him that is sick, so close that it renders him uneasie by its nearness, whereby it leaves a Scar behind it.'[46]

There were eleven outbreaks of cholera in Goa between 1543 and 1680. The first was the worst; we are told that of those afflicted, only one in ten survived.[47] The Italian merchant Sassetti described it in Cochin in the 1580s:

There is current here a certain disease which kills a person in just 24 hours and which is called mordaxi, which is a revulsion of the stomach and of the entire body which rejects itself; all the humours quit the body and the blood too, so that one dies; and it comes from eating much sweet fruit, much pork, many preserves, and from drinking much water; whence the poor stomachs, when they have suffered much, throw themselves on the ground. It is the accident which makes it known, that suddenly the patients lose the sense of touch in their external parts, so that they feel nothing if they are struck blows or pierced with a needle.[48]

The Venetian Manucci, a self-taught doctor, later in the seventeenth century noted that mort-de-chien, cholera, was the main killer, describing it as colic of the bowels with vomiting and laxity. The best cure, the usual one at this time, was to burn the heel of the patient with a red-hot iron

[45] *Intrepid Itinerant: Manuel Godinho and his Journey from India to Portugal in 1663*, trans. and ed. by John Correia-Afonso (Bombay: Oxford University Press, 1990), p. 38; J. H. van Linschoten, *The Voyage of John Huyghen van Linschoten to the East Indies*, ed. by Arthur Coke Burnell and P. A. Tiele, 2 vols (London: Hakluyt Society,1885), I, 235–36.

[46] John Ovington, *A Voyage to Surat in the Year 1689*, ed. by H. G. Rawlinson (London: Oxford University Press/Milford, 1929), pp. 204–05.

[47] Alberto C. Germano da Silva Correia, *La Vieille-Goa* (Bastorá: Tipografia Rangel, 1931), pp. 268–307. For the outbreak of 1567 see the contemporary Jesuit account in *Documenta Indica*, ed. by J. Wicki *et al* (Rome: Institutum Historicum Societas Iesu, 1948–), VII, 384, letter of Fr Gomes Vaz, 12 December 1567. For the outbreak of 1570 see João Manuel Pacheco de Figueiredo, 'Goa dourada nos séculos XVI e XVII: O hospital dos pobres do padre Paulo Camerte, esboço de sua reconstituição histórica', *Studia*, 25 (1968), 136–40.

[48] John Correia-Afonso, 'On the Fourth Centenary of Filippo Sassetti (1540–1588): Scientific Observations from Cochin', *Indica*, 26 (1989), 15–24 (p. 19). Sassetti was the only sixteenth-century European to try to learn Sanskrit, and he also talked with Hindu healers and got one of them to translate Sanskrit texts on pharmaceuticals for him. He spent most of his time in Malabar (1583–88) though he died in Goa. He was a well-educated and observant inquirer. See Lach, I, 477, and II, Book 3, 541.

until the heat was felt. In this way the pain was allayed and the discharge and vomiting stopped.[49]

The cauterization of the feet described by two of these authors may well have been an Indian method which the Portuguese adopted, for d'Orta was the first European to describe cholera, and he noted the Indian treatment of applying a hot iron to the feet.[50] An account from the 1750s seems to confirm these earlier Portuguese sources which say this was an Indian remedy, though the observer still thought it worked quite well:

There is likewise known on the Malabar-coast chiefly, a most violent disorder they call the Mordechin, which seizes the patient with such fury of purging, vomiting and tormina [sic] of the intestines, that it will often carry him off in thirty hours. For this the physicians among the natives know no more effectuall remedy, than the actual cautery applied to the soles of the feet, the powerful revulsion of which rarely fails of a salutary efficacy.[51]

One part of the treatment widely used by Hindu doctors was however apparently not picked up by the Portuguese. Hindu doctors would throw pepper into the eyes of the patient in order to gauge the intensity of the attack. This is presumably what Charles Dellon described in Daman in 1673, when he noted a young Portuguese girl was gravely ill, but 'the Indian physician, instead of letting her blood, had covered her head with pepper, which I immediately caused to be removed'.[52] I assume that the point was that if patients did not react to the pepper they were given up for dead.

These two treatments were combined with various other measures. First the patient was purged of the contents of his stomach. We have already described various methods of doing this. Costa said that in the case of cholera Indian doctors thought that a mixture of tamarind and young coconut oil provided a good but mild purge. In Goa local doctors used a particular variety of 'mirobólanos' ('terminalia chebula') to purge for cholera. We may note, incidentally, that many of these purging agents were known to the Portuguese already, from Galen and especially from Ibn Sina.[53] Costa said that Indians used canafistula ('cassia fistula') to purge the cholera and the humours which were affecting the stomach. To clarify

[49] Niccolao Manucci, *Storia do Mogor, or Mogul India*, trans. with intro. and notes by William Irvine, 2nd edn, 4 vols (Calcutta: Editions Indian, 1965–67), II, 157. The word used for cholera in Goa was *mordexim* or variants thereof. Dalgado tells us that the word is local, deriving from the Konkani *modxi* or *morxi*. The French later converted it to their term, as above, of *mort-de-chien*. See Sebastião Rodolfo Dalgado, *Glossário Luso-Asiático*, 2 vols (Coimbra: Imprensa da Universidade, 1919–21), II, 69–71, under 'mordexim'. According to Rawlinson the word came from the Marathi *modashi* through the Portuguese *mordexim*. See Ovington, p. 204, n. 1.
[50] *Coloquios*, no. 17.
[51] John Henry Grose, *A Voyage to the East Indies . . . to which is added A Journey from Aleppo to Busserah, over the Desert, by Mr. Charmichael*, 2nd edn, 2 vols (London: 1772), I, 250.
[52] A. K. Priolkar, *The Goa Inquisition* (Bombay: Priolkar, 1961), p. 14 of Dr Dellon's account.
[53] Costa, pp. 35, 43, 177. For myrobolan see Rosu, p. 191, n. 64.

XII

the blood a little rhubarb was used, and they often also gave some grains of cinnamon in order to cure flatulence.[54]

Following on from the purge, if the patients survived, they then had to be built up again. The Hindus gave kanji, in this case a mixture of rice water with pepper and cumin seed, that is cardamom, added. Canarin pepper was considered to be the best variety to use; Costa noted that both brahmin and Canarin doctors preferred it to other types.[55] D'Orta said that the Hindus also bound up most of the body of the sufferer to prevent cramps, and administered betel. He added that 'all these things are not wanting in reason, though they are done roughly'. The Portuguese method again typically allowed more food. Indians gave only kanji, but the Portuguese preferred to first purge the patient in order to clear the stomach, and then anoint it with oil in order to comfort it. After this chicken or partridge could be eaten.[56]

All this may well point to the difficulties of using these Portuguese sources as much as to their value. It is true that they sometimes, at least in the present state of my knowledge, appear to be contradictory and confused. It is very difficult to identify many of the particular plants which they mention. The diseases themselves are not always easy to name, for 'fever', for example, could refer to a range of quite different maladies. Nevertheless, they are all we have, and I hope this brief account will encourage much more research in this area, so that we can begin to describe Hindu medical practice, as opposed to theory, in this early modern period.

---

[54] Costa, p. 86.
[55] *Coloquios*, nos 17 and 46; Costa, p. 16. On cummin see Rosu, p. 202, n. 110.
[56] *Coloquios*, no. 17.

XIII

THE PORTUGUESE STATE AND MEDICINE
IN SIXTEENTH-CENTURY GOA

The Portuguese set up hospitals in several of their colonial areas in the sixteenth century. The one in Mozambique, for example, was often full of sick sailors.[1] As for the Royal Hospital in Cochin, few records seem to have survived. We do know that Christavão da Costa, a contemporary of Garcia d'Orta, and himself a very observant depictor of Indian medical practice, in 1569 was a doctor in the Royal Hospital in Cochin.[2] Like d'Orta, he often asked a brahmin doctor in Cochin about some local cures. This brahmin was a friend of Costa's, and very popular among both the local inhabitants of Cochin, and also the many Portuguese who lived there.[3] Costa also, unlike d'Orta most of the time, differentiates between different Hindu systems in different areas.

---

[1] On the hospital at Mozambique, see Gaspar Correa, *Lendas de India*, Coímbra, 1921-31, Lisbon, 1969, 4 vols., I, 785, and various studies by C.R. Boxer, collected in his *From Lisbon to Goa, 1500-1750: Studies in Portuguese Maritime Enterprise*, London, Variorum, 1984, especially "The Principal Ports of Call in the 'Carreira da India'," and "Moçambique Island and the 'Carreira da India." For the hospital at Mozambique in 1541-2 see Georg Schurhammer, *Francis Xavier: His Life, His Times*, vol. II, *India*, Rome, 1977, pp. 63-7, and A.A. de Andrade, "Fundação do hospital militar de São João Deus. Moçambique," *Studia*, I, 1958, pp. 77-89.

[2] *Tratado das drogas e medicinas das India Orientais, por Christovão da Costa*, ed. Jaime Walter, Lisbon, 1964, p. 125.

[3] Costa, *op.cit.*, p. 28.

402

Thus brahmin, Canarin and Malabar treatments are specified. His work tells us more than any other about Hindu medical practice in Cochin in the late sixteenth century.[4] In particular, Costa noted that Hindus, brahmins, vanias, all of them, never started the day without bathing the whole body. Muslims did this at least every three days, while Europeans notoriously would have been much more parsimonious in their ablutions. In 1569 the king of Cochin was ill, but he told Costa that even if it cost him his life he still had to take his bath every morning.[5]

Unfortunately, I can say little more about medical practice in Cochin in the sixteenth century, or about the Royal Hospital there. The rest of this essay will deal almost exclusively with the much better documented situation in Goa, but first I will sketch the European background.

State concern with helping ill people, and secular involvement in financing hospitals, seem to have been quite new ideas in both Europe and Asia at the beginning of the early modern period. In earlier times it was religious authorities who sponsored most health care, sometimes it is true prompted by pious rulers.[6]

Before the middle of the fifteenth century in Portugal there were some hospitals maintained by religious Orders, and two set up by Prince Henry in the early fifteenth century to cure "African" diseases, but apart from this only asylums and places of seclusion, especially for lepers. But under João II and Manuel in the late fifteenth century the state in Portugal began to interest itself in health care. Hospitals and a House of Mercy were established,

---

[4] *Ibid.*, pp. 23, 28.

[5] *Ibid.*, pp. 125-6.

[6] See generally a succinct survey in Roderick E. McGrew, *Encyclopedia of Medical History*, London, Macmillan, 1985, s.v. "hospitals"

notably the splendid hospital of All Saints, founded in Lisbon in 1492, and completed ten years later.[7]

We also find in Europe increasing difference in the matter of professionalism. Over the fifteenth and sixteenth centuries in Portugal pharmacists became quite closely regulated and had to be certified to be able to practice as druggists. They had to have five books on drugs available, and three particular measures.[8] Physicians and surgeons had in theory been licensed since 1338, though until a reform in 1448 this was poorly observed. From this year certificates of proficiency were issued, and matters were further tightened up in 1515 by D. Manuel.[9]

We can now turn to the situation in the first large European settlement in India, the port city of Goa, for here we seem to find a reflection of the changes we noted occurring in Europe. The Portuguese may not have been better curers than their Indian interlocutors,[10] but they did set up official hospitals, and they did make some attempts to regulate and control healers.

---

[7] C.R. Boxer, "Some remarks on the social and professional status of physicians and surgeons in the Iberian World, 16th-18th centuries," *Revista de História* [São Paulo], vol. L, no. 100, 1974, p. 200. On this hospital, see a splendid book which reprints the "Regimento" which established it and which contains copious information on medical knowledge and regulation at this time: Abílio José Salgado and Anastásia Mestrinho Salgado, eds. *Regimento do Hospital de Todos-os-Santos [edição facsimilada]*, Lisbon, 1992.

[8] A.H. de Oliveira Marques, *Daily Life in Portugal in the Late Middle Ages*, Madison, 1971, p. 151.

[9] C.R. Boxer, "Some remarks," *Revista de História*, 1974, pp. 197-8.

[10] On this and related matters see an article and a book chapter by the present author: M.N. Pearson, "First Contacts between Indian and European Medical Systems: Goa in the Sixteenth Century," in David Arnold ed., *Warm Climates and Western Medicine: the Emergence of Tropical Medicine, 1500-1900*, Amsterdam, Editions Rodopi (The Wellcome Institute Series in the History of Medicine), 1996, pp. 20-41; "The Thin End of the Wedge: Medical Relativities as a Paradigm of Early Modern Indian-European Relations," *Modern Asian Studies*, XXIX, 1, 1995, pp. 141-70.

Goa was conquered by Afonso Albuquerque for the Portuguese king in 1510, and was their main town and capital during the sixteenth century and later. The town's population at 1600 was about 75,000. Of these about 1500 were Portuguese or *mestiços*, 20,000 were Hindus, and some 50,000 were local Christians who had been converted during the sixteenth century. In the countryside the population was still predominantly Hindu.[11]

We know very little about health care in Goa before the Portuguese conquest. Figueiredo claims that long before the Portuguese all branches of knowledge, including medicine, were taught in institutions of higher learning, and in settlements of brahmins. These attracted students from far and wide.[12] This information is so fragmentary as to be of little use, for we cannot distinguish between medicine and other scholarly disciplines. We can assume that healers in Goa were often brahmins, and their more book-based knowledge was supplemented by locally proven recipes and nostrums dispensed by village women healers. We have almost no evidence of hospitals, or of state involvement in health care, before the coming of the Portuguese. All we have is one reference (from the eleventh century) to a house of mercy, established by a chief minister of a local king in Goa Velha, which provided relief for the poor, sick, and pilgrims.[13]

Portuguese Goa was generally considered to have a very high mortality rate. One estimate finds that no less than 25,000 Portuguese soldiers died in the Royal Hospital between 1604 and 1634; by repute 500 a year died from syphilis and "the effects of

---

[11] For Goa in the sixteenth century see M.N. Pearson, *The Portuguese in India*, OUP, 1987, pp. 81-115.

[12] John M. de Figueiredo, "Ayurvedic Medicine in Goa according to European Sources in the Sixteenth and Seventeenth Centuries," *Bulletin of the History of Medicine*, vol. 58, 1984, p. 226.

[13] See generally João Manuel Pacheco Figueiredo, "Goa Pré-Portuguesa," *Studia*, 12, 1963, pp. 139-259; 13/14, 1965, pp. 105-225, and especially nos. 13/14, p. 160.

profligacy." As a proverb had it, "Of the hundred who go to India [from Portugal], not even one returns."[14] Linschoten noted of the Royal Hospital that "every yeare at the least there entered 500 live men, and never come forth till they are dead."[15]

In most medical matters, such as diagnosis and healing, the newly arrived Europeans had no decisive advantage as compared to their Hindu subjects.[16] The only area where the Portuguese were more advanced was in the matter of state concern with medical matters, and the provision of hospitals for their Christian population. We will consider first hospitals, and then attempts by the state to regulate healers.

By late in the sixteenth century there were several hospitals in Goa, but we do not yet have a definitive list of which hospitals existed when and where.[17] There was, for example, the Leper Hospital of St. Lazarus, which had been founded in 1529. The Municipal Council and the Misericórdia or House of Mercy financed it. In 1634 there were 15-20 lepers held there.[18] Another was a hospital for Indian Christians. This was run by the Jesuits.

---

[14] Alberto C. Germano da Silva Correia, *La Vieille-Goa*, Bastorá, 1931, pp. 274-5; F. P. Mendes da Luz, "Livro das Cidades," *Studia*, 6, 1960, f. 8

[15] J.H. van Linschoten, *The Voyage of John Huyghen van Linschoten to the East Indies*, London, 1885, 2 vols, I, 237

[16] See my "First Contacts between Indian and European Medical Systems."

[17] Generally see C.R. Boxer, *Portuguese Society in the Tropics*, Madison, 1965, pp. 24-6, and Silva Correia, *La Vieille-Goa*, pp. 295-300. By far the best modern survey is in Fátima da Silva Gracias, *Health and Hygiene in Colonial Goa: 1510-1961*, New Delhi, 1994, pp. 118-36. For the Dutch hospital in Colombo, built soon after the conquest in the 1660s and still to be seen in the Fort area, see C.G. Uragoda and K.D. Paranavitana, "The Seventeenth-Century Dutch Hospital in Colombo," *Medical History*, XXIX, 1985, pp. 182-92.

[18] On this leper hospital see Schurhammer, *Francis Xavier*, p. 211; King to Câmara, 26 March 1532 in Archivo Português Oriental, ed. J.H. da Cunha Rivara, Nova Goa, 1857-77, 6 vols., I, part l, p. 12; António Bocarro, "Livro das plantas de todas as fortalezas, cidades e povações do Estado da India Oriental," in *Arquivo Português Oriental*, ed. A.B. de Bragança Pereira, Bastorá, Goa, 1937-40, IV, ii, part 1, p. 256; and Fátima Gracias, p. 132.

It was envisaged in the official regulation of the Jesuit college of St. Paul in 1546. It was noted that the Jesuits needed to cure, or if they died bury, local converts, and so the hospital was decreed. It was to have a native doctor, the best available, and also a barber whose duties included bleeding and shaving the patients.[19]

This hospital, known as the Hospital of the Poor of Fr. Paulo Camerte, was set up soon afterwards thanks to the efforts of this same Misser Paulo Camerte, an elderly Jesuit who had come to India in the first party of members of this order to travel east, led by Francis Xavier.[20]

We have a detailed account of its early days in a Jesuit letter of 1552.[21] Fr. Paulo looked after orphans, and was also the main person in the hospital attached to the Jesuit college of St. Paul. All ill native Christians were welcome in it, both men and women, though the sexes were kept strictly separated. It was kept scrupulously clean, and seven or eight people ministered to the patients. The hospital was supported by being given rice and some money from the College, and a grant of 300 *pardaus* from lands in Bardes and Salcette, but this trifling sum was supplemented by the good father himself, who financed most of the enterprise from his own efforts, even, for example, raising hens to be used in the hospital. At any one time there were 30 or 40 patients, and some Portuguese even used it as a hospice in order to be consoled in their last hours by the father. Governors visited it many times. Fr. Paulo also raised funds to establish a

---

[19] Regimento for College of St. Paul, 27 June 1546, in *Documenta Indica*, ed. J. Wicki et al, Rome, 1948 - , 16 vols to date, I, 125-6. Generally on this hospital see an excellent article: João Manuel Pacheco de Figueiredo, "Goa dourada nos séculos XVI e XVII: O hospital dos pobres do padre Paulo Camerte, esboço de sua reconstituição histórica," *Studia*, XXV, 1968, pp. 117-46. Fátima Gracias, *op.cit.*, p. 132, claims that "in course of time" non-Christians were admitted also, but she gives no date for this change of policy.

[20] See generally on Misser Paulo, Schurhammer, *Xavier*, p. 65, f.ns. 120, 121.

[21] Fr. R. Pereira letter of 8 Dec 1552, in *Documenta Indica*, II, 507-9.

small chapel adjacent to the hospital, and he was active in baptising new converts, and hearing confessions. Another Jesuit letter three years later noted that the hospital was still attached to the College, and was for poor native Christians who had fallen sick.[22]

The later history of this "hospital of the poor" is obscure. In 1594 it seems that the state was providing some finance, for the viceroy in this year decreed that merchants were not to employ on their ships soldiers who should be serving the king. A range of fines for offenders was laid down, and one quarter of the proceeds were to go to "the hospital of the poor of this city."[23] It seems that it was later taken over by the Misericórdia, and that this body was helping to finance it, for in 1607 the Municipal Council, in a general complaint about the poor state of affairs in Goa, noted that the Misericórdia could not even keep up the hospital of the poor.[24] In 1608 Pyrard noted that Indians have "a hospital apart, endowed by the townspeople, wherein are received only Christian Indians. There is still another hospital for the women of the Christian Indians, also endowed by the town, to which women only may go."[25] In 1630 there was a hospital for the poor in Margão, which may have been the same one, now transferred to this provincial town. It was run by the Jesuits, and received the miserly sum of 600 *pardaus* a year from the state.[26] In 1634 the Misericórdia was running a hospital for locals, supported by a grant of 300-350 *xerafins* a month.[27] Boxer tells us of a hospital

[22] Fr. Antonio de Quadros, 6 Dec 1555, in *Documenta Indica*, III, 350.

[23] Alvará of 29 Aug. 1594, in *Archivo Português Oriental*, ed. J.H. da Cunha Rivara, III, 468.

[24] Câmara to King, letter of 1607, in *Archivo Português Oriental*, ed. J.H. da Cunha Rivara, I, ii, 201.

[25] François Pyrard de Laval, *The Voyage of François Pyrard of Laval to the East Indies*, vol. II, London, 1888, p. 7.

[26] Viceroy to king, 12 Nov 1630, printed in *O Chronista de Tissuary*, 1867, vol. II; see also Fátima Gracias, *op.cit.*, pp. 132-3.

[27] Bocarro in *Arquivo Português Oriental*, ed. Bragança Pereira, IV, ii, 1, p. 256.

of All Saints run by the Misericórdia and open to all races.[28] Possibly the two are identical.

In an Indian context the famous Royal Hospital of the Holy Spirit was very innovative. It had been founded by the conqueror of Goa, Afonso Albuquerque, to cater for Portuguese soldiers. He set up a rather primitive adobe one in 1510, when the city was first taken by the Portuguese. Late in 1512, in a major campaign, he recaptured the town of Benastarim from hostile Bijapuri forces, and then marched in triumph back to Goa, and "he immediately established a hospital of very large size, with beds and everything that was necessary for the care and cure of the wounded, who were very numerous."[29]

At first this Royal Hospital was run by the factor of the city with a state subsidy,[30] but in 1542 it was handed over to the care of the charitable organisation the Misericórdia, with a state subsidy of about 4000 xerafins. It is clear, however, that the Misericórdia had been influential long before they took over control, for as early as 1519 the king had to decree that all ill Christians, not just those recommended by the officials of the Misericórdia, were to be entitled to care in the hospital.[31] At mid century a large staff, consisting of a mordomo or chief administrator, a physician, a surgeon, a barber (who also did bleedings), a pharmacist, an

---

[28] Boxer, *Portuguese Society*, pp. 25-6.

[29] Afonso Albuquerque, *Commentaries of the great Afonso Albuquerque*, London, Hakluyt, 1875-84, 4 vols. III, 241, and see generally Schurhammer, *Xavier*, pp. 201-4. For an extended study of the regulation of this hospital, see Vasconcelos Freire, "Hospital Real de Goa: Estudo dos seus regulamentos", Lisbon, Universidade Clássica, Departmento de História, 1998. Many thanks to Dr. Maria de Jesus Celia dos Matires Lopes for bringing this work to my attention.

[30] For examples of payments to various hospital staff before 1515 see *Arquivo Português Oriental*, ed. Bragança Pereira, IV, i, 1, pp. 446, 556, 607, 608, 609, 894.

[31] King's alvará of 22 Dec. 1519, in *Archivo Português Oriental*, ed. J.H. da Cunha Rivara, V, 44-5.

orderly, chaplain, secretary, buyer, cooks, washermen and slaves, looked after some 40 patients at any one time, though the number rose greatly each year when the ships from Portugal came in with their cargoes of Portuguese ravaged by the long unhealthy voyage.[32] It was run from 1579 by the Society of Jesus, though they later gave it up and had to be persuaded to resume their mission in 1591.[33]

The way the state insisted that the Jesuits take over again the hospital in 1591 showed how concerned the state was with the hospital, as did events soon after. The *alvará* which handed it over to the Jesuits also gave the hospital the proceeds from three state *rendas*, or contracts, that is the proceeds of the taxes on the sale of food, soap, and opium. In total these were meant to raise about 12,000 *xerafins*, which was considered to be enough. These proceeds were to be handed over direct to the Jesuits. If it were not sufficient, extra funds were to be found from other sources.[34]

A change of administration did not solve all the hospital's problems. In 1593 the king wrote to the viceroy that he had been told that the hospital was in dire shape, falling down, and unable to care for the 400 to 500 patients it admitted each year. The king had decided that the hospital was to be totally rebuilt on the same site, for it was essential that his "poor soldiers who served in the armadas" be given good care when they fell sick. The new building was to be bigger than the old one, it seems, for the king provided that small houses around the existing building could be bought

---

[32] For an extended description of the hospital in 1542 see Schurhammer, *Xavier*, pp. 201-8.

[33] Fátima Gracias, *op.cit.*, pp. 122-3. Linschoten described their work in the hospital in the 1580s: Linschotén, p. 237. For the king's attempt to get them to take over again, see king to viceroy, 21 Jan 1588, in *Archivo Português Oriental*, ed. J.H. da Cunha Rivara, III, 115, and king to viceroy 6 Feb 1589, in ibid, 196.

[34] Viceroy's alvará of 12 Oct 1591, in *Archivo Português Oriental*, ed. J.H. da Cunha Rivara, III, 333-5.

and demolished if they were in the way. Additional finance was also provided.[35] This however was not enough, so next year the king granted the proceeds from a voyage to China for the work.[36] This then was a very major relocation of state resources towards health care. But as often was the case, orders from Portugal took some time to be obeyed in Goa. In 1597 the king noted that the Jesuits were now much less keen on their new charge, for the voyage to China had still not been given to them. He ordered that all other claimants to the proceeds of a voyage to China would have to wait their turn until the Jesuits had been given theirs.[37] But the Jesuits were not prepared to wait, and gave up the hospital. It was handed over to the Municipal Council, who had no more success in extracting money from the local officials.[38] Even in 1603 the king was still complaining that almost no work had been done on the hospital.[39] In this same year the Municipal Council explained what had happened. Work had stopped, but this was because they had run out of money. They had indeed been given the proceeds of a voyage to China, which was sold for over 24,000 *xerafins*. However, they only got 4000 of this, as the rest was taken as a loan to the state. In 1605 they asked for another voyage

---

[35] King to viceroy, 20 March 1593, in "Livros das Monções do Reino," Historical Archives of Goa, 2B, f. 145v; see also king to viceroy, 10 March 1593 in *Archivo Português Oriental*, ed. J.H. da Cunha Rivara, III, 386-7.

[36] King to viceroy, 1 March 1594, in "Livros das Monções do Reino," Historical Archives of Goa, 2B, ff. 255v-256; printed in *Archivo Português Oriental*, ed. J.H. da Cunha Rivara, III, 433; see also-King to viceroy, Jan. 23, 1610, in *Documentos remettidos da India, ou Livros das Monções*, ed. R.A. de Bulhão Pato, Lisbon, 1880-1935, 5 vols, I, 303.

[37] King to viceroy, 5 Feb 1597, in *Archivo Português Oriental*, ed. J.H. da Cunha Rivara, III, 692-3, and cf. 689-90.

[38] King to Câmara, letter of 25 Jan 1598, in *Archivo Português Oriental*, ed. J.H. da Cunha Rivara, I, i, 121, and Câmara to king, letter of 1601, in ibid, I, ii, 86.

[39] King to viceroy, 12 Feb 1603 in "Livros das Monções do Reino," Historical Archives of Goa, 7, 139v.

so that they could continue construction.[40] Some time after this the hospital was finished, as Pyrard in 1608 has left us a glowing description of it. And the Jesuits had returned to take over its administration.

All this concerns extra expenses needed to build a new hospital, but the state also provided large routine sums each year. When the Misericórdia took it over in 1542 it was given about 4000 *xerafins*,[41] but later this was increased. Thus in 1576 the Royal Hospital was given 9000 *xerafins* a year for sustenance for the ill, and pay for the pharmacist, doctor, surgeon and other officials and servants.[42] Around 1600 the hospital received 12,000 *xerafins*, while by comparison the archbishop's establishment got 13,240, and the Inquisition 6,400. The hospital got about 1.5% of total state expenses.[43] Around the same time the great chronicler Diogo do Couto got about 360 *xerafins* a year for his work as the head of the state archives, and for writing a history of India.[44] In 1634 the hospital again got 12,000 *xerafins* to look after all sick Portuguese and soldiers.[45] It may be noted in passing that other hospitals in other Portuguese areas also received comparatively large sums. In Daman in 1565, and Diu in 1634, the hospital received in subsidy (mostly meaning salaries) a sum greater than the captain of the fort.[46]

---

[40] Câmara to king, 1603 and 1605, in *Archivo Português Oriental*, ed. J.H. da Cunha Rivara, pp. 117, 148-9. It should be noted that the price the Council received for selling the right to undertake this voyage is not the same as the profit the purchaser would hope to make from the actual voyage.

[41] Schurhammer, *Xavier*, p. 202.

[42] P.S.S. Pissurlencar, *Regimentos das fortalezas da India*, Bastora, 1951, pp. 63-5

[43] Ibid, pp. 528-30

[44] Royal Alvará of 25 Feb 1595, in "Livros das Monções do Reino," Historical Archives of Goa, 5, f. 47.

[45] Bocarro in *Arquivo Português Oriental*, ed. Bragança Pereira, IV, ii, 1, p. 254.

[46] Pissurlencar, *Regimentos das fortalezas da India*, pp. 394, 400; Bocarro in *Arquivo Português Oriental*, ed. Bragança Pereira, IV, ii, 1, pp. 108-13.

412

Admission to the Royal Hospital was restricted to Portuguese soldiers and a few indigent Portuguese. Pyrard said that no women, no householders, and no servants were admitted; nor were New Christians (converted Jews) allowed, though some managed to sneak in anyway.[47] Linschoten noted that the patients "are only Portingals, for no other sick person may lodge therein, I mean such as are called white men, for the other Indians have an Hospital by themselves."[48] It could hold a very impressive 1500 patients, and descriptions of it after it was expanded and rebuilt make it sound a most grand structure indeed. Pyrard noted that "Viewing it from the outside, we could hardly believe it was a hospital; it seemed to us a grand palace . . ."[49] Hospitals anywhere in the world at this time had deservedly low reputations, for they seem to have been most effective in transmitting communicable disease, or at best providing care but not cure. There was also a snobbish notion that hospitals were charitable, a resort only for those who could not afford care at home. But the Royal Hospital in Goa had a very high reputation, and this meant that, unusually for the time, even rich people were happy to use it.

Its staff included physicians, surgeons, apothecaries, barbers and bleeders, and Indian servants and slaves for the dirty work. Pyrard, who was a patient in 1608, has left an extended and glowing account of it. Even the beds were splendid, with mattresses and covers of silk or cotton. The meals were luxurious and ample, the plates, bowls and dishes of China porcelain or even silver. On admission the patient got a hair cut and wash, and was provided with bed clothes. There was even an out-patient facility: "He that wil not lie there, and hath any woundes or privie diseases, may come thether twice every day and be drest, and goe his way againe, without any question or deniall."[50]

---

[47] Pyrard, *op.cit.*, p. 12.

[48] Linschoten, *op.cit.*, p. 237.

[49] Pyrard, *op.cit.*, pp. 3, 7. It obviously then had been considerably enlarged since 1593, when it held only 400-500.

[50] Linschoten, *op.cit.*, p. 238.

Given all this expenditure, why the appalling mortality that we noted earlier? It seems that the organisation and funding of the hospital was more sophisticated than the medicine practised in it. The truly startling use of bleeding must have played a role, for as Tavernier noted bleeding could be "repeated, according to need, up to thirty or forty times, as long as bad blood comes."[51] Perhaps more important was a matter of patronage. Most governors brought their own doctors out with them from Lisbon as part of their vast retinues of relatives and hangers-on, all of them hoping to make a fortune in India during the three-year term of their patron.[52]

The problem with these newly arrived doctors was that they knew nothing of Indian medicine, yet the Portuguese had soon discovered that for Indian diseases Indian doctors were best. We find in Goa a very interesting and ad hoc mixture of Indian and Portuguese medical ideas.[53] The newly arrived Portuguese doctors were nearly always rewarded by being made the chief doctor of the Royal Hospital, but several contemporaries noted that this was a prime cause of mortality, for they knew nothing of Indian diseases, and just as they began to acculturate they returned to Portugal with their gubernatorial patron.[54] In 1605 the

---

[51] Jean-Baptiste Tavernier, *Travels in India of Jean-Baptiste Tavernier*, trans. V. Ball and W. Crooke, New Delhi, 1977, 2 vols, I, 160.

[52] Sometimes indeed they seem to have stayed on. Late in 1613 the viceroy recommended to the king that the *fisico-mor*, Dr. Paulo Ximenes, be rewarded, as had others with his position, with the habit of Santiago. He had come out with the previous viceroy, Ruy Lourenço de Tavora (1609-12), and had stayed on in the job after his patron's term ended. He had done well, and treated poor people without charging. Viceroy to king, date illegible but late 1613, "Livros das Monções do Reino," Historical Archives of Goa, 12, f. 54.

[53] I have discussed this matter fully in "First Contacts between Indian and European Medical Systems."

[54] See Silva Correia, *op.cit.*, p. 275, and Pyrard, *op.cit.*, intro. p. xii, and II, 14. For the career of one such *fisico-mor*, Dimas Bosque, who was attached to the viceroy D. Constantino de Bragança, 1558-61, see Jaime Walter, "Dimas Bosque, fisico-mor da India a as sereias," *Studia*, XII, 1963, pp. 261-71.

Municipal Council complained to the king that there were some 800 people in the Royal Hospital, and each day 15 or 20 died as a result of being treated by inexperienced newly arrived Portuguese doctors. These doctors were appointed by their viceregal patrons so that they could enjoy the pay attached to this position. Just as they acquired enough local experience they were replaced by another new comer. They asked the king not to allow these new comers, both doctors and surgeons, to hold this position; rather preference should be given to those who had greatest local experience.[55] Next year the Council wrote a similar complaint,[56] and finally in 1610 the king ordered that this practice cease and that the doctors and surgeons who went out with the viceroys not be allowed to practice in the Royal Hospital, "because they have no experience of the region and its medical methods." Surprisingly, this order seems to have provoked a storm of complaints from Goa, and three years later it was lifted.[57] Another problem raised by these itinerant doctors was that this resulted in a pronounced shortage of practitioners in Goa. A letter from Goa in 1644 complained of this, and noted despairingly that the present *fisico-mor* was a "negro," by which apparently is meant a Goan. The king was urged to take measures to make Portuguese doctors stay in Goa.[58]

More basically to explain mortality, the underlying health problems of Goa, stagnant water and porous soils, could not be met by the existing state of medical knowledge. The causes of tropical diseases such as cholera, dysentery and malaria were not

[55] Câmara to king, letter for 1605, in *Archivo Português Oriental*, ed. J.H. da Cunha Rivara, I. ii, 145.

[56] Câmara to king for year 1606, in *ibid*, I, ii, 186.

[57] King to viceroy. Jan. 23. 1610, in *Documentos remettidos da India*, ed. R.A. de Bulhão Pato. I. 304. and king to viceroy, Jan. 30, 1613 in ibid., II, 300.

[58] Archivo Historico Ultramarino, Lisbon. caixa 16A. no. 160, letter of 7 Sept. 1644. My thanks to Prof. Timothy Coates for this reference. See also John M. de Figuereido. "Ayurvedic Medicine." pp. 231-2.

diagnosed until the discoveries of the last century or so. To make matters worse, it is clear that even by the middle of the seventeenth century the hospital was in decline. Tavernier's account is quite revealing: "The hospital at Goa was formerly renowned throughout India; and, as it possessed a considerable income, sick persons were very well attended to. This was still the case when I first went to Goa; but since this hospital has changed its managers, patients are badly treated, and many Europeans who enter it do not leave it save to be carried to the tomb. . . . Generally all the poor people who begin to recover their health cry out from thirst, and beg for a little water to drink; but those who wait upon them, who are at present blacks and Mestifs [mestiços] - avaricious persons, and without mercy, do not give a drop without receiving something, that is to say, unless some money is placed in their hands, and to give colour to this wickedness they give it only in secret, saying that the physician forbids it."[59]   Similarly, Careri in 1695 found it to be "small, and ill Govern'd, tho' the King allows it four hundred pieces of Eight a Year. For this reason, and through the Pestilential Air of the Country there dye Thousands of sick Persons in it, and particularly of wretched Portuguese soldiers."[60]

If then the Royal Hospital reflected all too faithfully the problems of contemporary medical knowledge in both India and Europe, some of the resulting problems were alleviated by another state-supported institution, the *Santa Casa da Misericórdia,* or Holy House of Mercy. Like the Royal Hospital, the Misericórdia reflected a transfer to Goa of a new sort of institution from Portugal, for the Goa one was closely modelled on the mother house in Lisbon, which had been founded under royal patronage in 1498, the very year of da Gama's voyage. The Goan version was established by Albuquerque, probably in 1510. In both Lisbon

---

[59] *Ibid.*

[60] Careri in S.N. Sen. ed., *Indian Travels of Thevenot and Careri.* New Delhi. 1949, p. 194.

and Goa this organisation did excellent work for the poor and needy, providing them with food, cloths, drink and health care; to be sure, it was only Christians, indeed nearly always only Portuguese, who were served by this body.[61] Membership of its Board of Governors was a very high honour, and the Goan elite often rotated between service on this body and on the Municipal Council.[62]

The state also played a role, even if indirectly, in one other area of health care, for some pharmacies in Goa were in effect controlled by the state. In the early years of the seventeenth century the dowries for one or two nuns entering the convent of Santa Monica were pharmacies, and indeed in 1618 the convent, only recently founded, already owned eight pharmacies, three on Chorão Island, four on Divar Island, and one on Juá. The right to own these properties was ratified by a royal decree of 22 March 1617.[63] We can assume that the nuns leased out these rights; the ownership of Goa's other pharmacies cannot at present be determined.

Despite the sort of mingling of Hindu and Portuguese practice which we have discussed in detail elsewhere, the Portuguese did try to limit the prestige of Indian doctors. In 1563 all Hindu doctors were ordered to be expelled, but this order

---

[61] Boxer, *Portuguese Society*, pp. 24-5; C.R. Boxer, *The Portuguese Seaborne Empire*, London, 1969, pp. 286-8; Schurhammer, *Xavier*, pp. 168-72 for the Misericórdia in the time of Xavier; and for an extended, though now dated, coverage, see José Frederico Ferreira Martins, *História da Misericórdia de Goa, 1520-1910*, 3 vols, Nova Goa, 1910-14. We eagerly await a new study by Dr. Fatima Gracias.

[62] Boxer, *Portuguese Society*, p. 25.

[63] "Titulo dos bens que tem o convento das religiosas de Santa Monica da Cidade de Goa feito no mez de Janeiro de 1618 . . ." in *Documentos remitidos da India*, vol. VIII, p. 85. Many thanks to Timothy Coates for this reference. Dr. Coates'· dissertation at the University of Minnesota titled "Exiles and Orphans: Forced and State-Sponsored Colonizers in the Portuguese Empire,· 1550-1720," 1993 has been published in Portuguese. An English edition is in preparation.

was never enforced. In 1574 the governor decreed that Hindu teachers and doctors were not to go about on horseback or in palanquins. A first offence attracted a fine of 10 *cruzados*, a second 20 *cruzados* and the loss of the offending horse or palanquin, and a third meant being sent to the galleys. However, the doctor who served the governor's own household was exempt from this,[64] and in fact this prohibition also soon lapsed. Linschoten in the 1580s noted that "There are in Goa many Heathen phisitions which observe their gravities with hats carried over them for the sunne, like the Portingales, which no other heathens doe, but onely Ambassadors, or some rich Marchants. These Heathen phisitions doe not onely cure there owne nations and countriemen but the Portingales also, for the Viceroy himselfe, the Archbishop, and all the Monkes and Friers doe put more trust in them than in their own countrimen, whereby they get great store of money, and are much honoured and esteemed."[65]   As we noted, the Portuguese doctor Cristovão da Costa used to ask a local brahmin doctor in Cochin about local cures; this doctor was popular among both Indians and Portuguese in the town.[66]   In 1620 patients in the convent of Madre de Deus in Goa were treated by a pandit, and Portuguese soldiers wanting sick leave used letters from a pandit.[67]

What we have here are unsuccessful attempts first to expel, and then to limit the prestige, and patronage, of Hindu doctors using Hindu, that is ayurvedic, methods. Foiled in this attempt,

---

[64] *Ibid*, p. 178.

[65] Linschoten, *op.cit.*, I, 230.

[66] *Tratado das drogas e medicinas das India Orientais, por Christovão da Costa*, p. 28. This experimental, or perhaps better experiential, attitude was found early on in the Portuguese presence in the Indian Ocean. In 1505 some Portuguese engaged in taking Mombasa were hit by poisoned arrows. The Portuguese surgeon Mestre Fernando treated the wounds with wicks of pork fat, which soaked up the poison. He had learnt this technique from a Muslim healer. Fernão Lopes de Castanheda, *História do descobrimento e conquista da India pelos Portugueses*, 3rd ed., Coímbra, 1924-33, 9 vols., II, 6.

[67] John M. de Figuereido, "Ayurvedic Medicine," pp. 231-2.

mostly because its own elite were inconvenienced by this, the colonial state then moved to at least control and limit the numbers of its subjects who were allowed to practice European style medicine. We have eight published certificates (there are over a hundred in manuscript) given by the Portuguese chief physician to allow local doctors (*vaidyas*), from their names apparently all brahmins, to practice. This was a result of a decree of the Goa Senate in 1618 that no one might practice medicine unless he had passed an examination. The decree ran "no person of any religion, category, or nationality can exercise the medical or the surgical profession without passing a qualifying examination given by the *físico-mor* or the *cirurgião-mor*, and they will be obliged to take out a certificate of examination, so that those found practicing without this certificate will be fined twenty *pardaus*." The number of Hindu healers was to be limited to 30, and this restriction was to be enforced by the requirement that the certificate from the chief physician or surgeon was to be endorsed by the Municipal Council, in order to check the numbers. We do not know what areas of medicine were covered, or what the exam consisted of, but as these certificates gave the holders license to practice anywhere in the Portuguese empire they must have, as one would expect, tested European medicine, not *ayurvedic*.[68] This is also shown by the fact that the examiner is described as the *físico-mor*, normally a man from Europe. It is interesting, however, that the doctors so tested trained in traditional *ayurvedic* methods outside of Portuguese Goa before coming to the town to sit the examination which allowed them to practice this other form of medicine, that is European.[69]

---

[68] Figueiredo, "The Practice of Indian Medicine," pp. 53-60; Boxer, "Some Remarks," p. 207; John M. de Figueiredo, "Ayurvedic Medicine," p. 230.

[69] *Breve relação das escrituras dos gentios da India Oriental a dos sues costumes*, pp. 52-3, quoted in João Manuel Pacheco Figueiredo, "Goa Pré-Portuguesa," *Studia*, 12, 1963, pp. 139-259; 13/14, 1965, pp. 105-225, nos. 13/14, pp, 179-80, and also quoted [in English] in John M. de Figueiredo, "Ayurvedic Medicine," p. 231.

We have more detail from this same year concerning the attempt of the Municipal Council to regulate closely medicine in Goa. Physicians, surgeons, bleeders and pharmacists were fined 20 *pardaus* if they practiced without a city certificate. Bleeders were required to display at their door a painting of a man being bled, the object presumably being to make sure only these publicly known people engaged in bleeding. Hindu physicians were forbidden to leave Goa and travel to the mainland without a license, for fear they would engage in improper activities there. Municipal officers were to visit every pharmacy every six months and were to burn useless or adulterated medicines. The decree also controlled the prices of medicines, and banned the sale of some considered to be harmful.[70] As usual, one would expect that this sort of ambitious attempt at social engineering was observed more in the breach than otherwise; the rural majority of the population of Goa would certainly not be affected by this and would continue to use their traditional healers.

---

[70] "Livro de Posturas," Historical Archives of Goa, 1618, quoted in R.R.S. Chauhan, "Life in 17th Century Goa vis-a-vis Senate bye-laws," in P.P. Shirodkar, ed., *Goa: Cultural Trends*, Panaji, 1988, pp. 211-2.

XIV

The Thin End of the Wedge
Medical Relativities as a Paradigm of Early Modern Indian–European Relations

The Rise of the West, the creation of the Third World, the beginnings of disparity between Asia and Europe, or whatever other phrase is used, is obviously the great event of world history; hence the attempts to explain and date it, going back to the time when the Rise was actually beginning in the later eighteenth century. The literature is vast, complex and mostly of high quality. Some of it is concerned with causation—how did 'the West' get ahead, why did 'Asia' fall back or perhaps just stay the same? Others are interested in trying to date the beginnings of inequality—when can we see the beginnings of dominance, where did this occur and in which sectors of human life was this first to be seen? The first matter is, of course, the more important for an historian. It has been argued that, in the most general way, the fundamental cause of the beginnings of inequality is the series of changes in western Europe, and at first in England, known collectively as the Industrial Revolution. I will use this term as a shorthand for these collective changes, which Marshall Hodgson called the 'Great Western Transmutation.' Put most crudely, western Europe advanced and changed in a paradigmatic way, while Asia did not. At the most, Asia kept doing what it had been doing for centuries; Europe changed basically.[1]

Parts of this article are extracted from the text of my 27th James Ford Bell lecture, presented to the Associates of the James Ford Bell Library, University of Minnesota, at the American Association of University Women's Club, Minneapolis, 3 May 1989. The lecture was called 'Initial Contacts between European and Indian Medicine', and subsequently was pubished by the library under the title 'Towards Superiority: European and Indian Medicine 1500–1700'. More recently this paper has benefited from comments by Professors Donald Simpson and David Arnold.

[1] In what follows, I will be writing about India most of the time, rather than all of Asia, though I have drawn some examples from Persia. I have discussed in some detail elsewhere these broad changes, and the reader is referred to these for a fuller analysis and quite large bibliography. See M. N. Pearson, *Before Colonialism: Theories on Asian–European Relations, 1500–1750* (Delhi, 1988), and 'Merchants and States', in

These changes are seen as beginning from around the middle of the eighteenth century, though the culmination came perhaps even a century later. Most scholars, however, correctly see the Industrial Revolution as the capstone of a long process, going back even some centuries in England and in other parts of western Europe. Studies are made of the commercialization of land, of earlier industrialization, of various forms of capitalism, of the beginning of inter-continental trade and of scientific, intellectual and technological changes which preceded, and perhaps made possible, the Industrial Revolution.

Many studies of the relations between Asia and Europe have been concerned to delineate when European traders began to appear to be 'different' in the Indian Ocean. Europeans had, of course, traded in these waters since the very late fifteenth century. The consensus today seems to be that these traders operated on a basis of equality with their Asian peers, and indeed often partners, until some time in the later eighteenth century. Then, the beginnings of the Industrial Revolution in Europe, really England, began to be felt, and this translated into the displacement of 'traditional' Asian trades by Europeans who until this time had been in no way remarkable or dominant. Wallerstein's important work finds Europeans 'participating' in Asian trade for some time; 'the qualitative shift in the situation [of India and its relations with the European world economy] occurred in the hundred years following 1750...'. This was, however, not a result of the 'so-called Industrial Revolution' but of the expansion of the European world-economy, which began c. 1730–40. Political penetration into India occurred from 1750 to 1850, and economic, more concentrated, mostly in the nineteenth century.[2]

Several scholars have claimed that we can advance the date of this superiority to earlier in the eighteenth century, thus long before the

James D. Tracy (ed.), *The Political Economy of Merchant Empires* (New York, CUP, 1991), pp. 41–116.

[2] See Immanuel Wallerstein, 'Incorporation of Indian Subcontinent into Capitalist World-Economy', *Economic and Political Weekly*, XXI (4 Jan. 1986), pp. 28–39; also published in Satish Chandra (ed.), *The Indian Ocean: Explorations in History, Commerce and Politics* (New Delhi, 1987), pp. 222–53. The version here is focused on India, and is thus more accessible than the comparable study scattered through his *The Modern World-System III: The Second Era of Great Expansion of the Capitalist World-Economy, 1730–1840s* (New York, 1989). See also S. Arasaratnam's fine *Merchants, Companies and Commerce on the Coromandel Coast, 1650–1740* (Delhi, OUP, 1986); Holden Furber's classic, *Rival Empires of Trade in the Orient, 1600–1800* (Minneapolis, 1976); Om Prakash, *The Dutch East India Company and the Economy of Bengal, 1630–1720* (Princeton, 1985); Ashin Das Gupta and M. N. Pearson (eds), *India and the Indian Ocean, 1500–1800* (Calcutta, 1987).

Industrial Revolution. Steensgaard cautiously claims that European demand had become a major feature in Indian Ocean trade in the first half of the century, perhaps from the 1720s or 1730s.[3] Subrahmanyam finds the Europeans playing a very large role in Coromandel trade even in the second half of the seventeenth century.[4] It should be stressed, however, that this was a superiority in trade, derived perhaps from better transportation, or better business methods, including forms of credit, not necessarily in the whole gamut of economic organization.[5]

Other historians have seen the first insertion of the wedge coming when European traders in Asia got an advantage not because they were superior in certain sectors of economic organization, but because they had a military edge over their Asian rivals. A dramatic specific example is what the Dutch did to cinnamon prices once they had gained control of the coastal areas of Sri Lanka in 1659. The price had been 15 stuivers a pond. They immediately raised it to 36, and in 1660 to 50.[6] A recent study by Subrahmanyam finds an end to Indian ships voyaging between Masulipatnam and the Arabian Sea in the later seventeenth century. The point, however, is that Indian trade continued, in European ships, so that what this shows is 'not the superior economic organization of their rivals [the Europeans], but their inability to withstand the use of force in trade.'[7] Similarly, Geoffrey Parker, in his exemplary comparative study, very pertinently notes, 'Although the Machine Age helps to explain how the Europeans extended their control over the total land area of the globe from 35 per cent in 1800 to 84 per cent in 1914, it cannot explain how they managed to acquire that initial 35 per cent.'[8] He finds the answer in differing Asian responses to the more advanced military

[3] Niels Steensgaard, 'The Indian Ocean Network and the Emerging World-Economy, c. 1500–1750', in Chandra (ed.), The Indian Ocean, pp. 125–50; cf. Steensgaard, 'Asian Trade and World-Economy from the 15th to 18th Centuries', T. R. de Souza (ed.), Indo-Portuguese History: Old Issues, New Questions (New Delhi, 1985), pp. 225–35.

[4] Sanjay Subrahmanyam, 'Asian Trade and European Affluence? Coromandel 1650–1740', review article in Modern Asian Studies, XXII, 1 (Feb. 1988), pp. 179–88.

[5] See Tracy (ed.), The Political Economy of Merchant Empires.

[6] Arasaratnam, p. 137.

[7] S. Subrahmanyam, 'Persians, Pilgrims and Portuguese: the Travails of Masulipatnam Shipping in the Western Indian Ocean, 1590–1665', Modern Asian Studies, XXII, 3 (July 1988), pp. 503–30, and especially 524–30. The quotation is from p. 530.

[8] Geoffrey Parker, The Military Revolution: Military Innovation and the Rise of the West, 1580–1800 (CUP, 1988), p. 117; a revised and amplified version was published in Tracy (ed.), The Political Economy of Merchant Empires, pp. 161–95.

knowledge of the Europeans. And Habib agrees, for in a recent article he asks, 'Could it be that the European triumph against Indian (and Asian) merchants was not, then, one of size and technique, of Companies against pedlars, of joint-stock against atomised capital, of seamen against landsmen? Might it not have been more a matter of men-of-war and gun and shot to which arithmetic and brokerage could provide no answer, whether in the earlier "Age of Partnership" of after Plassey.'[9]

One should see the military revolution, European superiority in military techniques and tactics, as being part of a much wider complex of changes, indeed a true conjuncture, in the economy and society of western Europe. These included not just technological advances, but also the intellectual and scientific developments which made possible the technology and so the Industrial Revolution. Among these were changes in medical theory and practice, and in the medical profession. The present article contributes to this general debate, perhaps in a way which at first may seem extraneous or perverse, for it sketches a history of medical relations between Europe and Asia, these to be seen as exemplifying wider relations between the two. David Arnold noted that his main concern 'is not so much with disease and medicine as such as with their instrumentality — what they reveal about the nature and preoccupations, the ambitions and the methods of an encompassing imperialism.'[10] Along similar lines, I am describing the beginnings of this process. As it happens, I can date fairly precisely when the new European medicine was first seen in India and some other parts of Asia.[11] We can see clearly the beginnings of European superiority and Asian failure to keep up in

---

[9] Irfan Habib, 'Merchant Communities in Pre-colonial India', in James D. Tracy (ed.), *The Rise of Merchant Empires* (CUP, 1990), pp. 371–99.

[10] David Arnold, 'Introduction: Disease, Medicine and Empire', in David Arnold (ed.), *Imperial Health and Indigenous Societies* (Manchester, 1988), p. 2.

[11] Previous discussions of this matter were often written by people with better training in medicine than in history, so that they tend to be descriptive rather than analytical. Examples are P. D. Gaitonde, *Portuguese Pioneers in India: Spotlight on Medicine* (Bombay, 1983); João Baptista Amancio Gracias, 'Médicos Europeus em Goa e nas cortes Indianas nos séculos XVI a XVIII', *O Oriente Portugues*, XXIV–XXV (1939), pp. 335–91; and the various compilations of O. P. Jaggi: *Western Medicine in India* (3 vols, Delhi, Atma Ram and Sons, 1979–80); O. P. Jaggi, *Medicine in Medieval India*, vol. VIII of History of Science and Technology in India (Delhi, Atma Ram and Sons, 1977) (on yunani medicine); and *Indian System of Medicine* (Delhi, 1974) (on ayurvedic medicine). A good brief overview is K. K. Roy, 'Early Relations between the British and Indian Medical Systems', in *Proceedings of the XXIII International Congress of the History of Medicine* (2 vols, London, 1974, Wellcome Institute), I, 697–703.

this particular area; this to be seen as both an example of change to modern in Europe, and also as a contributor to the culmination of this modernity, that is, the Industrial Revolution.

Traditional Medical Systems

This is not the place to attempt a detailed description of early modern medical history. Nevertheless, a sketch is necessary in order to establish that there was a large degree of commonality in Eurasia concerning diseases and their cures.[12]

Identifying diseases from early modern sources is a hazardous business. It is often not possible to be sure what illness they are describing. Thus while the aptly named 'flux' was dysentery, the even more appropriately-titled 'bloody flux' could describe any disease where blood mixed with stools, for example bowel cancer. Similarly, typhoid and typhus are but two of many different enteric fevers, and can be identified only by autopsy; the prevalent 'fevers' of our period could be either of these, or some other quite different malady such as malaria. Diseases can change over time; indeed, some have suddenly appeared and then mysteriously vanished, such as the English sweating sickness of the sixteenth century.

The plague, smallpox and syphilis were three of the most threatening diseases in Europe. The most feared was plague. Some authorities distinguish between pulmonary plague and bubonic plague, but in fact the two are the same disease. Bubonic plague was first seen in Europe in the Black Death of 1347–51, which cut Europe's population by 40%. In this 'normal' version of plague the bacteria stayed in the bloodstream. Death occurred within one to five days for between 60 and 90% of those afflicted. However, this form was not contagious from human to human. The pneumonic variant was much more deadly. The bacteria entered the lungs, and as a result sufferers were highly contagious. They usually died in a matter of hours. Plague retreated in Europe in the early eighteenth century, the last major occurrence ravaging Marseilles in 1720.

It was considered that all forms of the plague were infectious. The rich, of course, could afford to flee, and did so at the first sign of

[12] Apart from specific works cited in footnotes, in this section I have used as a basic reference Roderick E. McGrew, *Encyclopedia of Medical History* (London, Macmillan, 1985). I also found much curious information in Deborah Manley (ed.), *The Guinness Book of Records 1492* (Guinness Publishing, 1992).

an outbreak. The poor stayed behind and died. Counter-measures included quarantine and isolation. As early as the fourteenth century Italian cities had introduced quarantine to keep out ship-borne bubonic plague from the Middle East. Once the disease appeared, affected areas were cordoned off; in the sixteenth century national policies evolved to achieve this.[13] In 1663 the Jesuit overland traveller, Manuel Godinho, arrived in Malta but was not allowed ashore 'despite our carrying health certificates, for having come from the East, because it is always presumed there is plague there.' He was more lucky in Marseilles: 'The lazaretto, or quarantine, at this port is not as strict as at Lyons and Venice and the health officers discharged me from it in seven days.'[14]

As spectacular in its own way as the Black Death was the very rapid spread of what was apparently a new and much more virulent form of venereal disease; that is, syphilis, from America, which even in the late 1490s was epidemic in areas which had contact with men returning from America. It spread all over Europe with remarkable rapidity, and also to Asia, for it was found in India in 1498, Canton in 1502 and Japan in 1505. In this same year the Italian Varthema in Calicut claimed that the ruler had 'the French disease ['Frangi'] and had it in the throat.'[15] Less dramatic maladies were endemic. Various fevers, smallpox, intestinal disorders, tuberculosis, dropsy (that is, oedema) and skin diseases were very widespread indeed, and were more effective because of poor diet, often deficient in some vitamins. What we need to remember here is that some diseases are more dramatic (cholera especially) than others. Owen distinguishes between crisis mortality and background mortality. The former, the dramatic and much described causes of mortality, include cholera, smallpox, plague, influenza and various 'fevers,' such as malaria and

---

[13] Fernand Braudel, *Civilization and Capitalism, 15th–18th Century*, vol. I, *The Structures of Everyday Life, The Limits of the Possible* (New York, 1979), pp. 78–88; E. L. Jones, *The European Miracle* (Cambridge, 1981), pp. 140–1. On plague, see McGrew, *Encyclopedia of Medical History*, s.v., and a useful survey of the literature by R. S. Roberts: 'The Question of the History of Plague', in *Proceedings of the XXIII International Congress of the History of Medicine* (2 vols, London, 1974, Wellcome Institute), II, 1291–4.

[14] John Correia-Afonso (trans. and ed.), *Intrepid Itinerant: Manuel Godinho and his Journey from India to Portugal in 1663* (Bombay, Oxford University Press, 1990), pp. 223, 224.

[15] Ludovico di Varthema, *The Itinerary of Ludovico di Varthema of Bologna from 1502 to 1508*, ed. R. C. Temple (London, 1928), p. 63. Generally on syphilis, see Ann G. Carmichael, 'Syphilis and the Columbian Exchange: Was the New Disease really New?', in Mario Gomes Marques and John Cule (eds), *The Great Maritime Discoveries and World Health* (Lisbon, 1991), pp. 187–200.

typhoid. However, maybe three-quarters of deaths were in fact caused by the less glamorous background category, things such as tuberculosis, dysentery and infantile diarrhoea.[16]

Underlying European medical practice was the notion of the four humours or bodily fluids, which indeed remained influential in western medicine until the mid-nineteenth century. The basis of medical education at the time was humoral pathology. Disease was a result of an imbalance or impurity of one of the four cardinal humours; that is, blood, phlegm, choler (red or yellow bile) and melancholy (black bile), these in turn being analogous to the four elementary substances of earth, water, air and fire. These in turn affected one's temperament, which would be respectively sanguine, phlegmatic, bilious or melancholic. In a healthy person the four humours were in equilibrium. The relative balance of the four was tested by means of urine samples, which were very widely used in diagnosis. A fever came from hot and dry causes and showed excess choler, and so was to be treated with cooling medicines such as coriander. Other cures included enemas, purging, the use of stimulants, tonics and drugs compounded from medicinal herbs and plants, and especially by bleeding, which was something of a universal specific and was done not only to cure illness but also as a preventative, being done routinely perhaps every two months or so. Renaissance doctors were ferocious venesectors, hacking away vast quantities of blood by incision or leeches. The time to bleed was often determined by astrology, which indeed was widely used in general diagnosis and cure. A very influential medical book in sixteenth-century Europe was Jean Gavinet's 'The Directory of Astrology made Medical,' written in 1431 and passing through five editions between 1496 and 1614.

This reliance on astrology points to a more general matter. It can be heuristically useful to distinguish three foci in medical practice, namely care, cure and causation. In this early modern period one could argue that the emphasis was on care; studies of cure, let alone cause, at this time were still primitive, having as much to do with astrology and malignant forces as with science. Even so, an accumulation of empirical data did mean that healers at this time were comparatively much better at cures than at causes. Early modern Europeans, indeed Eurasians, had almost no accurate ideas about the causes of disease. Rather than considering microbes, rats and fleas, they tended

---

[16] Norman G. Owen (ed.), *Death and Disease in Southeast Asia: Explorations in Social, Medical and Demographic History* (Singapore, OUP, 1987), introduction, pp. 4, 12.

XIV

148

to look to wider social and cultural matters to expain their illnesses. Among the favourite general explanations were the phases of the moon, the presence of 'foreigners,' especially Jews, and for the moralistic, 'the effects of profligacy.' It is thus not surprising that the most influential medical book from the twelfth to the eighteenth century was a book which dealt not with cause or cure, but with diet. This was 'The Salerno Regimen of Health,' published in 1480 but first written in the late eleventh century in Salerno, which went through no less than 300 editions. Also contributing to the long survival of these pre-modern notions was the fact that very few people had access to medical care. Physicians were scholars and so to be found only in centres of learning. Surgeons were low-status craftsmen, and more widely available.

When we look at disease, its transmission and cure, in our period we must take seriously the concept of Eurasia. Plague in the fourteenth century, and cholera in the nineteenth, both spread from Asia to Europe, while syphilis came from America via Europe to Asia. Eurasia was one disease zone. Thus the recently influential notion of 'ecological imperialism,' where 'virgin soil epidemics' spread rapidly in areas newly opened to Europeans and their exotic diseases, such as the Americas, Australia and the Pacific, has little currency in Eurasia. The most that can be said is that improved communications in the nineteenth century facilitated a more rapid spread of disease, the great exemplar of this being cholera.[17]

Similarly with medical practice. European medicine drew heavily on Islamic knowledge, but this in turn had been influenced by Hindu achievements as well as by Greek. India's earliest texts, the *Vedas* (c. 1500 BC), show a very primitive medical knowledge, but by 600 BC at least the *ayurvedic* system was established. This Hindu system thus pre-dated the classical Greek system associated with Hippocrates, who was born around 460 BC, and Galen, who lived from AD 129 to 199. In India, by the early centuries of the Christian era we find a fully evolved system. The basic texts are by Caraka (first and second centuries AD, or possiby much earlier) and Susruta (around the fourth century AD), both of which merely codified existing knowledge dating

[17] For ecological imperialism, a somewhat biological determinist notion anyway, see Alfred W. Crosby, *The Columbian Exchange: Biological and Cultural Consequences of 1492* (Westport, 1972), and Crosby, *Ecological Imperialism: the Biological Expansion of Europe, 900–1900* (CUP, New York, 1986). For useful general discussions, see Philip D. Curtin, *Disease and Imperialism before the Nineteenth Century* (Bell Library, University of Minnesota, 1990) (Bell Lecture no. 28), and David Arnold, 'The Indian Ocean as a Disease Zone, 1500–1950', *South Asia*, XIV, 2 (1991), pp. 1–21.

back some centuries. Caraka's work consisted of a massive eight books. This system was far from fixed and static. For example, at first Indian doctors used only drugs, mostly vegetable products, but from around the seventh century metals were used too, especially mercury but also compounds of iron and other minerals. By the thirteenth century the pulse was being examined, and in the sixteenth century an important ayurvedic healer in Varanasi, Bhavamisra, identified the new form of syphilis which had been introduced by the Portuguese. Significantly, he called it 'the Frank [European] disease,' and said it was usually caused by intercourse with Frank women.[18]

As in medieval Europe, the basic notion was of humours. Five elements were recognized in ayurvedic medicine: earth, water, fire, air and ether. Health was maintained through keeping an even balance between the three vital bodily fluids, wind, gall and mucus, to which some added a fourth, blood. Bodily functions were maintained by five winds. Food digested by one of these, the stomach, became chyle, which proceeded to the heart, thence to the liver, and so to blood, which in turn was converted to flesh. There was no clear idea of the brain because, like Homer, these Hindu doctors believed that the centre of consciousness, thought and feeling was the heart. Nevertheless, the importance of the spinal cord was recognized, and cleanliness was acknowledged to be medically valuable. There was copious use of drugs. A major problem was the Hindu taboo against contact with dead bodies. There was thus very little dissection, and obviously anatomy suffered as a result.

It is important to stress the way medical ideas circulated freely in the pre-modern world. In the case of India, some Hindu medical texts were influenced by Galen and Hippocrates. In the period of the Abbasid *khalifat* in Baghdad (AD 750 onwards) Muslim scholars travelled to India to study medicine, and also recruited Hindu doctors to come back with them to Baghdad, where some of them became very influential physicians at court, and translated Sanskrit works on medicine, pharmacology and toxicology into Arabic. In effect some parts of the knowledge of the Greek masters were preserved in India, and copiously added to. Then the new synthesis was taken to the Muslim world and so returned to Europe.

The Arabs also found Greek medicine closer to home. As they conquered Persia in the seventh century they acquired Greek treat-

---

[18] Gaitonde, pp. 82–8; Julius Jolly, *Indian Medicine*, 2nd edn (New Delhi, 1977) [1st pub. 1901], p. 3. For recent research on traditional Hindu medicine, see G. Jan Meulenbeld and Dominik Wujastyk (eds), *Studies on Indian Medical History* (Groningen, 1987).

ises. Arab doctors built on them, thus producing the *yunani* or *unani* (that is, 'Greek') school of medicine which later spread to India and was the system used by Indian Muslims. Rhazes (Al Rhabi, *b.* 865) wrote on smallpox, measles and other diseases, and challenged the authority of Galen long before this was done in Europe. His main work was a vast compilation of Greek, Arabic and Indian knowledge. A century later Avicenna (Ibn Sina, *b.* 980) wrote his huge *Canon of Medicine* (Al-Qanun), the most infuential text ever written in either Asia and Europe. For diagnosis all these great doctors relied on taking the pulse, a close study of urine and general external observation.[19]

As in the other two systems, notions of humours and elements were important. The Arab version was the same as the European one: the four humours of blood, phlegm and yellow and black bile were considered to correspond with the four elements of earth, water, air and fire. Illness was a sign that the balance of these four was disturbed. In 1637 in Persia a European visitor saw a man who had become gravely ill from drinking too much brandy and as he 'lay a Dying, I saw a Moor-Physician, who had the sick party in hand, order a great piece of Ice to be laid on his Stomack, maintaining his procedure by this general Maxim, that a Disease is to be Cur'd by what is contrary thereto.'[20]

It is often claimed that Muslims were not good surgeons, and indeed this was the received wisdom among the European commentators we will be quoting shortly. As dissection was abhorred, no advances in anatomy could be made, and so surgery was done blind. We should, however, remember that dissection had been considered to be antithetical not just to the Muslim tradition but also to the Jewish and Christian. The common dislike of vivisection meant that in both Christian and Muslim areas surgeons, in terms of status, were far inferior to physicians. Great physicians like Ibn Sina disliked the

---

[19] H. D. Isaacs, 'Some Clinical Methods used by the Arabs in the Middle Ages', in *Proceedings of the XXIII International Congress of the History of Medicine* 2 vols, London, 1974, Wellcome Institute), I, 82–7. The mixture in Persia was briefly noted by a traveller in 1637, who said: 'In Physick, or Medicine, they follow the Maxims of *Avicenna* and their Physicians are all *Galenists*.' Adam Olearius, *The Voyages & Travels of the Ambassadors sent by Frederick Duke of Holstein to the Great Duke of Muscovy, and the King of Persia. Begun in the year MDCXXXIII and finish'd in MDCXXXIX . . .*, trans. John Davies (London, 1662), p. 338. For *yunani* medicine in Persia in the seventeenth century, see Dr John Fryer, *A New Account of East India and Persia*, ed. W. Crooke (London, 1909–15), 3 vols, III, 97.

[20] Olearius, p. 338.

very notion of surgery, and left it to surgeons and bone-setters. However, he and other scholars did deal with surgery in their books.[21]

Working out precise flows of knowledge is obviously a difficult task. Ayurvedic medicine in India today is very little different from Susruta, except for the use of some new drugs like mercury, opium and sarsaparilla, which came to India perhaps a millennium ago with the Arabs. These newcomers to India introduced what became the still-influential Perso-Islamic yunani school of Indian medicine. Heuritically it and the Hindu ayurvedic system are considered to be distinct, even though there is a very substantial degree of interaction between the two. The earliest Indian book on the yunani tradition was written in the early fourteenth century, and drew on Muslim authorities such as Ibn Sina and also on Hindu practitioners. Hindu knowledge continued to contribute importantly to the yunani system, and vice versa. One notable divergence was over the use of bleeding, which was used occasionally in the yunani system, but not in the ayurvedic.[22] Generally the yunani doctors (usually referred to as 'hakims'), like the Europeans later, thought that at least some 'Indian' diseases were best treated by 'Indian' methods. As one practitioner wrote around 1500, 'By experience I found that Unani medicine did not suit the temperament of the people living in the changed climatic conditions of India.'[23]

Disease and Medicine in Early Modern India

Several early modern Muslim rulers in India left valuable descriptions of disease. They reveal an often impressive empirical interest in disease and even death, profound powers of observation and, at times, an unsettling reliance on fate and magic. The *Memoirs* of the emperor Babur, founder of the Mughal dynasty, cover the first two decades

---

[21] See *The Encyclopedia of Islam*, 2nd edn, s.v. djarrah [surgery].
[22] Generally on all this, see A. L. Basham, *The Wonder that was India* (London, 1963), pp. 500–2, for an excellent summary, and also A. L. Basham (ed.), *A Cultural History of India* (Oxford, 1975) pp. 48, 147–50, 438. See also a good survey in Edwin H. Ackerknecht, *A Short History of Medicine* (Baltimore, 1982), pp. 35–43. For Indian Muslim medicine, see S. M. Ikram, *Muslim Rule in India and Pakistan* (Lahore, 1966), 2nd edn, pp. 181–3. For Ibn Sina's influence on Indian medicine, see Hakim Abdul Hameed and Hakim Abdul Bari, 'Impact of Ibn Sina's Medical Works in India', *Studies in History of Medicine*, VIII (1984), pp. 1–12.
[23] Quoted in Gaitonde, p. 101.

or so of the sixteenth century, and are full of curious medical information. Most of them relate to his time in what is now Afghanistan,
that is, in a predominantly Muslim area. To quote a few examples,
dried Bukhara plums were an excellent laxative. In 1505 his mother
had a fever. Very significantly, for a Hindu doctor would not have
done this, blood was let. This had no effect, so they tried Khurasan
practice, and gave her water-melon; she died anyway. Later Babur
himself had a fever, and was bled. After ten or twelve days his doctor
gave him 'narcissus mixed with wine; I drank it once or twice; even
that did no good.' A good purgative was rose water, in English julep.
As for antidotes for poison, the water in which the fibre of a lime had
been boiled was considered to be efficacious, as was milk in which had
been dissolved stamped clay [terra sigillata?] and the best theriac. On
one occasion he 'elected to take opium because of earache; another
reason was the shining of the moon [which was considered to be
harmful and cold].' In India he got painful boils. An Ottoman Turk,
in an incident which points clearly to the transmission of medical
knowledge, used a remedy which had been recently discovered in
Turkey. He boiled pepper, and Babur held the sores in the steam,
and then washed them with the hot water. It took two hours to do
this treatment, but when he did it again a week later the water must
have been too hot, for it blistered his body and hurt him.

In certain specific areas it seems that surgery was relatively
advanced at the Mughal court, though their general anatomical
knowledge was inferior to Europe. Head wounds were routinely tre-
panned. On one occasion a skilled surgeon was presented to Babur.
'If a man's brains had come out, he would cure it, and any sort of
wound in an artery he easily healed. For some wounds his remedy
was in form of a plaister, for some medicines had to be taken. He
ordered a bandage tied on the wound in my leg and put no seton in;
once he made me eat something like a fibrous root. He told me himself, "A certain man had his leg broken in the slender part and the
bone was shattered for the breadth of the hand. I cut the flesh open
and took the bits of bone out. Where they had been, I put a remedy
in powder-form. That remedy simply became bone where there had
been bone before." '[24]

Equally valuable are the other great Mughal *Memoirs*, those of the
emperor Jahangir, who reigned from 1605 to 1627. Again, a curious

[24] Babur, *Babur-Nama*, trans. A. S. Beveridge (New Delhi, 1970), pp. 82, 106–9,
169–70, 246, 399, 400, 511, 543, 608, 657 660.

mixture is seen, ranging from acute empirical observation to reliance on fate. His *Memoirs* are full of his trying new foods, and considering the effects of fever. There are many references to his doctors, some of whom rose to very high positions at court, and his taking or ignoring their advice. On one occasion he tells of a rabid dog which bit two elephants. Over a month after they were bitten they died, one after having had water run out of its mouth for seven days. Once Jahangir had a severe headache, which went into a fever.

At night I did not drink my usual number of cups [of alcohol, or a mixture of alcohol and opium], and after midnight crop-sickness [that is increased crapulousness] was added to my fever, and till morning I rolled about on my couch. On Wednesday, the 16th, at the end of the day, the fever diminished, and, after asking the advice of my doctors, I took my usual number of cups on the third night. Although they urged me to take some broth of pulse and rice, I could not make up my mind to do so. . . . When they brought food for me this day, I had no inclination for it. In short, for three days and two nights I remained fasting.[25]

Perhaps most interesting of all is his dispassionate account of the death of the noble Inayat Khan, an account which in the way it looks analytically at the human body, and at the actual effects of illness, can be compared to Leonardo da Vinci's similar observations. Inayat Khan was addicted to opium and, when he could get it, to alcohol. As he got sicker he became a compulsive eater, and later became dropsical. Even his bones had dissolved, we are told, and he was so extraordinary a sight that Jahangir had his portrait painted on the day before he died.[26]

   In our period of the sixteenth and seventeenth centuries, and indeed both before and after this, smallpox is surprisingly little commented on in India, though this could be because our sources conflate it with general fevers.[27] Jahangir's *Memoirs* show that the plague, much opinion to the contrary, was certainly found in northern India.[28] The second decade of the seventeenth century saw several

   [25] Jahangir, *The Tuzuk-i Jahangiri*, trans. A .Rogers, ed. H. Beveridge (Delhi, 1968), 2 vols in 1, I, 330, 243; II, 12–13.

   [26] *Ibid.*, II, 43–4.

   [27] See a useful discussion in David Arnold, 'Smallpox and Colonial Medicine in Nineteenth-century India', in Arnold (ed.), *Imperial Health and Indigenous Societies* pp. 46–7.

   [28] In the late sixteenth century Linschoten said that the 'plague hath never been in India,' and his modern editor footnoted: 'Correct. The plague seems never to have extended beyond Scinde.' (J. H. van Linschoten, *The Voyage of John Huyghen van Linschoten to the East Indies* (London, 1885), 2 vols, I, 240 and fn.) According to H. G. Rawlinson the first recorded instance of bubonic plague in India was in 1616 but, given Jahangir's familiarity with it, this seems to be far too late a date. Later in the

154

calamitous outbreaks. As in Europe, it is clear that Indians knew the plague was infectious, and even that rodents had something to do with its spread. Several accounts mention the buboes which appeared, as the emperor noted, 'under the armpits, or in the groin, or below the throat.' He also described how a girl touched an infected mouse, and soon after the buboes of the plague appeared in her. She had a high fever, her colour changed to 'yellow inclining to black,' and on her last day she vomited, had a motion and died. The emperor, in a fuller account from Kashmir, noted of the plague that 'The symptoms were that the first day there was headache and fever and much bleeding at the nose. On the second day the patient died. In the house where one person died all the inmates were carried off. Whoever went near the sick person or a dead body was affected in the same way. In one instance the dead body was thrown on the grass, and it chanced that a cow came and ate some of the grass. It died, and some dogs that had eaten its flesh also all died.' In another outbreak most of those affected died within twelve hours. The symptoms were a very high temperature, and as the patient was dying 'broad spots of a black and blue colour appeared on their breasts.'[29] Some learned men said it came because there had been two years' drought, others because the air had been corrupted by drought and scarcity. Jahangir commented on this debate that 'Wisdom is of Allah, and we must submit to Allah's decrees.' Perhaps for this reason, I have found no mention of attempts in Mughal India to quarantine sufferers from infectious diseases. This is a strong contrast with the situation we noted prevailing in Europe at the same time.

We get useful information on Indian diseases and medicine from the accounts of early European travellers in the area.[30] Christopher Farewell wrote a vivid account of his bout with 'a burning fever' near Surat in 1614:

I here suddenly fell sicke of a burning fever and (thankes be to God) as sodainly recovered. For, fearing the extremity of that raving and uncomfort-

century it was a great killer, raging, for example, in Surat for six years in the 1680s. It caused great mortality among Indians, but Europeans were miraculously exempt. See John Ovington, *A Voyage to Surat in the Year 1689*, ed. H. G. Rawlinson (London, 1929), pp. 203–4 and fn.

[29] Jahangir, I, 442, II, 65, 66–7.

[30] The following discussion is merely a cursory survey of European descriptions of early modern Indian medicine. In particular, the Portuguese accounts, especially those by d'Orta and Costa, contain copious information on local medical practice in western India in the sixteenth century. I intend to produce a fuller analysis of this matter on some later occasion.

able sicknesse, against his will I prevayled with our chyrurgion to let me bleed till I fainted againe, as foreseeing it to be my remedy; applyed all comfortable things to my head; tooke my bed; and, full of perplexity to dye sencelesse, I commended myselfe to God. After some idle talke to my friends about me, I fell into a slumber; but quickely wakened by a desire to ease my stomacke, and had at least a dozen vomits naturally, which gave mee a most comfortable night...[31]

This account points to the prevalence of bleeding in European practice at this time. Two years later another case also, in a reverse way, seemed to show the efficacy of this method. Captain Larkin died 'of a fever which held him eight days, in which time he would neither be let blood nor once take anything for the recovery of his health, thinking to wear it away. So upon the sudden, finding himself very sick, he was let blood the morning before he died, but then it was too late; for his blood being grown so thick, he could not bleed.'[32]

An English chaplain in the second decade of the seventeenth century noted that 'The common diseases of the countrey are bloudie fluxes, hot fevers and calendtures [calentures, that is, tropical delirium]; in all which they prescribe fasting as a principall remedie. That filthy disease, the consequence of incontinencie, is common among them. The people in generall live about our ages; but they have more old men.'[33] Another visitor who lived in western India in the 1670s, Dr John Fryer, noted that Indians drank very little: 'Notwithstanding this Mortality to the *English*, the Country People and naturalised *Portugals* live to a good Old Age, supposed to be the Reward of their Temperance; indulging themselves neither in Strong Drinks, nor devouring Flesh as we do.'[34]

The comments of François Bernier, a French doctor who was in India from 1659 to 1667, are particularly valuable as he was himself well trained and, as we will see later, up-to-date with European advances. But on general matters of disease and medicine his account was restrained and moderate; he apparently saw little qualitative difference between what he knew and what he saw done in India. Like Fryer later, he noted that Indians drank very little, and that

---

[31] *The Voyage of Nicholas Downton* (London, Hakluyt, 1938), p. 135. See pp. 135–6 for an affecting account of a death from the 'bloudy fluxe.'

[32] John Browne letter of 30 May 1616 in William Foster (ed.), *Letters Received by the East India Company from its Servants in the East* (London, 1896–1902), 6 vols, IV, 106–7.

[33] Edward Terry in W. Foster (ed.), *Early Travels in India, 1583–1619* (Delhi, 1968), p. 310.

[34] Dr John Fryer, *A New Account of East India and Persia*, I, 180, and see also *ibid.*, II, 83–4.

156

the local version of venereal disease was relatively benign: 'Even the venereal disease, common as it is in *Hindoustan*, is not of so virulent a character, or attended with such injurious consequences, as in other parts of the world.' Nevertheless, people tended to be lethargic, and there were pronounced differences in their treatment of some diseases.[35]

Bernier was writing as an expert commenting on his peers, in his case the yunani practitioners, often Persians, who ministered at court, where he lived. But, as in Europe, folk remedies and supernatural notions coexisted more or less easily in India with this relatively academic medical knowledge. Several European visitors reflected the state of folk medical knowledge in Europe when they commented on popular practice in India.[36] This was seen especially in the treatment of cholera.

Cholera was probably the most feared disease, especially on the west coast and in the south. This disease had been endemic in India for at least 2000 years. It became pandemic and spread from Bengal all over the Indian Ocean area and to Europe and America in the second decade of the nineteenth century. Some 50% of those affected died in these great pandemics. It spread through polluted water, and as public health improved in Europe and America it thus declined. Arnold claims that the nineteenth-century version was a new and more virulent strain, but early modern accounts are united in their presentation of a feared and usually fatal disease. As just two examples, Fr. Godinho said it was 'so fatal that the end comes in a matter of hours,' while Linschoten noted that 'The sicknesse is very common, and killeth many a man, whereof they hardly or never escape.'[37] Ovington, an educated man and a clergyman, reflected a

[35] François Bernier, *Travels in the Mogul Empire, 1656–1668*, trans. and ed. A. Constable and V. Smith (London, 1914), pp. 253-4, 338-9. These pages constitute an excellent account of Indian medicine by an informed and experienced observer.

[36] When I write of 'quacks' and 'folk medicine,' I do not mean to be overly influenced by what we think are modern medical methods, and to test the past in accordance with what we, social historians with only a spotty expertise in medicine anyway, think is 'correct' and 'scientific' practice today. Andrew Wear claims that in his recent edited collection of studies 'the nineteenth- and twentieth-century values of the medical profession which in past history of medicine had been applied to earlier periods to condemn empirics, quacks, magical and religious practitioners have been discarded. In the process a much richer medical world has been uncovered.' Andrew Wear (ed.), *Medicine in Society: Historical Essays* (CUP, 1992), introduction, p. 2.

[37] Correia-Afonso, *Godinho*, 38; Linschoten, I, 235-6. For the claim that nineteenth-century cholera was new, see Arnold, 'The Indian Ocean as a Disease Zone',

European consensus concerning cause and cure when he wrote that cholera ['mordechine'] is 'violent Vomiting and Looseness, and which is caus'd most frequently by an Excess of Eating particularly of Fish and Flesh together. It has been Cur'd by a Red-hot Iron clapt to the Heal of him that is sick, so close that it renders him uneasie by its nearness, whereby it leaves a Scar behind it.'[38] For fevers in general the remedy was to 'Take an iron ring about an inch and a half in diameter and thick in proportion. Then heating it red hot in the fire, extend the patient on his back, and apply the ring to his navel, in such a manner that the navel may be as a centre to the ring. As soon as the patient feels the heat take away the ring as quick as possible when a sudden revolution will be wrought in his intestines.'[39]

A seventeenth-century Venetian healer, Niccolao Manucci, showed in some of his stories how little difference there was between his knowledge and folk medicine. In Bassein, he tells us, there was a woman of good station who produced a girl after a pregnancy of three years. The girl married at twelve years and also had a pregnancy of three years. As to rabies, a newly married man on his wedding night cut his bride to pieces, gnawing her breasts, plucking out her eyes and biting her face and body. The reason was that he had been bitten by a mad dog three months before. The remedy for rabies was to cauterize the wound at once. Alternatively, if the bitten person went on a sea voyage he would recover immediately.[40]

pp. 7–8. The vexed matter of the newness of cholera in the nineteenth century is too complex to be gone into here, but certainly cholera takes various forms, and it is my understanding that a disease which produced death so quickly from diarrhoea and dehydration can be nothing but some sort of cholera. It is also worth noting that the 'bloody flux' was not cholera, as this disease does not produce blood in the stools.

[38] John Ovington, pp. 204–5. These accounts point to the Europeans using the hot-iron method as a cure, but an account from the 1750s seems to say this was an Indian remedy, though the observer still thought it worked quite well: 'There is likewise known on the Malabar-coast chiefly, a most violent disorder they call the Mordechin, which seizes the patient with such fury of purging, vomiting and tormina [?] of the intestines, that it will often carry him off in thirty hours. For this the physicians among the natives know no more effectuall remedy, than the actual cautery applied to the soles of the feet, the powerful revulsion of which rarely fails of a salutary efficacy.' John Henry Grose, *A Voyage to the East Indies ... to which is added a Journey from Aleppo to Busserah, over the Desert, by Mr. Charmichael*, 2nd English edn, 2 vols (London, 1772), I, 250.

[39] Denis Kincaid, *British Social Life in India, 1608–1937* (London, 1973), p. 37.

[40] Niccolao Manucci, *Storia do Mogor, or Mogul India* (Calcutta, 1966–67), 4 vols, III, 114, 117. He notes on II, 90, that he simply took up doctoring because the demand was there: 'little by little I began to turn myself into a physician...'.

158

At least two European travellers in the seventeenth century noted a pronounced shortage of local doctors in India, the reason presumably being that most villagers relied on non-professional healers, or merely dosed themselves with local drugs and simples. Tavernier, commenting in a very valuable passage on health care in a very extensive area of India, said

It should be remarked that in all the countries we have just passed through, both in the Kingdom of Carnatic and the Kingdoms of Golkonda and Bijapur, there are hardly any physicians except those in the service of the Kings and Princes. As for the commonalty, when the rains have fallen and it is the season for collecting plants, mothers of families may be seen going in the mornings from the towns and villages to collect the simples which they know to be specifics for domestic diseases. It is true that in good towns there are generally one or two men who have some knowledge of medicine, who seat themselves each morning in the market-place or at a corner of the street and administer remedies, either potions or plasters, to those who come to ask for them. They first feel the pulse, and when giving the medicine, for which they take only the value of two farthings, they mumble some words between their teeth.[41]

A little later the Abbé Carré was sick, but a Persian noble told him 'as to providing someone who can give you remedies and treat your illness, you are aware that there is no doctor or surgeon amongst us; we hardly know what such a man is, and Europeans are only consulted when one of them happens to be passing in this country.'[42]

Europeans and Indian Medicine

This sketch of disease and curing in early modern India shows no particular advantage in knowledge or skill on the part of the newly-arrived Europeans. Rather it seems that, despite specific differences with regard to particular diseases, overall the situation was one of equality. In particular, no Eurasian at this time had what we would today call a 'scientific' knowledge of causation. Perhaps the closest they got was when they blamed polluted drinking water (on one occasion water 'whereinto a multitude of grasshoppers fell and poisoned the water'), 'inordinate drinking of a sort of wine that dis-

---

[41] Jean-Baptiste Tavernier, *Travels in India of Jean-Baptiste Tavernier*, trans. V. Ball and W. Crooke (New Delhi, 1977), 2 vols, I, 240.

[42] Abbé Carré, *The Travels of the Abbé Carré in India and the Near East, 1672–1674* London, Hakluyt, 1947–48), 3 vols, p. 271.

tilleth out of the Palmetto trees, called Tadie [toddy]' or emanations from a recently excavated moat.[43]

Europeans were aware that some Indian diseases were specific to the area. The Italian merchant Sassetti noted in Malabar malaria, several sorts of apoplexy, and elephantiasis, or filaria. He also commented on different cures. Bleeding was very seldom used, and nor were such standards of European pharmacopoeia as rhubarb and aloe.[44] Many other commentators also thought that Indian diseases were different, and should be treated by Indian methods. In the late seventeenth century an English doctor stressed the differences, and said gloomily that 'we are here, as Exotick Plants brought home to us, not agreeable to the Soil.'[45] But most European visitors were more sanguine and this in turn led to a very interesting eclectic mixture of European and Hindu medical systems. These data, incidentally, run quite contrary to David Arnold's finding that 'for a brief historical moment [in the first half of the nineteenth century] there was much that Western doctors thought they might (with reservations) practically learn from Indian medicine.'[46] The phenomenon goes back to the sixteenth century.

That some Indian diseases were different and peculiar to the subcontinent was widely acknowledged, and not just by Europeans. We noted Muslim medical practice being modified in India; indeed one Muslim author considered that there were major problems in applying the Perso-Islamic yunani ('Greek') system to Indians.[47] The eccentric alchemist and important early medical innovator Paracelsus in a book published in 1537–38 stressed that Asian and African prescriptions did not work in Europe, and he also was not certain that his prescriptions would work outside Europe.[48] In the late seventeenth century a French visitor said that for local diseases European medicines were no use. 'For this reason the Physitians that go out of Portugal into these parts must at first keep company with the Indian Surgeons to be fit to Practice; otherwise, if they go about to cure these

---

[43] Respectively *Letters Received*, I, 286, III, 4, and Correia-Afonso, *Godinho*, p. 37.

[44] John Correia-Afonso, 'On the Fourth Centenary of Filippo Sassetti (1540–1588): Scientific Observations from Cochin', *Indica*, XXVI (1989), pp. 15–24, esp. p. 19.

[45] Fryer, I, 180.

[46] David Arnold, 'Occidental Therapeutics and Oriental Bodies: Bengal, 1800–1860', typescript of a paper read at a subaltern studies conference, Calcutta, December 1989. An amplified version of this paper will appear as part of David Arnold, *Colonising the Body* (Berkeley, 1993).

[47] Ikram, p. 183.

[48] D. S. Lach, *Asia in the Making of Europe*, vol. II, book 3 (Chicago, 1977), p. 424.

160

Distempers, so far different from ours after the European manner, they may chance to Kill more than they Cure.'[49] Thirty years later another Frenchman, this one a doctor, complained of the quality of Indian medicine, but still said that the extensive local experience of the pandits (that is, practitioners of ayurvedic medicine) meant that they often did better than foreigners, who therefore 'sont obligez en certaines occasions de suivre leur methode...'.[50]

The major divergence between European and Hindu medicine was the routine use of bleeding by Europeans. As Pyrard noted, Indians, that is, Hindus, did not use bleeding at all.[51] Europeans, however, often used it to what seems to be excess. In January 1542 Francis Xavier, later to be a saint, was ill. He ended a letter by writing: 'I would very much like to write at greater length, but sickness does not now permit it. I have been bled seven times today, and I am only passing well.'[52] In the 1670s the Abbé Carré fell ill with a fever, and insisted on being bled. Great quantities were hacked out of him by enthusiastic but amateur bleeders, and 'This made me so feeble that I cannot bear to speak of it. Yet, though I felt very weak, I was not surprised that the fever grew less, as it no longer had the cause [that is, excess of blood] which had kept it up; and I further reduced it by refusing for eight days to eat many little delicacies that I would have liked—sometimes one thing, sometimes another, though I must confess I refrained with very great difficulty. For eight or ten days I still had my sight, my memory, and my senses, but so feebly that I did not remember anything that happened to me.'[53]

Earlier European practice had combined bleeding with feeding up the patient. By the 1640s in Goa the Europeans had decided that a much scantier diet was more appropriate, as in fact we just noted in the case of the Abbé Carré's self-cure. The procedure now was to try

---

[49] Careri in S. N. Sen (ed.), *Indian Travels of Thevenot and Careri* (New Delhi, 1949), p. 162.

[50] Luillier-Lagaudiers, *Nouveau voyage aux grandes Indes, avec une introduction pour le commerce des Indes Orientales, et la description de plusieurs isles, villes, & rivieres, l'histoire des plantes & des animaus qu'on y trouve; avec un traite des maladies particulieres aux pays orientaux, et dans la Route, et de leurs remedes* par Mr. D. L. F., Docteur en Medecine, qui a voyagé et sejourné dans les principales Villes des Indes Orientales, [pp. 199–236], Rotterdam, 1726. The quotation is from Mr. DLF, p. 213.

[51] François Pyrard de Laval, *The Voyage of François Pyrard of Laval to the East Indies*, vol. II (London, 1888), p. 13.

[52] Georg Schurhammer, *Francis Xavier: His Life, His Times*, vol. II, *India* (Rome, 1977), p. 96.

[53] Abbé Carré, *Travels*, pp. 284–5.

and build up the patient, using a Hindu specific, after the bleeding was finished. Bleeding was

repeated, according to need, up to thirty or forty times, as long as bad blood comes. . . . I forgot to make a remark upon the frequent bleedings in reference to Europeans—namely, that in order to recover their colour and get themselves in perfect health, it is prescribed for them to drink for twelve days three glasses of pissat de vache [cow's urine], one in the morning, one at midday, and one in the evening; but, as this drink cannot but be very disagreeable, the convalescent swallows as little of it as possible, however much he may desire to recover his health. This remedy has been learnt from the idolaters of the country, and whether the convalescent makes use of it or not, he is not allowed to leave the hospital till the twelve days have expired during which he is supposed to partake of this drink.[54]

The situation, then, was basically one of blending and cross-fertilization. In Surat a *vaidya* (Hindu practitioner), using urinalysis, albeit not very scientifically, was consulted by an Englishwoman: 'A *Bramin*, who had spent some Years in studying the Art of Physick, was invited to visit an *English* Gentlewoman, labouring under a Chronical Disease; who when he came desir'd a sight of her Urine, and pouring it into a small *China* cup, he let fall upon it one drop of Oyle, upon which he made this Remark in my presence. That if the Oyl sank to the bottom, it inevitably betoken'd Death; the spreading of it self immediately upon the Urin, prognosticated a Increase of the Distemper, but if slowly, and little by little, an abatement of the Disease.'[55] An account from the 1750s similarly describes pandits using urinalysis frequently.[56]

In the 1670s two travellers noted other Europeans using local doctors. Dr John Fryer, while generally not impressed with Indian surgical practice, did recognize that for certain problems Indian doctors were useful. A particular Brahmin doctor, or vaidya, was used by the English traders in Surat. 'This *Brachmin* comes every day, and feels every Man's Pulse in the Factory, and is often made use of for a Powder for Agues, which works as infallibly as the *Peruvian* Bark; it is a Preparation of Natural *Cinnaber* [that is, a form of mercury].'[57]

[54] Tavernier, *Travels*, I, 160–1.
[55] Ovington, pp. 205–6. Yet the hostile Dr Fryer could claim that 'the Urine they will not look on.' Fryer, I, 287.
[56] Mr. DLF in Luillier, pp. 216–17.
[57] Fryer, I, 288. It is another good example of Fryer's biased attitude that he tells on the previous page that Indian doctors 'pretend to understand the pulse . . .' yet now it seems all the English in Surat trusted this doctor to do exactly this. The matter is complicated, for Ovington at the same time and place also claimed 'I could

162

About the same time, in Golconda, the ailing Abbé Carré was helped by a Dutch trader, who, 'seeing I was still feeble and delicate, advised me strongly not to start on my journey so soon, and kindly invited me to stay some days in their house, where I could be treated by a very clever Hindu doctor, saying that they all had received much benefit from his care in the illnesses from which they had suffered for some time in that factory.'[58] The Hindu doctor 'had treated [the Dutch factor] for eight months with simples and local herbs, which are very efficacious when their use is known, and he had been much relieved thereby.'[59]

This use of Indian practice even, on at least a few occasions, led to some transference from India to Europe. At least in this early modern period, it is then by no means a matter only of European treatments spreading to India, but rather of a mixture in India itself, and some reverse flow also. Ovington noted late in the seventeenth century, 'The general Ease and Cure, which the White Powder [?] in *India* gives to Feavers, makes that a very common and acceptable Receipt there; and it has, with very good Success, been administered in *England*, sent from thence by the *Indian* Physicians. And all their Medicines here are generally of the cooler sort, because of the Heats to which the Climate naturally inclines them.'[60] A decade or so earlier Manuel Godinho said that some medicinal drugs were sent to dispensaries in Europe from India. They included miramulanos (a particular small medicinal fruit), asafoetida, spikenard and opium.[61] And despite the general European contempt for Asian surgery, India did make one important contribution here. The main activity in early plastic surgery was nose reconstruction, which in sixteenth-century Europe was done using a flap of skin. However, the church was opposed to this and the practice fell into disuse. The same method had been used in India for centuries. Information on this Indian practice reached Europe in the late eighteenth century, and revived European interest in rhinoplasty. On this foundation was built modern plastic surgery.[62]

never learn that our *Indian* physicians could pretend to that wonderful Knowledge in the Pulse, which those in *China* could confidently boast of...', Ovington, p. 206. Yet as we saw above, it seems that Indian doctors monitored the pulse from the thirteenth century.

[58] Abbé Carré, *Travels*, p. 345.

[59] *Ibid.*, p. 367.

[60] Ovington, p. 205.

[61] Correia-Afonso, *Godinho*, p. 70.

[62] T. J. S. Patterson, 'The Transmission of Indian Surgical Techniques to Europe at the End of the Eighteenth Century', in *Proceedings of the XXIII International Congress of the History of Medicine*, 2 vols (London, 1974, Wellcome Institute), I, 694–6.

Perceptions of Inequality

The beginnings of scientific medicine in Europe have been much studied. Beginning in the Renaissance, European medicine made fundamental advances, and began to transcend methods based on the Greek authorities and to escape the influence of the church. There were some advances in medicine, as seen especially in the work of Paracelsus (1493–1541). He was an eccentric and controversial figure in the development of new medical knowledge in Europe. He made major advances in the field of chemical medicine and generally contributed substantially to the rise of modern medicine. It is fascinating to remember that in 1527 he burnt in public (shades of Luther!) the books of Ibn Sina and Galen, yet in fact his own work was solidly based on his profound knowledge of the ancients.[63]

At first greater strides were made in anatomy and so surgery. In the sixteenth century the authority of Galen and Ibn Sina began to be questioned. The publication in 1543 of the first complete anatomy textbook, *De Humani Corporis Fabrica* by Andreas Vesalius (1514–64), marks a paradigmatic advance. While his work actually made few important changes in knowledge of human anatomy, his method was new for it was based on dissection and actual observation and both he and Paré (1510–90) found Galen to be wrong in several important areas. The Greeks had thought that blood ebbed and flowed in the human body. In 1616 Harvey, basing his anatomy on Vesalius, gave his pioneering lectures on the circulation of the blood, and in the middle of this century a microscope was invented. A short way to see the change in medical theory in the seventeenth century is to note a change 'from a humoral to a chemical and/or mechanical view of the body.'[64]

The list could go on and on. Two points are important. First, these and other advances at the time and later mark the beginnings of

---

[63] For a good discussion, see Walter Pagel, 'Paracelsus: Traditionalism and Medieval Sources', in Lloyd G. Stevenson and Robert P. Multhauf (eds), *Medicine, Science and Culture* (Baltimore, 1968), pp. 51–75.

[64] Andrew Wear, 'Introduction', in Andrew Wear (ed.), *Medicine in Society*, p. 5. See also on these general changes other articles in this excellent collection, and two other compilations: Andrew Wear, Roger French and I. M. Lonie (eds), *The Medical Renaissance of the Sixteenth Century* (CUP, 1985), and Roger French and Andrew Wear (eds), *The Medical Revolution of the Seventeenth Century* (CUP, 1989). For the fifteenth century, see a short useful study by Roger French: 'Medicine in Western Europe during the Fifteenth Century', in Mario Gomes Marques and John Cule (eds), *The Great Maritime Discoveries and World Health*, pp. 39–54.

164

scientific medicine, based essentially on empirical, testable and replicable observation. Second, it is important not to see these changes as introducing modern medicine overnight. Quite the reverse; a major disease was mastered for the first time in human history only in the 1790s, when Edward Jenner produced his vaccination (much more effective than the widely practiced inoculation) against smallpox. Harvey's ideas met with far from universal acceptance, so that Galen remained a prescribed text at the Cambridge medical school until the middle of the nineteenth century, and the notion of the four humours remained influential into the nineteenth century. Blood letting also continued. The great surgeon Paré was a ferocious bleeder. As late as the 1830s there was a bleeding craze in France, and some 20 million leeches a year were required to keep up with the demand. A connection between bodily cleanliness and good health began to be accepted only in the nineteenth century. In many areas there were fits and starts, and blind alleys. The first uses of anaesthetics in the middle of the nineteenth century actually increased mortality for a time.

Advances in knowledge were accompanied by improvements in professionalism. The College of Physicians of London was founded by charter in England in 1518, and used the title 'Royal' from 1682. From 1540 physicians in England were allowed to practice surgery. In this same year the Company of Barber-Surgeons was given corporate status by the English crown, but they were not allowed to prescribe medicines. Surgeons in England and France were separated from barber's guilds only in the 1740s. What is interesting here is that the College of Physicians was organized on a completely different basis from earlier medico-craft groups. Clark tells us that the College was not a craft guild, and did not have apprentices. 'It was not, like the Barber-Surgeons' Company bound by the Acts of Parliament which made the ordinances of the London crafts, guilds, mysteries, and fraternities subject to the approval of the lord chancellor, the lord treasurer, and the two lords chief justice or any two of them.'[65] In other words, it was 'modern' rather than 'medieval.' In other countries also professional bodies appeared to regulate and give solidarity to particular occupational groups. The consequences of this growing exclusiveness were two-fold: on the one hand, quacks were

[65] Sir George Clark, *A History of the Royal College of Physicians of London* (Oxford, 1964–66), 2 vols, I, 61, 337.

gradually weeded out but, on the other, so were were non-members of the exclusive group, such as midwives once obstetrics became 'professionalized.'

We can now turn to the comments of the French doctor François Bernier. He was born in September 1620 to a family of peasant-leaseholders in Anjou, received medical degrees from the University of Montpellier in 1652 and died in Paris in 1688. Bernier's remarks on the Mughal empire, where he worked at court and also travelled widely between 1659 and 1667, are generally regarded as being thoroughly ethnocentric and biased. In particular, he was very critical of the system of land tenure and payment of the nobility which he found in the empire, and compared these unsympathetically with the prevailing practice in his native France. His version of 'Asiatic Despotism,' total penetration by an all-encompassing state into the lives of all its hapless subjects, has been remarkably influential. But where he is most interesting is in the fact that he seems to be the first European doctor to represent in India the dramatic changes which were occurring in western European medicine in the sixteenth and seventeenth centuries. Unlike several other European doctors in India both before and after him, such as Manucci, who was merely a quack and knew little of the changes occurring in Europe, Bernier was well up with them.

To use accounts by Bernier, and indeed other European travellers, raises the important question of the underlying perceptions of these early European travellers. Michael Adas in his recent excellent book notes that these travellers considered themselves to be superior to Indians in most areas, including science and technology. However, until the eighteenth century this was little commented on or used as a standard to demonstrate this assumed superiority. Up to this time the key determinant and method of showing European advancement was religion.[66] Nevertheless, Adas himself in his discussion of Bernier and Fryer stresses how critical they were of Indian practice.[67] It is unclear whether he sees them as being an exception to a usually silent observation of this matter by Europeans, or whether, as I would think correctly, he sees them as harbingers of a future intolerance and overt assumption of superiority. Certainly they had no doubts about European superiority, and were quite open in expressing this; in turn

[66] Michael Adas, *Machines as the Measure of Men: Science, Technology and Ideologies of Western Dominance* (Ithaca, Cornell UP, 1989), pp. 6, 21–2.
[67] *Ibid.*, pp. 55–6.

this casts doubt on David Arnold's claim that 'before 1800, western medicine was far less domineering in its relationship with indigenous societies ...'.[68]

These scientific advances increasingly set off western medicine from all other systems. Comments from Bernier and Fryer, which we will come to in a minute, represent for the first time this change. However, we need to consider whether or not the seeds of this assumption of superiority were sown earlier, in the way in which early observers did find differences between Europe and Asian medicine, and diseases, even if they did not specifically find one better than the other. In other words, the difference was, as Adas notes, always there, at least implicitly. Once a benign phenomenon, it later moved into the more threatening things that Arnold discusses so well, such as the notions that Indians were bodily different, and later in the nineteenth century not just different but also inferior. Similarly, while in the early nineteenth century Orientalist doctors saw parallels between the humoral pathology of ancient and modern India and recent European notions, later in this century it was considered that European medicine had advanced enormously, but the ayurvedic and yunani systems had stood still and thus were exemplars of an inert and timeless India.[69]

It is my contention that Bernier in particular represents the first manifestation of an overt claim to European advancement. Several of Bernier's comments make clear how well read he was on the latest techniques in Europe. He often talked to his patron at the Mughal court of the recent discoveries of Harvey and Pecquet in anatomy, and we may note that Harvey died only in 1657 while Pecquet lived until 1674 and was more or less a contemporary of Bernier's. The former, as noted, had lectured on the circulation of the blood in 1616, while Pecquet contributed to the discovery of the lymphatic system. As we saw, Bernier's attitude to Indian medicine was rather neutral,[70] but the following passage shows clearly how much more advanced he considered himself to be in anatomy and so surgery.

It is not surprising that the *Gentiles* understand nothing of anatomy. They never open the body either of man or beast, and those in our household always ran away, with amazement and horror, whenever I opened a living goat or sheep for the purpose of explaining to my *Agah* [patron] the circulation of the blood, and showing him the vessels, discovered by *Pecquet*, through

---

[68] Arnold, 'Introduction', p. 11.
[69] Arnold, 'Occidental Therapeutics and Oriental Bodies'.
[70] Bernier, pp. 253–4, 338–9.

which the chyle is conveyed to the right ventricle of the heart. Yet notwith-standing their profound ignorance of the subject, they affirm that the number of veins in the human body is five thousand, neither more nor less, just as if they had carefully reckoned them.[71]

Similarly, Bernier represented advanced European medicine in that he considered copious bleeding to be old-fashioned, done as a result of the influence of Galen but not now considered to be very advisable. He noted that the yunani doctors at court 'generally bleed once or twice, not in the trifling manner of the modern practitioners of *Goa* and *Paris*, but copiously, like the ancients, taking eighteen or twenty ounces of blood, sometimes even to fainting; thus frequently subduing the disease at the commencement, according to the advice of *Galen*, and as I have witnessed in several cases.'[72] What Bernier is saying is that while he was convinced Europeans were much better on ana-tomy, this was not necessarily the case for medicine, where he took a pronounced agnostic attitude, making no claim as to whether or not 'these [Indian] modes of treatment be judicious.'

Bernier was not the only one to show that in the area of surgery a perception of a pronounced gap had appeared between India and Europe. Garcia d'Orta in Goa in the mid-sixteenth century was the first, but by no means the last, European doctor to be critical of Indians' anatomical knowledge: 'As for anatomy, they do not know where the liver is, nor the spleen, nor anything else.'[73] Dr John Fryer, whom we have quoted several times as being roughly on a par with his Indian peers in medical knowledge,[74] *did* in a modern way think too much bleeding was detrimental, and he noted how they knew nothing of veins:

They are unskill'd in Anatomy, even those of the *Moors* who follow the *Arabian*, thinking it unlawful to dissect Human Bodies; whereupon Phlebot-omy is not understood, they being ignorant how the Veins lye; but they will worry themselves Martyrs to death by Leeches, clapping on an hundred at

---

[71] *Ibid.*, p. 339.
[72] *Ibid.*, pp. 338–9.
[73] Clements Markham, *Colloquies on the Simples and Drugs of India by Garcia da Orta* [a translation of Conde de Ficalho, Lisbon, 1891–5] (London, 1913), no. 36.
[74] See, as one more example to add to those already quoted from Fryer in the text, Fryer, I, 285–6, where he begins a long description of disease in Surat by saying 'The Diseases reign according to the Seasons, the *North* blowing, Bodies are rendered firm, solid and active by exhausting the Serous Humours...'. In fairness, however, it must be noted that some diseases are seasonal in India. Cholera is most prevalent in the rainy season. Smallpox spreads better in dry weather, that is, from February to May, which is also the time of much travelling for pilgrimage and weddings in India. See Arnold, 'Smallpox and Colonial Medicine', pp. 46–7.

168

once, which they know not how to pull off, till they have filled themselves, and drop of their own accord. Chirugery is in as bad a plight, Amputation being an horrid thing.[75]

Fryer in fact was conscious, in his ethnocentric way, that European practice was innovative, for he noted of Persian medicine that although 'it be here in good Repute, yet its Sectators are too much wedded to Antiquity, not being at all addicted to find out its Improvement by new Enquiries; wherefore they stick to the *Arabian* Method as devoutly as to the Sacred Tripod...'.[76] Similarly, a traveller in Persia in 1637 said: 'They have nothing of Anatomy...'.[77] Even the self-taught quack Manucci could claim that all the doctors at the Mughal court were Persians, but 'Few of them know anything about, or can cure, the stone, paralysis, apoplexy, dropsy, anaemia, malignant fevers, or other difficult complaints. They follow the ancient books of medicine, which say a great deal but tell very little.'[78] In 1726 a French doctor wrote of the lack of anatomical knowledge, and the conservatism, of Indian doctors. 'Les Medecins Gentils, que l'on appelle, Pandites, sont gens sans étude sans science & sans aucune lumiere de l'anatomie, qui n'ont por toute connoissance, qu'un certain nombre de receptes que leurs peres leurs ont laissé...'.[79]

As a consequence, by the mid-seventeenth century European doctors were often in demand for surgery. One French doctor 'grew so famous in *Persia*, that the King himself profer'd him very considerable allowances, to engage him to continue in that Court. Nay, he grew into such repute, after he had recover'd persons who had been given over by others, that the people began to look upon him as an extraordinary man, insomuch that they brought to him some that were lame and blind from the Birth, to recover their limbs and sight who never had had them.'[80] Fryer in Persia after describing local medicine pointed out that if a particular cure failed, 'another Physician is consulted; for among such store they think it hard to miss of a Cure; and in that are so opinionated, that if their own Nation cannot give them Remedy, they think none other can. (Though as to Chyrurgery they are of another mind, thinking the *Europeans* better at Manual Operation than themselves.)'[81] In India the Abbé Carré in the 1670s several

---

[75] Fryer, I, 287.
[76] Fryer, III, 94.
[77] Olearius, p. 338.
[78] Manucci, II, 333.
[79] Mr. DLF in Luillier, p. 213.
[80] Olearius, p. 338.
[81] Fryer, III, 96.

times commented on a local preference for European surgeons. When he himself was to be bled, one of his Indian servants was eager to do it, for 'He himself (he said) had lived with a French surgeon, both at Surat and Rajapur, had witnessed many fine operations by him, and remembered what he had seen done.' This servant even apparently thought he would be qualified to do an amputation, again because he had seen a French surgeon do one.[82] Later a Muslim officer approached him in Madras and 'begged me first of all to send them a good French surgeon to look after one of their camp-marshals, who had been badly wounded by two musket-balls...',[83] and soon after he noted how two 'badly wounded Moor officers had withdrawn to the suburbs of Madras, hoping to find English surgeons.'[84] In the early eighteenth century we even hear of an Indo-Portuguese woman who was considered to be a skilled surgeon.[85] This prestige seems to mark a pronounced difference as compared with the situation in the previous century.

We described earlier how European medicine was being professionalized. Fryer noted how in Surat in 1675 medicine was still a craft, not a profession. 'Physick here is now as in former days, open to all Pretenders; here being no Bars of Authority or formal Graduation, Examination or Proof of their Proficiency; but every one ventures, and every one suffers; and those that are most skilled, have it by Tradition, or former Experience descending in their Families; not considering either alterations of Tempers or Seasons, but what succeeded well to one, they apply to all.'[86] Ovington also noted how medicine was really still a craft, and governed by caste rules. Brahmins were meant to do theology, but they also did arithmetic, astrology and physic. 'But such as addict themselves to the Practice of Physick, are bound to pay an Annual Fine to the rest of their Sect, because Physick is both Advantagious and Foreign to their Profession.'[87] And Fryer in Persia again commented how 'Here is no

---

[82] Abbé Carré, pp. 284–5.

[83] *Ibid.*, p. 598.

[84] *Ibid.*, p. 624. Not, however, that all Europeans were particularly expert. See *ibid.*, pp. 369–70, for the story of a French quack, who did at least examine an ill Portuguese 'by all the laws of Hippocrates and Galen...'.

[85] Jadunath Sarkar, *Studies in Aurangzib's Reign*, 3rd edn (London, 1989), p. 56.

[86] Fryer, I, 286. I am planning a separate study of the professionalization of medicine in Portuguese Goa.

[87] Ovington, p. 205. David Arnold tells me that in the first half of the nineteenth century bleeding, well on the wane in Europe, was all the rage in India, for it was thought that drastic remedies were needed in such tropical places. Personal communication from Prof. Arnold.

170

precedent License of Practising, but it is lawful for any one to exercise this Function who has the impudence to pretend it.'[88]

This new prestige for European surgery seems to have spilt over into the beginnings of an influx of western medical ideas into India. This could, however, be a double-edged sword, for one instance from the 1720s shows Indian doctors adopting bleeding with great enthusiasm. We noted that bleeding had never been used in ayurvedic medicine, but in 1726 we are told that it was now very widely used by pandits. One used to bleed his patients up to twenty times. Such ferocious treatment was now less common in Europe, and indeed it appears that European patients were no longer prepared to tolerate this sort of treatment, for the French doctor added regretfully that this pandit could do this 'sans que les malades en murmurent, étant bien plus obeissans aux ordres de leur Medecin qu'on ne l'est en France.'[89]

In the most general sense what Bernier and the others represent is the beginning of the process by which Europe achieved mastery over Asia. The accepted sequence, very crudely, is that for at least 250 years the Europeans did not represent an economically and technologically more advanced civilization than the ones they saw in Asia. Only with the Industrial Revolution late in the eighteenth century did a disparity in terms of power appear between Asia and western Europe. But the Industrial Revolution was built on, among other things, fundamental scientific advances in Europe, encouraged by the various learned societies which sprang up in several countries in the seventeenth century. Thus the seeds of later European advance and subsequent dominance must be found in scientific and other achievements, not least in the medical sphere, from at least two centuries before the culmination of the Industrial Revolution. This, then, is what Bernier represents; the first example in India of the medical aspect of this paradigmatic change in Europe.

---

[88] Fryer, III, 95.
[89] Mr. DLF in Luillier, p. 215.

XV

First Contacts between Indian and European Medical Systems: Goa in the Sixteenth Century

Until the sixteenth century medical knowledge in Europe, in the Muslim world and in India seems to have been relatively evenly spread. No area had any decisive advantage, although in different specialties different areas were ahead. Most obviously, healers in India had been practising 'tropical medicine' long before Europeans reified the concept and appropriated it to describe their own halting attempts to deal with 'warm climate' diseases. There was a considerable degree of interaction between the traditional systems of these three areas, yet there was also a recognition that some illnesses were geographically specific. Some Indian illnesses, for example, were seen by foreigners as 'different'. This interaction, and also the notion of difference, was seen in India in the sixteenth century, especially in the Portuguese capital of Goa. Indeed, these themes are plain to see in the career and writing of sixteenth-century Goa's greatest savant, the New Christian Garcia d'Orta and a study of his work will conclude this essay.

Plague, smallpox and syphilis were three of the most threatening diseases in Europe at the time. In Portugal in the period of the discoveries, that is in the fifteenth and sixteenth centuries, all three of these diseases were found in abundance. There were several major plague epidemics in the sixteenth century. Plague had originated in Asia, but we cannot tell whether these particular epidemics came from within Europe, or from India, or indeed whether the plague went from Portugal to India. It is possible that both areas had indigenous sources for this malady. In the major Portuguese plague epidemic of 1569–70, mortality in Lisbon in June 1569 was 50 to 60 a day, in July 300 to 400, and later up to 700. In this city of about 100,000 souls, some 50,000 died. Royal mortality in Portugal gives a good impression of general mortality, keeping in mind that royalty received the best care and had the best diets. D. Manuel, king from 1495 to 1521, had 13 children by three wives. Four of them predeceased him, and nine in all died before the age of 40. His successor, D. João III (1521–57), had ten children, whose average life span was 7.6 years: the oldest died at 22. Medical knowledge in Portugal, as in the rest of Europe, was incapable of dealing with these diseases.

As a result of the Muslim period of dominance in Portugal, which ended only in the late thirteenth century, Muslim authorities were widely used. Of the five books which in theory a druggist had to know before he could practise, four were of Muslim origin.[1] More generally, in Portugal, and indeed all of Europe, medicine was a blend of Latin, Arabic, Greek and Hebrew knowledge. In Portugal the most widely quoted authors were Hippocrates, Galen, Isaac and Ibn Sina (Avicenna). But these relatively scientific authorities blended easily into folk medicine, and belief in witches, astrology and sorcery. In other words, book-based medical practice co-existed with folk oral traditions.

One cure for diarrhoea was to rub the abdomen with egg whites, or with well-sifted goat dung, or a mixture of the two. In the thirteenth century Pedro Hispano, a very famous doctor and later to be Pope John XXI, said that a good cure-all was a little bag containing the eyes of a magpie, crab or wolf, worn around the neck. Badger powders were a very popular remedy:

> One began by inebriating a badger on a wine filtered through camphor and blended with a compound of gold, seed pearls, and coral. The animal then was decapitated, all of his blood drained, and his heart and liver removed. The mixture of the blood with the powders should be effected under a 'slow sun' or in the 'heat of a fire'.... Two ounces of paté resulting from pulverizing the heart, liver and even the skin and teeth of the badger completed the mixture. This compound, dissolved in wine or in water seasoned with vinegar, was given to the patient.[2]

We need more research on this interaction between formal and folk medicine, and must be careful not to ridicule folk practice. Andrew Wear claims in his recent edited collection of essays that 'the nineteenth- and twentieth-century values of the medical profession which in past history of medicine had been applied to earlier periods to condemn empirics, quacks, magical and religious practitioners have been discarded. In the process a much richer medical world has been uncovered.'[3]

First Contacts between Indian and European Medical Systems

Important advances occurred in European medicine, and especially surgery, during the Renaissance, but from the middle of the
sixteenth century Portugal lost all chance of taking part in these
changes. Medical education at the university in Lisbon in the early
sixteenth century was traditional in the extreme. This university
moved between Lisbon and Coímbra several times, until in 1537
Lisbon was definitively replaced by Coímbra. It seemed that this
university was poised to take account of, and contribute to, medical
and scientific advances in Renaissance Europe. Unfortunately, a
relatively open intellectual atmosphere in Portugal early in the
sixteenth century, and a Portuguese version of humanism, was stifled
in the 1550s by the new Society of Jesus, and by the Inquisition,
founded in 1536 and by mid-century dominant in the country. Its
influence was especially detrimental at Coímbra, for many of the
teachers there were New Christians.[4] As C. R. Boxer notes, until they
were forced to convert in the late fifteenth century over 60 per cent
of Portugal's doctors in Portugal had been Jews.[5] Persecution of them
thus crippled medicine in Portugal. Indeed, in 1583 there was such a
pronounced shortage of doctors in the kingdom that only one could
be spared for India that year.[6]

By the late 1550s Hippocrates and Galen were firmly reestablished
as the unquestioned and unquestionable authorities on all matters
medical. This was doubly unfortunate for Portugal (and Spain) for the
discoveries had opened up new horizons in all sorts of fields in the
Iberian countries. In the case of medicine, Portuguese doctors and
botanists soon found a host of new diseases and remedies. Garcia
d'Orta and Cristovão da Costa listed these, but this was not considered
to be acceptable knowledge in Portugal and the opportunity to pioneer
in tropical medicine, and even contribute on the basis of this to new
paradigms in European medicine, was never taken.

In most areas of disease and curing in early modern India there
appears to have been no particular advantage in knowledge or skill
on the part of the newly arrived Europeans. Rather it seems that,
despite specific differences with regard to particular diseases, the
situation overall was one of equality.[7] In certain areas, which could be
loosely called 'tropical medicine,' Indian healers with their millennia
of experience obviously knew more than did the Europeans.

We can now turn to the situation in the first large European
settlement in India, the port of Goa which was conquered by Afonso
Albuquerque for the Portuguese king in 1510, and was their main
town and capital during the sixteenth century and later. The town's
population in 1600 was about 75,000. Of these about 1,500 were

First Contacts between Indian and European Medical Systems

Portuguese or *mestiços* (ethnically mixed), 20,000 were Hindus, and some 50,000 were local Christians who had been converted during the sixteenth century. In the countryside the population was still predominantly Hindu.[8] Looked at from the late twentieth century, the prevalent diseases in sixteenth-century Goa make up a still familiar list. Late in the century a Dutch resident, Jan Huygen van Linschoten, said the main ones were *mordexijn* (in other words cholera), the bloody flux (or dysentery), and fevers, especially malarial ones. The term 'fever'could cover a range of illnesses, which at this distance in time can hardly be specified. 'They have many continuall fevers, which are burning agues, and consume mens bodies with extreame heate, whereby within foure or five dayes they are eyther whole or dead,' wrote van Linschoten.[9] Pyrard de Laval, a visitor in the early seventeenth century, said burning fevers, presumably enteric fever (typhoid), and dysentery were common, as was venereal disease.

In Goa, syphilis, the disease which had devastated large parts of Europe after its probable introduction from America in the 1490s, was considered to be a Portuguese import. A local sixteenth-century Hindu work called it 'firangi roga', that is the 'European disease'.[10] Similarly, Pyrard claimed it was found only 'where the Portuguese are'.[11] It seems that a milder venereal disease was already widespread in India, so we can assume that he is referring here to the new, more virulent, American disease of syphilis. But van Linschoten in Goa in the 1580s must have been writing of the mild indigenous form when he noted:

> pockes and piles, with other secret diseases, they are in those countries verie common and not hidden or concealed, for they thinke it no shame, more then to have any other disease. They heale them with the roote China; there are some that have had them at the least three or foure times, and are not any thing at all shunned or disliked for the same, but dare both boast and bragge thereof. It is not anything perillous for the bodie...[12]

The question of cholera in sixteenth-century India is a controversial one. Some have claimed that cholera was first seen in the great pandemics that spread from India in the nineteenth century. But there is no doubt that what our sources describe in India in the sixteenth century was cholera. This is shown by the fact that all of the accounts stress rapid morbidity as a result of dehydration caused by acute watery diarrhoea: this must have been cholera, though it should be noted that the commonly described 'bloody flux' was not, for cholera does not produce internal bleeding. The point, presumably, is that there are various strains of the disease. One of these was epidemic in the sixteenth century, and possibly it was a variant of this that was so devastating three centuries later.

Cholera was a major killer in Goa. There were outbreaks in the town in 1543, 1563, 1567, 1570, 1580, 1588, 1610, 1635, 1639, 1670 and 1680. The first one was the worst; we are told that of those struck by it, only one in ten survived.[13] The Italian merchant Sassetti described it in Cochin in the 1580s:

> There is current here a certain disease which kills a person in just 24 hours and which is called *mordaxi,* which is a revulsion of the stomach and of the entire body which rejects itself; all the humours quit the body and the blood too, so that one dies; and it comes from eating much sweet fruit, much pork, many preserves, and from drinking much water; whence the poor stomachs, when they have suffered much, throw themselves on the ground. It is the accident which makes it known, that suddenly the patients lose the sense of touch in their external parts, so that they feel nothing if they are struck blows or pierced with a needle.[14]

The Venetian quasi-doctor Manucci later in the seventeenth century noted that *mort-de-chien,* or cholera, was the main killer, describing it as colic of the bowels with vomiting and laxity. The best cure, the usual one at this time, was to burn the heel of the patient with a red-hot iron until the heat was felt. In this way the pain was allayed and the discharge and vomiting stopped.[15]

Goa was generally considered to have a very high mortality rate. One estimate finds that no less than 25,000 Portuguese soldiers died in the Royal Hospital between 1604 and 1634; by repute 500 a year died from syphilis and 'the effects of profligacy'. As a proverb had it, 'Of the hundred who go to India [from Portugal], not even one returns.'[16] Many in fact never even made it to India, such was the mortality on the voyage out from Lisbon. Vasco da Gama on his first voyage lost over half his crew to scurvy. Duncan shows that between 1497 and 1590 some 171,000 people left Lisbon for the east, and about 17,000 of these were lost to disease or shipwreck.[17] When the great ships from Portugal arrived each year in Goa they brought with them many newcomers with bad ulcers, the result of scurvy.[18] Accounts of the state of health on board the great carracks arriving in Goa from Lisbon are harrowing in the extreme.[19] A contemporary list shows that in the period 1629–34 5,228 people left Portugal for India, but only 2,495 completed the voyage – though to be sure some would have deserted, and two ships of the 17 that left Portugal in this period were lost at sea.[20] As one other indication of mortality, which reflects the mortality of the royal

First Contacts between Indian and European Medical Systems

family at home, of 50 governors of Portuguese India up to 1656, 22 died during their term of office or on their way home.

Several travellers speculated on the reasons for Goa's unhealthiness. Manucci and others put forward the notion that India was healthy for men over the age of 40, but not for younger men. As Dr John Fryer put it, 'For to the Lustier and Fresher, and oftentimes the Temperatest, the Clime more unkind; but to Old Men and Women it seems to be more suitable.'[21] Medical practice at the time also contributed to high mortality, a point we will return to shortly. One problem was Goa's porous soil, so that sewage sank into drinking wells, and thus faecal-borne disease was spread. There seems also to have been an increase in the incidence of malaria due to stagnant waters lying around. Manucci left a vivid picture of illness and mortality in Goa. In his view, the unwholesome air in Goa was a problem. Also there was an island nearby which was a real graveyard:

> The reason is that it is full of courtesans, Mahomedan and heathen, who bear on them the unhappy poison by which they take the life of so many wretched men, after they have like leeches sucked from them every penny in their purse. It is, above all, the soldiers newly arrived from Portugal who succumb to this sad fate. Having exhausted both their bodily strength and their scantily-stored purses in the infamous dens allowed to exist there, misery and feebleness overtake them so completely that they are forced to enter the hospital. That is a place from which they hardly ever come forth alive, the number of men dying there being astonishing, every day five to 25 dead bodies being carried out, sometimes more, sometimes less, a fact that I have myself observed several times. By this means that island becomes the cemetery of all those newly arrived from Europe, and I honestly believe that at the end of the year not an eighth part survives of those who landed.[22]

Others, too, noted the effects of 'profligacy'. There was, of course, a real medical, as opposed to moral, basis for these comments, for the 'profligate' risked catching the new and more malignant venereal disease, syphilis, which the Portuguese had brought with them to India. Van Linschoten claimed that a fundamental cause of Portuguese ill health was that they

> use much company of women ... which often times costeth them both life and limme, for although men were of iron or steele, the unchaste life of a woman, with her unsatiable lustes were able to grinde him to powder, and sweep him away like dust, which costeth many a mans life.[23]

Whatever the reason, the health situation in Goa was so poor, and deteriorated so greatly during the seventeenth century, that in the eighteenth century the town was abandoned and the capital moved down river to the more healthy Panaji.

While some Indian diseases were well known from European experience others, such as cholera and enteric fever (typhoid), were unfamiliar to Portuguese doctors. The Italian merchant Sassetti noted in Malabar malaria, several sorts of apoplexy, and elephantiasis (or filaria). He also commented on different cures. Bleeding was seldom used, nor were such standards of European pharmacopoeia as rhubarb and aloe.[24] Many other commentators thought that Indian diseases were different, and should be treated by Indian methods. In the late seventeenth century an English doctor stressed the differences, and said gloomily that 'we are here, as Exotick Plants brought home to us, not agreeable to the Soil'.[25] But most European visitors were more sanguine and this in turn led to a very interesting eclectic mixture of Portuguese and Hindu medical systems.[26] David Arnold has noted how 'before 1800, Western medicine was far less domineering in its relationship with indigenous societies'. After this time, in the nineteenth century, the British rulers of India sometimes seemed to blame the Indians themselves for their ill health and high mortality. These were caused, it was claimed, by Indian culture and customs; the contribution of British colonialism was played down or ignored.[27] This seems to be a small illustration of the pronounced differences between the colonial impact of the two European powers. It is commonplace that an industrialized Britain had a much more overwhelming effect on India than did the Portuguese; indeed, I have several times made the case that the Portuguese had a very slight impact on most aspects of Indian life.[28] In the medical field, this smaller impact, even in their capital of Goa, and the essentially pre-modern nature of the Portuguese, meant that acculturation could flourish, and also that Indian mortality was seen as no different from Portuguese. Hence Hindu custom and medical practice were not blamed for disease and death.

The basic idea seems to have been that for certain diseases Indian doctors were much preferable to European ones. An extended contemporary Jesuit account noted how Hindu doctors

> come to the lands of the Portuguese, and they are examined by the Físico-Mór [the chief official Portuguese doctor], a man from Europe, whom I often heard stating that the said Brahmans called Panditas cure better than the European physicians who practise in India. I knew a friar of St Augustine, of the Portuguese nation, who taught medicine in Portugal, and lectured on it for sixteen years, who after coming to India treated some Portuguese patients, all of whom passed

First Contacts between Indian and European Medical Systems

away; seeing this happening, the said priest called the Panditas and asked them how they went about curing their patients; they replied that the properties and the composition of the drugs were well taught in the books; however, this was not sufficient to heal the patient unless his complexion, and the ruling humour, and the connection with the local climate were first known, and that they ordered their remedies according to these principles. Knowing they were giving him a good reason, the Priest took some information from them in order to succeed in curing, and according to this and his science he later made some wonderful cures.[29]

The acceptance of this notion meant that for most of our period Indian medical practice was described, but usually without comment. Even though some of the 'cures' prevalent in India at this time seem today to be bizarre in the extreme, Europeans apparently found them different but not qualitatively better or worse than those they already knew. Van Linschoten even made a specific comparison of rival treatments of fevers:

This sicknes is common and very daungerous, and hath no remedie for the Portingalles, but letting of blood: but the Indians and heathens do cure themselves with hearbes, Sanders, and other such like oyntments, wherewith they ease themselves. This sicknes consumeth many Portingalles every yeare.[30]

The related notions of a lack of qualitative difference, and the idea that Indian diseases were 'different', meant that even governors and clerics used Hindu healers because of their supposed better local knowledge. In 1548 an Indian Brahmin was practising in the Jesuit College of St Paul, and another *vaidya* (Hindu doctor, also sometimes called *pandit*) was doctor to Governor Barreto in 1574.[31] Governor Manuel de Sousa Coutinho (1588–91) and his wife were accused by the Inquisition of using Indian doctors, and dealing with Hindu sorcerers ['feiticeiros'].[32]

Portuguese racism sometimes tried to limit the prestige of these Hindu doctors. In 1572 the Governor decreed that Hindu teachers and doctors were not to go about on horseback or in palanquins. A first offence attracted a fine of ten cruzados, a second 20 cruzados and the loss of the offending horse or palanquin, and a third meant being sent to the galleys. However, the doctor who served the Governor's own household was exempt from this,[33] and in fact the prohibition soon lapsed. Van Linschoten noted in the 1580s that:

There are in Goa many Heathen phisitions which observe their gravities with hats carried over them for the sunne, like the Portingales,

First Contacts between Indian and European Medical Systems

which no other heathens doe, but onely Ambassadors, or some rich Marchants. These Heathen phisitions doe not onely cure there owne nations and countriemen but the Portingales also, for the Viceroy himselfe, the Archbishop, and all the Monkes and Friers doe put more trust in them then in their own countrimen, whereby they get great store of money, and are much honoured and esteemed.[34]

The Portuguese doctor Cristovão da Costa used to ask a local Brahmin doctor in Cochin about local cures; this doctor was popular among both Indians and Portuguese in the town.[35] In 1620 patients in the convent of Madre de Deus in Goa were treated by a *pandit,* and Portuguese soldiers wanting sick leave used letters from a *pandit.*[36]

The reverse of this sensible arrangement was that most governors brought their own doctors out with them from Lisbon as part of their vast retinues of relatives and hangers-on, all of them hoping to make a fortune in India during the three-year term of their patron. These newly arrived Portuguese doctors were nearly always rewarded by being made the chief doctor of the Royal Hospital, but several contemporaries noted that this was a prime cause of mortality, for they knew nothing of Indian diseases, and just as they began to acculturate they returned to Portugal with their gubernatorial patron.[37] In 1610 the king ordered that this practice cease and that the doctors and surgeons who went out with the viceroys not be allowed to practise in the Royal Hospital, 'because they have no experience of the region and its medical methods'. This order seems to have provoked a storm of complaints from Goa, and three years later it was lifted.[38] Another problem raised by these itinerant doctors, who usually returned to Portugal with their patron, was the resulting shortage of practitioners in Goa. A letter from Goa in 1644 complained of this, and noted despairingly that the present *fisico-mor* was a 'negro', in fact a Goan. The king was urged to take measures to make Portuguese doctors stay in Goa.[39]

There seems to be a contradiction here in Portuguese racial policies. As we have and will see, converted Jews, the 'New Christians', were greatly discriminated against, and Indian doctors were not allowed to practise in the Royal Hospital. Muslims generally were feared and disliked. As opposed to this, most Portuguese in India used Hindu doctors, and liked Hindu healing practice. It is inappropriate here to go into such a complex topic in any depth, but it may be suggested that the difference was between theory and practice, or perhaps normative as opposed to actual behaviour. Thus while Hindus and Jews, even New Christians, were to be discriminated against at an official or normative level, so that the former could not practise in the Royal Hospital, nor

First Contacts between Indian and European Medical Systems

hold tax-farming contracts, in actuality they were still popular doctors, and held most of the contracts. Garcia d'Orta, of whom more later, seems to represent a paradigmatic figure in this respect. During his life he treated the Goan élite, from the governor on down. By contrast, after his death normative or official behaviour took over; he was accused of being a crypto-Jew and his bones were exhumed and ceremoniously burned.

Despite this discrimination, what we find overwhelmingly in Goa is a mixture of European and Hindu practice. As Arnold notes in the introduction to this book, tropical medicine appears more and more to have been the result of a synergistic relationship between core and periphery. Portuguese Goans seem to have had a quite *ad hoc* and experimental attitude to health, and tried different systems quite freely. An Augustinian friar with a very painful swelling in the testicles was cured by a poultice of stewed leaves applied by an old woman. A Hindu doctor was considered to know a perfect cure for scrofula, a swelling of the glands caused by tuberculosis. The Jesuits jealously guarded the recipe for their cordial stone, a bezoar stone with an amazing list of other ingredients added. It was used for heart problems, and was a good example of a mixture of Indian and European practice.[40] In the Portuguese settlement of Daman in 1673 a French visitor found a young Portuguese girl with fever, whose 'Indian physician, instead of letting her blood, had covered her head with pepper'. The European insisted on bleeding her with leeches, and perhaps surprisingly she recovered quickly. The use of pepper is obscure, but it may refer to the local practice of throwing pepper into the eyes of a sufferer. This was designed to gauge the severity of the malady. I assume that the point was that if patients did not react to the pepper they were given up for dead.[41] This incident points to a major divergence between European and Hindu medicine, which was the routine use of bleeding by Europeans.[42] Pyrard claimed Indians, that is Hindus, did not use bleeding at all.[43] There were clearly problems with this method of dealing with fevers, especially when it was used so often; patients in the Royal Hospital could be bled 30 or even 40 times.

Earlier European practice had combined bleeding with feeding up the patient. In the following description of medical practice in Goa's Royal Hospital from the 1640s we find that the Europeans had now decided that a much scantier diet was more appropriate. But we can also note that they were at least worried enough about the effects of bleeding to try to build up the patient, using a Hindu specific, after the bleeding was finished.

First Contacts between Indian and European Medical Systems

I forgot to make a remark upon the frequent bleedings in reference to Europeans – namely, that in order to recover their colour and get themselves in perfect health, it is prescribed for them to drink for 12 days three glasses of *pissat de vache* [cow's urine], one in the morning, one at midday, and one in the evening; but, as this drink cannot but be very disagreeable, the convalescent swallows as little of it as possible, however much he may desire to recover his health. This remedy has been learnt from the idolaters of the country, and whether the convalescent makes use of it or not, he is not allowed to leave the hospital till the 12 days have expired during which he is supposed to partake of this drink.[44]

We have seen Europeans using Indian methods, and incorporating them into their medical practice. There was also some transfer of medical knowledge from India to Europe. John Ovington noted late in the seventeenth century:

The general Ease and Cure, which the White Powder [?] in India gives to Feavers, makes that a very common and acceptable Receipt there; and it has, with very good Success, been administered in England, sent from thence by the Indian Physicians. And all their Medicines here are generally of the cooler sort, because of the Heats to which the Climate naturally inclines them.[45]

A decade or so earlier, Manuel Godinho said that some medicinal drugs were sent to dispensaries in Europe from India. They included miramulanos (a small medicinal fruit), asafoetida, spikenard and opium.[46] And despite the general European contempt for Asian surgery, India did make one important contribution here. The main activity in early plastic surgery was nose reconstruction, which in sixteenth-century Europe was done using a flap of skin. However, the church was opposed to this and the practice fell into disuse. The same method had been used in India for centuries. Information on this Indian practice reached Europe in the late eighteenth century, and revived European interest in rhinoplasty. On this foundation was built modern plastic surgery.[47]

What, however, of a reverse flow? Did Indians learn from the Portuguese? Certainly the great Portuguese healer and scholar Garcia d'Orta treated various rulers in the Deccan, especially the ruler of Ahmadnagar and his family, though he was often in competition with Muslim authorities at the court.[48] He claimed that the king 'taught me the names of illnesses and medicines in Arabic, and I taught him the same in Latin'. Hindu doctors often used Portuguese methods, 'But most of them not correctly.' Nevertheless, they had learned some things from European practice, just as d'Orta had from them.[49] At a meeting of the Portuguese Council of State in 1629 the ambassador of neighbouring Bijapur, who was meant to attend, excused himself because he was sick; he asked that the viceroy send him his *fisico-mor*, which the Portuguese agreed to do.[50] There is evidence from the seventeenth century of European surgeons being much in demand in India. This reflects the fact that Indian anatomy, and so surgery, was by this time well behind European knowledge, a point which Peter Boomgaard also notes in his essay in this book.

As for the universal European practice of bleeding, it seems to have been picked up by Hindu healers from the Portuguese quite early. D'Orta wrote acerbicly that 'they say there is bleeding [that is, that they practised it], and they never bled before we were in the land'.[51] By the later seventeenth century the method was more firmly established in areas where Europeans were numerous. In 1674–6 Dr Dellon was held in the prison of the Inquisition in Goa. Such was his despondency that he tired of life, and decided to end it, but wished to avoid a mortal sin by using someone else for the purpose. He feigned illness, and sure enough a doctor was introduced who prescribed five bleedings on five successive days. This remedy did indeed bring Dellon close to death, but more to the point the doctor was 'a Pundit, or Pagan Physician'.[52] Bleeding had never been used in Ayurvedic medicine, but in 1726 we are told that it was now very widely used by *pandits*. One used to bleed his patients up to 20 times. Such ferocious treatment was now less common in Europe, and indeed it appears that European patients were no longer prepared to tolerate this sort of treatment, for the French doctor added regretfully that this *pandit* could do this 'sans que les malades en murmurent, étant bien plus obeissans aux ordres de leur Medecin qu'on ne l'est en France'.[53]

The only area where the Portuguese were more advanced was in the matter of health care. Official bodies concerned themselves with the provision of medical facilities; apparently this was innovative for India. By late in the sixteenth century there were several hospitals in Goa. Among them was the Leper Hospital of St Lazarus, which had been founded in 1529.[54] The famous Royal Hospital of the Holy Spirit was Goa's main hospital. It had been founded by the conqueror of Goa, Afonso Albuquerque, to cater for Portuguese soldiers. Its main financing always came from the state, and in this it was truly new. At one time the revenues from the sale of the very valuable licensed voyage to China (Macao) were devoted to the hospital, and the king told the viceroy that if this did not suffice he was to write

First Contacts between Indian and European Medical Systems

and say how much more was needed.[55] Admission was restricted to Portuguese soldiers and a few indigent Portuguese. It could cater for a very large total of 1,500 patients, and descriptions of it after it was expanded and rebuilt in the 1590s make it sound a most impressive structure indeed. Its staff included physicians, surgeons, apothecaries, barbers and bleeders, and Indian servants and slaves for the dirty work. No Indian doctors were allowed. Pyrard, who was a patient in 1608, has left an extended and glowing account of it. From his description the building looked like a grand palace. Even the beds were splendid, with mattresses and covers of silk or cotton. The meals were luxurious and ample, the plates, bowls and dishes of Chinese porcelain or even silver. On admission the patient had a hair-cut and wash, and was provided with bed-clothes.[56]

Why such a lavish establishment, apparently in advance of European hospitals at the time? The context is important. Such grandeur had a symbolically reassuring function. The hospital catered mostly for Portuguese soldiers, single men isolated in a precarious frontier society. In Portugal they could expect to be cared for by their families, but not in India. To maintain their loyalty (for many 'deserted' and sought greener pastures in neighbouring Indian states) it was important for the state to reassure them that they would be cared for if they were sick, and if they died, would die well. There is a similar divergence from European practice in the way that even the élite of Goa were happy to be cured in the hospital; in Europe at this time they would have seen a hospital as being only for the poor and indigent.

Given all this, why the appalling mortality in the hospital that we noted earlier? Among other reasons, the truly startling use of bleeding must have played a role, as also, no doubt, did the lack of Indian experience of the chief doctors. More basically, the under-lying health problems of Goa, stagnant water and porous soils, could not be met by the existing state of medical knowledge. The causes of 'tropical diseases', such as cholera, dysentery and malaria, were not diagnosed until the the last century. Nevertheless, in the area of state involvement in public health and especially hospitals the Portuguese had an innovative role in India. Can we say the same about the greatest scholar of sixteenth-century Goa, the New Christian Garcia d'Orta (*c.*1500–68)? D'Orta was the first major naturalist to study the main medicinal plants and other therapeutic substances used in the East; he was also a doctor and historian of medicine, a pharmacist and a wide-ranging savant interested in history and anthropology. His famous work, *Colloquies on the Simples and Drugs of India,* was one of the first books (and one of

First Contacts between Indian and European Medical Systems

the very few secular books) to be published in Goa in the sixteenth and seventeenth centuries. The rare first edition (only 24 copies are known) is dated 1563.[57] It is divided into 57 chapters, each of them in the form of a dialogue or colloquy. Each deals with one drug or simple. In each case he describes the drug, says where it grows, and comments on its therapeutic use. Most of the drugs are vegetable, but he also deals with ivory and diamonds. It is an excellent comprehensive and accurate empirical study of Indian materia medica and botany in general. It does not really discuss medicine as such, although he was a famous doctor in sixteenth-century Goa, serving as the physician of the Royal Hospital at the time of St Francis Xavier's stay in Goa in the early 1540s, and ministering to the Portuguese élite of the town and to local rulers.[58]

D'Orta's medical knowledge was not advanced. This can be seen from his description of cholera. Goa was hit by a major cholera epidemic in 1543: all classes and ages were struck by it in the winter, that is the monsoon period, of that year. The Portuguese doctors could do nothing, and of every 100 who were affected, only ten survived. Twelve, 15, even 20 victims were buried each day. The Governor, Martim Afonso de Sousa, even ordered an autopsy in a fruitless attempt to find the cause of the affliction.[59] D'Orta was the first European to publish a description of cholera in India. In the *Colloquies* he mentioned the Hindu and Arabic names for it, and compared what he saw in Goa with what he knew of Europe. He believed that there was a toxic humour which had to be expelled. It was caused by over-eating, or by too much sexual intercourse. He noted that the local *vaidyas* used rice with pepper and cardamom, cauterized the feet of the patient, tied up the patient's limbs and applied pepper to the eyes.[60] As to fevers, d'Orta followed European practice and treated fevers with bleeding and purging, and rich foods – the latter, as we noted, later lost favour in Goa. Thus we must not make too much of d'Orta's work. He seems to have been thoroughly grounded in early modern European practice of the first half of the sixteenth century. He learned of Muslim or Yunani medicine from its local practitioners, the *hakims,* and usually appreciated the abilities of the local *vaidyas* with whom he had contact, considering their cures as often superior to those he knew. However, he had no inkling of the vast and ancient body of Ayurvedic theory. The main influences on his medical thinking were the thoroughly predictable ones: Aristotle, Hippocrates, Galen and Ibn Sina. The basis of his work was, in essence, humoral pathology. His book goes into very elaborate detail as to whether various drugs were 'in the fourth, warm and dry', or 'in the second part of the third'.[61] D'Orta never went beyond this. He did correct and criticize his authorities on occasion, once, for example, writing 'Let not any text of any author deny what my own eyes have observed.... Frighten me not with Dioscorides or Galen, for I do not say but the truth and what I know.' [62] Nevertheless, he did not transcend them. It is especially revealing that he also quoted his contemporary Vesalius, but not on anatomy, in which he was the great paradigmatic innovator, but rather on a cure for syphilis.[63]

An important reason for this was the fact that d'Orta was a New Christian, and, apparently, a far from convinced convert. Born in *c.*1500, he studied at the Spanish universities of Salamanca and Alcalá de Henares, where his medical training consisted of memorizing Hippocrates, Galen and Ibn Sina. Subsequently d'Orta taught at Lisbon from 1526 until he left for India. It seems very likely that his departure for Goa in 1534, as the personal physician of the later Governor Martim Afonso de Sousa, was a result of increasing intolerance in Portugal. Two years after he left the Inquisition was set up in Lisbon, and was in full swing four years later. As a New Christian he was forced to step carefully, and no doubt he was also detrimentally affected by the mid-century attack on open inquiry which we mentioned above. As a result, the massive compilation that was the *Colloquies* was generally ignored in Portugal, though it was widely used in other parts of Europe in the later sixteenth century and subsequently, thanks to a Latin translation which went through five editions, the first one being published in 1567 in Antwerp. D'Orta himself suffered posthumously from this intolerance. He died in 1568, but in 1580 he was condemned as a Jew by the Inquisition, and his remains were dug up and burned at an *auto de fé*. A sister was burned by the Inquisition in Goa in the year after his death. Such intolerant bigotry symbolizes the stranglehold of the Counter Reformation as seen in the Inquisition on intellectual life in Portugal. While d'Orta certainly described many new (to Europeans) medicinal drugs and cures and diseases, and thus in a minor way contributed to undermine the authority of Hippocrates and Galen, it is incorrect to see him as representing a new paradigm for European medicine based on his Asian discoveries. Rather his contribution was to add to the store of European descriptive knowledge. [64]

First Contacts between Indian and European Medical Systems

Notes

Parts of this article are a much revised version of my 27th James Ford Bell lecture, presentèd to the Associates of the James Ford Bell Library, University of Minnesota, at the American Association of University Women's Club, Minneapolis, 3 May, 1989. The lecture was called 'Initial Contacts between European and Indian Medicine', and subsequently was published by the library. I am most grateful to Professor John Parker, the now retired Curator of this library, for inviting me to deliver this lecture. The present essay was greatly improved as a result of criticisms and comments at the conference from which this book comes. I must also thank Professor Donald Simpson, and my wife Denni, for helping to avoid at least some errors of medical fact. The present article could be read in tandem with my other venture into the history of medicine, 'The thin end of the wedge: Medical relativities as a paradigm of early modern Indian-European Relations', in *Modern Asian Studies,* 29 (1995), 141–70, which concentrates on the broader changes which occurred in the seventeenth century. Finally, much of my research into this subject was done, most appropriately, at the Xavier Centre of Historical Research in Goa. My thanks to its Director, Fr Teotonio de Souza, for his continued kindnesses over many years.

1. These were: *Pandectae Medicinae* by Matthaeus Sylvaticus; Mesua's *De Simplicibus; Antidotarium* by Nicolau Myrepso; *Liber Servitoris;* and the Fifth Book of the *Canon* of Ibn Sina. A. H. de Oliveira Marques, *Daily Life in Portugal in the Late Middle Ages* (Madison: University of Wisconsin Press, 1971), 151. A recent excellent introduction to Western European medicine in the fifteenth century is to be found in Roger French, 'Medicine in Western Europe during the fifteenth century', in Mario Gomes Marques and John Cule (eds), *The Great Maritime Discoveries and World Health* (Lisbon: Escola Nacional de Saúde Pública, 1991), 39–54.
2. Marques, *op. cit.* (note 1), 143–4.
3. Andrew Wear (ed.), *Medicine in Society: Historical Essays* (Cambridge: Cambridge University Press, 1992), Introduction, 2.
4. See P. D. Gaitonde, *Portuguese Pioneers in India: Spotlight on Medicine* (Bombay: Popular Prakashan, 1983), 75–81, for sketches of the careers of numerous doctors who left Portugal, often from Coímbra, as a result of religious distrust or even persecution, because they were Jews or 'New Christians' (that is, converted Jews).
5. C. R. Boxer, 'Some remarks on the social and professional status of physicians and surgeons in the Iberian World, 16th–18th centuries', *Revista de História* [São Paulo], 50 (1974), 199, 201.
6. King to Camara of Goa, 24 March, 1583, in J. H. da Cunha Rivara

(ed.), *Archivo Português Oriental* (Nova Goa: Imprensa Nacional, 1857–77, 6 vols), I, i, 95.

7. See Pearson 'The thin end of the wedge' for documentation.

8. For Goa in the sixteenth century, see M. N. Pearson, *The Portuguese in India* (Cambridge: Cambridge University Press, 1987), 81–115.

9. J. H. van Linschoten, *The Voyage of John Huyghen van Linschoten to the East Indies* (London: Hakluyt Society, 1885, 2 vols), I, 235–9. The quotation is from 236.

10. John M. de Figueiredo, 'Ayurvedic medicine in Goa according to European sources in the sixteenth and seventeenth centuries', *Bulletin of the History of Medicine*, 58 (1984) 227. This article provides a familiar sketch of some aspects of interaction, though the author's use of sources is occasionally careless (e.g., his footnote 14). An exhaustive search has failed to find any further publications by this author. For a recent and authoritative discussion of syphilis and its origins, see Ann G. Carmichael, 'Syphilis and the Columbian exchange: Was the new disease really new?' in Marques & Cule, *op. cit.* (note 1), 187–200.

11. François Pyrard de Laval, *The Voyage of François Pyrard of Laval to the East Indies* (London: Hakluyt Society, 1888), Vol. II, 11.

12. Linschoten, *op. cit.* (note 9), 239. See the following chapter by Boomgard for the 'China root' and its uses.

13. Alberto C. Germano da Silva Correia, *La Vieille-Goa,* (Bastorá: Tipografia Rangel, 1931) 268–307; see also his many other publications listed in the bibliography of this book. For the outbreak of 1567, see the contemporary Jesuit account in J. Wicki *et al.* (eds), *Documenta Indica,* (Rome: Jesuit Historical Institute, 1948 f., 16 vols to date) VII, 384, letter of Fr Gomes Vaz, 12 December, 1567. For the calamitous outbreak of 1570, see João Manuel Pacheco de Figueiredo, 'Goa dourada nos séculos XVI e XVII: O hospital dos pobres do padre Paulo Camerte, esboço de sua reconstituição histórica', *Studia,* 25 (1968), 136–40.

14. Quoted in John Correia-Afonso, 'On the fourth centenary of Filippo Sassetti (1540–1588): Scientific observations from Cochin', paper presented at the Fifth International Seminar on Indo-Portuguese History, Cochin, January 1989, and published in *Indica,* 26 (1989), 15–24. The quotation is from 19.

15. Niccolao Manucci, *Storia do Mogor, or Mogul India* (Calcutta: Editions Indian, 1966–67, 4 vols), II, 157. The word used for cholera in Goa was *mordexim* or variants thereof. Dalgado tells us that the word is local, deriving from the Konkani *modxi* or *morxi.* The French later converted it to *mort-de-chien.* See Sebastião Rodolfo Dalgado, *Glossário Luso-Asiático* (Coímbra: Imprensa da Universidade, 1919–21, 2 vols), s.v. 'mordexim', II, 69–71. According to H. G. Rawlinson the word came from the Marathi *modashi* through the Portuguese *mordexim.* See John Ovington, *A*

First Contacts between Indian and European Medical Systems

Voyage to Surat in the Year 1689, H. G. Rawlinson (ed.), (London, 1929), 204, footnote.

16. F. P. Mendes da Luz, 'Livro das Cidades', Studia, 6 (1960), fo. 8.

17. T. Bentley Duncan, 'Navigation between Portugal and Asia in the sixteenth and seventeenth centuries', in Cyriac K. Pullapilly et al. (eds), Asia and the West: Encounters and Exchanges from the Age of Explorations: Essays in Honour of Donald F. Lach (Notre Dame: University of Notre Dame, 1986), 3–25.

18. Pyrard de Laval, op. cit. (note 11), 11–14.

19. See Correia-Afonso, op. cit. (note 14), and Anthony Disney, 'The world of long-distance voyaging in the seventeenth century: The Lisbon-Goa fleet of 1629 as a case study', read at the International Symposium on Maritime History, Pondicherry, February 1989, and published in K. S. Mathew (ed.), Studies in Maritime History (Pondicherry: Pondicherry University, 1990), 143–58. See also A. J. R. Russell-Wood, 'Men under stress: The social environment of the Carreira da India, 1550–1750', II Seminario Internacional de História Indo-Portuguesa, Actas (Lisbon: Centro de Estudos de História e Cartografia Antiga, 1985), 19–35. For seventeenth-century mortality on board ship see da Cunha Rivara, op. cit. (note 6), I, ii, 197, Camara to King, letter of 1607, and J. H. da Cunha Rivara, 'A India no governo do ViceRei Conde de Villa Verde, 1693–1698', O Chronista de Tissuary, ii–iii (1868), 26: entry for 26 September, 1699. Philip Curtin has recently raised the matter of relocation costs in imperialism: evidence is lacking for the Portuguese, but I would strongly suggest that there was in fact a relocation cost in their empire, especially as even the actual relocation, that is the voyage out, was so expensive of life. Philip D. Curtin, Disease and Imperialism before the Nineteenth Century (Minneapolis: James Ford Bell Library, 1990) (Bell Lecture no. 28), and, more fully in Death by Migration: Europe's Encounter with the Tropical World in the Nineteenth Century (Cambridge: Cambridge University Press, 1989).

20. 'Livros das Monções do Reino', Historical Archives of Goa, Vol. 19B, f. 607, list of Barreto de Rezende.

21. Dr John Fryer, A New Account of East India and Persia, W. Crooke (ed.) (London: Hakluyt Society, 1909–15, 3 vols), I, 180; Manucci, op. cit. (note 15), II, 157.

22. Ibid., III, 265.

23. Linschoten, op. cit. (note 9), I, 236–7.

24. Correia-Afonso, op. cit. (note 14), 19.

25. Fryer, op. cit. (note 21), I, 180.

26. I am aware that to write of 'Hindu' or 'Indian' medical practice is to ignore the pronounced regional differences evident at this time. Thus the important Portuguese commentator Cristóvão da Costa differentiated between Brahmin, Canarin and Malabar treatments. See Jaime Walter (ed.), Tratado das drogas e medicinas das India

Orientais, por Christovão da Costa, (Lisbon: Junta de Investigações do Ultramar, 1964), 23, 28.

27. David Arnold, 'Introduction: Disease, medicine and empire', in David Arnold (ed.), *Imperial Medicine and Indigenous Societies* (Manchester: Manchester University Press, 1988), 11; idem, 'Occidental Therapeutics and Oriental Bodies: Bengal, 1800–1860', paper read at Subaltern Studies conference, Calcutta, December 1989.

28. See, for example, my *Portuguese in India,* (note 8), passim.

29. *Breve relação das escrituras dos gentios da India Oriental a dos seus costumes* (Lisbon: 1812), 52–3, quoted in de Figueiredo, *op. cit.* (note 10), 231. This and other descriptions of medical practice in sixteenth-century Goa raise an interesting general question. The generally accepted four stages of Western medical practice are: *library,* where practice was based on Galen and other authorities, and the healer had little contact with the patient; *bedside,* where observations were carried out; *hospital,* in other words huge wards of people, which developed in the nineteenth century; and *laboratory,* where doctors reveal the results of tests. What we find in Goa is a mixture of the first two of these typologies, or perhaps even the first three. Thanks to my colleague Dr Susan Hardy for introducing me to this matter.

30. Linschoten, *op. cit.* (note 9), I, 236.

31. J. M. Pacheco de Figueiredo, 'The practice of Indian medicine in Goa during the Portuguese rule, 1510–1699', *Luso-Brazilian Review,* 4 (1967), 52–3.

32. João Manuel Pacheco Figueiredo, 'Goa Pré-Portuguesa', *Studia,* 12 (1963), 139–259; 13–14 (1965), 105–225. The quotation is from 13–14, 163–4.

33. A. K. Priolkar, *The Goa Inquisition* (Bombay: 1961), 140.

34. Linschoten, *op. cit.* (note 9), I, 230.

35. Costa, *op. cit.* (note 26), 28. This experimental attitude was found early on in the Portuguese presence in the Indian Ocean. In 1505 some Portuguese engaged in taking Mombasa were hit by poisoned arrows. The Portuguese surgeon Mestre Fernando treated the wounds with wicks of pork fat, which soaked up the poison. He had learnt this technique from a Muslim healer. Fernão Lopes de Castanheda, *História do descobrimento e conquista da India pelos Portugueses* (Coímbra: Imprensa da Universidade, 1924–33, 9 vols, 3rd edn), II, 6.

36. de Figueiredo, *op. cit.* (note 10), 231–2.

37. See Silva Correia, *op. cit.* (note 13), 275, and Pyrard, *op. cit.* (note 11), introduction, xii, and II, 14. For the career of one such *fisico-mor,* Dimas Bosque, who was attached to the viceroy D. Constantino de Bragança, 1558–61, see Jaime Walter, 'Dimas Bosque, fisico-mor da India a as sereias', *Studia,* 12 (1963), 261–71.

38. King to Viceroy, 23 January, 1610, in R. A. de Bulhão Pato (ed.), *Documentos remettidos da India, ou Livros das Monções* (Lisbon: Typografia de Academia Real das Sciencias, 1880–1935, 5 vols), I,

304, and King to Viceroy, 30 January, 1613, *ibid.*, II, 300.

39. Archivo Historico Ultramarino, Lisbon, caixa 16A, no. 160, letter of 7 September, 1644. My thanks to Timothy Coates of the University of Minnesota for this reference.

40. Ann Maria Amaro, 'Goa's famous cordial stone', *Review of Culture* [Macau], 7–8 (October 1988–March 1989), 82–103. Many thanks to Fr Charles Borges for this reference.

41. Priolkar, *op. cit.* (note 33), 14 of Dr Dellon's account.

42. On the use of bleeding in Portugal at this time, see, for copious and gory detail, Costa Santos, *Sobre barbeiros sangradores do hospital de Lisboa* (Porto: 1921).

43. Pyrard, *op. cit.* (note 11), II, 13.

44. Jean-Baptiste Tavernier, *Travels in India of Jean-Baptiste Tavernier*, trans. V. Ball and W. Crooke (New Delhi: Oriental Books Reprint Corporation, 1977, 2 vols), I, 160–1.

45. Ovington, *op. cit.* (note 15), 205.

46. John Correia-Afonso, (trans and ed.), *Intrepid Itinerant: Manuel Godinho and his Journey from India to Portugal in 1663* (Bombay: Oxford University Press, 1990), 70.

47. T. J. S. Patterson, 'The transmission of Indian surgical techniques to Europe at the end of the eighteenth century', in *Proceedings of the XXIII International Congress of the History of Medicine*, 2 vols (London: Wellcome Institute, 1974), I, 694–6. This paragraph is based on my article 'The thin end of the wedge'.

48. Clements Markham, *Colloquies on the Simples and Drugs of India by Garcia da Orta* (London: H. Sotheran, 1913), nos. 11, 13, 24, 36.

49. *Ibid.*, no. 36.

50. P. S.S. Pissurlencar (ed.), *Assentos do Conselho do Estado* (Bastorá: Tipografia Rangel, 1953–57, 5 vols), I, 237, meeting of 20 November, 1629.

51. D'Orta, *op. cit.* (note 48), no. 36.

52. Dellon in Priolkar, *op. cit.* (note 33), 42.

53. Luillier-Lagaudiers, *Nouveau voyage aux grandes Indes, avec une introduction pour le commerce des Indes Orientales, et la description de plusieurs isles, villes, & rivieres, l'histoire des plantes & des animaus qu'on y trouve; avec un traite des maladies particulieres aux pays orientaux, et dans la Route, et de leurs remedes* par Mr. D.L.F., Docteur en Medecine, qui a voyagé et sejourné dans les principales Villes des Indes Orientales (Rotterdam: 1726), 215. Portuguese records include copious detail on Hindu medical practice on the west coast of India in the sixteenth century, especially works by d'Orta, and Costa. These records will be used for a separate study on Hindu medicine in this period, but in terms of the present study the point is that the sources seem to show not superiority but acculturation and equality; the authors betray no feeling of contempt for Indian practice.

54. See C. R. Boxer, *Portuguese Society in the Tropics* (Madison: University

of Wisconsin Press, 1965), 24–6, and Silva Correia, *op. cit.* (note 13), 295–300. For another hospital founded in Goa in about 1550, called the 'Hospital dos pobres do Padre Paulo Camerte', see João Manuel Pacheco de Figueiredo, 'Goa dourada nos séculos XVI e XVII', 117–46.

55. King to Viceroy, 23 January, 1610, in Bulhão Pato, *op. cit.* (note 38), I, 303.

56. Pyrard, *op. cit.* (note 11), II, 2–17, provides the classic contemporary account of the Royal Hospital, while J. N. da Fonseca, *An Historical and Archaeological Account of the City of Goa* (Bombay: Thacker, 1878), 228–36, gives a good overview and references to documentary sources. The location of the Hospital can be worked out from the plan of Old Goa in his book; see also M. S. Commissariat (ed.) *Mandelslo's Travels in Western India, A.D. 1638–9* (Bombay: Oxford University Press, 1931), 70. I have in hand a separate study of the way the Portuguese tried to regulate medical practice in Goa, not only in their hospitals, but also in their attempts to license Hindu healers.

57. For d'Orta (and not Horta, da Orta, or Orta) see Garcia d'Orta, *Coloquios dos simplos, e drogas he cousas mediçinais de India* (Goa: Ioannes de Endem, 1563); Garcia da Orta, *Coloquios dos simples, e drogas he cousas mediçinais de India* ... Conde de Ficalho (ed.), (Lisbon: Imprensa Nacional, 1891–5, 2 vols); Markham, *op. cit.* (note 48), [a translation of Conde de Ficalho, Lisbon, 1891–5]. Especially important is C. R. Boxer, *Two Pioneers of Tropical Medicine: Garcia d'Orta and Nicolas Monardes* (London: Wellcome Institute, 1963). See also Conde de Ficalho, *Garcia da Orta e o seu tempo* (Lisbon: Imprensa Nacional, 1886); Luis de Pina, *Subsídios para a história da medicina portuguesa indiana do século XVII* (Porto: Araujo e Sobrinho, 1931); Luis Filipe de Sousa Barreto, 'Garcia da Orta e o dialogo civilizacional', in *Seminário internacional de história Indo-Portuguesa, Actas* (Lisbon: Centro de Estudos de História e Cartografia Antiga, 1985), 541–69, for a textual and semiotic study, and João Manuel Pacheco de Figueiredo, 'Coloquios dos simples de Garcia d'Orta, 1563–1963', *O Medico*, no. 602 (1963) (also published in *Boletim do Instituto Meneses Bragança*, 83 (1963), 161–86), for a useful summary, and also Gaitonde, *op. cit.* (note 4), 118–40. For more bibliography see Daya de Silva's excellent *The Portuguese in Asia: An Annotated Bibliography of Studies on Portuguese Colonial History in Asia, 1498–c.1800* (Zug: IDC, 1987), entry no. 2336, 252–3. There is even a journal named after him: *Garcia de Orta: Revista da Junta das Missões Geográficas e de Investigações do Ultramar*, Lisbon, 1952 – . This journal had an emphasis on scientific matters, and in 1963 in Vol. 9 no. 4, a special number commemorated the 400th anniversary of the publication of the *Coloquios*. The hagiography continues up to today. See Ivan A.

First Contacts between Indian and European Medical Systems

D'Cruz, 'Garcia da Orta in Goa: Pioneering tropical medicine', *British Medical Journal*, 303 (1991), 1593–4, and Fernando A. R. Nogueira, 'Garcia de Orta, physician and scientific researcher', in Marques & Cule, *op. cit.* (note 1), 251–64.

58. See Tomé Pires, *The Suma Oriental of Tomé Pires and the Book of Francisco Rodrigues* (ed. Armando Cortesão) (London: Hakluyt Society, 1944), 512–18, for an earlier and smaller account of Indian drugs; Jaime Walter, 'Simão Alvares e o seu rol das drogas da India', *Studia*, 10 (1962), 117–49 for a list from the mid-sixteenth century, neither of which have anything on the uses of these drugs, nor on medicine, and D. S. Lach, *Asia in the Making of Europe,* Vol. II, book 3 (Chicago: Chicago University Press, 1977), 427–45 for knowledge of Asian botany in Europe.

59. For a dramatic description, see Gaspar Correa, *Lendas de India* (Lisbon: Academia Real das Sciencias, 1858–66, 4 vols), IV, 288–9.

60. See d'Orta, *op. cit.* (note 48), no. 17 for a description of *mordexim* in 1543.

61. *Ibid.,* no. 5, and cf. no. 12.

62. *Ibid.,* no. 9.

63. See especially Boxer, *op. cit.* (note 57), 7–13, Georg Schurhammer, *Francis Xavier: His Life, His Times,* Vol. II, India (Rome: Jesuit Historical Institute, 1977), 203; and M.B. Barbosa and J. Caria Mendes, 'Garcia d'Orta, pioneer of tropical medicine and his descriptions of cholera in his Colóquios (1563)', in *Proceedings of the XXIII International Congress of the History of Medicine* (London: Wellcome Institute, 1974), II, 1258-9.

64. We may also note that d'Orta was followed by Cristovão da Costa, who arrived in Goa in the year of d'Orta's death. Modern libraries often list him as 'Cristobal Acosta, *c.*1515–*c.*1592.' His book in English was called *Treatises on Drugs and Medicines of East India* (1578); the best modern edition is Walter, *op. cit.* (note 26). Earlier scholars claimed that he basically summarized d'Orta, though his book did have numerous illustrations. However, Donald Lach has shown that while he knew of and used d'Orta, the two books differ widely. For example, Costa describes 47 plants, and of these 14 are not mentioned by d'Orta, while nine of d'Orta's are not in Costa. See Lach, *op. cit.* (note 58), Vol. II, book 3, 436–7.

INDEX